D1387834

JOHN MATUSIAK

MARTYRS OF HENRY VIII

REPRESSION, DEFIANCE, SACRIFICE

'Indignatio principis mors est.'
(The wrath of the prince is death.)

Proverbs, 16:14

First published 2019

The History Press
97 St George's Place, Cheltenham,
Gloucestershire, GL50 3QB
www.thehistorypress.co.uk

British Library Cataloguing in Publication Data.
A catalogue record for this book is available from the British Library.

ISBN 978 0 7509 8795 0

Typesetting and origination by The History Press
Printed and bound in Great Britain by TJ International Ltd

CONTENTS

THE ROAD TO TYBURN

This day, the Nun of Kent, with two Friars Observant, two monks and one secular priest, were drawn from the Tower to Tyburn, and there hanged and headed. God, if it be his pleasure, have mercy on their souls.

John Hussee to Lord Lisle, *Lisle Papers*, v, 95.

In the early morning of Monday, 20 April 1534, as the sun ascended balefully upon her appointed day of destiny, a 28-year-old Benedictine nun by the name of Elizabeth Barton was awoken from her no-doubt meagre slumbers in the Tower of London, along with two Benedictine monks, two Franciscan friars and a former secretary to the Archbishop of Canterbury, to face her ultimate ordeal as an enemy of the Tudor state. Since no one in England had hitherto been executed in clerical garb, or would be until the following year, she was dressed on departure, we may safely assume, in a plain shift typical of the kind worn by condemned women, while her male counterparts, likewise convicted of high treason, wore cast-off gowns donated by the charitable. Bound on their backs, without ceremony or sympathy, to four wooden hurdles, their ankles securely lashed together and their hands tied in the attitude of prayer, the condemned were watched over by members of King Henry VIII's Privy Council and in particular the Lieutenant of the Tower, Sir Edmund Walsingham, who had assumed responsibility for their handover after his superior, Sir William Kingston, the Tower's Constable, had been taken ill. It was a heavy responsibility: weightier, certainly, than any the deputy lieutenant is likely to have envisaged when in 1520 he first succeeded Sir Richard Cholmondley in his current post at an annual salary of £100. For, like others that day, he too was henceforth tightly harnessed, though not to an executioner's hurdle, but to a revolution that would lead he knew not where: one of unprecedented scale and significance, and one that would lead him before long to supervise a long line of illustrious prisoners, including Anne Boleyn, Catherine Howard, the Countess of Salisbury, the Marquess of Exeter, Lord Henry Montagu, the Duchess of Norfolk, and arguably the most famous, if not the most significant, of all the king's martyrs, Sir Thomas More, England's one-time chancellor.

It was to Walsingham, indeed, that More is said to have delivered his final ironic quip upon ascending the scaffold the following year: 'I pray you, Master Lieutenant, see me safe up, and for my coming down, let me shift for myself.' By that time, the full import of the government's intentions was clear: nothing less than the enactment of a seismic breach with the ancient Church of Rome and the systematic suppression of all those resolved to take that Church's part. Neither statesman nor theologian and certainly no freethinker, Walsingham, in keeping with the vast majority of others caught up in the tumultuous events of these years, would dutifully follow his government's lead, trusting its judgements and executing its wishes out of an unquestioning mix of inbred loyalty and solid self-interest. Nor, of course, was it ever remotely likely to have been otherwise. He was, after all, a long-standing servant of the Crown, knighted by Thomas Howard four days after the Battle of Flodden more than twenty years earlier, and appointed a sewer in the royal household in 1521. Then, with an eagle eye for the main chance and by a judicious combination of earnest enterprise and the sixteenth-century equivalent of modern-day political correctness, he had become both a freeman of the Mercers' Company, and, much more significantly still, a dutiful member of the packed jury that had tried and convicted Edward Stafford, 3rd Duke of Buckingham, a decade earlier. For such an upstanding member of England's elites, the royal will was sacrosanct, its dictates irresistible, its retribution ineluctable.

Yet, for an intractable few, such ready compliance was never so straightforward an option, and the humble nun now laid supine before the Tower's lieutenant in one of its many inter-connected courtyards was not only the first of that line chronologically, but at one point, arguably, a figure of no less potential significance than the altogether more exalted victims that succeeded her: a clear and present existential threat to the king's marital designs and the trigger for much that followed.

Such was Elizabeth Barton's celebrity, in fact, that, according to one likely eyewitness, the Protestant cloth merchant Richard Hilles, she was now afforded pride of place and the dubious distinction of a hurdle to herself, as Walsingham duly entrusted her sorry body, and those of her associates, to the capital's two High Sheriffs, Thomas Kitson and William Forman, in return for the written receipt invariably engendered by the niceties of Tudor bureaucracy. Whereupon, the waiting horses were harnessed to their wretched human cargo, and the heavy escort of soldiers in attendance duly shouldered pikes in readiness for a clattering departure over the fortress's cobbled pathways. Passing by turns through the successive portcullises of the Bloody Tower and over the groaning drawbridge releasing them to the outside world, troops and officials alike were from this point onwards self-conscious participants in a carefully stage-managed public spectacle – playing an indispensable supporting role to the helpless victims themselves, bound feet-first behind the horses as they bumped and jarred like cumbersome harrows over the uneven ground and unmade roads stretching far ahead of them through the heart of London and on to Tyburn Crossroads.

For the organisers, in particular, it was an occasion of much personal significance. High Sheriff Kitson, on the one hand, had come to London from Lancashire in his youth as an apprentice to the London mercer Richard Glasyer, but risen steadily to become Warden of the Mercers' Company in 1533, by which time only ten other English merchants could compete with his cloth-dealing activities in Antwerp, Middleburg, and elsewhere in Flanders. Nor would the smooth running of the day ahead be any less crucial to his further prospects. Already the owner of the Duke of Buckingham's former manors of Hengrave in Suffolk and Colston Basset in Nottinghamshire, he was indeed to be knighted within the month, which made the faultless prosecution of his current task all the more pressing, since it was he, along with his counterpart William Forman, an alderman from the Cripplegate Ward in the City of London, who now assumed primary responsibility for the safe delivery of the condemned prisoners to Tyburn and the attentions of a certain 'Mr Cratwell', the capital's newly appointed executioner who, as a man of considerable consequence in Tudor society in his own right, was likewise keenly primed that morning. For this was his debut, and along with his assistants

– who numbered the men in charge of the brazier for burning the victims'
entrails and the cauldron for parboiling their quartered remains – he too
had much to prove, sedulously calculating the precise degree of torment
entailed by the law and directing the various other underlings tending the
Tyburn gallows, which consisted of two dark oaken uprights, high enough
to ensure an unimpeded view for spectators, and a stout crossbeam, from
which hung several well-oiled and flexible ropes. 'A conninge butcher in
quartering of men', the executioner would himself be hanged for theft
before a crowd of 20,000 baying spectators at Smithfield only four years
later. But for now at least, on this spring day, he was lord of his calling,
caught up in the most significant political execution of its kind for more
than a decade, and surrounded by a busy throng of willing apprentices
anxious to learn his craft.

For the moment, in fact, the arrival of the condemned woman and
her associates was still some way off, since the distance from the Tower
to Tyburn was all of 5 miles, and the procession, if it was to achieve its
intended purpose as a potent affirmation of regal power, was not to be
rushed. Passing slowly along Tower Lane and Cheapside, under the Arch
of Newgate with its statue of the Virgin and Child, it was making, with
all due gravity, for the spot known today as Marble Arch, where Oxford
Street and its prolongation, the Bayswater Road, are intersected by Park
Lane and Edgware Road. And both the cruelty of the occasion and the
raucous carnival atmosphere surrounding it were intended to be savoured.
A year later, when processions of this kind had become less novel and
their implications altogether more ominous, a guild of charitable ladies
would offer posies and cups of mulled wine to the victims at the venerable church of St Sepulchre's before they left the City. But this time, there
was no such kindness to be had. On the contrary, the capital's citizens, still
unused as yet to the employment of terror as an everyday instrument of
government policy, played their full role as tormentors. Heartless brutes
and merry housewives harangued the victims on their way, flinging taunts
and missiles from the over-hanging houses under which the helpless slow-
moving targets passed, while buffoons with inflated pigs' bladders, buskers
and ribald ballad-singers, specially hired for the occasion by the government, tweaked the victims' noses, pulled their ears, mimicked their spasms
of pain, and inquired facetiously how they liked their rough passage.

Even the horses contributed their torrents of steaming piss and periodic bombardments of hot dung.

At the brook that gives its name to Holborn – the halfway mark of the journey, lying just outside the City, and the customary spot both for the horses to be watered and for the soldiers to relax after jostling their way through the crowded, narrow streets behind them – there was, at least, a break in proceedings. Yet the way ahead would offer no further respite once the journey was resumed along the Oxford Road, which today has become High Holborn. With dwellings here and there at considerable intervals, some of them high-gabled timber houses, others gentlemen's mansions with greenswards all around, the route now traversed pleasant fields on either side with spreading oak and elm trees and thick forests stretching out northwards and southwards beyond the high road to Tottenham. All around, in fact, there were varied undulations of both pasture and arable land, while to the north lay the wooded valley of the Kill-bourne, as well as the Mary-bourne, a stream noted for its grayling. Tyburn itself, indeed, notwithstanding its notoriety as a place of execution since at least 1196, was justly regarded as an otherwise wholesome location – the site, anciently, of the blue and sparkling stream of Teobourne, which passed very near to the place of execution and supplied the conduit at Cheapside with clear, untainted water. But from this point forward the road was entirely unpaved and therefore even rougher than previously, while brambles trailing from the uncut hedges round about tore the prisoners as they were dragged along before the noisily pursuing crowds – some riding, most walking, drawn from every section of society – the vast majority of whom were keenly intent upon witnessing the heady climax of the kill itself.

Just over one year later, when the Carthusian priors of Axholme and Beauvale made the same lamentable journey, along with the prior of the London Charterhouse, the Bridgettine monk, Dr Richard Reynolds, and John Hale, Vicar of Isleworth, the whole Boleyn clique turned out in force to witness the spectacle. On the one hand, the Duke of Norfolk was there with his nephew, Viscount Rochford, as was the Duke of Richmond, the king's bastard son. And to complete the ghoulish congregation, the royal chamberlain, Henry Norris, would also see fit to arrive with forty horsemen, all masked for additional dramatic effect. It was 'something new', wrote the Imperial ambassador, Eustace Chapuys, that Richmond, Norfolk, and other magnates, including Anne Boleyn's father, the Earl of Wiltshire, had stood 'quite near the sufferers' during their final agonies. Even the king himself, it was rumoured, had been present, since, among some courtiers disguised as Scottish borderers, there was one, or so some said, to whom extraordinary deference had been paid. Chapuys, indeed, considered Henry's presence 'very probable … seeing that all the court was there' to witness the crude castration and evisceration of those who had fallen victim to Thomas Cromwell's notorious law of December 1534 – a measure of unprecedented harshness that had extended the concept of treason to encompass all types of 'malicious' attack upon the king, Queen Anne or the succession, including those made even orally.

It was of no little significance either that this so-called 'law of words', designed to root out the seditious 'imps of the said bishop of Rome', had in fact been directly prompted by the visions and prophecies of Elizabeth Barton herself, though the nun, as a woman, was now merely to be hanged until dead and thereafter beheaded rather than endure the full rigour of hanging, drawing and quartering. At Canterbury in October 1532 she had denounced King Henry in his very presence, warning him of his death within the month, should he marry Anne Boleyn, and telling him in no uncertain terms how she had seen the place reserved for him in hell, were he to proceed. To those who sought to hear from heaven on the king's divorce, she had spoken, too, of other visions: of Christ re-crucified, as a result of the king's adultery, and of Anne Boleyn as a Jezebel whom dogs would eat. As such, there was no prospect of mercy either for her or for those unfortunate men who had endorsed her pronouncements and were now accompanying her to the gallows. But for the latter those same considerations of public decency, which would at least spare Barton the unspeakable agonies of ritual disembowelment, were not to apply. Indeed, by the time of their arrival at Tyburn, the tools of executioner Cratwell's trade were not only already honed and heated, but purposely placed on display before the victims, who, according to a Latin history of the English Franciscan martyrs, written by Father Thomas Bourchier and published in Paris in 1582, 'were obliged to inspect the instruments of execution, partly to increase their sufferings, partly in the hope of break-ing their holy resolution'.

In return for the usual private undertaking from the Crown that their families, friends and associates would remain unmolested if they professed their guilt, all, including Barton, delivered carefully contrived confessions from the gallows after the writ of execution had been read. Whereupon Cratwell, after first kneeling, as was customary, to receive his victims' forgiveness for what was to follow, warmed to his appointed task, dispatching the nun first before inflicting the more prolonged sufferings of the men. Continuing in prayer as the rope was tightened, each man in turn was duly positioned on a supporting ladder, which was finally kicked away at a signal from the supervising sheriff. After that the suspending hemp rope was cut, leaving what amounted to a demi-corpse to fall to the ground like a dead weight prior to the final desecration of its members. Crudely revived by slaps, punches, shaking and dowsing in cold water, and duly propped up so that they could witness the full horror of what ensued, the five members of the clergy then suffered, one after the other, the agony of seeing their entrails torn from their bodies and cast into the waiting brazier after their genitals had been hideously severed and thrust into their mouths.

The heart of one friar, Bourchier suggests, was still quivering after it had been squeezed and ripped from the gaping visceral cavity below, as was confirmed, it seems, when Cratwell 'held it aloft for the inspection of the crowd', though even by this point the whole ghastly spectacle had still not run its final course until the corpses were subsequently hacked into four parts and the severed heads parboiled 'to diminish the smell when later put on poles for the citizens to see'. Bagged up by Cratwell and taken back to the capital, 'the nun's head', we are told by John Stow, 'was set on London Bridge, and the other heads on the gates of the City', though as a result, it seems, of some dwindling regard for clerical privilege, which was to have disappeared entirely only fourteen months later, the quarters themselves were not, on this occasion, exhibited as gruesome symbols of royal might. Instead, as the contemporary *Chronicle of the Grey Friars of London* makes clear, Barton's remains were eventually placed in the cemetery of the Grey Friars in Newgate Street, along with those of the two friars, while the others found a final resting at the London cemetery of the Dominican Fathers at Blackfriars.

It was the day after the feast of St Alphege, martyred by the Danes in 1012 for refusing to ransom his life with the funds of the Church, and the eve of the feast of St Anselm, who had also battled and suffered for the Church's rights against William II and Henry I, founding in the process Elizabeth Barton's own Benedictine convent of St Sepulchre's in Canterbury. But by the time that Anselm's feast had dawned for those nuns still present there, the remains of both their executed sister and her fellow martyrs had already been quietly gathered by the Hospitallers of St John of Jerusalem at Clerkenwell, who, as one of the seven corporal works of mercy to which they were sworn, had by long tradition undertaken to fetch the corpses of plague victims, suicides, and felons executed at Tyburn for burial – usually in the Pardon Churchyard, a cemetery between their own priory and the adjoining London Charterhouse. Placing the bodies of Barton and the other victims upon the cart kept specially for the purpose, which was covered in a black pall, with a large white cross running its length, and a small cross of St John in front, they went about their sombre task at dead of night to the sound of a solitary bell, signalling their approach to those in the vicinity.

Only five years later, the same Knights of St John would themselves be objects of suspicion and attack, their Clerkenwell headquarters dissolved by Thomas Cromwell with his sovereign's avid consent, and two of their number, Sir Thomas Dingley and Sir Adrian Fortescue, executed, like Barton before them, not according to the rights laid down by the Common Law of the land, but by Bill of Attainder, as the summary justice of the day had by that time come to dictate. On the night of Elizabeth Barton's death, moreover, the net was already tightening not only for the so-called Knights Hospitaller bearing her remains to their chapel for distribution thereafter, but for the Carthusian monks of the adjacent London Charterhouse, some of whom are certain to have heard the melancholy ringing of the hand bell announcing her passing. Indeed, within the year, ironically enough, they too would be ripped from the seclusion of their austere lives of prayer and contemplation by the self-same swirling winds of religious change engulfing the kingdom. Sir Adrian Fortescue, by curious coincidence, had once enjoyed high favour at Henry VIII's own court as the son of Alice Boleyn, Anne Boleyn's aunt, and had been made a Knight of the Bath in 1503, along with the king himself, whom he later accompanied to Calais and the Field of Cloth of Gold. And a similar privileged status had also been the lot of 35-year-old Sebastian Newdigate, a former courtier of the king's own Privy

Chamber, who had some time since renounced the world of politics and ambition after his wife's death, to seek instead the consolations that only the Carthusian life seemed fully able to offer. Though he did not know it at the time in the shelter of his lonely dwelling within the Charterhouse, young Newdigate, too, was bound for a cell of an altogether less inviting kind, and eventually a martyr's fate of his own at Tyburn. For, like Fortescue after him, he would make his way by turns to the infamous jail at Marshalsea, where, along with two fellow Carthusians, he was tied to a post by an iron collar, his legs riveted to 'great fetters', and left for seventeen days, loaded with lead, unable to sit and 'never loosed for any natural necessity', before meeting his own grisly end at executioner Cratwell's accomplished hands.

Notwithstanding personal visits from the king himself, who allegedly offered him wealth and preferment in return for compliance with the royal supremacy, Newdigate would remain unyielding. And there was to be one further twist to his eventual martyrdom on 14 June 1535. For not only was he by then following the road to Tyburn already travelled five weeks earlier by the man most instrumental to his spiritual development at the Charterhouse, his prior, Father John Houghton, he was also preceding to a martyr's fate – and by only one week – the very individual who had ordained him a deacon barely four years earlier and gone on to become the most dogged and dangerous of all the king's opponents. Described by Chapuys as the 'paragon of Christian prelates, both for learning and holiness', Bishop John Fisher had in fact been an outspoken adversary of the royal divorce from its very inception, defending Queen Catherine at Blackfriars in 1529 and declaring openly that he would willingly die like St John the Baptist on behalf of the indissolubility of her marriage. And that bold promise had indeed been made good six years later when, already emaciated and dying from consumption, he knelt before his masked executioner at Tower Hill on 22 June 1535. Described by one eye-witness as 'a very image of death and (as one might say) Death in a man's shape and using a man's voice', he was nevertheless to 'suffer cheerfully his impending punishment'. After which, his 'headless carcass' was left 'naked on the scaffold for the rest of the hot June day, saving that one, for pity and humanity, cast a little straw upon it'.

From the king's perspective, of course, Fisher, like Barton and Newdigate before him, was both wilful and deluded, and, above all, threatening – fully meriting the treatment meted out to him. Nor were such opinions confined solely to those within the king's circle. To the MP and chronicler Edward Hall, for instance, 'the bishop was a man of very good life, but wonderfully deceived therein'. He stood accused, after all, of entering into a treasonous correspondence with Emperor Charles V, which had been intercepted on the Continent by Thomas Cromwell's spies, and by September 1533 was urging the emperor to invade England and depose Henry altogether, in what amounted to a religious war: a crusade, which, he maintained, would be as pleasing to God as war against the Turk. Under such circumstances, the king's subsequent remark that Fisher's death had been the least cruel that could be devised, since he had been neither hanged, nor quartered, nor burned, nor boiled in lead but merely 'sworded', may not seem quite so casually callous – or any more insupportable, for that matter, than the tag of 'hypocrite nun' applied by government propaganda to Barton, who, in the view of Chancellor Thomas Audley, expressed to Parliament in November 1533, had manufactured her visions and 'feigned prophecies' purely in search of celebrity, and thereby inveigled a number of great personages into questioning her sovereign's marriage to Anne Boleyn.

From a similar perspective, too, even the monks of the London Charterhouse, cut off though they were from the outside world in their abode of peace and seclusion, could be neatly construed by Thomas Cromwell as intolerable threats to the new and better order he was feverishly engaged in creating. Certainly, for an administrator of Cromwell's tremendous energy and breadth of vision, the liberal anachronisms and genteel prejudices that typify twenty-first-century attitudes to selective political terror were utterly foreign, warranting no more consideration than the stubborn adherents of papal authority themselves or the hidebound religious attitudes to which they clung. He was, after all, first and foremost an institutional thinker, a bold and original statesman and patron of like-minded political philosophers, who was convinced of the rectitude and creativity of his revolutionary work in delivering his countrymen from servility to foreign interference and religious error. And if a Barton, a Newdigate or a Fisher saw fit to block the way to progress in God's name on grounds of conscience, then that same way might just as cheerfully be cleared by force, or so Cromwell believed, in God's name. He made this clear in a long letter delivered to Bishop Nicholas Shaxton in March 1538, in which he professed that he aimed only for constructive results and was no less engaged upon God's work than any cleric protecting his flock:

> I do not cease to give thanks that it has pleased His goodness to use me as an instrument and to work somewhat by me, so I trust I am as ready to serve him in my calling as you are … My prayer is that God give me no longer life than I shall be glad to use mine office in edification and not in destruction.

Nor, manifestly, was Cromwell the only statesman or public servant of early Tudor England to exhibit little sense of the 'tears of things'. On the contrary, his peers, to a man, would surely have marvelled that the imagination of later generations should find cause to linger at any length at all over a deluded nun, a disobedient monk or a recalcitrant bishop.

But whether the claim made by Cromwell to Shaxton really did spring from the honest operation of a 'higher' morality and the harsh necessities imposed by circumstance upon a suitably supple conscience, or reflected rather the self-justifying sophistry of a cynical political hatchet man, ideally suited to further the interests of the tyrant he served, remains a matter for dispute. Plainly, his was a stance that not only set his master's kingdom on a new and perhaps necessary course, but one that would also ensure a steady income for executioner Cratwell and his successors for years to come – long after John Fisher had mounted the scaffold on Tower Hill and the road to Tyburn had been traced by Elizabeth Barton and Sebastian Newdigate. Yet if Cromwell's methods were undoubtedly ruthless, were his victims themselves no more than holy innocents? Each, after all, had chosen the path of resistance at a time when opposition to the Crown's designs might engender untold repercussions for the peace and future development of the kingdom as a whole, not least because the very violence of the State was, from many perspectives, as much a token of its weakness as its strength. If so, then where, if at all, are blame and guilt actually to be laid? And why, equally intriguingly, had a religious faith considered moribund and decadent by its critics nevertheless continued to generate such fervour among those who saw fit to lay down their lives on its behalf? What were the stakes and allegiances, passions and principles involved, and what, ultimately, the underlying events and processes – not to mention the misconceptions, miscalculations and twists of chance – that finally brought Barton, Newdigate and Fisher to their fatal pass? More than four and a half centuries later in our own troubled age, when martyrdom for a sacred cause is once again a cherished goal for some, the need for reflection is surely far from over. And if timeless lessons are indeed to be had from the bloody precedents of the past, what might they prove to be?

1

A CHURCH TO DIE FOR

They all attend Mass every day and say many Paternosters in public — the women carrying long rosaries in their hands, and any who can read taking the Office of Our Lady with them, and with some companion reading it in church, verse by verse, in a low voice after the manner of churchmen. They always hear Mass every Sunday in their parish church, and give liberal alms, because they may not offer less than a piece of money, of which fourteen are equivalent to a golden ducat; nor do they omit any form incumbent on good Christians; there are, however, many who have various opinions concerning religion.

From *The Italian Relation*, an account of the island of England, written by a Venetian in 1497.

For those in search of English history's most momentous documents, a worthy candidate may surely be found approximately 6 miles south-west of the bustling Spanish metropolis of Valladolid, on the road to Zamora and the right bank of the river Pisuerga, in the small but picturesque town of Simancas. Home to slightly more than 5,000 souls, the place is these days primarily an agricultural centre, boasting a deserved reputation for its poultry. But it remains also the location of an impressive citadel, built in the sixteenth century by the architects Juan de Herrera, Alonso Berruguete and Juan Gómez de Mora, which has the distinction of being the first building of the modern era created exclusively to house a nation's archives. Lodged in some forty-six rooms and arranged in upwards of 80,000 bundles containing no fewer than 33 million documents, are to be found each and every major record produced by government bodies relating to the Spanish monarchy since the time of the Catholic Monarchs, dating from 1475, through to the establishment in 1834 of what became known as the

Liberal Regime. And it is within this same Archivo General de Simancas, established by Philip II in 1563 and sometimes called the Archivo General del Reino, that there resides a striking parchment of outstanding significance, lettered in gold and beautifully embellished with the royal arms of Spain and red rose of Lancaster, which would change the course of history: the marriage treaty between the future Henry VIII, at that time newly heir to the Tudor throne, and the Trastámara princess known to posterity as Catherine of Aragon, daughter to Ferdinand and Isabella of Spain. Finally signed by Henry VII on 3 March 1504, after its agreement at Richmond during the previous summer, the treaty set the seal upon a marriage like few others before or after – one that was to prove problematic from its very conception, and which marked, unbeknown to its progenitors, the beginning of the end for the entire fabric of Roman Catholic influence in England.

Yet never, arguably, had the Roman Catholic Church in that realm been more securely entrenched nor the prospect of Catholic martyrs from within its ranks more remote than upon Henry VIII's succession in 1509. On the one hand, the so-called *Ecclesia Anglicana* – a term encompassing the entire clerical estate within the kingdom – was not only firmly protected by sanctions and support from its base abroad, but strengthened by wide-ranging privileges and immunities enshrined in native law and consecrated by long custom. At the same time, its leading bishops were central to the council of the king, whose bureaucracy, such as it was, still largely comprised clergymen. Its services were necessary on all important occasions in life – at christenings, marriages and funerals. Its courts determined all matrimonial cases, ratified or refused to ratify all wills, and took cognisance, too, of all transgressions of the moral law, rendering both the fornicator and the village scold alike subject to its punishment. And this was merely the iceberg tip of the Church's more general prominence in the fabric of everyday life. For merchant guilds and craft guilds still boasted their own thriving chantry chapels to succour the souls of their departed, and besides administering all charitable funds, the clergy almost entirely controlled education and hospitals, amply assisted at other levels by the kingdom's parish churches, which remained indispensable centres of social life.

Shortly before his death at the age of 88 early in the next century, Roger Martyn, churchwarden of Long Melford in Suffolk, left a rich and vivid account of a religious world that was by then already a distant memory: a world closely replicated, moreover, throughout the other 9,500 parishes of Tudor England, and, in consequence, one that was never likely to be lightly supplanted when the time for reformation finally dawned. For Martyn, unlike the small minority of Protestant sceptics who actively endorsed the changes, would find the spiritual reorientation from a Catholic mental universe of supportive saints and saving sacraments to a Protestant one of justifying faith, nurtured by sermons and Bible-reading, a decidedly painful one. And for most others too, if only out of long familiarity with its everyday rhythms and undoubted consolations, the abandonment of the old religion's ways was equally perplexing. On the one hand, Martyn lovingly recalled the festivals of the Church's year, when on Palm Sunday, for example, the people of Long Melford processed around their churchyard with the consecrated host (a communion wafer) borne aloft under a canopy carried by four yeomen of the village. On Maundy Thursday, meanwhile, candles were set in a painted frame before the Easter sepulchre, and on Good Friday the priest sang the Passion service from the rood loft, standing next to the rood itself, which had been veiled throughout Lent. On St Mark's day, too, and at Corpus Christi there were processions around Long Melford's green, once again with the consecrated sacrament featuring prominently, along with bell-ringing and singing, while in Rogation week there were prayers 'for fair weather or rain, as the time required', as well as great celebrations involving ale and a parish dinner on Rogation Monday, a breakfast of cheese at the rectory on Tuesday, followed later by ale at the manor house chapel, and ale at Melford Hall on the Wednesday.

And this, of course, was only one limited segment of a packed parish calendar that bound the Church of Rome so inextricably to the habits and sentiments of ordinary Tudor men and women. On the eve of St James's day there was a village bonfire, with a tub of ale and bread for the poor, and there were bonfires and ale, too – this time in front of the Martyns' own house – on Midsummer eve as well as the eve of Saints Peter and Paul. For the St Thomas's eve bonfire, in its turn, the family provided mutton pie and peascods in addition to the usual bread and ale, 'and with all these bonfires', Martyn tells us, some of the friends and 'more civil poor neighbours' were called in to dine by candlelight with his grandfather, as a taper burned before the image of St John the Baptist in the hall. Always there were priests on hand, and usually in numbers, since Long Melford was a prosperous cloth-producing village, boasting no fewer than four chaplains, three of whom were chantry priests, whose main duty was to perform the all-important task of celebrating Masses for the salvation of souls nominated, more often than not, by wealthy benefactors. Reducing by their prayers the time spent by dead souls in purgatory, these same chantry priests were also responsible for assisting in the daily worship of the parish at large, and in some cases teaching at schools supported by patrons' endowments. And when it is remembered that these same men were frequently assisted by additional clergy, sometimes employed for a year or two by a local guild, as well as the sixty or so monks housed at the great Benedictine monastery of nearby Bury St Edmunds, the scale of the Church's presence, as well its ability to intervene in everyday life, becomes all the more apparent.

No doubt, Martyn paints an idyllic picture of a merry Melford of yesteryear, where goodwill flourished, and parish life followed a timelessly untroubled course. He makes no mention of the fact that the village's poorer workers had joined an anti-tax rebellion in 1525, or that, for much of his childhood, his local church was in the spiritual charge of William Newton, a frequently absent pluralist rector, who held various ecclesiastical offices throughout East Anglia. Enjoying an annual income of £28 2s 5d from Long Melford alone – more than three times the average income of most English priests, and perhaps ten times that of an agricultural worker – Newton was hardly the most shining example of priestly diligence, let alone Christian poverty. Yet he, and others like him much less worthy still, were nevertheless rendered wholly credible to the vast majority of their flocks by the huge and complex organisation that sustained them. For each and every one of the 2.5 million men, women and children of early Tudor England were automatically members of the Church of Rome. All were required to attend Mass on Sundays and festivals, to fast on appointed days, and to make confession to a priest and receive communion at least at Easter, while those with wages, profits or produce were bound to contribute to the upkeep of their parish priests and churches by tithes.

And in the meantime, clerics of various types and categories continued to abound, as did the ceaselessly chiming bells in town and village steeples, calling the king's subjects to prayer and devotion. For although the recruitment of clergy had slumped in the late fourteenth century, by the mid-fifteenth it was booming once again, not least as a result of energetic lay endowment of Masses, and the improved reputation of priests resulting from the fact that criticism of churchmen had become associated with heresy and threats to the social order. Between the Parliament of 1410 and that of 1529, there had even been less lay complaint about the customary bugbear of clerical wealth, so that new recruits to the priesthood came forward confidently and with healthy prospects for the future. In Kent, where parishes were small, there were nevertheless two clerics on average to serve their parishioners' needs, while in Lancashire, where parishes were very large, there might sometimes be as many as seven or eight, even excluding those other clergy, found in Long Melford and up and down the country at large, who, as we have seen, said Masses for cash and found occasional work where they could. As a result, there were some 40,000 so-called 'secular' priests, alongside another 10,000 in the 'regular' orders of monks and friars, complemented by a further sub-category of deacons and subdeacons progressing towards priesthood, and as many as 2,000 nuns. No other body could compare in scale or boast a bureaucracy to rival the king's own, and no other organisation could potentially offer such resistance to the Crown, in the unlikely event of a contest. For Church professionals numbered roughly one fortieth of the population, and about 4 per cent of all males, and the Church itself controlled enormous wealth, derived from ownership of at least one fifth of the kingdom's land. Should any ruler therefore attempt a challenge, let alone a wholesale frontal assault, the enterprise was likely be risky. To attempt a root and branch dismantlement was sure to be. Certainly, there would be resistance: the only question its scale, intensity and duration. And where resistance occurred, there were equally sure to be casualties – particularly among those representing figureheads, however unconsciously, reluctantly or otherwise.

Even so, under all normal circumstances, the likelihood of any significant confrontation between State and Church remained minimal, not least because the Church itself was so anxious, wherever possible, to accommodate the wishes of the princes falling under its theoretical ambit. In 1208, Innocent III had suspended all church services in England, and excommunicated King John, to impose Stephen Langton as Archbishop of Canterbury. But even Henry II, who had made humble submission to Rome after Thomas Becket's murder, ultimately achieved most of his objectives, while the confrontation between Edward I and Archbishop Winchelsey in 1297, over royal taxation of the clergy, had resulted in a speedy resolution in the king's favour. Even in 1341, when Archbishop Stratford claimed that Edward III was infringing the privileges of the clergy over jurisdiction and taxation, and subsequently excommunicated Crown servants, the eventual outcome was a compromise solution, in which both sides backed down. And when Clement VI's appointments of clerks to English benefices proved too numerous, the result was the Statute of Provisors – a countermeasure enacted in 1351 and followed by further restrictions four decades later. Churchmen themselves, significantly enough, had protested against papal intrusion at that time, and when Martin V appointed Bishop Beaufort his legate *a latere*, the nomination was successfully rejected by both Henry V and Archbishop Chichele. Thereafter, there was no serious conflict between England and the Holy See, merely disputes over abuse rather than struggles over principle. Never were there martyrs. And nor was it ever likely to be otherwise when so many leaders of the English Church were themselves royal officials, with no taste for constitutional crises, and when hard political reality guaranteed that a king, with the assistance of his lay magnates, could invariably bend the clergy to his will. As a result, English bishops gladly embraced royal authority, and in return kings readily supported churchmen against heresy and lay critics of their role.

Yet this is not to suggest, of course, that an organisation so pervasive was without flaws, or to deny that there were those all too ready to rail against ecclesiastical abuses of various descriptions. In *The Obedience of a Christian Man*, published in 1528, William Tyndale scoffed at the 'wily tyranny' of ecclesiastical authority and exhibited nothing but cold contempt and sarcasm for the clergy in general and bishops in particular, who, in his view, were not merely content 'to reign over king and emperor and the whole earth', but sought to 'challenge authority also in heaven and in hell'. From the highest to lowest ranks of the Church hierarchy, if Tyndale is to be believed, there was nothing but unbridled avarice. 'The parson sheareth,' he wrote, 'the vicar shareth, the parish priest polleth, the friar scrapeth, and the pardoner pareth; we lack but a butcher to pull off the skin'. And in the meantime, through practices like confession, whereby they 'knew all secrets', the clergy kept their flocks in passive subservience, though they themselves could often scarcely read – a bone of particular contention, it seems, for many reformers of Tyndale's scholarly mould:

I daresay that there are some 20,000 priests, curates this day in England, and not so few that cannot give the right English unto this text in the Paternoster, *Fiat voluntas tua, sicut in coelo et in terra*, and the answer thereunto.

The supposedly heavy financial burdens imposed in the form of tithes, mortuary and probate fees, Peter's Pence, annates, indulgences, dispensations, etc., were another regular source of dissatisfaction for those with axes to grind. 'Is it not unreasonable,' asked Thomas Starkey, 'the first fruits to run to Rome, to maintain the pomp and pride of the Pope, yea, and war also, and discord among Christian princes as we have seen by long experience?' Similarly, the materialism and worldliness of cardinals and bishops, which contrasted so starkly with the ideals of apostolic poverty and Christian humility that they claimed to espouse was also being loudly condemned in some quarters. It was John Colet, for instance, who first coined the phrase 'wolves in sheep's clothing' in connection with the English episcopacy, and nepotism, simony, pluralism and absenteeism had all become favourite targets of anticlerical bile. To cap all, the leading clergyman in England, Thomas Wolsey, seemed to epitomise all that was wrong with the institution whose power he wielded so domineeringly. 'One cross,' declared the Italian Polydore Vergil, 'is insufficient to atone for his sins.'

Monks, in their turn, attracted more than their fair share of criticism at a time when tales of decadent 'abbey lubbers' abounded and it was widely mooted that if the Abbot of Glastonbury bedded the Abbess of Shaftesbury their bastard would surely become the richest landowner in England. Christopher St German, on the other hand, pointed to priests who played 'at Tables' and other illicit games, while even Thomas More observed of the parish clergy that 'many were lewd and naught'. Erasmus's *Colloquies* make taunting reference to prebendaries and their concubines, and parsons who were sots, while as early as 1486 Cardinal John Morton had condemned priests addicted to field sports, as well as those who wore secular clothes and let their hair grow long, or who loitered in taverns. And before the 1520s were out, Simon Fish, a barrister of Gray's Inn, would publish his famous *Supplication of Beggars*, which amply reflected the full venom of the Church's most vociferous critics. In it, among other things, he denounced the pope as a 'cruel and devilish bloodsupper drunken in the blood of saints and martyrs of Christ'. The clergy, too, were depicted as immoral perverters of God's word, and Fish beseeched his sovereign accordingly 'to tie these holy idle thieves to the carts to be whipped naked about every market town'.

Yet a prudent judge reads the work of an agitator like Fish with appropriate caution and, in spite of his passionate rantings, the old religion, though embattled, was far from crisis. In fact, complaints about corrupt or decadent clergy were neither new, as any student of Langland and Chaucer can attest, nor especially widespread. By no means all members of the episcopacy were as corrupt as Wolsey, and the much maligned parish clergy were, in the main, a willing enough bunch, in spite of all the anticlerical vitriol that Fish and others might pour upon them. Nor were the judicial and financial burdens imposed upon the king's subjects as intolerable as high-profile scandals and lurid tales of the day might suggest. Besides which, many of the Church's deficiencies were, in any case, readily acknowledged by some of its most eminent leaders, while schemes for improvement remained ongoing. Indeed, when denunciations of the Church's worldliness occurred, they tended in the main to come from priests themselves: from moral reformers such as Thomas Gascoigne, chancellor of Oxford University at various points between 1439 and 1453, or from humanist scholars such as John Colet, enthused by their exposure to the so-called 'New Learning'.

Colet, in fact, had returned from study in Italy in 1496 and thereafter lectured in Oxford on St Paul's epistles, bringing with him a new style of scriptural exegesis, which applied the principles of Renaissance classical scholarship to the biblical text, and led him to a renewed fervour for the re-creation of primitive Christianity. As a result, in 1498 he condemned the Church's compromises with the world and its values, and demanded that bishops and priests should eschew royal service and the race for profits and promotion. After which, as Dean of St Paul's, he preached the same message to the Canterbury Convocation in 1510, pointing out that the clergy were guilty of 'pride of life', 'lust of the flesh', 'covetousness', and 'worldly occupation', and calling for 'the reformation of ecclesiastical affairs' on the grounds that 'never was it more necessary'. Elsewhere, moreover, he was even more outspoken. In his lectures on the *Hierarchies of Dionysius*, for example, he seemed so obsessed with the wickedness of the day that he could see nothing else:

O Priests! O Priesthood! O the detestable boldness of wicked men in this our generation! O the abominable impiety of these miserable men, of whom this age contains a great multitude, who fear not to rush from the bosom of some foul harlot into the temple of Christ, to the altar of Christ, to the mysteries of God.

Yet even so outspoken a critic as Colet recognised, too, that 'the diseases which are now in the Church were the same in former ages', and acknowledged that canon law had provided the requisite remedies. 'The need, therefore,' he concluded, 'is not for the enactment of new laws and constitutions, but for the observance of those already enacted.'

This, then, was certainly no proto-Protestant, embittered to the point of rebellion by either the ecclesiastical structure or the Church's sacramental system. On the contrary, Colet was a high clericalist, anxious to maintain the privileges of priests by raising their prestige. And the same was equally true of John Fisher, Bishop of Rochester from 1504, whose famous preaching skills were often turned to good effect in echoing Colet's themes. The clergy, in Fisher's view, 'were wont, and indeed ought still, like lights to the world to shine in virtue and godliness', though at the present time 'there cometh no light from them but rather an horrible misty cloud or dark ignorance'. For as Fisher made clear in his *Penitential Psalms*, only the ministrations of a virtuous priesthood could bring the laity to Christ and through him to salvation:

All fear of God, also the contempt of God, cometh and is grounded of the clergy, for if the clergy be well and rightfully ordered, giving good example to others of virtuous living, without doubt the people by that shall have more fear of Almighty God. But contrary-wise, if the clergy live dissolutely in manner, as if they should give no account of their life past and done before, will not the lay people do the same?

Like Colet, therefore, Fisher clearly held the highest possible view of the priesthood and its privileges, since both his theology and personal spirituality led him to stress the prevalence of sin and the necessity of repentance to avoid God's fearsome punishment. And it was this, above all else, that explains his fears that the worldly clergy of his day were failing to proclaim Christ's call for penitence with proper evangelical fervour. Yet just like Colet, too, he was conscious of the deficiencies of the clergy, not because they were acute or worsening, but because any defects – even comparatively minor ones – were bound to threaten the salvation of men and women. As such, it was Fisher's pastoral concern to save souls rather than the actualities of clerical life that made him such a critic of priests. And it was this self-same concern for souls that made him a model bishop in his own right, amply fulfilling the episcopal ideal set before Convocation by Colet.

No member of the episcopacy could, in fact, have embodied more effectively the self-same diligence that Fisher demanded from his peers, though most already were doing much of what both he and Colet demanded. For while Bishop James Stanley of Ely, a son of the first Earl of Derby, did indeed sire three children (apparently by his housekeeper) and live the life of a great lord – hunting with neighbours and retainers, building magnificently, especially at Manchester, and neglecting his pastoral duties at every turn – he remained a striking exception to the general rule: an unworthy aristocrat foisted on the Church by family connection and royal patronage. By contrast, bishops like Blythe of Lichfield, Mayhew of Hereford, Nykke of Norwich, Oldham of Exeter, Sherburne of Chichester, Smith of Lincoln, and, of course, Fisher of Rochester were all energetic administrators, determined to maintain clerical discipline, along with the highest possible level of pastoral care. And while Archbishop William Warham's attention may have been distracted from Canterbury by his responsibilities as primate and Lord Chancellor, he too found time to take part in a careful diocesan visitation of 1511–12 and employed effective deputies, such as Cuthbert Tunstall, to meet those needs he himself could not. Likewise, Fox of Winchester, who had previously been immersed in his role as Lord Privy Seal, nevertheless withdrew from government in 1516, to throw himself into diocesan business, while only two English bishoprics – those of Bath and Wells, and Worcester – were held by absentee Italians, hired by the king as his representatives in Rome.

Even the sullied reputation of the papacy itself, for that matter, had no more destroyed the allegiance of most Englishmen to the See of Rome than the commitment of their kings to the faith they considered themselves born to protect. Lewd tales heard outside the Flaminian Gate in Rome had certainly lost nothing in the telling by the time they reached English shores, while stories that in Italy were lightly dismissed as little more than merry yarns continued to excite grating indignation in London taverns and Cotswold cottages alike. Some popes, as not a few of the king's subjects well knew, had become far more renowned for their toxicological wizardry than for their pastoral gifts as 'Vicars of Christ', while others, such as Julius II, seemed to confirm the papacy's widespread reputation for greed and immorality. Not only did this particulary dazzling example of papal excess personally conduct an armed vendetta against his rivals in vice, the Borgias, but he did so in specially commissioned silver armour. Moreover, when not demolishing his enemies, Julius seemed to busy himself mainly with marvellously extravagant building projects, involving Raphael, Bramante and Michelangelo. It was he, for instance, who laid the foundation stone of the new Basilica of St Peter and bequeathed to posterity the Sistine Chapel. But, in the meantime, he also saw fit to fashion a family of at least three illegitimate daughters before finally falling prey to the scourge of syphilis in 1513. And his successor, Leo X, was, it seems, no less inclined to cherish visibility. The son of Lorenzo de Medici, he had been an abbot at the age of 7, a canon at 8 and a cardinal at 13, while later, as pope, he would trade in more than 2,000 ecclesiastical appointments with a value of 3 million ducats and be accompanied on procession by Persian horses, a panther, two leopards and, for additional effect, his pet elephant, Hanno, whose portrait was painted by Raphael.

Yet when Julius II was elected in 1513, the mayor and aldermen of London attended a *Te Deum* at St Paul's in honour of the occasion, and nationwide prayers for the Holy Father and the good of the Church continued to be conducted long afterwards. In 1490, they had been commanded in conjunction with similar prayers for the king and his realm, but as late as 1527 they were directed to the restoration of the pope's liberty, following the sack of Rome. In the meantime, as papal appeals for assistance against the advance of Islam in the eastern Mediterranean and along the Danube valley continued to attract support in England, the Holy City remained a popular destination for English pilgrims. Records of the English College in Rome, for example, reveal a constant stream of visitors who were received in the English hospital there: eighty-two in the six months from November 1504 to May 1505; 202 in the year between May 1505 and May 1506; and 205 in the year after that. Not all, it is true, were necessarily pilgrims, since some described as merchants and sailors may well have been in Rome in the normal course of their work. But a letter to Thomas Wolsey written in 1518 made clear that increasing numbers of pilgrims were indeed creating extra costs for the hospital, and there is little doubt either that some Englishmen were already prepared to hazard their lives on the Church's behalf. For according to a contemporary Durham register, three men – from Brancepeth, Chester-le-Street and Morpeth – made vows of commitment in 1499 in response to a crusading indulgence issued by the pope the previous year. And while Henry VII resisted papal attempts to levy a crusading tenth directly, he, too, nevertheless agreed to donate money to the fight against the Turk, as did Henry VIII later. Various English Knights of St John are known at the same time to have served in Rhodes, and when English representatives at Valladolid reported on Spanish campaigns against the Moors, there were references not only to English fighters but to those English soldiers captured and in need of ransom.

Similar enthusiasm had, in fact, also infected the very king who would eventually see fit to sunder all ties with Rome – not least because crusading ideals conformed so neatly with his own ongoing perception of himself as a Christian warrior-prince. Piety was, after all, an integral part of the chivalric culture that Henry VIII had absorbed from his Burgundian forebears, and his own Knights of the Garter, in their turn, remained every bit as devoted to their faith as they were to deeds of heroism. Henry saw himself, in fact, quite literally in the mould of the Arthurian Sir Belvedere, and early in the reign when his blood was running especially freely, he had not hesitated to speak boldly of conquering Jerusalem with a mighty army of 25,000 men. Indeed, he had even seen fit to request four galleys from Venice to assist his proposed exploits. And although this particular rush of blood had soon abated, it was not long before he was stirred to even wilder flights of fancy. For when, in 1516, Selim the Grim's Ottoman Turks subdued the Holy Land, Henry was soon aflame once more after Leo X's earnest appeal for aid from Christian knights, proclaiming at the time of Cardinal Campeggio's visit to England two years later how he would not hesitate to place everything in his possession at the pope's disposal. His personal wealth and treasure, his royal authority and even his kingdom itself, he declared, might all be gladly rendered up in the sacred cause of defending Christendom against the infidel.

But no less important to the Church's well-being, arguably, than the endorsement of kings was the ongoing support and devotion of altogether humbler folk, held fast, on the one hand, by the grip of long-standing custom, and consoled, on the other, by a range of practices offering hope at a time when life expectancy was low, pain an unavoidable price of life, and divine judgement ever-impending. For every parish church in Tudor England had on its walls the sad fading garlands betokening the death of young virgins, while both purgatory and hell itself – with its everlasting agonies 'more grievous and hard than all the nails and pikes in the world' – were never more than a failed heartbeat or horse's stumble away, making the Church not only an indispensable prop in this life but an equally compelling investment for the next. In consequence, even individuals like Etheldreda Swan, a woman of very modest means who lived in a village near Cambridge, saw fit to endow their parish churches with what little they had left upon their deaths – in her case, a shilling apiece for the local church's high altar, bells and torches; 20d towards its repairs; her best coverlet and a sheet to one of the chapels, along with 6s 8d to another church nearby. Most significantly of all, perhaps, she gave 13s 4d to 'Our Lady's light' in comparison to merely 7d for her own funeral (including 2d for the bellringers).

Nor was the piety prompting such death-bed generosity confined to the poor and sparsely educated. In July 1532, in the western extremity of Somerset, an affluent gentleman called James Hadley left one shilling to every church in four of the county's hundreds and one shilling to every parish priest. He left a shilling, too, to every unbeneficed cleric in the diocese of Bath and Wells, and £1 to every religious house – except Glastonbury, which was to have £2. The sum of 5s was bequeathed to the high altars of six named churches and a shilling to their side altars, so that he might have his name entered on their beadrolls (the list of deceased folk to be remembered at Mass). And still the list of Hadley's bequests went on: £2 for the repair of a reliquary in his parish church; money for thousands of Masses; 4d for every householder in eight towns; and gifts of money not only for his tenants, but for prisoners in Wells and Bristol, as well as for a bridge, some hospitals and a lazar house. And as a final benevolence, 'forasmuch as I have been negligent to visit holy places and going on pilgrimage', he also left gifts of money to twelve shrines, including

Walsingham, Canterbury, Hailes Abbey, Henry VI's tomb and pilgrimage centres nearer home, along with a further £5 for the construction of a chapel in honour of the Visitation and St Christopher.

Hadley's will and the sheer volume of others like Etheldreda Swan's could not, in fact, have demonstrated more aptly either the ongoing vitality of the old religion or the belief system that sustained it, however vulnerable they both eventually proved to be. For the intellectual and political ferment that would ultimately underpin the drive to reformation was still a gaping gulf away from the sympathies, sentiments and concerns of ordinary, and indeed more exalted, folk, who continued to adhere so comfortably to those habits disdained by the standard bearers of religious change. No amount of detailed reasoning or high-browed biblical exegesis could, for example, dislodge believers from their long-held devotion to the saints, which had rendered St Apollonia a tried and trusted cure of toothache, St Osyth an indispensable aid to women who had lost their keys, and left even pickpockets with their very own patron in St Nicholas. The females at Arden made offerings to St Bridget for their sick cows, while in St Paul's Cathedral stood the statue of St Wilgefort, known appropriately as the Maid Uncumber, who was said to rid women of their unwanted husbands, if they offered her oats. And where there was the prospect of saintly assistance, so there was once again ample scope for pious endowments. At Morebath in Devon, for instance – a parish consisting of no more than thirty-three households in 1531 – there were nevertheless regular bequests from comparatively poor folk like Alice Obelye, a servant, for the veneration of St Sidwell and the gilding of his image. And when, in November 1534, a thief broke into the church and stole the saint's silver shoe, the 'young men and maidens of this parish' swiftly 'drew themselves togethers and with their gifts and provisions' attempted to make good the loss. At Ashburton too, to take but one example from innumerable others, there were substantial contributions from the laity for saints' images: an improved St George between 1526 and 1529, a new St Thomas Becket in 1529, along with a new St Christopher as late as 1538. The parish of Wing in Buckinghamshire, in the meantime, was only one of many to set up separate funds in its accounts to supply candles before its altars – for Saints Katherine, Margaret, Thomas and Mary Magdalene – while at Bassingbourne in Cambridgeshire one of the local church's main benefactors was the guild of St John the Baptist, another figure attracting widespread devotion throughout the kingdom, including the capital, where parish processions on the feast day of his heavenly counterpart, St Barnabas, frequently rivalled those conducted on Corpus Christi itself.

Plainly, there could be no doubting the powerful hold exerted over the popular imagination by the Church's saints and their wondrous images, nor of the awe generated by the endless stock of relics that were readily available to heal the sick, save the sinner and comfort the forlorn. As early as the fourth century, St Augustine had denounced men who, in the habit of monks, wandered about North Africa peddling spurious relics, and almost a thousand years later Chaucer was equally dismissive of pardoners travelling his own land with their fardels stuffed with 'pigges bones'. But righteous indignation had failed to stem the influx of sham memorials and faked religious curios originally palmed off by enterprising Levantines on credulous Crusaders, or the systematic dismembering of saints' corpses finally prohibited by Gregory the Great. And when one marvels at the later childlike naivety of our Tudor forebears, it is worth remembering, too, how even Blaise Pascal, some 200 years later, would attribute the sudden recovery of his little niece from illness to her touching of the holy thorn. At Hailes Abbey, a crystal vase was purported to contain the very blood shed by Christ on Calvary, and the people, wrote Hugh Latimer in 1533, 'came by flocks to see it', believing that the sight 'certified them that they be of clean life, and in state of salvation without spot of sin, which doth bolden them to many things'. Such, indeed, was the celebrity attached to possession of holy objects that one particular Bishop of Lincoln was said to have bitten off and brought home part of Mary Magdalene's finger, which had been on display at Fécamp, while elsewhere, at Caversham, the head of the lance of Longinus, apparently delivered by an angel with a single wing, sat in a little chapel – not far from the 'holy halter' with which Judas had hung himself – as fresh as the day it had pierced the Saviour's side.

And when a handful of more rationalistically inclined critics like the London merchant Richard Hilles publicly demurred, they generally foundered on an unyielding coral reef of popular prejudice and hostility. In 1531, for example, the outspoken Hilles was forced to seek employment from Thomas Cromwell, because other merchants refused to deal with him.

Yet five years later he was still declaring himself hated by his neighbours for refusing to contribute towards candles set before images. Likewise, when Grace Palmer of St Osyth's in Essex attempted in 1531 to dissuade her neighbours from participating in pilgrimages to holy images – 'for there you shall find but a piece of timber painted' – she was promptly turned in by those she sought to enlighten: a fate reserved, too, for John Hewes of Farnham in Surrey, who was reported in the same year for scorning a man who had knelt in the street as a crucifix was borne aloft by a passing procession. 'Thou art a fool!' declared Hewes. 'It is not thy maker, it is but a piece of copper or wood!' Elsewhere, when a couple of Wiltshire heretics expressed similar sympathies, they swiftly lost their cattle – to the hearty approval of their peers – and when in 1537 William Senes of Rotherham stood up for common sense in preference to the old-established ways, the result was a tongue-lashing from the Earl of Shrewsbury. 'Come near, thou heretic and kneel near!' declared the outraged nobleman. 'Thou art an heretic, and but for shame I should thrust my dagger into thee!'

But it was the Virgin Mary, above all, who had captured the imagination of contemporaries and inspired such unquestioning devotion, triggering a cult of Our Lady that continued to flourish at a host of pilgrimage centres and eventually underpinned much of Elizabeth Barton's extraordinary prestige. Curiously enough, even the arch-heretic John Wycliffe had written how 'it is impossible for us to be crowned in heaven without Mary's good offices. She was the cause of Christ's Incarnation and Passion, and consequently of all the world's salvation.'

And on this issue at least, his sentiments were wholly at one with the sympathies of those Tudor men and women who, in 1516, almost a decade before Barton's emergence, provided a dramatic demonstration that images and miraculous stories – especially those involving the Blessed Mother of Christ – could still inspire not only the king's subjects but also queens and cardinals. For in East Anglia the convulsions suffered by the daughter of Sir Roger Wentworth had apparently been alleviated by a vision of Our Lady of Ipswich, and when the child subsequently made pilgrimage to the shrine at Gracechurch, where a famous image of the Madonna resided, she was escorted by no fewer than 1,000 devotees who had swiftly caught wind of the rumour. When, furthermore, the girl's parents delayed a promised return visit to Gracechurch, it was alleged that her fits had recurred until a further pilgrimage – this time with upwards of 4,000 in attendance – achieved a complete cure. Inspired by her experience, the girl urged the people to be 'more steadfast in their faith', and proceeded to relieve her brother of a similar affliction. Nor was it long before a local notable had reported the episode to Henry VIII, with the result that both Queen Catherine and Cardinal Wolsey made pilgrimage to the shrine. More importantly still, by 1526 the latter had ensured Gracechurch's lasting fame by obtaining a new indulgence for anyone visiting it. Three years later, indeed, even that confirmed sceptic Sir Thomas More was prepared to relate the story in print, as proof that miracles could still happen:

> Miracles we find largely reported in the godly books of St Gregory, St Augustine, St Jerome, St Eusebius, St Basil, St Chrysostom and many other holy doctors of Christ's Church whose books were not unwritten this thousand year. And when ye say yet of miracles many be now-a-days feigned, so may it be that some were then also: but neither then nor now neither were all feigned.

Since the early days of Christian worship, in fact, churches had been devoted to Christ's mother, and in AD 431 the Council of Ephesus had not only acknowledged that she was widely held in 'special veneration' but laid down that every church should have some special place where the faithful could revere her. The eventual result in England was the flowering of the so-called Lady Chapel in each and every parish church, usually containing a representation of the Madonna herself, sometimes in the form of wall paintings like those surviving at St Mary's Church, Dalham, near Newmarket, or icons, such as the example at West Grinstead, which was copied from one brought by St Eusebius from the Holy Land in the fourth century. More often still, the representation would take the form of a statue or statuette, frequently dubbed in accordance with one or other of the specific virtues locally associated with the Blessed Mother: 'Our Lady of Pity' (London); 'Our Lady, Mother of Mercy' (York); 'Our Lady Refuge of Sinners' (Stone in Kent); 'Our Lady of Perpetual Succour' (Liverpool); 'Our Lady of Grace' (Ipswich). And in many cases these images themselves had come to acquire miraculous reputations, helping to fuel the medieval proliferation of shrines, which had seen the emergence of at least sixteen in Suffolk alone: at Beccles, Cherington, Eye, Ipswich, Ixworth, Melford, Mildenhall, Mutford, Norton, Stoke-by-Clare, Stowmarket, Sudbury, Thetford, Weston, Woodbridge and Woolpit.

Not infrequently, it seems, such intensity of devotion went hand in hand with superstitions and corruptions that became the easy object of attack by religious reformers. *The Golden Legend*, compiled by Jacobus de Voragine in 1260 and published by William Caxton in 1483, still enjoyed a wide readership and told, among other things, of a lecherous monk condemned by Christ but nevertheless rescued by Our Lady on the grounds that he had always saluted her image. Likewise, when Christ's mother was alleged to have brought the first scapular to the Carmelites with the promise that 'whosoever dies in this garment will not suffer everlasting fire', it was not long before wicked men were wearing similar strips of brown cloth around their necks on the assumption that they might pass straight through purgatory to heaven. Rosaries, too, were prone to the same kind of abuse, as Sir Thomas More made clear in his account of a Franciscan friar who conducted a mission at Coventry, proclaiming eternal salvation for those reciting the prescribed cycle of prayers, notwithstanding the protests of the local rector who 'found his flock infected with such a disease that the very worst were especially addicted to the rosary for no other reason that they promised themselves impunity in everything'.

Yet in spite of – perhaps in part because of – its abuses, the veneration of the Blessed Virgin remained unstinting and had also made Walsingham in particular one of the greatest religious centres not only in England but in Europe as a whole. Rivalling both Glastonbury and Canterbury, it had come to serve as a popular substitute for visits to Jerusalem, Rome and Compostella, when warfare and political upheaval rendered them inaccessible during the period of the crusades. And the reputed Marian apparitions to Lady Richeldis de Faverches in 1061 had lost none of their ability to inspire by the start of the sixteenth century. A noblewoman known for her good works who was married to the lord of the manor of Walsingham Parva in Norfolk, Lady Richeldis, or Rychold, lived during the reign of Edward the Confessor, and experienced, it was said, a series of three visions in which she was shown the house of the Annunciation in Nazareth and instructed to build a replica of it in the Norfolk village of Walsingham as a place of pilgrimage where people might honour the Virgin Mary. 'Whoever seeks my help there will not go away empty-handed', she was allegedly told, and this promise was reinforced, it seems, by angelic intervention after Richeldis had heard singing in her garden and witnessed the miraculous completion of the 'Holy House' – some 200 yards from its original site, where she had been endeavouring with no little difficulty to build it. This alone, it seems, was enough not only to inspire the local populace but to generate a nation-wide cult and enlist substantial royal patronage from the time of Henry III through to the reign of Henry VIII himself. By 1513, indeed, even Erasmus was overwhelmed by what he witnessed at the shrine's so-called Slipper Chapel, constructed in 1340, where visitors left their shoes before tramping barefoot the final mile to the shrine itself. 'When you look in,' he wrote, 'you would say it is the abode of saints, so brilliantly does it shine with gems, gold and silver.' And the magnetism of Walsingham's appeal was enough not only to make Catherine of Aragon a regular visitor, but to attract even Anne Boleyn, who publicly announced an intention to stage a pilgrimage, although this was never eventually made good.

Yet it was not altogether surprising, perhaps, that contemporary men and women should also have indulged a rather less respectable fascination for the other side of the same superstitious coin. For alongside the teachings and practices of 'official' religion, there co-existed a parallel world of even more irrational elements that lapped against them at every level, loading nature itself with various layers of occult meaning. There were charms, for example, to be spoken during childbirth and at the foaling of horses, while others helped ale to brew and milk to churn more quickly. In time of sick-ness, incantations were recited to staunch bleeding, and fevers and rheums were abated by a magical process known as 'casting of the heart'. Country folk, in the meantime, hung rue around their necks as a safeguard against witchcraft, and put boughs of mountain ash and honeysuckle in their barns on the second day of May to turn aside spells cast on their cattle. Hot wax from a paschal candle dropped between the beasts' horns and ears gave addi-tional protection, while burying an aborted calf in the roadway prevented cows from miscarrying. Equally, just as the future might be gauged from the chattering of birds, so lumps of coal could be relied upon to keep the evil one at bay. And where pre-Christian traditions of this kind existed, so the Church had readily supplemented the existing stock with colourful tales and images of its own, so that few doubted how the world of human affairs was intimately linked to an ever-present celestial world, populated with highly corporeal and active agents in the form of cherubim and seraphim and other supernatural intelligences, including angels and archangels, who, it was said, conducted divine services 'all the day long' and only took time off to listen to the appeals of men 'just before their matins and their evensong'.

No less for many wealthy London merchants than thousands of illiterate Tudor plough-hands was there any serious doubt that hailstones the size of eggs fell freely from the sky with the devil's face upon them, that rain might readily turn to blood by wondrous means, or that decapitated traitors regularly chased about the country holding their heads in their arms. And when a high wind blew down St Alkmund's church steeple in Shrewsbury, the news that Satan's very own talons had left great scratches on the fourth bell would have come as no real surprise to either unschooled Shropshire housewives or their God-fearing sheep-farmer husbands. Well into the sixteenth century and long after the yoke of Rome had finally been cast off, enlightened bishops were still forbidden to denounce the existence of so-called 'dismal days' on which weddings, travel, blood-letting etc. were to be avoided. And nor at any stage of his reign would Henry VIII himself submit to his own Archbishop of Canterbury's request that he assign both astrology and physiognomy to the list of 'unlawful and superstitious crafts'. For this, after all, was a king who, of his own confession, saw much greater need 'to contemplate the severe and inflexible justice of God than the caprice of his mercy', and one who in 1512, when his male child lay close to death, had not hesitated, albeit in vain, to ensure the infant's life by conducting, over all of ten days, a secret and barefoot pilgrimage to the shrine of Our Lady at Walsingham, where he said his prayers, kissed the relic of the Virgin's milk and made offerings of £1 13s 4d.

Nothing, moreover, could have demonstrated more eloquently the hold of the ways of the old religion in England than the very obsequies accompanying the death of Henry's own father. Henry VII had breathed his last at Richmond in April 1509, and on the morning of 10 May a solemn funeral Mass was celebrated at St Paul's by the Bishop of London and the Abbots of Reading and St Albans. Appropriately enough, it was Bishop John Fisher, generally acknowledged as the finest episcopal preacher of the day, who delivered the funeral sermon, emphasising the transitoriness of human existence and the role of Mother Church as intercessor, by pointing out how even so great a king had ultimately had to forgo 'all his goodly houses, so richly dekte and apparayled, his gardens large and wylde' at his Creator's summons. And it was no less fitting either that the Gothic tomb in which the former king was laid, originally prepared for the remains of his miracle-working predecessor, Henry VI, should have been so suitably embellished with sacred relics: a piece of the True Cross set in gold and adorned with pearls and jewels, as well as 'oon of the legs of St George set in silver parcel gilt'.

For when the first Tudor made such provisions, he could never have doubted that the religious system in which he had been brought up would endure as long as the world itself. His kingdom, after all, like Europe as a whole, was still at religious peace, while he himself was always his pious mother's son: a man as committed to a magical conception of the Mass and a mechanical conception of prayer as any of his predecessors, and equally convinced that only by membership of the mystical body of Our Lord, under the guidance of the Holy Father in Rome, could both he and his subjects ultimately achieve political harmony in this life and eternal salvation in the next. That the precious relics of his magnificent tomb might one day be lost or that a Protestant granddaughter would come to sit in the chapel that housed it beneath a canopy fashioned from the confiscated Florentine copes of his priests, was almost as unimaginable as the thought that the Puritan, Sir Robert Harley, might eventually cast down its altar and hack in pieces its reredos – that miracle of Torrigiano's art. But such desecrations would indeed become fact, before a certain 'Captain Walter Lee of the Yellow Regiment, haberdasher' ultimately saw fit to complete the vandals' task by breaking the tomb's stained glass windows, more than a century after its occupant's own son had proclaimed himself Supreme Head of the Church, laid waste the monasteries and left a scarlet trail of martyrs' blood in his wake.

No less inconceivable, of course, was the prospect that the very bishop entrusted to preach at the first Tudor's funeral service would himself be awaiting execution on Tower Hill little more than a quarter of a century later. For the only martyrs in Henry VII's kingdom were a tiny handful of Lollard heretics, who, without organisation, learning or leaders of distinction, went largely unrecorded by history. More often feared and hated by their peers, these courageous but isolated adherents to the fourteenth-century teachings of John Wycliffe had long since declined in prominence from their heyday at the time of Sir John Oldcastle's uprising in 1415, and were now mainly to be found in London and the eastern counties. Where they or their offshoots appeared at all, moreover, they were quickly and effectively suppressed, as the ambassador of Ludovico Sforza made clear in 1499 when he wrote from London of a sect of heretics who declared 'baptism unnecessary for the children of Christians, marriage a superfluous rite, and the sacrament of the altar a fiction', before adding how the bishops had already begun to eradicate them. Francis Bacon, too, would note in his history of Henry VII's rule how proceedings against heretics were 'rare in this king's reign', observing that where action was taken at all, it was in most cases 'rather by penance than fire' – as, indeed, in 1498 when Henry himself converted a Canterbury heretic at the stake, not only sparing the man from imminent burning, but rewarding him with a coin thereafter for his good sense in recanting.

For a quarter of a century of the next reign, too, it must be said – until the watershed of Elizabeth Barton's execution at Tyburn – religious martyrs remained a comparative rarity, consisting exclusively of known and recalcitrant heretics. In 1511, it is true, Andreas Ammonius wrote a gossiping letter from London to Erasmus, full of sprightly exaggeration:

> I do not wonder that the price of faggots has gone up, for many heretics furnish a daily holocaust, and yet more spring up to take their place. And, so please you, the brother of my man Thomas – more a stick than a man – has not only started a sect, but has disciples.

Erasmus, moreover, loving warmth and yearning for a Dutch stove, played along with the joke by declaring from his Cambridge residence how, with winter upon us, he will hate heretics all the more for raising the price of fuel. But the hard evidence to the contrary was overwhelming. For, shortly after Henry VIII's accession, Bishop Fitzjames of London began a heresy hunt in the capital, which exposed little more than Richard Hunne's suspect Bible with all its 'naughty' annotations. And even John Foxe's martyrological scourings years later could uncover nothing more than forty cases between 1509 and 1527 in the entire diocese of London, which included Essex. In all instances but the two cases involving the relapsed heretics Sweeting and Brewster, the accused duly abjured and did penance by standing, as was customary, with faggots on their shoulders before Paul's Cross during Sunday sermon time.

Nor should it be assumed that the burning of heretics excited much resentment on those occasions that it did occur, or that their cause had much appeal. When Thomas Bennet went to the stake at Exeter in 1532, for example, he was threatened by one zealot in the crowd brandishing a blazing furze-bush on a pike, who declared to him: 'Ah! whoreson heretic! Pray to Our Lady and say *Sancta Maria, ora pro nobis*, or by God's wounds I will make thee do it!' Whereupon the crowd raged at the victim and threw sticks and furze into his fire. Likewise, when Thomas Harding was burned at Chesham in 1532, even children took wood to the fire as the crowd rejoiced at his suffering. Before James Bainham's burning in the same year, there were similar scenes, which left the victim in further agonies for the fate of his innocent wife. 'For my sake she shall be an approby unto the world,' he declared, 'and be pointed at of every man on this sort, "Yonder goeth the heretic's wife!"'. And it was no mere coincidence, of course, that Dr John London would seek to deter his nephew from heresy in 1534 by emphasising the resulting shame to his family:

> Your mother, after that she shall hear what an abominable heretic she hath to her son, I am well certain that she will never eat more bread that shall do her good. Alas, remember that hitherto there was never heretic of all our kin.

Known heretics, after all, including those who had abjured, were widely ostracised and ill-treated. When Humphrey Monmouth, for instance, acquired a reputation as 'a Scripture man', even his poor neighbours in Barking refused to take charity from him, or to borrow money. And after John Hig, a Dutch Lutheran living in London, abjured his heresy in 1528, he was soon forced to petition for release from his so-called 'faggot badge', since no one would employ him wearing it.

By that time, of course, as the impact of Lutheranism became more pronounced, there was greater government concern and a sprinkling of higher-profile victims. Thomas Bilney, for example, who was eventually executed in July 1531, had been born around 1495 in Norfolk, most probably in Norwich, and entered Trinity Hall, Cambridge, to study law, before taking Holy Orders in his mid-twenties. Introspective by nature, and with a supersensitive conscience to boot, he had tried and failed to establish his own righteousness in the eyes of God, until rescued from his spiritual torment by the words of St Paul in Erasmus's translation of the New Testament, which convinced him, not unlike Luther before, 'that Christ Jesus came into the world to save sinners of whom I am the chief and principal'. 'Immediately', he later recorded, 'I felt a marvellous comfort and quietness, insomuch that my bruised bones leapt for joy,' after which 'the Scripture began to be more pleasant unto me than the honey or the honeycomb; wherein I learned that all my labours, my fasting and watching, all the redemption of masses and pardons' were valueless 'without truth in Christ, who alone saveth his people from their sins'. Preaching throughout the diocese of Ely from 1525 onwards, denouncing the veneration of saints and relics, together with pilgrimages to Walsingham and Canterbury, he was eventually pulled from the pulpit of St George's, Ipswich, after producing a series of inflammatory sermons, which resulted in his arraignment before Cardinal Wolsey, Archbishop William Warham of Canterbury, and Cuthbert Tunstall, Bishop of London, in the chapter house at Westminster Abbey where he was convicted of heresy.

But such was the comparative moderation of the court that Bilney's sentence was actually deferred while efforts were made to induce him to recant, which, to his subsequent overwhelming remorse, he duly did after two days of intensive cross-examination. The result was his eventual release from the Tower in 1529 and subsequent return to Cambridge where he experienced the full agony of conscience accompanying his apostasy and finally resolved to 'come again like one rising from the dead', as one of his protégés, Hugh Latimer, later put it. Delivering passionate sermons in the open fields of Norfolk, since his licence to preach in church had been revoked, he returned to his former themes, distributing New Testaments and exposing the errors of Rome – all of which, wholly predictably, led to his arrest by Bishop Nykke of Norwich and sentence to burning by the civil authorities at the so-called 'Lollards Pit'. The night before his death, after eating his last meal, Bilney had, it was said, placed his finger in the flame of a lamp and only withdrawn it after it had been burned down to the first joint. And when questioned by friends about such an extreme course of action, he had replied: 'I am only trying my flesh; tomorrow God's rods shall burn my whole body in the fire.'

Plainly, then, the fortitude required to resist unto death was not confined to Catholics, and the types of personality involved in both cases were not always dissimilar. Just under two years later, for example, John Frith, the son of a Kentish innkeeper, took a similar route to martyrdom for denying that either purgatory or transubstantiation were founded upon Holy Scripture. Born in 1503 in Westerham and educated initially at Sevenoaks Grammar School and Eton College, Frith had finally been admitted as a scholar at Queens' College, Cambridge, where he encountered both Thomas Bilney and William Tyndale as a frequenter of the White Horse Tavern – a well-known meeting place for evangelically inclined intellectuals. While at Cambridge, too, his tutor was none other than Stephen Gardiner, the eventual Bishop of Winchester who would later take part in condemning him to death. But it was at Oxford, where, after graduating in 1525, he became a minor canon at Thomas Wolsey's new Cardinal College, that he first ran foul of the authorities. For, like other Cambridge emigrants, he was already tainted with heresy and found himself imprisoned – in a cellar where fish were stored – for possession of heretical books, only to escape to Antwerp after Wolsey had himself rescued him on condition that he travel not more than 10 miles from Oxford.

Renewing his connection with William Tyndale, Frith may well have assisted in the translation of the former's New Testament. But it was his polemical writing against John Rastell's defence of purgatory, for which he gained more lasting fame, along with two return visits to England, that brought him once more to the attention of the authorities. For in 1530, probably while attempting to make contact with the heretical Prior of Reading, he had been arrested as a vagabond and confined to the stocks upon refusal to disclose his identity. There the town schoolmaster encountered him, conversed with him in Latin and heard him recite lines from Homer's *Iliad*, which was enough, it seems, to secure his release. Even so, like other restless souls of his kind, Frith could not accommodate himself to compliance for long, and by 1532 he had returned to his activities, this time to be arrested in Essex and lodged in the Tower, as a result of what John Foxe later attributed to 'the great hatred and deadly pursuit of Sir Thomas More, at that time chancellor', irrespective of the fact that Frith had arrived in July, a full two months after More had already resigned the Great Seal. In fact, the grounds for the reformer's arrest are unknown, though he was soon engaged, in spite of his incarceration, in a literary controversy with More over the issue of transubstantiation, which would ultimately cost him his life.

Frith's death for what he – and indeed the authorities responsible for his condemnation – believed to be the salvation of his soul casts much additional light, moreover, on the kinds of drives and personal psychology that, in some cases, inspired both Protestants and Catholics alike to resist to the limit. Certainly, during the five months before a commission was finally appointed to examine him, Frith had received at least one letter from Tyndale enlarging upon the glories of martyrdom:

> Fear not threatening therefore, neither be overcome by sweet words, with which twain the hypocrites will assail you. Neither let the persuasions of worldly wisdom bear rule in your heart. No, though they be your friends that counsel you. Let Bilney be a warning to you. Let not their vision beguile your eyes. Let not your body faint. He that endureth to the end shall be saved.

There were references, too, to the heroic men in the Netherlands and France who had already sacrificed their lives 'to the glory of God', and a final message delivered on behalf of Frith's own wife: 'Your wife is well content with the will of God, and would not for her sake have the will of God hindered.'

After such exhortations, what else could a sensitive young man do? Suitably exposed to the comradely inducements and self-propagating fixations of a persecuted underground circle comprised of charismatic individuals like Tyndale, who had themselves become cut off from the mainstream attitudes of contemporary society, Frith and others like him found their resistance fuelled not only by the white-hot coals of a faith offering eternal salvation, but, likewise by the promptings of those they held most dear. Indeed, it was sometimes the love of those nearest and dearest – almost as much as service to God and the principle of a higher truth, to which only they were privy – that consecrated such individuals for the flames so readily.

Even so, however, every effort was in fact made to save Frith, like Bilney before him, from the agonies of the stake – efforts of a kind that would often be strikingly absent only a little later when the king's own hand was more directly involved in proceedings. The bishops examining Frith, for example, had, as Thomas Cranmer was at pains to point out, in a 'fatherly manner, laboured and travailed for the amendment of that ungracious child'. Cranmer, indeed, who had presided over the commission, recorded how 'I myself sent for him three or four times, to persuade him to leave that his imagination', before even encouraging what appears to have been an abortive escape attempt. For on his way to a meeting with Cranmer at Croydon, Frith's guards suggested that he should slip away into the woods of Brixton and make for Kent, while they pursued him in the direction of Wandsworth: an offer that Frith promptly refused, with the result that he was subsequently referred to John Stokesley, Bishop of London, who by that point had no option other than to pronounce the sentence of excommunication. Handed over to the lord mayor and sheriff, as laid down by the law, *De Haeretico Comburendo*, which had been passed by Henry IV in 1401 for the specific purpose of punishing those who 'do wickedly instruct and inform people ... and commit subversion of the said catholic faith', Frith was then duly burned at Smithfield in the company of a young disciple named Andrew Hewet. A tailor's apprentice, Hewet could only confess at his trial that he believed as Frith believed, and was ready to die with him, though such loyalty evoked no apparent sympathy from the presiding London parson, Dr Cooke, who informed the watching crowds that it was as wrong to pray for the condemned as to pray for a dog.

In such circumstances, of course, it is easy to feel that the heavy hand of the State had been applied with excessive force to men of genuine principle whose direct threat was always likely to be limited. Thomas Bilney, indeed, had to the very end remained entirely orthodox on the authority of the pope, the sacrifice of the Mass, and the doctrine of transubstantiation. But peace and order were always fragile prizes in Tudor England, rarely to be taken for granted and therefore all the more worthy of protection at any cost against those who threatened them, intentionally or otherwise. No one, moreover, had digested this principle more thoroughly than Henry VII or his successor – and for very good reason. Never wholly at ease on his throne and never personally popular, the first Tudor had nonetheless overcome all obstacles. But the effort involved encouraged the blind court poet, Bernard André, to compare his achievements with the twelve labours of Hercules. And André's analogy was undoubtedly a good one; 1497, in particular, had proved a year of especial crisis, as Scots continued to threaten the border, and Cornishmen led by the lawyer Thomas Flamank and a giant blacksmith from St Keverne called Michael Joseph saw fit to march in anger across the breadth of England against the 'crafty means' by which the king had elicited his 'outrageous sums'. Not until they reached Blackheath, in fact, did the rebels finally 'suffer vengeance', but only then after some 15,000 of them, 'stout of stomach, mighty of body and limb', had encamped at Farnham, causing London's citizens to pile up great mounds of timber against the city's gates. And the need thereafter for absolute obedience and unwavering uniformity would never, in consequence, desert either the king or the son who came after him, as the grave mounds left at Blackheath in the aftermath of the 1497 rebellion attested all too graphically. Still visible two centuries later, they were potent reminders not only of the Tudor state's authority but of its very fragility, and the clearest possible warning that any attempt to provoke a religious revolution of the kind launched in the 1530s could only succeed in a largely orthodox kingdom on the back of systematic and uncompromising repression. For the Catholic Church in England would continue to retain the leadership of its flock as a moral, spiritual and indeed social force right up to the moment of its unexpected demise: an organisation not so flawless, it is true, as the idealists may have wished, but neither so diabolically mired as its most passionate critics contended.

Certainly, when Roger Martyn was a small child, not only his own Long Melford church, but the Church in England as a whole had seemed effectively impregnable. For if, on the one hand, there was an occasional bishop like James Stanley to breed scandal, there was always a John Colet to denounce him and a John Fisher to set a saintly example. And if there were opportunities for clashes of interests involving what was, after all, a great national institution boasting integral relations with the king, secular courts and civic authorities, the Church's officials nevertheless muddled on dutifully enough in the main and got on with their business in the time-honoured fashion. No doubt there was some local contention between priests and people, since the Church was ultimately, of course, a collection of parish communities, each with their own idiosyncrasies. But while few would eventually refuse whatever gains might fall their way, neither king nor nobles, nor gentry nor Parliament were systematically plotting to seize its wealth and jurisdiction. And just as there was no organised resistance to Long Melford's tithes or, once again, the Church's tithes in general, so the few heretics who denied parts of the Church's teachings, even in Long Melford, had been around for a century and more, with little hint of lasting damage.

Whatever undoubted difficulties *Ecclesia Anglicana* may therefore have faced, there were no Reformations on any horizon as the sixteenth century dawned. On the contrary, for the vast majority of its adherents, the Church remained a homely sanctuary – familiar, tolerable and sacrosanct out of long habit, while offering security in this world and eternal bliss in the next. And if the Catholic Church in England had, perhaps, grown flabby from undue comfort, it remained, too, an organisation to be respected by lay rulers, especially when, for a tiny minority of its adherents, it was something much more potent still: nothing less, in fact, than a divinely appointed institution meriting defence unto death itself, and therefore a challenge of formidable proportions to any hoping to destroy it. For if prophetic visions of doom like those proclaimed by Elizabeth Barton were to receive credence among common folk, let alone those in high places, or, worse still, become combined with active resistance from the likes of John Fisher or passive non-compliance from otherworldly monks like Sebastian Newdigate and his Carthusian colleagues, the ramifications might well prove momentous, since Tudor England was not an easy country to govern at the best of times. On the contrary, even on the smaller, day-to-day scale, the threat of disorder was an ever-present feature of contemporary society, making the prospect of what Henry VIII and Thomas Cromwell were ultimately prepared to attempt all the more daunting. As such, there seemed but one conclusion to be drawn by those in power when the time of reckoning finally beckoned: if the yoke of Rome was to be broken, the recalcitrant minority who refused to bow would have to be broken, too.

2

MARTYR-IN-WAITING

He was in holiness, learning and diligence in his cure and in fulfilling his office of bishop such that of many hundred years England had not any bishop worthy to be compared unto him. And if all countries of Christendom were searched, there could not lightly among all other nations be found one that hath been in all things like unto him, so well used, and fulfilled the office of bishop as he did. He was of such high perfection in holy life and strait and austere living as few were, I suppose, in all Christendom in his time, religious or other.

The opinion of a young contemporary of John Fisher, recorded by William Rastell, nephew of Sir Thomas More.

It was not until 10 May 1509, after a long and creaking descent into illness and old age, that Henry VII was finally consigned to dwell 'more richly dead than he did alive' in his splendid tomb of black marble at Westminster. But by then, as spring was quickening and 17-year-old Henry VIII was bursting upon his unsuspecting kingdom, a new government, peppered with remnants of the old order, had already taken shape. For the young king's chief councillors remained largely his father's men: weighty, substantial, grave and elderly. Prominent among them was Thomas Howard, the 66-year-old Earl of Surrey – a thick-shouldered old warhorse who, until his death in 1521, would sally northward from time to time to sharpen his sword against marauding Scots. But the balance lay with the clerical interest, all of whom, in stark distinction to their new ruler, were conservative in outlook, cautious by nature, and, to a man, wholly unable to bridle the young man's restless temperament. Though he retained the Great Seal, William Warham, Archbishop of Canterbury, seems to have taken little or no responsibility at all for moulding his sovereign's outlook. Unambitious and almost certainly weary of twenty years of official life, his hang-dog expression in his most famous portrait seems merely to imply a long life-time of mild regrets, and though Erasmus rightly described him as 'witty' and 'generous', the Dutchman was by no means altogether unfair either in adding the epithet 'laborious' to the archbishop's description. Overall, he was a pliant, sceptical character who, it was said, 'only read' and would die with merely £30 in hand, 'enough for my funeral', all of which contrasted markedly with, on the one hand, his fellow councillor, Richard Fox, Bishop of Winchester – who, as a result of Warham's comparative indifference, came to assume direction of affairs as Lord Privy Seal – and, above all perhaps, Thomas Ruthall, Bishop of Durham, whose narrow devotion to the everyday drudgery of accumulating vast lands made him the richest prelate in the realm.

None of these, it seemed, could hold the king indefinitely from war and breakneck marriage, and none, more obviously still, was made of martyr's stuff. Yet among their number, of comparatively junior status but altogether more tenacious fibre, was John Fisher, who was to become by turns the most outspoken and challenging opponent of the king's eventual divorce two decades later. Born at Beverley in Yorkshire around 1469, his home town's history explains in part, perhaps, his own, and in particular that religious zeal and independence of mind, which, along with his outstanding intellect, rendered him so capable and determined an opponent when roused. For his birthplace nestled at the foot of the eastern slopes of the wolds of East Yorkshire, an area well known both for the jealous protection of its liberties and unwavering orthodoxy, which it advertised boldly by its famous Minster, as well as two long-established Dominican and Franciscan houses, a commandery of the Knights Hospitaller, and the hospitals of St Giles and St Nicholas, not to mention Fisher's own parish church of St Mary. And if Beverley's 5,000 inhabitants were well served by the Church whose rituals and rulings they observed so readily, their interests were no less adequately furnished either, it seems, by those self-same merchant governors who had ensured its place as one of the leading cloth-making and marketing centres of the kingdom. A thriving agglomeration of fine houses, paved streets and public buildings, protected by a surrounding moat and guarded by five sturdy gates, its people were not to be lightly offended, as Edward IV wisely appreciated when he led his army through their midst in 1461 on his way to Towton, carefully avoiding all hint of indiscipline or offence. And it was a precedent not lost on his rivals, who likewise acknowledged the need to leave the tenth largest town in the kingdom untouched through all the arduous twists and turns of what became known to posterity as the Wars of Roses.

If a later king had been equally judicious in his dealings, of course, John Fisher might have proved no less compliant himself than the townsfolk whose steadfast loyalty to the Crown he instinctively shared. For there was certainly nothing about the future bishop's family background to imply anything other than law-abiding pragmatism, in addition to honest, unquestioning piety. Indeed, as a mercer of moderate prosperity, his father Robert's final will and testament bore every routine hallmark of the characteristically rock-like, late medieval bourgeois, whose bequests to local churches and almshouses were as conventional as the in-built faith that underpinned them, and the earnest endeavours of a lifetime that made them possible in the first place. Hailing originally, it seems, from southern Lincolnshire, the head of the Fisher household left fitting sums to religious foundations in that county: one to the Premonstratensian monastery at Hagnaby, to which he left 10s for a trental of Masses for the repose of his soul; the other a smaller amount for the upkeep of a church at Holtoft. And there were similar payments directed closer to home – including one of 6s 8d to Robert Cook, chaplain of his parish church – likewise confirming the residing impression of a solid, if unassuming, pillar of his local community, whose main life's business, beyond God-fearing right behaviour, had been business itself, and the dedicated care and protection of his family. For there is mention, too, in his will of four children, who, though unnamed, can be safely assumed to include John, the probable eldest if an early manuscript version of his life is to be trusted, and his brother Robert who was later his steward at Rochester. All, including a daughter, were securely provided for by a father who had clearly been nothing less than dutiful in the execution of his parental responsibilities, and more likely still, a loving parent to each of his offspring.

Yet by the time of his eldest son's eighth birthday, Robert Fisher senior was dead and buried, at St Mary's, his parish church, whose vicar witnessed the will on 17 June 1477. And the result was a new stepfather for the boy John, whose mother, Agnes, had soon remarried to a William White by whom she had five further children: Thomas and another boy named John, who became merchants; Richard, a priest; Elizabeth, who entered the Dominican nunnery at Dartford in Kent; and a last named Edward. Certainly, if scope for tension arose as a result of the new arrangement, it was never apparently realised, since two of the three works Bishop John Fisher composed during his final imprisonment in the Tower were addressed to his half-sister, at which time his brother Robert was still attending him in the confines of his cell. Not long previous, moreover, according to a delightful vignette recorded by his earliest biographer – who wrote anonymously, but was probably Dr John Young, a fellow of St John's College, Cambridge, and sometime member of his household – he had provided lavish Christmas fare for his relatives at Rochester before seeking welcome refuge from their merry-making in the seclusion of his study. Always more at ease in solitude among his books or at the pulpit, declaiming upon the joys of heaven and perils of hell, Fisher had nevertheless retained a love for his family's company long after his horizons had shifted far beyond their own. And a similar pride and affection extended too, it seems, to his Yorkshire roots in general, as was amply indicated by his assiduous promotion of a northern presence at Cambridge, through fellowships and scholarships, once he had become the university's chancellor.

From numerous perspectives, then, the imprint of Beverley upon both boy and adult man should not be underestimated. For while John Fisher, true to character, was an impersonal writer who left us only two or three definite references to his childhood experiences, and although there are no other records or legends of his earliest years, we can nevertheless recreate with considerable accuracy the everyday environment of the bustling late medieval town in which he grew up, and fully imagine its lasting influence upon him. No doubt, the silver-gilt shrine of St John of Beverley, martyred in the eleventh century and to whom Henry V attributed his victory at Agincourt, will have left its mark upon young Fisher's spirituality. For it had made the town a major source of pilgrimage in the Middle Ages and, as such, contributed in no small measure to Beverley's prosperity – so much so that when it was destroyed on Henry VIII's orders in 1541, significant economic decline ensued. No doubt, too, Fisher watched the completion of the great west front of Beverley's Minster, the Collegiate Church of St John of Beverley, as it soared heavenwards, and we can also picture him witnessing the miracle plays for which his birthplace was famous – on Corpus Christi and the Feast of the Purification, and on the Sunday after the feast of St Peter ad Vincula, at which the Paternoster play was performed. All were sources of delight to any child, and episodes that, like the liturgy at the Minster and his own parish church of St Mary's, will all have left their trace upon the growing boy. Perhaps, indeed, the lasting emphasis that John Fisher was eventually to place upon the necessity for good preaching may well reflect further childhood impressions, good or bad, when local priests served up their own instruction to him from the pulpit. In any event, there would have been ample scope for him after such occasions to venture forth beyond Beverley's moated walls, and indulge his abiding appreciation of the countryside and country life in general, which is apparent in his sermons and writings of later years.

But it was at school and in study that Fisher spent the lion's share of his time, and it was in this area that he excelled particularly. For along with his brother Robert, he attended the Minster grammar school, which could trace its history back to the tenth century and continued to enjoy a high reputation. Boasting the unusually high number of three masters, the school seems, moreover, to have served his own specific needs to particularly good effect, since in 1483, to the especial satisfaction of his mother and stepfather, he was duly dispatched to Cambridge at an age when boys of similar background were mostly preparing for the more humdrum demands of life within the family business. Certainly, the path to university was not untrod by many others of Fisher's background, but only those of exceptional talent tended to take it. And nor was it insignificant that John Fisher should arrive at his new place of study without the need to earn his keep as either a sizar,[1] or as was sometimes necessary, a mendicant. Plainly, his family was determined to assist his success – and sufficiently confident of their own resources – to ensure his comfort and due dignity at any necessary expense. Nor was it any less noteworthy, perhaps, that as young John Fisher set out on the 150-mile journey along the old Roman road through Lincoln down to Cambridge, he did so in the paid-for company of one of the university's 'fetchers' – another sign in its own right of his family's means. No doubt excited by the

---

1 A sizar is an undergraduate of Trinity College, Dublin, or the University of Cambridge who receives some form of assistance.

opportunities ahead, but daunted, too, by the challenges involved, there would be ample scope for reflection as the week-long journey to his appointed destination unfolded before him. For one thing above all else will have impressed itself upon the talented 14-year-old: namely, that success or otherwise from this time forth was dependent upon no other thing than his native talents and diligence.

Cambridge, after all, was already slowly shedding its former reputation as the cosy nesting place of unguided youth, and gradually becoming a place of more exacting standards and competition. No longer quite the home to riotous high jinks and dissolute living it had undoubtedly become after the fleeting brilliance of its heyday, it was emerging, in fact, as a more ordered and rigorous society, as a result of reforms which Fisher himself, appropriately enough, would further encourage after his own eventual promotion within the university's hierarchy. New hostels and colleges were being built, and the first freshening breeze of an altered approach to learning was beginning to blow away the cobwebs from Cambridge's ancient cloisters, though, as its new student would eventually make clear in an oration before Henry VII delivered in 1506, there was still much ground to make up.

At the time when your majesty first showed your concern for us [Fisher observed], learning had begun to decline among us. This may have been the result of constant litigation with the town, or of the frequent plagues that beset us so that we lost many of our leading scholars, or of the lack of patrons of learning. Whatever the cause, we should indeed have been reduced to despair had not your majesty shone down upon us like the rising sun itself.

For a scholar of Fisher's uncompromising rigour and hard-edged honesty, of course, the comment was hardly surprising. And he was not alone in bemoaning his university's previous shortcomings. For in a letter of 1516 to his old pupil Henry Bullock of Queens' College, Erasmus himself commented that 'about thirty years ago, nothing was taught at Cambridge but Alexander [de Villa Dei], the *Parva Logicalia*, as they are called, those old dictates of Aristotle, and the questions from Scotus'.

But if the New Learning came later to Cambridge than to Oxford, and both the mode and manner of learning had changed insufficiently since the previous century to satisfy fully a perfectionist like Fisher, change, as he himself recognised, was at last afoot, and, for all the shortcomings elsewhere, his own college, Michaelhouse – which was soon to be absorbed into the new foundation of Trinity – was well placed to set him on his future path. Noted for its distinctly conservative theological orientation, it possessed, moreover, at least one tutor of no mean distinction in William de Melton, who was not only more open to humanistic scholarship but also more pastorally minded in outlook than many of his more hidebound peers, and a stickler for the kind of intellectual precision that became such a hallmark of Fisher himself. Later, the pupil was to refer to his master as 'a very eminent theologian' and recall in one of his rare autobiographical reminiscences how Melton 'used often to admonish me when I was a boy and attended his lectures on Euclid, that if I looked on the least letter of any geometrical figure as superfluous, I had not seized the true and full meaning of Euclid'.

And it was precisely because of such thoroughness that Fisher would steadily emerge as a student of such considerable prowess in his own right, notwithstanding his arrival at Cambridge at an age that was young even by contemporary standards. His success, indeed, was glittering and precocious, and would provide the first clear indication of those personal qualities – combining outstanding eminence with high moral seriousness, endurance and willpower – that eventually made him so illustrious, and formidable, a figure.

When he acquired his bachelor's degree in 1488, Fisher did so in the company of two other men of note. One was John Bouge, who later recalled how he and Fisher took their degrees 'both of one day', and went on to become parish priest at St Stephen's Walbrook and confessor to Sir Thomas More. The other was Nicholas West, a fellow of King's until 1498, who was a protégé of Bishop Richard Fox, and became Bishop of Ely in 1515. We know, too, that John Skelton, court poet and tutor to Henry VIII, was another of Fisher's contemporaries. Yet, unlike 'merrie Skelton', rank and reputation in the broader world outside were low on the young Yorkshireman's priorities as he applied himself to study for his MA, which he duly acquired in 1491. Instead, his eyes were squarely set upon an academic career and the priesthood, to which he was subsequently ordained by Thomas Rotherham, Archbishop of York, that same December, when

still some four years below the acknowledged canonical age. Facing thereafter at least ten or twelve long years of further study for his doctorate in
theology, Fisher's horizons did not, indeed, appear to have extended any
further than the fellowship at Michaelhouse that duly accompanied his
MA, or, at most, his subsequent promotion within the university's administrative hierarchy, which, in spite of his predominantly academic leanings,
was not long in coming.

Since 1246, in fact, Cambridge's supreme officer had been its chancellor, elected for two years by the so-called house of regents, which
consisted of those Masters of Arts who presided over the disputations that
constituted a key element of the academic curriculum. But as the chancellor himself was sometimes a bishop or statesman, his duties were often
delegated in turn to the vice-chancellor who, after much rankling, had
eventually become independent of ecclesiastical control, to bear primary
responsibility for a single area of overriding concern: the inculcation of
discipline and good order among the student body. For at a time when
Cambridge's provision for more general aspects of welfare was so limited,
and so many students were more widely known for their shortcomings
than their virtues, it was hardly surprising that priority should have lain
here. Yet even contemporary Cambridge had to be fed and paid for, and
it was for this reason that two other figures, the university's proctors, had
come to assume over the years an increasingly significant role in matters
both routine and more substantial. Elected annually to serve as executive
and administrative officers responsible for supervising all ceremonies and
disputations, they also managed finance, controlled market supplies and
bore the everyday task of keeping peace in the streets. No less importantly,
they usually represented the university in any negotiations with the town
authorities. And in 1494, at the unusually tender age of 25, John Fisher was
elected to this senior post by his fellow regents in recognition not only
of his outstanding scholarship but of his drive and efficiency, which had
singled him out so ideally for his new role.

Henceforth, though his efforts as a scholar and cleric remained undiminished, the rising young star was no less an administrator and man of
practical affairs. And from this point forward, too, he was to become not
only a familiar figure in the streets of Cambridge but, in all probability, a
particularly striking one. For the famous portrait by Holbein of a painfully

gaunt and careworn figure depicts him within two or three years of his
sixtieth year, by which time the troubles of the last decade of his life had
clearly taken their toll. Yet in his prime he was tall, lean and big-boned, with
auburn hair, prominent grey eyes and a strong jaw suggestive of a man not
easily turned from his purposes, though his speech was as spare as his person,
and his imposing appearance was belied by the mildness and modesty of his
demeanour. Always too earnest, it seems, to invite easy acquaintanceship, he
remained nonetheless a caring and trustworthy guide to those who pierced
his outward defences, while to those who gained his support he was a
brave and unyielding ally. Indeed, where loyalty, both to people and principles, was concerned, he was unsurpassed, and where truth was at issue, his
trenchant reasoning and natural tenacity made him a rock-like adversary.
For while there was no more ardent advocate of the established order, both
political and religious, or more passionate critic of opposition for opposition's sake, Fisher was invariably a servant, first and foremost, to his God,
his Church and his conscience: a man prepared to endure to the limit and
to champion the cause of any wrongfully persecuted underdog that others
might see fit to abandon for fear of the consequences.

For so young a man, doubtless, there was even now an implicitly forbidding edge – sufficient, presumably, to cow recalcitrant students scarcely
more callow than himself, not to mention hard-bargaining men of com-
merce with whom he now dealt regularly. But nor was the future bishop
without his fair share of intimates or admirers, among whom he numbered
John Syclyng, Proctor and Master of Godshouse, the college founded by
William Byngham in 1439 'for the free herbigage of poor scholars of
Grammar'. First thrown together in 1494 by the perennial controversies between the university and the town, involving disputed rights and
grants of royal privileges, it was this interminable wrangling over petty
local disputes that swiftly brought Fisher his first acquaintance with a
figure of national importance who would be critical for his own rise to
much wider prominence. For in their tussle with Cambridge's municipal
authorities, which had recently reached a new intensity, the university's
proctors were faced with numerous visits to London, not only for legal
appeals but in search of influential patrons at the royal court. And as a
leader in such negotiations, Syclyng had already emerged as a man with
connections in high places, who identified at once in his counterpart a

most reliable and capable ally. Sallying forth to the capital in the very first year of their acquaintance, therefore, they found themselves bound for a significant encounter that would mark a new development in the younger man's life, involving none other than Lady Margaret Beaufort, Countess of Richmond and Derby – mother of the king, patron of culture and learning, and one of the major powers behind the throne itself.

Intensely devout in her religious faith and no less devoutly intense, it must be said, in her political schemings, Lady Margaret was, in fact, one of the most remarkable women of the century: a figure who had not only been instrumental in the plots that finally brought her son the crown but one who had lived through more reigns, with more opportunity to influence their outcome, than any other person at his court. To the Spanish ambassador in 1498, she was among the half-dozen people with the greatest influence in England. And it was into her presence that John Fisher now arrived, with consequences that could hardly have been more momentous, either for him or his university, though his own response to his first entrée into the circles of the truly high and mighty could hardly have been more typically detached. More concerned with the minutiae of the journey and in particular its cost, the earnest young proctor seems to have been almost entirely unmoved by its potential personal significance. Certainly, he seems to have harboured no prior wish to impress, beyond supporting the university's interests as best he might, or demonstrated any appreciable excitement, as he made his way in Syclyng's company on the two-day journey from Cambridge to Greenwich – by way of Barkway, Ware and Waltham – that would bring him face to face with, arguably, the kingdom's most influential figure other than the monarch himself.

In the Proctor's Book of 1494, recorded in Fisher's own neat handwriting, is the following entry, detailing the expenses of the very trip.

For the hire of two horses for 11 days ... 7*s*.
For breakfast before crossing to Greenwich ... 3*d*.
For the crossing by boat ... 4*d*.

And with the young man's usual attention to detail, there are further references to expenditure on lodgings and refreshments, as the two men spent the first night of their trip 'at the sign of St John's Head' at Barkway.

Thus, 'for wine and fruit', we find a payment of 1s 3d, suggesting the enter-
tainment of guests, while another entry – 'for the use of altars at St Bride,
and bread, wine and candles … 1s 8d' – confirms that Fisher stopped to
say Mass at the famous church of that name in Fleet Street. But it was
another, typically laconic, item within the accounts where the real fascination lies, not only as evidence for a particularly significant historical event
but as confirmation of Fisher's own character. For without pause for further elaboration of any kind, or the slightest hint of the meeting's personal
importance, the proctor records how he had 'dined with the lady mother
of the king' and also, for that matter, 'supped with the [lord] chancellor'.

Probably known to the elderly lady already from her existing connections at Cambridge, Fisher's impact upon her sensibilities on this occasion
was nevertheless particularly profound, as he swiftly emerged thereafter as
her most intimate and trusted associate: first as one of her chaplains and
later as her confessor, in place of Richard Fitzjames, who would precede
his young counterpart as Bishop of Rochester in 1497. In the words of
his anonymous earliest biographer, Fisher 'ordered himself so discreetly,
so temperately and so wisely' that ultimately both Lady Margaret 'and all
her family were governed by his high wisdom and discretion'. 'Whereby
at last,' the account continues, 'he became greatly reverenced and beloved,
not only of that virtuous lady and all her household, but also of the king
her son with whom he was in no less estimation and credit all his life
than with his mistress'. Clearly, this was praise indeed. But the bond
between the two, notwithstanding the gaping difference in their years,
was hardly unpredictable since love of learning and deep devotion to the
Church were, after all, defining features of the 'Venerable Margaret', and
Fisher's scholarly achievements and reputation for integrity and discretion went before him. Indeed, the countess's exceptional spiritual intensity
and austerity, and finely honed intellect, not only closely mirrored her
young visitor's own but had already formed an essential ingredient of the
upbringing of the future Henry VIII – though hardly for the best in this
particular instance, since both her obsessions and ambitions were to leave
an indelible and fateful imprint upon her second grandson.

In effect all prayer and learning, she would become in fact, at one and
the same time, both the best and worst of influences upon the highly
impressionable grandson to whom she became a dominating presence.

At her happiest when reading and translating pious works, such as *The Imitation of Christ*, her devotions commenced at 5 a.m. every day, one hour before the general time of rising, after which, notwithstanding the agonies of acute rheumatism, she was never deterred from spending long periods on her knees in prayer. Next to her skin, she wore a hair shirt 'for the health of her soul' and instead of regal fineries dressed merely in modest robes, much like a nun's habit. Nor was this the sum of her austerities. For, like Fisher himself, who was always a sparing eater at best, she observed fast days meticulously, restricting herself during Lent to but one fish meal a day. Relentlessly self-mortifying, her final years would become almost an abnegation of earthly life itself, as she went about her remaining days maintaining twelve paupers in her house in Woking, washing their feet, serving them with meals when they were ill, and studying them as they approached death, so that she might thereby learn how to die well when her own eagerly awaited appointment with eternity arrived.

Although not permanently resident with her, the growing Prince Henry was therefore likely to have feared his grandmother no less than he loved her, since she represented an oppressive mix of sharp wits, high expectations and maudlin piety, leavened, for good measure, by a pinch of slowly gnawing anxiety that communicated itself to all those close enough to know her. She had never forgotten, after all, how history had hung in the balance at Bosworth Field and how her cherished son might have ended the day in King Richard's place, a broken and dishonoured corpse. Indeed, it was John Fisher, ever the impartial observer and never the syco-phant, who later noted her knack for 'marvellous weeping', and it was he, too, who remarked upon her morbid pessimism. 'Either she was in sorrow by reason of present adversities', he observed, 'or else when she was in prosperity she was in dread of the adversity to come,' though Fisher never forgot either her virtues or his personal debt to the lady herself. In particular, he would always commend her 'singular wisdom far passing the common rate of women', and in a dedicatory letter written in 1527 to Richard Fox, Bishop of Winchester, he paid this further tribute:

> Were there no other besides the great and sincere love which she bore to me above others (as I know for a certainty), yet what favour could equal such a love on the part of such a princess? But besides her love, she

was most munificent towards me. For though she conferred on me no ecclesiastical benefice, she had the desire, if it could be done, to enrich me, which she proved not by words only, but by deeds; among other instances, when she was about to leave this world … This only I will add, that though she chose me as her director to hear her confessions and to guide her life, yet I gladly confess that I learned more from her great virtue than ever I could teach her.

Elsewhere, perhaps significantly for the light it throws on his own priorities and aptitudes, Fisher would also praise the efficiency with which she managed her household, likening her to the biblical Martha:

First her own household with marvellous diligence and wisdom, this noble princess ordered, providing reasonable statutes and ordinances for them, which by her officers she commanded to be read four times a year … If any factions or bands were made secretly amongst her head officers, she with great policy did bolt it out and likewise if any strife or controversy, she would with great discretion study the reformation thereof.

And neither, it seems, would he forget the challenges of her youth, when, as an illegitimate descendant of Edward III through John of Gaunt and his mistress Katherine Swynford, she had been married to Edmund Tudor at the age of 12. For in a speech delivered in the presence of Henry VII and Lady Margaret herself, Fisher declared how the king, like Moses, was:

Wonderfully born and brought into the world by the most noble princess, his mother, who at the time of the king's birth, was not above fourteen years of age, and very small of stature, as she was never a tall woman; it seemed a miracle that at that age, and of so little a personage, any one should be born at all, let alone one so tall and of so fine a build as the king.

Plainly, there was a familiarity in the relationship between the king's mother and her confessor that allowed him scope for the kind of personal public utterance that might, for any other, have appeared awkwardly inappropriate in the formal context of the Tudor court. But the bond was obviously unusual and sufficiently intimate in due course for Lady Margaret to renew before Fisher the solemn vow of chastity she had undertaken earlier during her marriage to Thomas Lord Stanley. For after the death of Edmund Tudor in November 1456, she had subsequently been wed to Henry, Lord Stafford, and finally to Stanley himself after Stafford's death in 1481, whereupon, as Fisher put it, 'in her husband's days long time before he died [1504], she obtained of him license and promised to live chaste, in the hands of the reverend father my lord of London [Bishop Fitzjames] – which promise', Fisher adds, 'she renewed after her husband's death into my hands again'. By then 61 years of age and more devoted than ever, it seems, to the man with whom she had obviously consulted on this like all other matters, the step had nevertheless been a predictable one – and not only for what the countess termed 'my more merit and quietness of soul' but as a token of her undiminished esteem for Fisher, 'to whom I hath been, since the first time I see you, admitted, very determined (as my chief trusty councillor) to my own obedience in all things concerning the well and profit of my soul'.

Yet for all its significance to both parties, the precise chronology of Fisher's actual residence in Lady Margaret's household remains unknown. Unquestionably, he succeeded William de Melton as Master of Michaelhouse in 1497, the same year in which her previous confessor, Richard Fitzjames, became Bishop of Rochester. After which, according to his earliest biographer, 'he resigned the mastership of Michaelhouse and left the University for that time', in order to enter the Beaufort household. But if we subsequently allow at least two years of service in his new university role, then 1499 seems appropriate, notwithstanding the fact that he was back at Cambridge in an official capacity by 1501 when he was elected its vice-chancellor at the remarkably early age of 32 and received the highest of its degrees, the doctorate in divinity, upon completion of the stipulated ten-year intermission from the award of his MA. Even so, he retained his appointment as Lady Margaret's spiritual director, and would indeed continue to fill this role after he had taken up his role as Bishop of Rochester, since a papal dispensation of 6 January 1506 granted him leave of absence from his diocese to serve, as required, as '*confessor Reginae Anglia*' (Queen of England) – an interesting exaggeration of Lady Margaret's status, which nevertheless reflects the undoubted magnitude of her reputation.

Significantly, Fisher had been reluctant initially to accept his promotion to the episcopacy. But the influence of his friends seems to have prevailed, and on 24 November 1504 he was duly consecrated by Archbishop Warham. Only two days later, moreover, he was present in the Star Chamber at Westminster as a member of the king's council, alongside the Lord Privy Seal, Richard Fox, Bishop of Winchester, who had likewise played a key role in his rise. 'You also', he later told Fox:

Recommended me to King Henry VII, who then, with the greatest prudence, held the reins of this kingdom, so that by the esteem he had for me from your frequent commendations, and of his own mere motion, without any obsequiousness on my part, without the intercession of any (as he more than once declared to me) he gave me the bishopric of Rochester, of which I am now the unworthy occupant. There are, perhaps, many who believe that his mother, the Countess of Richmond and Derby, that noble and incomparable lady, dear to me by so many titles, obtained the bishopric for me by her prayers to her son. But the facts are entirely different, as your lordship knows well.

Almost obsessively at pains to distance his advancement from the kind of nepotism that was so common in ecclesiastical appointments, Fisher would also remain anxious subsequently to ensure that the purity of his intentions remained unquestioned. And this was uppermost, too, in the mind of the king himself who admitted in a letter to his mother, announcing Fisher's appointment, how, 'by the promotion of such a man', he hoped 'to encourage many others to live virtuously and to take such ways as he doth, which should be a good example to many others hereafter'. 'I have in my days promoted many a man unadvisedly,' he continued, 'and I would now make some recompense to promote some good and virtuous men which I doubt not should best please God.' Even during his last illness, according to Fisher, Henry had declared that 'the promotions of the church that were of his disposition should from henceforth be disposed to able men such as were virtuous and well-learned'.

Yet the gift of Rochester itself offered few rich pickings for its new incumbent. On the contrary, it was the smallest and poorest diocese in England, yielding Fisher a revenue of no more than £350 a year – a tenth of

that enjoyed by the Bishop of Winchester. Indeed, it was even smaller than
a map may suggest, since thirty-four of its parishes, forming the deanery of
Shoreham, actually fell under the jurisdiction of Canterbury. There were, it
is true, two episcopal palaces and several manors belonging to its bishops.
But in those days of horseback travel and bad roads, it was necessary for any
prelate to have access to several centres from which to carry out his work,
and the palace of Rochester, which had been built the previous century, was
far from grand in the broader scheme of things. Lying between Canterbury
Cathedral and the mud of the Medway, which did little to enthuse visitors
like Erasmus in particular, its remains today have disappeared, and the bishop's other episcopal residence in London, by Lambeth Marsh and adjoining
the archbishop's palace to the east, was hardly more salubrious. It was
from there that Fisher subsequently hurried off to show William Warham
Erasmus's *Novum Instrumentum*, but beyond building a brick wall around the
palace, and conducting routine repairs, he undertook no building works of
significance. Likewise, his manors at Halling and Bromley were little used,
while those at Stone, near Dartford, and Trottescliffe, near Wrotham, do not
appear to have been employed at all.

No more, then, than a humble first rung on the episcopal ladder,
Rochester did, however, hold out the promise of further promotion, were
Fisher to seek it. Thomas Savage, for example, was bishop there from 1492
to 1496, when he was translated to York, while his successor at Rochester,
Richard Fitzjames, was promoted to Chichester in 1504 and thence to
London in 1506. Certainly, the plum ecclesiastical appointments, including
the prospect of a rich abbacy held '*in commendam*', lay open to Fisher, as did
the possibility of high government office, especially in view of his considerable administrative capacity. Nor, it seems, was he without the personal funds
necessary to indulge altogether grander tastes, had he so desired. For, as he
recorded in his preamble to his statutes for St John's College, Cambridge:

> The noble princess, Lady Margaret, Countess of Richmond, the foun-
> dress of this college, in her great condescension had a great desire to
> procure me a richer bishopric. But when she saw that her approaching
> death would frustrate this desire, she left me a no small sum of money to
> use for my own purposes, which I mention lest anyone think that I have
> made this large endowment with other people's money.

But Fisher's priorities lay elsewhere, and his thirty-one years of episcopal service would indeed be spent as Bishop of Rochester – a uniquely long tenure. During the remaining years of Henry VII's reign, it is true, only three bishoprics fell vacant, and these were within two years of Fisher's appointment to Rochester. But when Henry VIII offered him Lincoln in 1514, followed by Ely the year after, he declined both. And over the same uniquely long period, after his appointment in 1504, he would also remain Chancellor of Cambridge, not content like many of his predecessors to be little more than a non-resident figurehead. On the contrary, he would be deeply concerned with the university's affairs, often facing an uphill task in executing Lady Margaret Beaufort's wishes after her death, while continuing to write extensively and conduct his theological studies at the highest level. He would remain, indeed, a student throughout his life, learning Greek and Hebrew as he approached the age of 50 and remaining singularly unconcerned with the goings-on at court and politics in general until fate intervened to force his hand otherwise. Instead, Cambridge and his bishopric were the effective limits of John Fisher's horizons, and with regard to the latter his contribution was both novel and significant for two main reasons.

Firstly, as a resident pastoral bishop, he was determined to create an effective preaching clergy, and secondly, at a time when episcopal office was conceived mainly in judicial-administrative terms and the ministry of preaching was often offloaded to friars, he determined to play his own part in the pulpit to the full. Indeed, at a time when most bishops never addressed a congregation at all, Fisher would emerge as the foremost preacher in the kingdom, notwithstanding the fact that his sermons bear all the highly structured and analytic hallmarks of the scholastic tradition from which he sprang. The 'four last things' (death, judgement, hell or heaven), repentance for sin, the passion of Christ, and, appropriately enough, the vanity and transitoriness of life were all recurring themes. And although they reflect a mind set in a medieval mould, albeit at its most austere and transcendental, their emphasis upon the problem of human sinfulness and advocacy of a primarily penitential religion still seems curiously attuned to the spirit of the age in which they were delivered. Salvation was critical and Fisher's terms for its attainment uncompromising, since mankind's propensity for sin was as limitless as its consequences were catastrophic, and the only resulting aid lay in the ministry of Christ's divinely appointed

Church, which no human agency could supersede or subvert, in spite of the fact, as Fisher also constantly repeated, that the Church itself was under threat – not only from the infidel without but, more lamentably still, from the inefficacy of a decadent clergy within, which had lost the evangelical spirit and ceased to proclaim Christ's call for repentance as the end of days approached.

It was a powerful message: more than sufficiently powerful, as events would prove, to propel a man to martyrdom. But it was a notion, too, that bedded Fisher's thought firmly within the kind of reforming impulses that would ultimately underlie the Reformation that he opposed so bitterly. For it comprehended the concerns of humanists like Erasmus, the evangelical revivalism of the Dominican friar Savonarola, and the revived Augustinianism of theologians such as Martin Luther. And if the themes of Fisher's preaching might well have been familiar to any congregation of the later Middle Ages, they exhibited, nonetheless, few stylistic resemblances, since there were none of the elaborate rhetorical devices so heartily commended in medieval treatises on the subject, and Fisher preached, just as St Augustine did, straight out of the Bible, familiarising his audience with the text that most could not read themselves by numerous scriptural quotations. For the Book was the key to revelation and the salvation that went with it, and Fisher knew its every nook and cranny. Hence, in his sermons on the Penitential Psalms, which were later published at the request of Lady Margaret Beaufort before whom they had been preached, there were no fewer than 160 biblical quotations, excluding those from the Psalms themselves: forty from the Old Testament; sixty from the Gospels, forty of which involved Christ's own words; and fifty-five from the Epistles, including thirty-six from St Paul. And where Fisher did not quote directly, he recounted tales from Scripture in his own words, including the parables of the Good Samaritan, and the Prodigal Son, as well as the story of the meeting between Jesus and the woman of Samaria, and the stories of Jonah, and David and Goliath by way of illustration.

Delivered on Sundays in August and September 1504, the sermons on the Penitential Psalms were manifestly not for the easily daunted. Fisher, after all, was a scholar and academic, and each lasted about an hour and a half. But for one of Fisher's bent, of course, the business of salvation was no light matter to be tripped over casually with the clock in mind.

And though quotations from the Fathers and Schoolmen are not numerous, neither did he shirk them, as a result of which St Augustine was cited ten times, along with St Jerome (four times), St John Chrysostom (three times), St Anselm and William of Auvergne (twice each), and both Origen and St Thomas Aquinas once. Of classical writers, meanwhile, Demosthenes was twice quoted, and there were additional single references to Cicero, Ovid, Vergil and Plato (*Gorgias*), though it should be remembered always, of course, that this was a time when printed books, let alone manuscripts, were still comparatively inaccessible, so that Fisher was far from engaging in pedantry for pedantry's sake. And if his style lacks the range of Sir Thomas More's prose, with its light touches of humour and leavening flashes of wit, he was also capable nevertheless of employing the commonplace to good effect. Hence the references to millstones, sore eyes, the snaring of birds, and the mending of a clock, as well as the following example of an everyday chore, to drive home a favourite theme:

> If a table be foul and filthy by a long continuance, first we rase [scrape] it, after when it is rased we wash it, and last after the washing we wipe and make it clean. Our soul is compared unto a table wherein nothing was painted, nevertheless with many misdoings and spots of sin we have defouled and made it deform in the sight of God. Therefore it is needful that it be rased washed and wiped. It shall be rased by the inward sorrow and compunction of the heart when we are sorry for our sin. It shall be washed with the tears of our eyes when we [ac]knowledge and confess our sin. And last it shall be wiped and made clean when that we be about for to make amends and do satisfaction by good deeds for our sins. These three things that we have spoken of cometh without doubt of the gracious pity of God. Thou art sorry for thy sin, it is a gift of Almighty God. Thou makest knowledge of thy sin weeping and wailing for it, it is a gift of Almighty God. Thou art busy in good works to do satisfaction, which also is a gift of Almighty God.

Clearly, Fisher was by no means incapable of expressing a fundamental principle of his Christian message both elegantly and cogently, and in terms fully comprehensible to the ordinary man or woman. And though the bishop's style in the sermons on the Penitential Psalms and elsewhere sometimes rings strange to the twenty-first-century reader, this too may well be partially explained by his own Yorkshire dialect, which differed significantly from the London strain that eventually shaped our own.

More notably still, of course, some of Fisher's images, like his account of how to capture monkeys, are especially curious to modern ears:

> Like as men say apes be taken by hunters by doing [putting] on shoes, for the property of an ape is to do as he seeth a man do. The hunter therefore will lay a pair of shoes in his way, and when he perceiveth the hunter doing on his shoes he will do the same, and so after that it is too hard for him to leap and climb from tree to tree as he was wont, but falleth down, and anon is taken.

Yet if Fisher's comprehension of the more exotic reaches of the natural world could be suspect, the appeal, or, more accurately, the power of his preaching was rarely in doubt, and never more so, perhaps, than in his sermon at Paul's Cross 'preached on a Good Friday' against 'the pernicious doctrine of Martin Luther', where the resulting celebration of the physical ordeal involved in Christ's crucifixion not only demonstrates his ability to produce a forceful image, but confirms an ongoing preoccupation with self-sacrifice and the suffering it necessitates:

> But you marvel peradventure why I call the crucifix a book? I will now tell you why. A book hath boards, leaves, lines writings, letters both small and great. First I say that a book hath two boards: the two boards of this book is the two parts of the cross, for when the book is open and spread, the leaves be couched upon the boards. And so the blessed body of Christ was spread upon the cross. The leaves of the book be the arms, the hands, legs and feet, with the other members of his most precious and blessed body. Never any parchment skin was more straightly stretched by strength upon the tentors [framework for drying] than was this blessed body upon the cross.

And it is at this point that Fisher extends his metaphor from the reverential to the more harrowing:

Thus you perceive that this book was full of lines and small letters, which were of divers colours, some black, some blue, some red, some blueish, that is to say full of strokes, and lashes, whereby the skin was torn and rent in a thousand places. Besides these small letters, yet was there also Capital Letters illumined with roset colour: roset is a red colour like unto the colour of a rose, which colour that most precious blood, which issued out of his hands and feet [whereby] was illumined the five great Capital Letters in this wonderful book. I mean by these Capital Letters the great wounds of his body, in his hands, and in his feet, and in his side. These five great wounds were engraved with sharp and violent pens, that is to say, the sharp nails and the spear.

Such preoccupation with Christ's agonies was not, of course, unique. On the contrary, it was central to the whole Christian message and, in particular, the soteriological assumptions of all Christian theologians. But when placed in the broader context of its author's life and destiny, it assumes, perhaps, greater significance, since death was, in effect, the almost obsessive object of John Fisher's daily meditation for many a year. 'And lest that the memory of death might hap to slip from his mind,' wrote one contemporary, 'he always accustomed to set upon one end of the altar a dead man's skull which was also set before him at his table as he dined or supped.' So when the time came, the martyr's option was always, arguably, a likely, if not preferable, outcome. For although suffering and death were not without terror, even for a temperament like his, not only faith but logic, too, upon which he set such especial store, would eventually leave him little choice other than to declare defiantly how he would willingly die like St John the Baptist on behalf of the indissolubility of the king's marriage.

In the meantime, however, as Fisher busied himself with the affairs of his diocese and university, and turned himself increasingly between 1522 and 1527 to literary warfare against Martin Luther – entailing well over half a million words of Latin polemic – there was still little hint of the destiny beyond the horizon. There were, as might be expected, glimpses of political involvement and even the pomp of high affairs, though Fisher continued a marginal, if not largely indifferent, figure on such occasions. He was summoned, for example, to the Parliaments and Convocations of 1510, 1512 and 1515, the last of which was notable for an early clash between the Crown and the Church when MPs sought to renew an act depriving criminals in minor orders of benefit of clergy, only to be opposed by the House of Lords, in which the bishops and abbots held a majority. The result was a conference of Lords and Commons called by the king and dominated by Friar Henry Standish, warden of the Greyfriars, who, in supporting the position of the Commons, subsequently found himself summoned before Convocation and appealing to the king for protection. Vindicated finally, after a further conference at which Henry VIII maintained the prerogatives of his predecessors and rejected Wolsey's plea that the matter be referred to Rome, Standish had, in effect, struck a significant blow for England's religious independence of the papacy. Yet nothing was heard of John Fisher's part in this momentous controversy, in which the judges had referred ominously to the fourteenth-century Act of Praemunire, with its curbs on the Church's ability to impinge upon the jurisdiction of secular courts.

Elsewhere, the records tell us of Fisher's role at great functions. Thus, on 15 November 1515, he was crosier to Archbishop Warham at Westminster Abbey when Wolsey received his cardinal's hat, 'in so solemn wise', according to George Cavendish, 'as I have not seen the like unless it had been at the coronation of a mighty prince or king'. And in the following year, it was the Bishop of Rochester who christened the son of Princess Mary, the king's sister and former Queen of France, who was by that time Duchess of Suffolk. Since Rochester lay on the road from Canterbury to London, moreover, visitors of distinction travelling to and from Dover would frequently expect to be entertained by him, and the letter he received from the royal council in 1514 when the sword and cap presented by Pope Leo X to Henry VIII arrived in England, is typical of numerous others:

> The prior of Christ's Church of Canterbury shall meet with the said ambassador and ... shall conduct him to some place convenient between Sittingbourne and Rochester, where the king hath appointed that your lordship, the Master of the Rolls and Sir Thomas Boleyn shall meet with him and so conduct him to London.

Certainly, Fisher was among the prelates present at Canterbury on 23 July 1518 to receive Cardinal Campeggio on his mission to create Wolsey a papal legate *a latere*, and on that occasion doubtless joined the cardinal's train as far as Rochester. So, too, in 1522 when Charles V came to England, the Bishop of Rochester was obliged to be at Canterbury with the archbishop to meet him, and to entertain the emperor along the way to London at Rochester during a Sunday.

But, as always at such times, he appears to have been a largely passive, if not reluctant, participant – civil always, but perhaps a trifle awkward too. 'If any strangers came to him,' his first biographer records, 'he would entertain them according to their vocations with such mirth as stood with the gravity of his person, whose talk was always rather of learning or contemplation than of worldly matters.' Lacking the easy urbanity of which Thomas Wolsey, for example, was undoubtedly capable, Fisher seems, in fact, to have been even peevishly uncomfortable at times amid the glitter of the Tudor court, as became strikingly clear when he later reflected upon Henry VIII's hugely lavish extravaganza at the so-called Field of Cloth of Gold – one of those notable occasions when Fisher's normally latent irascibility got the better of him, it seems. For his presence in the midst of such excess was clearly a source of irritation, as he made clear in a sermon shortly afterwards that bordered on the indiscreet. 'Never before was seen in England such excess of apparelment,' observed the flint-faced bishop, reflecting no doubt upon the king's decision to expend vast sums on rich fabrics, including 1,050 yards of velvet, and jousting clothes costing more than £3,000. And in emphasising the contrast between heavenly and earthly joys, he not only looked back with equal exasperation at the 'midsummer games' that had been played out between Guisnes and Ardres, but recalled, with somewhat more satisfaction, the strong winds that had blown dust into the faces of the mighty and shaken the dwellings erected for their pleasure.

Fisher's only recreation, in fact, appears to have been hunting, where we hear, in one case, of an invitation from Sir George Neville, Lord Bergavenny, Keeper of Ashdown Forest and owner of several manors in Kent and Sussex. Nor when the invitation came was it any mere formality, it seems, since Bergavenny would present the advowson of Ibstock, Leicestershire, to the Bishops of Rochester in perpetuity in 1531, suggesting that the two men were clearly on good terms, and leaving little doubt that the gift was a particularly appropriate one. For Fisher's comparison in both his sermons and writings 'between the life of hunters and the life of religious persons' suggests that he was not only soundly versed in the skills of the chase, but an enthusiastic practitioner in his own right. Indeed, as the nobleman's invitation confirms, he kept his own dogs for the purpose – one of his few extravagances: 'If it shall please you to see your greyhounds run at any time, either within or without, I have commanded my keeper to give you attendance and make you such disport as if I were there present.'

Yet where Fisher was sometimes forced by virtue of his status to stray into affairs of State, he continued to perceive such episodes as wasteful distractions from his more serious concerns. Indeed, if his anonymous earliest biographer is to be believed, the bishop even said as much at the legatine synod called by Wolsey in 1518 to affirm his superiority in rank as cardinal-legate to that of Archbishop Warham:

> Truly, most reverend fathers, what this vanity in temporal things worketh in you I know not; but sure I am that in myself I perceive a great impediment to devotion, and so have felt a long time, for sundry times when I have settled and fully bent myself to the care of my flock committed unto me, to visit my diocese, to govern my church, and to answer the enemies of Christ, straightways hath come a messenger from higher authority by whom I have been called to business and so left of my former purpose. And thus by tossing and going this and that way, time hath passed and in the meanwhile nothing done but attending after triumphs, receiving ambassadors, haunting of princes' courts and such like, whereby great expenses rise that might better be spent in other ways.

And although Fisher's words are unlikely to have been recorded verbatim, they nevertheless encapsulate his known opinions – and indeed cantankerous streak – to perfection, since he, like many men with a mission, could become fractious, and when it came to his priorities, the rigorous routine of his everyday dealings as Bishop of Rochester, however mundane, invariably came first.

In this regard, during the first half of his episcopate, he carried out visitations in 1505, 1508, 1511, 1514 and 1517, and though assisted by his archdeacon, his thoroughness was characteristic. According to his first biographer, he began the first, on 15 May 1505, by:

Calling before him the priors and monks, exhorting them to obedience, chastity and true observation of their monastic vows; and where any fault was tried, he caused it to be amended. After that he carefully visited the rest of the parish churches within his diocese in his own person; and sequestrating all such as he found unworthy to occupy that high function, he placed other fitter in their rooms; and all such as were accused of any crime, he put to their purgation, not sparing the punishment of simony and heresy with other crimes and abuses. And by the way he omitted neither preaching to the people, nor confirming of children, nor relieving of needy and indigent persons; so that by all means he observed a due comeliness in the house of God.

Almost a decade later, Fisher was as diligent as ever. For both his episcopal Register, along with the Act Book of his Consistory Court, not only still exist but confirm his activity. Occasional intervals of a month or two indicate when he was away on State or university business, but the routine affairs of his diocese were never neglected, as the records for 1513, by way of example, amply demonstrate. The first entry, dated 5 March, notes an abjuration of heresy before the bishop in his chapel at Halling, after Henry Potter of West Malling was accused of declaring publicly that he would not believe in the Last Judgement 'till I see it'. When brought before Fisher, the guilty party promised to avoid suspect persons in the future, as well as books of Scripture in English, and to give information about them as soon as possible. Whereupon he was duly absolved from excommunication and ordered to walk in procession to his parish church with the faggot on his back, and to do so again in the cathedral on the following Sunday unless dispensed from this by the bishop. In addition, he was to ensure that no harm came to those who had testified against him and make no attempt to leave the diocese without presenting himself to Fisher in person – all of which Potter seems to have agreed to without demur, leaving his cross upon the record.

On 12 March, meanwhile, also at Halling, Fisher ordained a deacon, before collating one priest at Rochester on 4 April and admitting another to vicarages. The same day, he confirmed the election of the new Abbot of Lesnes, William Ticehurst, formerly Prior of Bilsington, and received his profession of obedience, along with testimonies that the abbot-elect was of legitimate birth, discreet and circumspect. Thereafter, by 27 June Fisher was at his Lambeth residence admitting a cleric to a vacancy in Cobham College in conformity with the king's wishes, while on 20 August, at Bromley, he collated three priests to livings, and on 7 October, two others at the same place, notwithstanding his broader duties to the king. For, according to a letter dated 1 October, he had already found himself requested by the Barons of the Exchequer to organise the collection of the four-tenths ordered by the king – a task that he duly entrusted to the Augustinian canons of Tonbridge and Lesnes, and the prior of Rochester, after listing nearly forty benefices that he deemed too poor to be taxed. Interestingly, too, the episcopal Register contains a copy of a further letter from Fisher, instituting Richard Clarke to the vicarage of Halling, which had been made vacant by the deprivation of John Cotton, whose adultery is recorded in the Acts of the Consistory Court for 17 September when five cases of correction of his clergy came before the bishop. Cotton, it seems, came clean, declaring, 'I would my lord had put me in prison when he commanded Joan Hubbard to prison.' But the Bishop of Rochester was nothing if not meticulous in the execution of his judicial duties, since the investigation involved several sittings and was not concluded until 27 September.

It was not without irony, of course, that Fisher had earlier found himself in legal hot water of his own, after the escape of two men indicted from his prison at Bromley. On 11 December 1506, indeed, a pardon and release is recorded in the Patent Rolls for 'John Fisher of Rochester', though his involvement in his Consistory Court was, in any case, largely limited to more serious cases like the one he heard at Lambeth on 17 March 1511 when he absolved a priest from contumacy (the nature of which is not stated), but suspended him from saying Mass in his parish or elsewhere in the diocese. Instead, Fisher kept mainly to his primary objectives of ensuring a better-educated and more zealous clergy, and encouraging the zeal of his flock. Thus, on 29 November 1508, a certain Hugh Taylor of Foot's Cray came before him with letters of presentation from the canons of St Mary Overbury to that benefice, though Fisher was dissatisfied with the young man's attainments and ordered him to spend a year of study in a grammar school before proceeding. Clearly a stickler for standards, Fisher would not hesitate to embarrass any individual clergyman for failing to achieve them. But there were also happier duties for him to perform, as on 17 July 1508 when he received the profession of William Temple as a hermit in the chapel of St Blaise at Bromley. Accepting his eremitical habit from the bishop, Temple promised before God and the saints to direct his conduct and conversation according to the rule of St Paul, the first hermit, and was duly assigned to the hermitage of St Catherine at Dartford. And similarly, on 21 April 1511, Fisher confirmed a vow of chastity from Elizabeth Fitzwarren, a widow of Beckenham, who reverently undertook 'to be chaste of my body' and 'truly and devoutly' to remain chaste 'from this time forward as long as my life lasteth after the rule of St Paul [the hermit]'.

It was on such occasions, no doubt, that John Fisher felt particularly gratified, witnessing the spirituality of those entrusted to his care, not to mention the tangible fruits of his own example and diligence in a diocese whose affairs he had come to know like no other. For by 1520, certainly, he was familiar to the clergy under his charge both as a person and as a pastor to whom they might resort in times of difficulty – his own austere example serving as an inspiration to the faithful and reproach to the more easy-going. As one contemporary put it:

All pastors and curates used him for their lantern, as one of whom they might perfectly learn when to use action and when contemplation. For in these two things did he so far excel that hard were it to find one so well practised and expert in any one of them apart, as he was in both of them together.

And in the meantime, as he regulated his diocese through a period of steady work and quiet achievement, so his broader responsibilities as his university's chancellor had borne fruit of a more spectacular kind, with the encouragement of sound learning and preaching, the promotion of Greek and Hebrew, and above all the establishment of Christ's College and founding of St John's – all of which would help to lead Cambridge out of its past lethargy into the humming world of the new scholarship.

In this regard, Fisher was ably assisted by other talented administrators whom he astutely identified and employed to relieve him for the episcopal duties that he always considered his overriding priority. Henry Hornby (master of Peterhouse, and also chancellor of Lady Margaret), Robert Shorton (first master of St John's and later master of Pembroke, who served, additionally, in the households of Wolsey and Catherine of Aragon), and Nicholas Metcalfe (third master of St John's, and Fisher's right-hand man as archdeacon of Rochester) were all invaluable aids. But Fisher's guiding role and overall impact cannot be doubted. For until her death in 1509, he had remained Lady Margaret Beaufort's closest adviser, and it was under his influence that she re-founded Godshouse as Christ's College 'on account of her singular devotion to the most glorious and most holy name of Jesus Christ'. At the same time, she provided a Cambridge residence for him from which to carry out his heavy load of business and secured for him the presidency of Queens' College, where since the death of Henry VII's wife, Elizabeth, she had in effect wielded foundress's rights. And though he resigned that post in 1508, as a result of his other commitments, his association with the king's mother had, in the meantime, brought other benefits to the university, including the endowment of a readership in divinity, which fell initially to Fisher himself, and a preachership, paid for in part by the endowment of a chantry, and entailing, among other things, six sermons annually at Paul's Cross or at St Margaret's, Westminster.

Altogether more significant still, however, was Fisher's role in persuading his patroness to found St John's College, though her death prevented the proper completion of arrangements, and embroiled him ultimately in two long years of legal wrangles with none other than the new king, who was anxious for a share of the lands earmarked by his grandmother for the college's endowment. More than 1,500 acres were involved, along with a sum of £500, and since the relevant codicil to Lady Margaret's will had not been sealed, the full provision could not be granted by the courts. To compound matters, a number of her servants had put in claims of their own that also received royal support, so that from first to last, as Fisher openly acknowledged, Henry VIII was to prove 'a very heavy lord against me'. Indeed, a settlement of sorts was only reached ultimately, after the bishop had sacrificed around half of the lands undoubtedly intended by Lady Margaret for the endowment. 'Forsooth,' he wrote, 'it was sore laborious and painful unto me that many times I was right sorry that ever I took that business upon me.' Indeed, it is doubtful whether a less determined man would have completed what had seemed so often a hopeless task. But Fisher's tenacity in the courts was unwavering and, though the king himself was his adversary, he would not be bowed – a clear sign, it would seem, of things to come.

Speaking of his success in securing a reasonable interpretation from the judges, Fisher was typically terse. 'If this had not been obtained,' he reflected, 'here would have been a poor college.' But ultimately, as a result of his dogged pursuit of a principle, St John's would become in his own mind – and not without some justification – his chief hope for perpetuating his memory. For it was he who drafted the college's original statutes, which were promulgated in 1516, and he, too, who became engaged in almost constant revision of them right up to the time of his eventual imprisonment. Besides this, he also persuaded several other benefactors to add to St John's endowments and personally made over lands worth £500 for the establishment of a chantry chapel there, with several chapels attached both for the benefit of learning and salvation of his soul. While doing so, furthermore, he remained unstinting in his broader activities as the university's chancellor, as a result of which his fifty-year association with Cambridge would witness not only the arrival of the first lecturers in Greek and Hebrew, but further lectureships in the arts and mathematics, the reform of the proctorial elections, the introduction of the office of public orator, and the establishment of the first – though short-lived – Cambridge press.

Significantly, too, Fisher would even prove willing to sacrifice his own status on behalf of what he perceived to be the university's better interests. For in 1514, he offered to resign as chancellor after his re-election for ten consecutive years. Instead, he proposed that Thomas Wolsey, then Bishop of Lincoln, should replace him, since Wolsey was already growing vastly in power and his patronage would have been to Cambridge's great advantage. Reluctantly, the university authorities actually accepted Fisher's proposal, only for Wolsey to reject it – and with a humility that seems strangely out of kilter with his later pretensions. As a result, Fisher was at once offered the unique distinction of election as chancellor for life, and immediately set about the task of renewing his links with the university and consolidating his legacy to it. For even when he was later attainted and lodged in the Tower, Cambridge remained faithful to him, refusing to win royal favour by rejecting him. And not without good reason either, since it has been rightly suggested that Fisher's chancellorship made Cambridge for the first time the intellectual equal of Oxford, notwithstanding the fact that he himself has frequently been depicted as an intellectual conservative, whose thoughts were firmly set in a medieval mould – an image reinforced, perhaps, by his own more general antipathy to any challenge to the religious status quo.

Certainly, he was no more built for breakneck innovation than he was for triviality. Yet he remained acutely aware of the intellectual issues of the day, and, though his statutes for St John's provided for disputations on the *doctor subtilis*, Duns Scotus, they also encouraged regular teaching in Greek for junior students as well as Hebrew for seniors. Nor, of course, should it be forgotten that while in his forties, Fisher launched himself with almost schoolboy enthusiasm into the study not only of Greek but of Hebrew, too, which he learned under Robert Wakefield. As such, he was a figure who, like Duns Scotus himself, arguably, looked both backwards and forwards: a powerful and vigorous thinker who, though imbued with the best elements of the scholastic tradition emphasising dialectical skill and rigour, nevertheless bridged epochs. Only thus, of course, could he have seriously sustained his undoubted reputation throughout Europe and only thus, moreover, could he have enjoyed such close and cordial relations with the man usually considered to be the most renowned humanist figure of his day, Erasmus of Rotterdam. For although the two men seem unlikely to have formed an acquaintance during the Dutchman's first visit to England in 1499, or even during his second stay when he was entered as a pensioner at Queens' College between August 1505 and April 1506, the third trip tells a different story, when in the summer of 1511, John Colet appears to have been pressed by Erasmus for financial aid and saw fit to pass the load on to Fisher.

'I am going to show a specimen [of Erasmus's translation of Basil on Isaias],' wrote Colet, 'and see if he [Fisher] is prepared to lighten my labours with a small reward.' Fisher duly complied, albeit with a noteworthy hedging of his options regarding any future payments, and a final suggestion to the Dutchman himself that any other funds might best be supplied by Lord Mountjoy, Erasmus's primary patron in England:

> Greetings to you Erasmus. I beg you don't be too offended that I did
> not write when I sent to you recently. The messenger was in a hurry to

leave town, and I met him just as I was going out. So, as I was unable to write, I gave him the small gift you asked for; it was not however from the fund you assume to be at my disposal and to be of some size. Believe me, Erasmus, whatever may be said, I have no funds that I can use at my sole discretion. The use of that money is restricted and cannot be varied. I feel that you are so much needed in our University that I will not let you be in want as long as there is anything to spare out of my own modest resources. At the same time, I will do all I can, whenever an opportunity comes, to beg help from all others when my own means are insufficient. Your Mountjoy, nay, mine also, will I am sure remember you if he has promised to do so, and I will gladly encourage him since he is now at court. The best of health, Erasmus. From London.

Yet this not altogether uncharacteristic partial palm-off by a thrifty Yorkshireman did not, it seems, diminish Erasmus's genuine admiration of Fisher. On the contrary, in 1512 he would write in glowing terms to Thomas Halsey, the English Penitentiary in Rome, of the man who would go on to become both his friend and admirer: 'Unless I am sadly mistaken, he is the one man at this time, who is incomparable for uprightness of life, for learning, and for greatness of soul.' And by the time that Erasmus returned to England in May 1515, the two men were indeed on the most cordial terms, as Fisher confirmed in a letter penned at Halling in the following month: 'When the time comes for your journey to Basle, do arrange to come here as I need your advice. I beg you not to let this slip your memory. Long may you be healthy. Yours, John of Rochester.'

Most striking of all, perhaps, was Fisher's response to Erasmus's *Novum Instrumentum* – his edition of the New Testament – which was published in 1516 and provoked a response from the bishop that, by his own exacting standards of self-restraint, verges on uncontrollable excitement:

Although I am up to my eyes in business – in fact I am just setting out for Cambridge for the opening of the College [St John's] which is at last to take place – I could not let your Peter [Meghen] return without a letter. You have put me greatly in your debt by the gift of your *Novum Instrumentum* translated from the Greek. As soon as I received it and saw some of the notes in which you extol your Canterbury

Maecenas [Archbishop Warham] with many compliments, I hurried to him to show him these passages. When he had read them, he promised he would do much for you, and begged me, if I should write to you, to urge you to return. Indeed I do not doubt if you do he will be more generous to you than ever.

It was the *Novum Instrumentum*, moreover, that stirred Fisher at the age of 48 to learn Greek, initially from Erasmus himself, who appears to have given some preliminary instruction during a ten-day sojourn at the episcopal palace in Rochester, which incidentally left the Dutchman bemoaning the palace's condition 'ten times over'. Writing some years later, indeed, his visitor actually warned the bishop of the dangers of residing there:

The near approach of the tide, as well as the mud which is left at every ebb of the water, makes the climate unwholesome. Your library, too, is surrounded with glass windows which let the cold air through the crevices. I know how much time you spend in the library which is to you a very paradise. As for me, I could not live three hours in such a place without being ill. You would be better in a room with a wooden floor, with wainscoted walls; brick and lime give off unhealthy vapours.

Apart from Fisher's own company, it seems, the only real compensation for the inconveniences of the scholar's stay was a visit from Sir Thomas More. Yet Fisher accepted his guest's grumbling in good spirit, studiously ignoring, it must be said, his advice on more comfortable living, while continuing to admire his guest's achievements at a time when conservative critics of his work were numerous. For after a further brief stay at Rochester as he made his way to Dover in April 1517, and what would prove to be the last meeting of the two men, Erasmus received the following letter of encouragement, plainly demonstrating its author's receptivity to what might be considered the most laudable elements of the New Learning:

No sensible person could be offended at your translation [into Latin] of the New Testament for the common benefit of everyone, since not only have you made many passages clear by your learning but have indeed provided a full series of comments on the whole work; thus it is now possible for everyone to read and understand it with more gratification and pleasure ... I owe it to you, Erasmus, that I can to some extent understand where the Greek does not quite agree with the Latin. Would that I could have had you as my tutor for a few months.

In the event, Fisher's only criticism was that the text contained a number of misprints. Nor did he hesitate to sign himself 'Your disciple'. And the same openness to progressive scholarship was extended to Johann Reuchlin, whose works on Hebrew studies were later sent to him by the Dutchman. One of these, *Caballistica*, took some time to reach Rochester, since both Thomas More and John Colet had found it so interesting that they had delayed passing it on, though Reuchlin's promotion of Hebrew had, in general, received much opprobrium, and Fisher displayed no small measure of bravery, not only in defending the German scholar, but arranging at one point to visit him. For in a letter to Reuchlin of August 1516, Erasmus makes clear that his English friend was intending a trip to Stuttgart for the purpose of meeting the scholar:

> I cannot find words to express in what affection and veneration your name is held by that great leader of learning and piety, the Bishop of Rochester, insomuch that, whereas Erasmus had been hitherto in high esteem, he is now almost despised in comparison with Reuchlin ... I never have a letter from him (often as he writes) without some honourable mention of you. He had made up his mind to put off his episcopal garb, I mean the linen vestment which the bishops always wear in England (except when they are out hunting) and to cross the sea, mainly in order that he might have an opportunity of talking with you. And on this account, as we were hurrying to the ship, he detained us for ten days on purpose that we might make the passage together. Some later incident made him change his plan, but if he has put off its accomplishment, he has not changed his purpose.

Manifestly, then, Fisher was no obscurantist or dyed-in-the-wool revenant of the Middle Ages. On the contrary, at a time when most theologians looked askance at Erasmus and altogether shunned Reuchlin, the Bishop of Rochester warmly embraced both – perhaps in no small part because of his perennial willingness to stand firm against the crowd in championing the underdog. The otherworldly man of God was also sufficiently skilled managerially to retain the confidence of his university's authorities while committing himself to the advancement of reform on a moderate scale and at a reasonable pace. Certainly, his encouragement of *bonae litterae* and the New Learning at Cambridge was never his main priority. Nor were the developments he engineered in this area even remotely root and branch in kind. For at both St John's, and more so still Christ's, the training remained essentially scholastic, and Fisher's own religious outlook, unlike Erasmus's, would always remain more transcendental and charismatic than anthropocentric – more concerned, that is, with penance and the ultimate dependence of mankind upon the Church as both the yardstick of God's intentions and designs. If men and women were to be saved, Fisher resolutely contended, they could not tread the path to salvation unaided. Nor could they opt for various routes according to taste or whim. Accordingly, the Church of Rome was not to be challenged under any circumstances or at any cost, however unsatisfactory some of its ways or superficially questionable certain its teachings. And on this, as both Martin Luther and Henry VIII himself would discover, John Fisher would never back down.

THE COURTIER
AND THE MAID

And I looked up, and, behold, a hand was sent to me, wherein a book
was rolled up: and he spread it before me: and it was written within and
without; and there was written in it lamentations and canticles and woe.

Ezekiel 2:9

As winter beat its familiar dogged retreat in 1512, John Fisher made
ready to attend the fifth Lateran Council in Rome as one of a team
of England's representatives that included Silvestro de Gigli, absentee
Bishop of Worcester, who was already present in the Holy City, Richard
Kidderminster, Abbot of Winchcombe, and Sir Thomas Docwra, senior
lay baron and Grand Prior of the Knights Hosptaller. And although political developments would eventually frustrate his plans, Fisher, on this
occasion at least, appears to have been a more than willing candidate for
his appointed role – so much so, indeed, that when the offer of attendance was renewed in 1514, he readily appointed the Priors of Rochester
and Leeds (in Kent) to act for him at home during his absence. For
when it came to the internal politics of the Church, especially where
the issue of ecclesiastical reform was concerned, Fisher was invariably
ready, if only for limited periods, to divert his gaze from the bustle and
hugger-mugger routine of his diocesan and academic involvements. It
was on these grounds, indeed, that he had played a leading part at the
Convocation of 1510–11, and for this reason, too, that he remained a
prominent ecclesiastical politician throughout the 1520s, though the
wider world of secular politics would always remain decidedly cold
fare for one of his temperament. Never a State official of any kind and

never one of the royal council's inner circle, his attendance at its more infrequent larger sessions was initially conscientious enough, but his last recorded attendance occurred, nonetheless, as early as 25 January 1512. If he had sought it, there seems little doubt that advancement as a royal councillor was his for the taking, particularly in light of his administrative expertise. But high principles and high office, as Fisher wisely appreciated, were uneasy bedfellows at the Tudor court, and he kept his distance accordingly.

Yet there was an irony, too, about Fisher's reluctance, since from the time of Henry VII, and especially under Henry VIII, the central importance of the council had, in any case, begun to shift elsewhere. Certainly, the king's councillors were numerous and active, consisting of as many as forty individuals, all appointed by the monarch personally for their expertise and political weight. But they rarely met as one body. Instead, the council's only regular members were, in effect, the kingdom's state officials, while others, like John Fisher, might be called upon to render advice solely when occasion demanded. And it was for this very reason, in fact, that the so-called 'Privy' Council would eventually harden into a discrete organ of state under Henry VIII. Throughout, the council's major advisory role was maintained. During the reign of Henry VII, moreover, its various 'committees' or 'by-courts' had already become the key executive instruments of Tudor government. But despite this role, the council had no independent authority of its own. On the contrary, it gave advice merely when the king asked and exclusively on those subjects he chose to lay before it, while the 'by-courts' were not true committees of the council at all, since they reported back not to it but to the king once again, who alone defined their areas of activity and conferred their power, making him, to all intents and purposes, not only his own prime minister and treasurer, but, likewise, his own *de facto* secretary of state.

And this independence would have crucial ramifications for the entire nature of Tudor politics. For while the gravity of the council and glitter of the royal court remained essential ingredients of government, the centre of power came increasingly to lie beyond the richly carved door known as the King's Threshold, and within the apartment of the royal household, known as the Privy Chamber. Here, as in the court itself, hung rich tapestries behind heavy oak sideboards heaped with gold and silver plate.

Here, too, resided guards, musicians and attendants in silk and gold chains, all playing their carefully prescribed parts in the great moments of the court day, when the king processed to chapel, or dined, or received a foreign ambassador. But the Privy Chamber was also much more besides, since it was the intimate arena where an altogether smaller cast of servants, more highly favoured and still more magnificently dressed, attended the king himself in his more private hours, making it a centre of unofficial yet potentially limitless political power, depending upon the personality of the monarch concerned. For if a king were to prove impressionable or frustrated by, say, the age and conservatism of his council, the Privy Chamber's upper servants stood poised to become the lynchpins of government, both at the centre and on the periphery. And if the king concerned was none other than Henry VIII, not only impressionable and frustrated by his councillors at one and the same time, but infinitely prone to whim and flattery, the implications were obvious.

At first, the so-called 'Great Chamber' of the royal household had been precisely that: one great, draughty, largely 'open plan' room, in which, as in a royal bedsit, too many conflicting functions – political, administrative, personal and recreational – had been crammed. But in the course of the fourteenth and fifteenth centuries, as the desire for greater privacy increased in tandem with the wish to emphasise the majesty and mystique of the monarch himself, the single room of the Great Chamber had evolved into a suite of three more-or-less specialised apartments, which the early Tudors came to describe as: the Great or Watching Chamber, the Presence Chamber and the Privy or Secret Chamber. The first was primarily a guard room, staffed by the Yeomen of the Guard, while the Presence Chamber served as the throne room, the king's public dining room, and a thronging rendezvous for the court, where everyone who mattered met to gather news and to gossip. As such, the Tudor Presence Chamber closely resembled the Great Chamber of the Middle Ages: a humming, bustling, semi-public reception room, constantly astir with comings and goings and continually awash with the more trivial everyday etiquette, ceremonial and formalities of court life – all of which made the secluded world of the Privy Chamber increasingly important, not only as what amounted to a regal refuge but, much more importantly still, as a political melting pot where whispers, casual asides and innuendoes might mould and shape, or make and break. For Henry VII had been an altogether more private person than his predecessors, and under the Tudors in general, the Privy Chamber would become the monarch's personal space in a way that the old, unitary Great Chamber never could be: his private realm, peopled by those he liked best and those who became most intimate with him, as well as those whom he could trust, since men like Francis Marzen, who was described in 1501 as 'oon of the groomes of the privie chamber', not only monopolised access to the king, but frequently undertook confidential missions, both within the kingdom and abroad.

Henry VII, it is true, was not without his pleasures or, for that matter, a carefully constructed public persona, which he was keen to cultivate studiously. Certainly, he enjoyed hunting, cards and shooting, and at the same time performed his courtly obligations dutifully. But perhaps because of the very slenderness of his claim to the throne, he took particular pains to invest the notion of kingship with a mystique all of its own. It was he, after all, who introduced the very term 'majesty' into the English language, and he, too, who came to ensure that solemn processions, the shouting of loyal salutations, the doffing of caps and reverent genuflexions in the royal presence all formed part of the underlying propaganda message that such spectacle was designed to drive home. The grooms, pages, servers and sundry menials in constant attendance were suitably attired in the Tudor livery of white and green embossed with the Tudor rose, and lest any should doubt or forget the might and splendour of England's new dynasty, there were, likewise, not only roses in the chains and necklaces worn by the king and queen, but on the wooden ceilings and tiled floors of all royal dwellings, and even on the gilded harnesses of royal horses. Most important of all, however, the king made sure that his accessibility was strictly limited, so that when it came to the jousts and revels and other public entertainments of the court, he carefully kept his distance. Never taking part personally, Henry VII remained, in fact, 'a princely and gentle spectator' at all times, and, in doing so, applied the same principle institutionally, by reforming the royal household and developing the role of the Privy Chamber within it. Hitherto, as one contemporary put it, those responsible for tending the king's most private needs had been 'persons of little worth except in the matter of giving good personal service'. But an ordinance of 1494 laid down that only specifically chosen gentlemen 'ought to array and unarray the king, and noe man else to sett hand on the Kinge', while by that time, too, the Groom of the Stool – the person responsible for assisting the king's toileting – had emerged as a figure of unique standing in his own right, heading the entire Privy Chamber establishment.

In short, then, for Henry VII, the private royal apartments were the place in which he could put off his 'magnificence' and be unobserved by the outside world. Indeed, in 1501 he had specifically restricted access to his 'Secret Chamber' to 'the groom of the stoole, with a page with hym, or such as the kyng woll commande ought to wayte in the Kinges secrete Chamber especially and no one else'. And by the reign of Henry VIII, attendance upon the king in what had become his increasingly complex 'privy lodging' of bedrooms, libraries and closets beyond the Presence Chamber had swiftly come to rank among the most prized of courtly appointments, carrying with it not only boundless opportunity for patronage and preferment but greater potential than ever for influencing the political agenda. For as the second Tudor's reign opened, the 'ancient and grave' members of his council were, as we have seen, ill-matched to either his personality or his priorities. Faced with a new ruler, nine weeks and four days short of his eighteenth birthday at the time of his accession – a glittering, massive, puffed up and impressionable young man, bent on ushering in a new golden age of glory, light and learning – Henry VIII's advisers were, indeed, both baffled by his impetuosity and burdened by their residing fear that, as John Stow put it, 'such abundance of riches … the King was now possessed of should move his young years into a riotous forgetting of himself'. Yet the conservatism that had made the new king's councillors so highly valued in the previous reign, where consolidation was the watchword, and, in particular, their strenuous efforts 'to acquaint him with the politique government of the realm, with which at first he could not endure to be much troubled' served merely to compound their predicament, as the Privy Chamber progressively transmogrified from its original role as a place of concentration and austerity – an orderly, harmonious zone where unobtrusive efficiency and discretion were the highest virtues – into a teeming playground in which the new monarch could enjoy 'pastime with good company', surrounded not only by a vastly swollen formal establishment of grooms and pages, but a boisterous host of musicians, revellers and 'boon companions' or 'minions', unashamedly intent upon bringing him up 'in all pleasure', so that he might be prevented, as one contemporary suggested, from growing 'too hard upon his subjects as the King his father did'.

Among this hugely influential intimate circle were the Earl of Surrey's second son, Sir Edward Howard; Sir Thomas Knyvet, who had married Surrey's eldest daughter; and Sir Thomas Boleyn, who had married the Earl of Wiltshire's eldest daughter. All equally patrician and some years older than the king, they were joined in turn by Henry Bourchier, Earl of Essex; Sir Henry Guildford, who as Master of the Revels was responsible for the fairy-tale entertainments so beloved of his sovereign; William Compton, chief gentleman of the bedchamber; and another who towered, it seemed, above all: the hulking, broad-shouldered, spade-bearded Charles Brandon – seven years older than the king, and, though 'brought up out of nought', in all respects the kind of dashing, reckless individual whom any hot-blooded boy with a showy streak was sure to follow. For while Brandon's blood pedigree was humble enough for Erasmus to refer to him later as a 'stable boy', and notwithstanding the indisputable fact that his gifts of mind were few, he more than made up for this by sharing to the full with his royal companion a marked physical exuberance and a headstrong delight in excelling at wrestling, hunting, tilting and jousting that would lead him ultimately to be regarded as 'a second king … one who does and undoes'. Larger than life in every respect, no figure could have encapsulated the spirit of the new reign more fully, nor embodied more aptly the gaping gulf between the prevailing ambience of the Privy Chamber and the king's council, whose members were old indeed at 55 and 60, and among whom only Thomas Wolsey, it seems, offered sufficient dynamism for the new ruler's taste.

But even Wolsey was in his forties by the time he achieved his ascendancy, and he, too, could not entirely ignore the possibility of being somehow circumvented. For while by 1513 Knyvet and Howard had been killed fighting the French, and others of their circle had lost favour, the result was not only an influx of new blood but a further, more worrying sea-change in the Privy Chamber's ambience, as a smaller, younger and even more privileged group of individuals, closer to Henry's own age, came to enjoy an added status all of their own. They included Edward

Neville, Henry Courtenay and Nicholas Carew, all of whom would be condemned to traitors' deaths in later life by the young man with whom they now revelled, and the first, in particular, achieved an especial significance. Indeed, as a kinsman of Warwick the Kingmaker, Neville enjoyed the particular distinction of sharing Henry's colouring and husky physique to such an extent that he was even rumoured in some quarters to be the prince's bastard brother, and together the two young men had achieved an unusually close bond – enjoying the same boisterous pastimes and, on other occasions, donning exotic costumes at splendid court functions that invariably offered the chance to pose brashly before the fairest females on hand. As Neville shone and thrived, moreover, so he and his colleagues came to form what amounted to an exclusive private club with their sovereign as president. Letting him win at tennis, while taking his money at dice, this self-same laughing crew not only shot with the king at the butts, served at his table and formed the glittering stage army for the innumerable court masques he loved so heartily, but caroused, carolled and cavorted with him into the small hours, fuelling his ego all the while by reflecting, or so he believed, his own physical prowess and zest for all things martial.

But as the distinction between service and camaraderie became increasingly blurred, so concern among the older heads at court grew more pressing, and for none more so than Thomas Wolsey, who came to see in the influence of the Privy Chamber's members a dangerous counterweight to his own. According to the chronicler Edward Hall, all were increasingly guilty of over-exuberance and lack of due deference in the company of the king. 'Not regarding his estate or degree,' said Hall, they were too 'familiar and homely with him and played such touches with him that they forgot themselves,' while the Abbot of Woburn, in a specific to reference to Henry's favourite of favourites, Sir Francis Bryan, observed not only how 'the said Sir Francis dare boldly speak to the King's Grace the plainness of his mind' but 'that his Grace doth well accept the same'. Not only was such familiarity irreverent, of course, it was also breeding the kind of intimacy that threatened the cardinal's own monopoly of the king's ear, and it was this, above all, that made a reckoning of the kind that occurred in May 1519 inescapable. For at a meeting held at Greenwich in that month, Henry's council, led by

Wolsey, finally called upon him to put a stop to the intolerable effrontery that was being given free licence within the confines of the court.
And though no formal criminal charges were preferred against them,
the king duly complied, dispatching Carew to govern a fort in Calais,
and admonishing Neville, Bryan and a selection of other culprits to tend
their other commitments outside the court more dutifully.

'Within the past few days,' wrote the Venetian ambassador, 'King Henry
has made a great change to his court' by dismissing some of those young
companions 'who had enjoyed very great authority in the kingdom, and
had been the very soul of the king'. And the accompanying change to
the ethos of the Privy Chamber was swift in following. For the mantle of
callow youth, which the king himself had encouraged so enthusiastically,
had become, in any case, increasingly inappropriate to a ruler who now
stood on the threshold of his thirties. True, his preference for the company
of younger men would abide, and his devotion to the members of his
Privy Chamber would remain as intense as ever. But the need now was
for an infusion of more sober blood, and a relationship more paternalistic
in nature. The same intimacy with the king would apply, yet on a more
reverential basis. And while the glitter, the pomp, the courtly graces would
also still hold, the gentlemen of the Privy Chamber were henceforth to
become persons capable of bridling their worldliness and bearing their
high status with dignity and decorum: individuals of solid background,
appropriate to royal service, yet humble enough in origin to appreciate
their promotion and be suitably awed by their access to their sovereign's
private world. Service, in short, rather than camaraderie, was once again
to become the order of the day. And from Thomas Wolsey's perspective
especially, the denizens of the king's secret world were to be figures disinterested in political influence. No longer sources of 'evil counsel' or figures
'intent on their own benefit to the detriment, hurt and discredit' of their
sovereign, they were to be immune, likewise, to the broader temptations
entailed by their proximity to the king. For according to the Venetian
agent Giustiniani, the cardinal had at one point perceived the former minions 'to be so intimate with the king that in the course of time they might
have ousted him from the government'.

That new entrants to the Privy Chamber should be otherworldly to the
point of sanctity or, even less likely, to the level of accepting martyrdom

in defence of their principles was not, of course, a prerequisite. But these, remarkably enough, were precisely the hidden characteristics of one particular young man who entered the king's service in the wake of Wolsey's purge of the royal inner sanctum. Born in 1500 at Harefield Place in Middlesex, which lies midway between Northwood and Rickmansworth, at a distance of about 2.5 miles from either place, Sebastian Newdigate appears to have displayed few outward hints of distinction, let alone saintliness, when he first arrived at court in his early twenties. He was the son of John Newdigate, Esquire, lord of the manor of Harefield, and his wife Amphelissa, daughter and heiress of John Nevill, Esquire, of Sutton, in the county of Lincoln, who was the son of Anne Holland, daughter of John Holland who was the son of Elizabeth, Duchess of Exeter, herself the daughter of John of Gaunt. As such, Sebastian was descended on his mother's side from the royal house of Lancaster – a fact that would be crucial to his entrance to the Privy Chamber in the first place – but beyond his blood line there was little, it seems, to distinguish him significantly from similar young men of his class. On the one hand, he was neither his father's principal heir, nor remembered for his exploits at Cambridge where he was educated. Indeed, there is no record even of the college he attended, or the subject he studied, though John Newdigate is known to have been a product of Lincoln's Inn, making the son's preparation for a career in law a distinct likelihood.

Of Sebastian's nine brothers and seven sisters, meanwhile, we know that John was the eldest and that at least five others took seniority over him. Silvester and Dunstan would become Knights Hospitaller, while George took monastic vows, Jane went on to marry the knight Sir Robert Dormer of Wenge in Buckinghamshire, and another sister married into the Stonor family, well-known recusants of the reign of Elizabeth I. Two other brothers died early – an unusually low number, given the number of siblings involved – and two sisters also became nuns: Mary, at Syon, and Sybil who became Prioress of Halliwell in Middlesex. And if there is nothing to support the proud family legend that their estate was first awarded by the king to a great hunter who, in ancient times, cleared large tracts of Surrey from wolves, neither is there any doubt that the Newdigate line can actually be traced back over some twenty-two generations to the reign of King John. The first to settle at Harefield, Sir John de Newdigate, had been knighted by Edward III for his services in the French wars and awarded a fleur-de-lys argent for his crest, before obtaining in 1356 what would become the long-term family manor and residence through his wife Joanna, heiress of Richard de Bacheworth and sister of William de Swanlond, Lord of Harefield, who died without issue and left his estate to her. It was there, moreover, that the red brick mansion of Old Harefield Place eventually arose – a little to the north of the nearby church lying about half a mile from the village of Harefield – and there too that Sebastian eventually came to spend the peaceful years of his happy boyhood, before the edifice was finally burned down in the seventeenth century, leaving only traces of its former character to later observers: some fragments of walls jutting out from the turf; a curious row of fifty or so arched recesses that formerly supported a terrace overlooking a garden; a portion of the walls of the adjoining farm buildings; and a moat, along with the reservoirs that once fed it.

But while the house is no more, the connection of the area with the Newdigates is still maintained vividly enough within the walls of the local church, which bears ample testament to their local prominence. Built of flint and stone, with a square tower to the north-west corner, St Mary the Virgin continues to stand proudly on the side of a gentle slope, set amid ancient yew trees and vast cedars, and, save for the lengthening of an aisle, it has endured no change major enough to make it unrecognisable to those who might have worshipped within its walls, alongside Sebastian Newdigate himself, some five centuries since. His family's tombs and monuments, indeed, have survived in almost every conceivable form to this day, from a fourteenth-century brass, with its pious appeals for prayers, to the post-Reformation mural tablet proclaiming the virtues of a later Newdigate clearly wishing to be commemorated as a champion of Protestantism. Along the south aisle, encompassing the Brackenbury Chapel where the greater part of the Newdigate monuments reside, there is also an altar tomb, placed under the east window, where the remains of Sebastian's parents still lie, though not in the place initially intended by John Newdigate himself, since his will, dated 'June 23, 20 Henry VIII', i.e. 1528, had directed his body to be buried in his 'chapell at Harefield at the north end of the awter'.

Clearly, even a figure of Newdigate's undoubted substance could not withstand from his grave the tide of future events, which not only shifted his tomb from its original site, but left its Latin inscription upside down after the relocation:

> Here lie buried the bodies of John Newdegate, sergeant at law, and Amphelys his wife, daughter and heiress of John Nevill, Esquire: the which John Newdegate died August 12, 1528, and the aforesaid Amphelys July 15, 1544, on whose souls may God have mercy.

Yet the worthy sergeant is finely represented, nevertheless, on his brass in coif, gown and hood, his hands folded in prayer, while from his mouth proceeds a scroll bearing the invocation, *Sancta Trinitas Unus Deus* (Holy Trinity One God). Opposite him stands his wife in the kind of headdress familiar to us in portraits of Catherine of Aragon, a long girdle bearing a pomander encircling her waist, while her shoulders are draped with a cloak bearing the Neville arms, including arguably the proudest device in all England, a saltire ermine. Even more significantly, perhaps, her scroll, in its turn, bears a prayer to the Virgin Mary, *Miserere nobis miseris* (Pray for us sinners), confirming her dedication to the old religion in whose defence her son had been martyred some nine years before her own death and ten years before the death of her eldest son, John.

How she reacted to Sebastian's eventual martyrdom may well be imagined. But if one tantalising possibility holds true, then even a mother's natural grief may well have been magnified beyond all normal bounds by another of her son's dealings. For while Sebastian held fast to Rome to the point of agonising death, his eldest brother seems to have embraced the new religious changes with no little enthusiasm. In St Mary the Virgin's chancel, indeed, stands his own impressively appointed altar tomb, surmounted by a canopy of perpendicular work in accordance with a man of some considerable status, but otherwise bearing all the hallmarks of the reformed religion, complete with an English inscription and a marked absence of references to either the Blessed Virgin or the saints, or to prayers for his departed soul.

> Off your charite [the inscription runs] pray for the soules of John Newdigate Esquyer and Anne | his wyff y^e whiche John decessyd the xix^th day of June in the year of o^r Lorde | God a thousand fyve hundred fourtie fyve and y^e said Anne decessyd y^e | __ day of _____ in the year

of o^r lorde God a thousand five hundred _____ On whose Soules and all Christen soules Jhū have mercy Amen.

Curiously, the date of the wife's death was never specified, and it is equally curious in its way, perhaps, that John himself should have died on the tenth anniversary of his martyred brother's death, by which time, it seems, he had profited in no small measure from the religious changes of the time. For St Mary the Virgin itself had come into his hands in 1542 in the wake of the dissolution of the monasteries, and while the eldest of his seven sons, George, had himself become a monk at Chertsey, the eventual marriage of another, Francis, to the widow of Edward Seymour, Lord Protector and uncle of Edward VI, confirmed not only the father's thoroughgoing Protestant credentials but, much more significantly still, the family's strikingly successful integration into elite circles under his auspices. And nor is this the end of either the curiosity or the irony, since a John Newdigate Esquire is found not only among the jurors who eventually condemned John Fisher to death, but on the self-same jury responsible for the condemnation of Sebastian himself.

Whether the juror and the lord of the manor of Harefield were indeed one and the same is unknown, but, in other respects at least, John Newdigate was certainly not alone in advancing his fortunes by surfing the tides of religious change in sixteenth-century England. On the contrary, opportunism was, as might be expected, far more common than martyrdom, and the Newdigates were in any case already making hay by loyal compliance long before their king saw fit to break with Rome. John's father, for instance, had been advanced to the Order of the Coif on 18 November 1510, opening the way for his appointment as a justice of the Court of Common Pleas and the King's Bench, and ten years later he had been appointed King's Sergeant – promotions that eventually opened the way, no doubt, for his son Sebastian's career at court, first as a page and then, much more prestigiously still, as a gentleman of the Privy Chamber. Probably about 21 at that point, and in all likelihood married, Sebastian was already, according to Henry Clifford's *Life of Jane Dormer, Duchess of Feria*, 'a gentleman of good parts' and 'not a little favoured by the king'. And there is no reason to believe that either his domestic circumstances or the fascinating splendours of court life did anything initially beyond captivating him. For if the tone of the Privy

Chamber had indeed by that time changed, not least because of the king's wish to affirm his own maturity, its prestige and attractions for any young man remained as potent as ever.

Within a year of their banishment, Neville, Bryan, Carew and their colleagues had, in fact, re-surfaced at Henry's side at the Field of Cloth of Gold for what would be the most extravagant chivalric spectacle in which any of them, including Henry himself, had yet been involved. And both they and now Sebastian Newdigate, too, would continue to earn their keep, not least by parading as striking embellishments to great ceremonial spectacles, such as those involving Emperor Charles V's state visit of 1521. Sumptuously attired in black or blue velvet, as occasion demanded, and emblazoned with golden fleurs-de-lys and other majestic emblems, they acted as escorts and outriders, and, if both the laughter and politics of the Privy Chamber were henceforth more muted, its members enjoyed the same intimacy with the king as before, and perhaps for the newcomers an altogether deeper emotional bond, as Henry now embraced more and more fully the posture of an older, wiser head and father figure, nurturing the altogether more awed, respectful and less flamboyant members of his private brood. Though no pious wet, if the comments of his sister Jane are to be trusted, Newdigate's discretion and comparative moderation are likely to have rendered him particularly dear to the king, who often admired most in others what he most signally lacked himself, not the least of which was the kind of model family life also apparently enjoyed by his fresh young servant. For during the courtier's three-year residence within the Privy Chamber a daughter named Amphelys was born, who is mentioned in the will of Richard Newdigate, dated 1545, which cites 'Amphilis Newdigate, daughter of Sebastian Newdigate, of Herefilde, co. Middlesex'.

Nor, in spite of his eldest sister's warnings about 'the deceits of the world and the snares of the devil' entailed by life at court and the king's company, does the young courtier appear to have served his wife's needs any less dutifully than those of his royal master. For although he would imply to his sister that he had lived the courtier's life fully and on one occasion even defended his 'infamous behaviour' when she laboured the point, he nevertheless downplayed his excesses and, in doing so, also suggested that 'the report and her opinion of the king were worse than he merited'.

Yet if Newdigate maintained, as duty required, as judicious a silence on his master's shortcomings as he might, those flaws were already assuming increasing prominence around the very time of his own arrival at court. Certainly, the king's extra-marital excursions were already old news when sister Jane saw fit to counsel her brother, and the brother's response had not, in any case, been entirely unequivocal. For when pressed, Newdigate duly conceded that 'if the king should prove as bad as the world suspecteth or speaks of him', he would 'have in memory what she advised him'. Much more curiously still, however, he then concluded with an astonishing revelation that betrayed for the first time the true extent of his inner turmoil: nothing less indeed than an admission of his intention to abandon the court altogether, as Sir Thomas More had once considered, in preference for the solitude of London's famous Carthusian monastery.

The episode is described thus by Clifford, who was a trusted retainer of long-standing in the household of Jane's granddaughter and namesake, the Duchess of Feria:

> At which word, pausing awhile, leaning his head upon his hand, he replied: 'Sister, what shall you say if the next news you hear of me shall be that I am entered to be a monk in the Charterhouse?'

And the sister's response was one of wonderment – not only further confirming her suspicions about the kinds of influences to which her brother had been subject, but reflecting too, perhaps, the unrivalled rigour of the particular monastic order to which he was now on the verge of committing himself: '"A monk!" she saith. "I fear, rather, I shall see thee hanged. I pray God keep thee a good Christian, for such perfection is fit for men of other metal than loose courtiers."'

The Carthusian way of life could hardly have been more starkly at odds with the splendour and pitfalls of the Tudor court. On the contrary, the Order founded by St Bruno in 1084 was a model of austerity at a time when other monastic brotherhoods had become a byword for corruption and soft living. *Nunquam reformata quia nunquam deformata* (never reformed, because never deformed) ran the saying, and if their everyday lifestyle was any guide, it is easy to see how the claim that their Charterhouses had never been reformed because they had never been defiled in the first place held true. Eating only bread, fruit, herbs, and vegetables, and fasting at least once a week on nothing more than bread, water and salt, Carthusians tradition-ally lived out their silent lives confined to two-storey cells: the lower floor a workshop in which they spent part of their day labouring, and an upper level consisting of two rooms, one for sleeping, furnished with a board cov-ered with a blanket, and the other containing a stall and *prie-Dieu*, a work table, bookshelf, two chairs, and a 'refectory' set in the window recess. And the broader rigours of their lifestyle were no less taxing, since the Carthusian left the confines of his cell only for the three daily services held in the mon-astery chapel and for the community meals on Sundays and solemn feast days, which were also held in silence. Indeed, his only other relief from med-itation and prayer were his private garden, in which he was required to grow food for himself and the broader community, and the twice-yearly, day-long community recreations, which consisted of a walk in the Charterhouse's surrounding grounds in the company of his fellow monks.

Plainly, it was the furthest possible cry from what Newdigate had expe-rienced for at least three years. But by 1524 his wife had died and with rumours awash everywhere concerning the security of the king's mar-riage, the young courtier set his course accordingly. Notwithstanding 'the favour of the king, nor his hopes of higher advancement', he would retire from court and leave its frequenters to their own devices, offering neither judgement nor condemnation, and maintaining to the end the loyalty to his royal master's name that he had demonstrated to his sister before inti-mating his decision. Martyrdom, of course, was as yet unthinkable, and not least because the full ramifications of the coming course of events were still obscure to all, including the king himself. But it was a remarkable turn of circumstance, nevertheless, when, within a year of his conversation with his sister, Newdigate did indeed make good his prediction. By which time, another individual of far less exalted but altogether more explosive potential – a young serving girl from south-east England's rural hinterland, with a gift for 'prophesy' and, as it happened, an insouciant disregard for the sensibilities of the high and mighty – was also on the verge of surpris-ing one and all around her.

Known variously as the Holy Maid of Kent, the Holy Nun of Kent, and the Nun of Canterbury, Elizabeth Barton was born – if Dom Edward Bocking, the man who was to become her spiritual mentor, is to be relied upon – in 1506. But her birthplace is unrecorded and we have only local tradition to tell us that it was the village of Aldington, about 12 miles from Canterbury. To complicate her origins even further, Barton's parentage remains completely unknown, though her surname suggests that her forebears may once have earned their livings on church lands, the manager of which in the Middle Ages was known as a *bertonarius*. If so, it was by curious coincidence, therefore, that in 1525, she entered history for the first time, employed in the household of Thomas Cobb, *bertonarius* of Aldington on behalf of the Archbishop of Canterbury, whose residence had been at the manor since the eleventh century. Yet even her relation to Cobb is unclear, since in one early account produced by her contemporary biographer, Edward Thwaites, she is described as 'servant to one Thomas Cobb', while in the Act of Attainder responsible for her death, there is reference only to her 'having dwelt with one Thomas Cobb'.

Since the status of servants in Kentish households of the period, as elsewhere, was in fact surprisingly fluid, it is far from inconceivable, therefore, that Elizabeth Barton was either a needy relation who worked for her keep, or even that she was an illegitimate connection, though no mention is made of her in Thomas Cobb's will, dated 1528, and at no point was she ever smeared with the stigma of bastardy amid the barrage of charges ultimately levelled against her by hostile propagandists. Indeed, an undated letter written to her by Archbishop Warham's secretary, Henry Gold, probably in 1532, suggests that she had a sister, though this was almost certainly the limit of any blood relatives she may have possessed. For none were named or interrogated upon her arrest in 1533, as was usual in such cases, and at no stage was she accused of attempting to bring material advantage to either herself or her family by her activities. As such, it seems that death may have deprived her of her parents before she was of marriageable age and that it was for this reason that she found herself from around the age of 8 onwards at the Cobb family home of Goldwell – situated in the parish of Aldington, which lay on the land-locked cliffs overlooking the Marsh and the port of Hythe – where she became part of a large and thriving rural establishment, presided over by a man of no little substance in his own right, whose connections to influential local figures, not to mention the highest levels of the ecclesiastical hierarchy at Canterbury, would play an indispensable role in bringing her ultimately to national prominence.

For as land agent to the Archbishop of Canterbury, Thomas Cobb was responsible not only for the management of his own farm, but the archbishop's land, too, and for supervising the entire manor of Aldington with all that this entailed: the collection of rents and tithes; the sorting, storing and recording of his ecclesiastical landlord's produce; and the supervision of other local farms to ensure that they were kept, as the saying went, 'in good heart'. Such was its extent, indeed, that in former days the manor of Aldington had stretched practically from Dover to Hastings, and though it had shrunk over the centuries and was subjected to royal depredations shortly after Thomas Cobb's death, in 1608 it still had more than 200 tenants on its rent-rolls, including eighteen Kentish knights with total holdings amounting to 6,000 acres in twenty-three parishes, exclusive of forty-four enclosures in the Weald. How much of this may have fallen under the ambit of the Archbishop of Canterbury's *bertonarius* is unfortunately unknown, but Thomas Cobb was nevertheless certainly responsible for at least the ecclesiastical lands of Aldington and Stowting, of which the demesne lands attached to the archiepiscopal residence in Aldington, including the park, alone accounted for more than 1,000 acres. And as manager of such an estate, he therefore became a man of virtually unchallengeable authority in the locality, particularly since Archbishop Warham himself spent much of his time commuting between Canterbury and Lambeth. Deals involving the interests of the manor of Aldington and those of neighbouring landowners were, indeed, negotiated by Cobb as a magnate among magnates, and it was a measure of his standing that upon his death in 1528, it was a Baron John Hales of the Exchequer whom he named as overseer of his will.

Not only land agent to the Primate of England, but boasting a family coat of arms in his own right, consisting of a ducal coronet and demi-leopard on its crest, Thomas Cobb's bloodline was, in fact, without question very old and reasonably wealthy into the bargain – traceable to at least 1324 when a certain John Cobb, Esquire, was said to have been awarded the manor of Organers in the parish of Newchurch on the levels of Romney Marsh. The farm of Aldington itself, meanwhile, also appears to have enjoyed a number of special advantages over its neighbours, not least because the village from which it drew its name was comparatively densely populated and even seems to have had the makings of a small town, complete with what amounted to a budding high street and, of course, the archiepiscopal residence itself – with its five kitchens, six stables, nine barns, seven fodder-houses and eight dove-houses – where Warham's predecessor, Cardinal Morton, staged amateur theatricals featuring Sir Thomas More, who was by no means the only illustrious visitor of his kind. For in 1511, Erasmus of Rotterdam, the celebrated scholar, was appointed rector of Aldington by Archbishop Warham, and lived at the rectory next to the church in what is now called Parsonage Farm. Speaking only Latin and Dutch but no English, the new incumbent was unable to preach to the English congregation, and resigned one year later as a result of a kidney complaint, which he blamed on the local beer. But he would certainly have been known to Cobb and was equally certain to have been a visitor to Cobb's own house, which still stands today – on the road running from Aldington Corner to join the A20 between Ashford and Sellinge – looking in its modern incarnation more like a comparatively modest Victorian villa, but substantial enough, even now, to be divided comfortably into two, and with much more room than the current frontage, which is all that can be glimpsed from the road, might suggest.

Named, according to tradition, as a result of the perpetual spring that rose in its cellar, Goldwell remains a treasure trove of architectural detail, which allows us to capture tantalising snapshots of the domestic surroundings and everyday life of the young woman who began her rise to cult status while employed within its walls almost five centuries ago. For although extensively refaced, cut about and shaken by Second World War landmines into the bargain, the house still retains a number of contemporary features, particularly in the upstairs of the north-east end of the house, where the original plan seems not to have been modified at all, beyond the fact that the ceilings have been raised a little. A large bedroom, for instance, with south aspect, contains an ogival stone fireplace, which was almost certainly the master bedroom belonging to Thomas Cobb himself, since in Kentish farmhouses of the day, a bedroom with a fireplace was the exclusive privilege of the master. Equally intriguingly, on the landing outside the bedroom, a window dating to the period exactly frames the parish church and the length of the footpath that ran across the fields from the farm itself to the churchyard, ensuring that Thomas Cobb had merely to step out of his bedroom door to command a sweeping view not only of the church itself, but of the parson's house slightly to the right, not to mention the archbishop's country palace slightly to the left, and the nine enormous tithe barns, mentioned in Purley's *Weald of Kent*, for the filling of which he, as *bertonarius*, was responsible. Should Archbishop Warham, on a visit from Canterbury, have therefore chosen to dispatch a nimble cleric up the unfinished church tower to hoist a signal, or if Mistress Cobb or a dawdling servant lingered on the way home from Mass, the master of Goldwell would have been sure to notice from this vantage point. And it was in this spot, too, that his wife and servants gathered at night, for, to the right of the bedroom door, on the landing outside, resides a rectangular recess, which was once home to a 'praying cross' around which domestic prayers were said before the household retired for sleep. Mustered conveniently outside the master's chamber, on the same landing made sufficiently wide for the purpose, the servants of Goldwell, including young Elizabeth Barton, would have made their nightly devotions before making finally for their own quarters, which lay in a vast attic running the length of the original house and as high as the pitch of the roof.

Lit only by a single dormer window, which was destroyed during the Second World War, the attic was still roughly floored with thick wooden planks as late as the 1970s and divided up into thirds in much the same way that it had been centuries earlier: one third lying over the master bedroom, extending as far as the central chimney, while the remaining area was divided in half by an ancient partition, of which the wooden framework still stood only fifty years ago, supporting panels of cow-dung plaster that were by then falling away to dust. In the middle of the partition, meanwhile, lay a wooden door, behind which the dimmest part of the attic was divided longwise by a low course of worm-eaten boarding. And it was beyond this securely fastened door, we may assume, that Elizabeth Barton and her fellow female servants took their rest, since it was usual for the men, who were more inclined to bedtime unruliness, to sleep within earshot of their master, directly above his own bedroom. Reclining on truckle-beds, palliasses, bare straw or sacking, communicating from time to time perhaps in hushed voices through the thin cow-dung partition, it was in this spot that the day's labours ended for one and all, as they slumbered not only beneath open rafters but, where cracks existed, beneath the stars themselves. And it was here too that these self-same folk lay to be nursed if sick, just as happened in Easter 1525, when Elizabeth Barton, aged about 19, first fell prey to a very severe, persistent and curious illness, the details of which were recorded by a wealthy and cultured justice of the peace named Edward Thwaites, who visited Goldwell that December.

For what should have been a routine visit by a local office-holder – perhaps in his capacity as inspector of Romney Marsh's water table – actually proved nothing of the kind, since Thwaites was so struck by an extraordinary story related to him by Cobb about the apparently astonishing gift of the ailing girl in his employ that he would become her earliest biographer and indeed advocate. Consisting of twenty-four pages and printed in 1527 under the title *A Marvellous Work of Late Done at Court-of-Street in Kent and Published to the Devout People of this Time for their Spiritual Consolation,* Thwaites's account of what he was told and subsequently witnessed in person is largely preserved in William Lambarde's *Perambulation of Kent* (1570), and ascribes, not altogether surprisingly, a directly supernatural interpretation upon the events that would soon lead to the creation of a shrine centred upon his subject's visions of the Blessed Virgin. Indeed, his pamphlet was effectively a brochure for the shrine of Our Lady at Court-at-Street – which was known to contemporaries as Court-*of*-Street – popularising the findings of an episcopal commission of 1526, and explaining to the multitudes that visited as pilgrims the remarkable circumstances in which the shrine became active. Divided into two parts (the first dealing with Barton's girlhood, her supposed cure at Court-at-Street and subsequent entry into a nunnery; the second detailing the subsequent miracles performed at Court-at-Street by the intercession of the Virgin Mary) Thwaites's *Marvellous Work* remains, in fact, not only our sole eyewitness account of Barton's activities, but by far the most valuable, too, since the author was both an educated man and magistrate, and, as such, well used to hearing potentially suspect tales and appropriately equipped to weigh their reliability.

Even more than Thomas Cobb, Thwaites was a man of substance, influence and connections – a figure whose support and advocacy not only carried considerable weight in its own right, but extended far beyond Aldington and its confines. His marriage to the Kentish family of Elynden had, for instance, made him master of the very extensive manor of Easture and East Stour – 'held of the King by ward of the Castle of Dover by the payment of 7*s*' – with lands in six different Kentish parishes: Chilham, Godmersham, Waltham and Petham, all contiguous and in the immediate neighbourhood of Canterbury; along with Stourmouth and Preston, also contiguous, near Sandwich. Equally significantly, however, the marriage had also enabled him to claim that the so-called 'Lieutenancy of the Lantern' at Calais was his by right of inheritance, and when the first Mrs Thwaites died early, possibly in giving birth to his son Thomas, an even more advantageous union had followed – with the widow of Sir George Warham, nephew of the archbishop and brother of his archdeacon. For Thwaites's new bride, Dame Anne Warham, was a member of the St Leger family of Leeds Castle, whose head was frequently sheriff of the county and had been for the previous two decades, to all intents and purposes, the hereditary Member of Parliament for Kent. Indeed, the influence of the St Legers ran clean through Church and State alike – on into the nobility, and even into the royal family itself, since one of Dame Anne's great uncles had married a widowed princess, Anne, Duchess of Exeter, and another had married the daughter and heiress of the Earl of Ormonde, while her nephew was Sheriff of Kent and later Lord Deputy of Ireland.

Thanks to his second marriage, therefore, Thwaites found himself rubbing shoulders and sharing the local administration with individuals who constituted the sixteenth-century pantheon of Kent: the congeries of leading families, who, between them, by cousinship and alliance, controlled power-lines running straight into the royal household itself, as well as the Privy Council, the law courts, Convocation and the highest echelons of the clergy, not to mention the ecclesiastical courts, the magistrates' courts, the manorial courts, the local garrison towns, castles and ports, the customs and excise, and down into the marshes, where he and his peers determined the very height of the water table – itself no mere trifle, since this in turn materially affected the pasturage for hundreds of thousands of sheep. Wealthy by his first marriage, influential as a result of his second, it was only natural that Thwaites should have promoted the social rank of his relatives, with the result that Thomas his son would marry the younger daughter of his wealthy neighbour Sir William Finch, of the Mote near Canterbury, while Ursula Thwaites (his daughter?) was married to the same Sir William's grandson, becoming Lady Finch, mother of Baron Finch of Fordwich in Kent, aunt of the first Earl of Winchelsea and

Viscount Maidstone, great-aunt of the first Earl of Nottingham, and great-great-aunt of the first Earl of Aylesford.

So when Edward Thwaites became captivated by young Elizabeth Barton's tale on a routine visit to Goldwell and took up her cause, it was to prove an event of considerable significance, both for the girl herself and, as events would prove, for the king and government in faraway London. For in view of his rank, background and ongoing ambition, Thwaites is unlikely to have championed her lightly. Nor, in light of the style of the pamphlet that he wrote in 1527, did he do so for the sake of his own publicity. For *A Marvellous Work* suggests an individual of undoubted piety, who while conservative and orthodox and genuinely impressed by the unusual, was nevertheless admirably sympathetic to human suffering, and commendably ordered in his thoughts. Writing a more direct and uncluttered English than many of his more learned or famous contemporaries, and exhibiting a decided flair for telling an intriguing tale in a vivid and convincing manner, he was, in fact, eminently suited to deliver his account, which focused, initially at least, upon the onset and symptoms of her illness itself, which he described thus:

> About the time of Easter, in the sixteenth year of the reign of King Henry VIII [spring 1525], it happened a certain maiden named Elizabeth Barton (then servant to one Thomas Cobb of the Parish of Aldington, twelve miles distant from Canterbury) to be touched with a great infirmity in her body, which did ascend at divers times up into her throat, and swelled greatly; during the time whereof, she seemed to be in grievous pain, in so much as a man would have thought that she had suffered the pangs of death itself, until the disease descended and fell down into the body again.

Offering no further insight into the causes or nature of the girl's illness, beyond the fact that it 'continued by fits, the space of seven months and more', Thwaites does, however, make clear that the Cobbs were not only willing to accommodate the sufferings of their sickly servant girl but to delegate staff to nurse her during the seven busiest months of the farming year, and to bring her from her attic resting place to the comfort of the main house – by which time, it seems, 'a young child of her master's lay desperately sick beside her'.

And it was this somewhat unusual decision to place the sickly young woman with Thomas Cobb's ailing infant that would ultimately become the springboard for Barton's astonishing ascent to celebrity thereafter. For, as Thwaites tells:

> She, being vexed with the former disease, asked with great pangs and groaning whether the child were yet departed this life or no; and when the women that attended upon them both in their sickness, answered no, she replied that it should be anon. Which word was no sooner uttered, but the child fetched a great sigh and withal the soul departed out of the body of it.

In the presence, then, of at least two women, and with the greatest physical effort, Elizabeth Barton had, it seems, delivered her first 'divination and foretelling', under what had appeared some strong compulsion, as though she were forced to speak in spite of herself. Doubtless, the impact upon both her attendants and the Cobb household in general must have been considerable, and the implication, too, is that the incident was rapidly mooted more widely, since, as Thwaites makes clear, this was 'the first matter that moved her hearers to admiration'. Seen as much more than any mere coincidence, Barton had, it was believed, prophesied the child's demise with supernatural assistance. And further acts of clairvoyance, often relating to events occurring at some distance, coupled to utterances on religious matters – all delivered in writhing agony or trance-states – were not long in following: this time frequently witnessed by Thwaites himself who left accounts, like the one below, of what occurred:

> But after this in sundry of her fits following, although she seemed to the beholders to lie as still as a dead body (not moving any part at all), as well as in the trances themselves as after the pangs passed also, she told plainly of divers things done at the church and other places where she was not present, which nevertheless she seemed (by signs proceeding from her) most likely to behold as it were with her eye.

How she managed to speak in the first place, while 'not moving any part at all', is in itself a matter of some interest, of course, not least because the manner, as described in a letter written by Thomas Cranmer in 1533 – which drew, it seems, upon a passage from Thwaites's narrative later suppressed by Lambarde – was dramatic enough to leave little doubt about its impact upon those witnessing it:

> Then [Cranmer relates] was there a voice heard within her belly, as it had been in a tun [barrel] her lips not greatly moving; she all that while continuing … in a trance.
>
> The which voice, when it told anything of the joys of heaven, it spake so sweetly and heavenly that every man was ravished with the hearing thereof. And contrary, when it told anything of hell, it spake so horribly and terribly that it put the hearers in a great fear.

'She spake', moreover, not only of 'heaven, hell and purgatory', but, as Thwaites informs us, 'of the joys and sorrows that sundry departed souls had, and suffered, there'. And there were moral and spiritual messages, too. For, according to Lambarde's abridgement of Thwaites:

> She preached frankly against the corruption of manners and evil life: she exhorted repair to the Church, hearing of masses, confession to priests, prayer to our Lady and saints, and (to be short made in all points), confession and confirmation of the Popish creed and catechism, and that so devoutly and discreetly (in the opinion of mine author) that he thought it not possible for her to speak in this manner [i.e. with a level of knowledge and authority beyond the capabilities of a young woman of her age and background].

Revelations about the conditions of departed souls would continue, in fact, throughout the remainder of Elizabeth Barton's brief life. Indeed, they would eventually come to encompass not only the celestial fates of Cardinal Wolsey and Archbishop Warham, but of Henry VIII himself. Yet even in the winter of 1525–26, before she had emerged from the farmhouse into the world of national –– and indeed international – politics, her statements were already increasingly loaded with broader significance.

For her observations on the need for attendance at Mass, sacramental confession, the cult of saints, pilgrimages, prayers for the dead and so on, cut
straight to the heart of the clash between orthodox Catholicism and the
propaganda of the continental Reformation that was already combining
so potently with English anticlericalism.

It was a propaganda, moreover, as violent as it was diverse, and typified
by the 'great errors and pestilent errors' of William Tyndale, recorded in
the register of Archbishop Warham for 1530. In seven selected works, the
register noted, no fewer than 251 errors, blasphemies and heresies were
detectable to the eyes of orthodox theologians. But although Tyndale's
writings did not begin to appear in print in 1526, the ailing servant
girl of Thomas Cobb's household had already, in effect, identified and
forewarned against the most central a year in advance. For while Tyndale
might declaim against the pope and St Thomas Aquinas or contend that
there was no scriptural warrant for monasticism, it was his denunciation
of the Mass and the Church's sacramental system that represented the
most radical threat, and it was these, curiously enough, that Elizabeth
Barton was most inclined to defend in her trance pronouncements.
More importantly still, while the ploughboy in the field might be disinterested in the issue of whether Elijah and Elisha were or were not the
fathers of Christian monasticism or whether Aquinas 'savoured of the
spirit of God', he was sure to be vitally concerned about whether or
not to hear Mass, attend confession, 'go to sermon' or make pilgrimage
to Canterbury, all of which were powerfully endorsed by Barton – and
with an authority that impressed not only Edward Thwaites, but other
contemporaries like the anonymous biographer of John Fisher, who
also bore witness to it, though he did not reside even in the diocese of
Canterbury, and was equally impressed by her trenchancy, as the following observation makes clear:

> True it is, that divers times, being in her trance wherein she happened to
> fall very often, she uttered such words touching the reproving of heresies
> which then began fast to spread: declaring what mischief would ensue
> this realm by admitting the same, that it was thought wonderful to be
> heard at the mouth of such a woman.

Barring supernatural agency, then, it would seem that Elizabeth Barton was by no means the ignoramus later depicted in hostile propaganda. Certainly, Thomas Cobb was no hayseed himself and the fact that Barton was retained in his household even when unable to perform her duties, and indeed nurtured in illness with such care, leaves little doubt of the regard in which she was held. If she could not read, moreover, it is hard to see how she would eventually become a professed nun by October 1528, after entering the Benedictine novitiate only the year before. And this is not the only reason for acknowledging her intelligence. For, according to the government's own charges levelled against her in January and February 1534, we hear that by the early 1530s, even the brother of Archbishop Warham's chaplain had entrusted his two daughters to her as a competent and instructed person. Certainly, Thwaites makes no suggestion of meanness of background or provides the vaguest hint of any simple-mindedness on Barton's part. On the contrary, he praised her lucidity and discretion of speech, which appeared to contrast so markedly with the muddled lewdness of so many contemporary controversialists.

Doubtless, too, a quick-witted young girl could have learned much from Thomas Cobb himself, whose will was a model of orthodox piety and, as such, indicative of a man who may well have been inclined to voice his distaste for heresy both to Barton and anyone else at hand within his household. As was customary, he 'bequeathed' his soul 'to Almightyful God, to our blessed Lady S. Mary and to all the holy company of heaven', and, apart from bequests for a new north window in the local church and assistance totalling 12s for 'twelve of the poorest people being householders within the said parish of Aldington', there was a further sum of 40s left to the priory of Horton Monkyn (about 4 miles from Aldington) 'for to sing a trental of masses for my soul', along with the sum of 13s 4d yearly to 'have an obit done for my soul and all Christian souls in the church of Aldington by the space of seven years'. Certainly, Tyndale would have winced at the contents, just as Cobb was sure, while living, to have bristled at growing news of heresy and anticlericalism both in Kent and the broader world. And as a long-standing member of a business-like household where Catholic piety was habitual and where she may well have enjoyed a comparatively familiar relationship with that household's head, Barton herself, of course, was unlikely to have remained unmoved by the challenges to the religion of her upbringing or the opinions of her master, whose staunch conservatism in religious matters was effectively guaranteed by his position.

Nor is it difficult to see in such circumstances how the humble servant girl's pronouncements might also have acquired the sophistication that they do indeed appear to have done. For there was the influence, too, of another figure – no less substantial from another perspective than Thomas Cobb and cited in Cobb's own will: namely, the 'honest priest' who had been appointed at a cost of £7 13s 4d 'to sing for my soul and all my friends' souls in the church of Aldington aforesaid for the space of one whole year next immediately following my death'. The priest concerned was Richard Master, another of the distinguished men who had for some time been appointed, like Erasmus before him, to serve the parish of Aldington by direct appointment of the Archbishop of Canterbury himself. For prior to the Dutchman, Thomas Linacre – physician, classical scholar and another leading intellect of the day – had held the living between 1509 and 1511, before becoming Latin tutor to Henry VIII's eldest daughter, Mary. And when Erasmus, likewise, had eventually moved on to greater things, he in turn had been replaced by John Thornton, prior of St Martin's, Dover, who had already been consecrated as suffragan to Archbishop Warham in 1508 under the title Bishop of Smirnium. All three, in fact, were a far cry from the kind of hack curate to be found in so many contemporary parishes, and this was hardly surprising, since Aldington's church was, in effect, so closely associated with the archiepiscopal palace that it became nothing less than a local chaplaincy for the Primate of England's itinerant court. As such, it had become reserved only for men of genuine substance with a significant ecclesiastical career before them. And upon his appointment in 1514, Richard Master appears to have fallen squarely within this category.

Born at Maidstone in 1484, the latest incumbent of the parish of Aldington had been educated at the royal foundation of Eton, and in 1504 went up to Cambridge as a scholar of the twin foundation of King's College, where, after impressing with apparently lightning speed, he became a fellow from 1505 to 1515 and won the reputation of 'an excellent natural and experimental philosopher'. He had graduated Bachelor of Arts in 1506–7 and Master of Arts in 1510, before ordination to the subdiaconate at Lincoln in March 1511 and incorporation as a member of the University of Oxford in 1513, after which he served as Junior Proctor at Cambridge from 1513 to 1514, bringing him into direct contact with John Fisher. But by 1515 he had also been granted his degree of Bachelor of Divinity, by which time Erasmus was already acknowledging Master as a young man of promise, 'learned in divinity, and of good and sober life' – an opinion obviously shared by Archbishop Warham, who appointed him to the valuable living of Aldington, and all that that entailed, on 18 November 1514, in the thirty-first year of his life.

With Aldington, moreover, went not only the adjacent chapelry of Smeeth, as well as a further living of Eastry, 17 miles north-west of Aldington in the neighbourhood of Sandwich, but ultimately the friend-ship of Thomas Cobb, the closeness of which was demonstrated ultimately by the latter's last will. For when Cobb framed it just under fourteen years later, Master was the only legatee mentioned with any trace of affection. The others, in fact, including even Cobb's wife and five children, were so many names and no more, and in the wife's case, indeed, there had actually been the following undisguised threat:

> I will that, if my said wife be not contented with such portions as I have assigned to her in this my testament and last will, but she or any other person for her or in her name, will or do trouble, interrupt or vex my executors in anything concerning my said last will and testament, then I will that she shall lose and not have the aforesaid 53s. 4d. by year nor no part thereof.

But Richard Master, by contrast, remained 'my honest priest', who, by that time had effectively shared the rule of Aldington's affairs for more than a decade, presiding over its spiritual well-being just as Thomas Cobb controlled material matters, and becoming in the process, we may safely assume, one half of a firm friendship.

Significantly, when the inventory of his possessions was taken by gov-ernment agents in 1534, Master was the owner of a very sizeable library, consisting of 'forty-two great books covered with boards, and thirty-three small books covered with boards, and thirty-eight books covered with leather and parchment'. And it was this cultivated man, conscientious in his duties, up-to-date but orthodox, who, in befriending Thomas Cobb, became familiar with Elizabeth Barton, an impressionable young girl who, from the age of 8 to 19, heard his vernacular sermons, Sunday by Sunday, confessed her sins to him and received his visits when illness overtook her. According to *The Sermon against the Holy Maid of Kent and her Adherents* – composed by Nicholas Heath, amended by Thomas Cranmer, and delivered at Paul's Cross in London on 23 November 1533 – Master had supped at Thomas Cobb's table after those visits, before returning to his church, no more than a stone's throw away. And it was he, ultimately, who, in compliance with canonical regulations, became compelled to inform the relevant ecclesiastical authorities of young Elizabeth Barton's growing repute. Since his parish was exempt from the aegis of the Rural Dean of Lympne, as also from the Archdeacon of Canterbury, he would have no alternative, moreover, than to deliver his report to Archbishop of Warham, and, in doing so, elevate the whole affair to an entirely new level.

Doubtless, therefore, it was with some misgivings that Master rode forth from Aldington at some point in the winter of 1525–26, leaving behind him the parish church of St Martin's, where Elizabeth Barton herself was a worshipper, and which still stands today much as it did then – a potent link to the extraordinary events about to unfold. Though the bell tower begun by Archbishop Warham would take another four centuries to complete, it remains as impressive a structure as the day that Master set out, with its nave and chancel flanked by a south aisle and what used to be the Lady Chapel. In Barton's time, too, there were statues of the Blessed Virgin and St Martin as well as St Erasmus, a little known early martyr, whose image was installed in recognition of the church's association with his much better-known namesake. And these were not the only signs of the small collegiate church's comparative affluence, since the screen and parcloses of the choir, which dated from Cardinal John Morton's time, were unusually elaborate, not unlike the stalls themselves, which terminated in rich poupée-headed finials and boasted elaborate knee-boards carved with foliage and a pin-cushion device of the Five Wounds. As an added flourish, moreover, Master's own stall boasted an angel carved on its end-post, which still survives today, albeit as a mutilated, wingless, headless figure, seated with a scroll across its lap, but as another poignant link, nonetheless, to the past and, in its own way, the dilemma facing its occupant at this time. For the hand of Richard Master must often have touched it, as he sang his office and puzzled over the strange case presented by Thomas Cobb's servant, knowing full well that in spite of their willingness to acknowledge supernatural intervention in everyday life, the ecclesiastical authorities did not in fact do so lightly, thereby guaranteeing that any priest presenting such a possibility – particularly one of Master's status – risked his reputation accordingly.

When the time came, moreover, Archbishop Warham was indeed appropriately non-committal about Barton's revelations, merely instructing Master 'to be at them as nigh as he could mark them well'. Or this at least was the account of the meeting provided in *The Sermon against the Holy Maid of Kent and her Adherents* eight years later. But both the *Sermon* and the Act of Attainder, drafted under the supervision of Thomas Cromwell in January and February 1534, also went on to suggest that, upon his return to Aldington, Master now went much further than his brief, not only refusing to await the findings of the episcopal commission soon to be set up by Warham to investigate the case, but, in the meantime, actively encouraging Barton to continue with her oracles. As *The Sermon* put it:

[He] showed her that the said Archbishop took the matter very well and said it was notable, and commanded him to be present if she had any more speeches and to mark the same: [the parson] affirming that the speeches she had spoken came of God, and that she should not refuse, neither hide, the goodness and works of God. And likewise said unto Thomas Cobb, her master.

If true, the last part of the account clearly renders Master a provocateur – a cynical exploiter of a troubled young woman for his own nefarious purposes. Worse still, it was also suggested that the rector of Aldington directly persuaded her that 'her words proceeded of the inspiration of the Holy Ghost', and in doing so convinced both her and her circle of what amounted to her newfound celebrity status, bringing visitors from further afield – including Edward Thwaites, who now regularly travelled the not inconsiderable distance of some 11 miles across country to meet her – and elevating her own status within the Cobb household. For in the words of *The Sermon*: 'As soon as she was able to sit up, her master now caused her to sit at his own mess with her mistress and this parson of Aldington.'

Intoxicated by her new circumstances and prompted by a clerical Svengali, Barton would, it seems, be given free rein to deliver her pronouncements under the direct supervision of her exploitative guide and mentor.

But does this depiction of Master, let alone the Maid herself, square with what we know of a sometime proctor of the University of Cambridge, reckoned hitherto by all who recorded their thoughts of him to be 'of good and sober life'? And is it likely, too, that such a man would have stirred the coals so readily and pre-empt the findings of the impending episcopal commission at such potential risk to both his own career and Barton's personal safety? For there was always the possibility, of course, that any supernatural intervention at Goldwell might ultimately be deemed demonic in nature, with all the ramifications that might entail. Certainly, as early as 1528, William Tyndale was teaching that the Maid's visions and prophecies, if not the result of human trickery, were 'done of the Devil, to prove us [Protestants], whether we will cleave fast to God's word; and to deceive them [Catholics] that have no love to the truth of God's word, nor lust to walk in his laws', while by 1537 Richard Morison was declaring without reservation that at the outset of her rise to prominence 'she fell under the sway of a demon'. If true, then the risk clearly existed that Barton might be detained in an ecclesiastical gaol on suspicion of witchcraft, or that Thomas Cobb might be stripped of his honourable and lucrative position for nurturing such a woman.

That Cobb was closely involved with his servant's activities is demonstrated by the following passage from Thwaites, which also demonstrates the ongoing evolution of Barton's claims after Master's visit to Canterbury, by which time the claim that 'she should go home', i.e. to the chapel at Court-at-Street where she was supposedly transported in her trances, was 'ever much in her mouth':

> Whereupon, being in a time of another trance demanded where that home was, she answered: Where she saw and heard the joys of heaven, where St Michael weighed souls, where St Peter carried the keys, and where she herself had the company of our Lady of Court-of-Street, and had heartily besought Her to heal her disease; Who also had commanded her to offer unto Her a taper in Her chapel and to declare boldly to all Christian people that our Lady of Court-of-Street had revived her from the very point of death; and that Her pleasure was that it should be rung for a miracle.

> Which words when her master heard, he said: that there were no bells
> in that chapel.

Notwithstanding Cobb's need to correct her about the chapels bells, or more precisely the lack thereof, Barton's pronouncements were therefore clearly growing in scope, as the nearby shrine of Court-at-Street featured more and more prominently in her utterances. For there, she declared, 'Our blessed Lady will show more miracles shortly,' so that 'if any depart this life suddenly or by mischance in deadly sin … he shall be restored to life again to receive shrift and housel, and after to depart this world with God's blessing.'

In the context of the time, of course, this was a particularly potent claim, and one, as events would soon prove, with ample scope to transform the little tumbledown chapel that she revered so ardently from one of the many humbler shrines to the Virgin Mary, scattered up and down the kingdom, into a place where multitudes might visit – and not only to plead for the intercession of Christ's mother in their humdrum affairs, but to marvel at the 'Holy Maid' herself. Known in Barton's time as Court-of-Street, the chapel lay halfway between Aldington Corner and the old Roman port and fortress-town of Lympne, and had originated as the domestic chapel of a fortified manor house built by John de Hadlow in the early fourteenth century. With the disappearance of Hadlow's house, however, the chapel had ceased to be used for regular liturgical use and fallen into decay, so that by the start of the sixteenth century it was tended by no more than a solitary hermit, who was not a priest and could therefore neither say Mass nor administer sacraments. Nor were his efforts at the chapel's preservation from the meagre alms he received likely to have been particularly successful, for in 1504 we find the sum of only 3s 6d being spent on upkeep, and by 1527, some twenty years later, the building was still not equipped with the bare necessities required for divine worship – lacking, as Thomas Cobb noted, even a bell.

According to an architectural survey of 1929, there were indications of a large perpendicular east window, and by the 1970s there was still the remnant of the four-centred west doorway, enclosed in a rectangular hood mould with triangular spandrels, and within it, on the north side, a cavity once containing a holy water stoup. But even in Elizabeth Barton's day, Court-at-Street was hardly an architectural gem. On the contrary, it was a remote and dilapidated outpost of the local religious landscape, just under 3 miles away from Goldwell and set deep in vast woodland through which its hermit resident is said to have piloted those benighted wayfarers unfortunate enough to have become lost there. Yet it did have a venerable statue of the Virgin Mary, and henceforth it would now have the growing celebrity of the 'Holy Maid of Kent' herself to sustain it. For after a nine-day period during Lent in 1526, involving two separate visits and a prolonged fast during which she remained 'eating nothing and drinking little', Elizabeth Barton was finally promised a cure for her long-standing ailment, and thus emerged as a ready-made cult figure in her own right.

According to a supernatural voice heard at the scene, her abstinence had been proof in its own right of 'a true miracle', and although the cure itself was still to come, hereafter, we are told, the 'fame of the marvellous Maiden was to spread abroad' – on a scale, moreover, that now made the summons of the ecclesiastical commission, mooted earlier by Warham, a pressing priority. Were it to legitimise Barton's revelations, it might render the failing chapel of Court-at-Street a latter-day Walsingham, and the maid herself another in the long line of visionary mystics dating back to St Theresa of Avila and earlier. Indeed, the possibilities were virtually limitless. But they were also explosive. For if the prophecies issuing from Barton's lips were to become political, they would not be ignorable – by either the authorities in general or the king, in particular, who, at this very moment, was hell-bent on severing all ties with his long-suffering wife.

4

TYRANT'S WHIM

So far as I can see, this passion of the king is a most extraordinary thing. He sees nothing, he thinks of nothing but Anne; he cannot do without her for an hour and it moves one to pity to see how the king's life, the stability and downfall of the whole country hang upon this one question.

Cardinal Lorenzo Campeggio, letter to the Holy See dated 18 February 1529.

Just as Henry VIII had been at first a loyal son of the pope, so he was also for many years a diligent spouse to Catherine of Aragon. Soon after her marriage, indeed, Queen Catherine was described as being in 'the greatest gaiety and contentment that ever there was', and for almost a decade she and Henry were to live in harmony as, at the very least, close and devoted friends. On the one hand, they were happy partners at revels, dances and a host of other entertainments. Both rode together, likewise, in the hunt. And as the king jousted tirelessly in her honour, wearing her symbol, the pomegranate, on the trappings of his horse, the queen played her coyly simpering part to perfection, spending most afternoons with him in her apartments, discussing theology, reading books or receiving visitors. Finally, when evening came at last, it was his habit – 'taking his pleasure as usual with the Queen' – to enjoy supper in his other half's company, after which he invariably joined her for Vespers. Such, indeed, was his ardour that in 1513, shortly after she had sent him the blood-soaked garments of the fallen King of Scotland as a sign of victory and token of her love, Henry had declared to her father: 'If I were still free, I would choose her for wife above all others.' Catherine was, after all, a kindly, gracious, loving and humble partner, who had learned well the virtues of patience and discretion after the death of her first husband, the prince's elder brother, Arthur.

Yet, sad to say, none of these qualities would now serve to spare her from rejection at the hands of the very man around whom she had so gladly rebuilt her life.

There was, of course, still much outward affection and warmth in evidence when, on 18 February 1516 at Greenwich Palace, the royal couple's procreative exertions had borne their first lasting fruit, for at last the king's manly honour and his nation's future seemed less doubtful. So vital had the delivery of a healthy child been this time that, as the queen endured a difficult labour, clutching the girdle of her patron saint and namesake, the news of her father's demise had been kept from her, lest grief affect the final passage of her pregnancy. And in view of her harrowing catalogue of previous failures, such grave precautions seemed most apt. Catherine had already delivered a stillborn daughter in 1510 and at the end of November 1514 she had given birth to a premature child, 'a prince who lived not long after'. Indeed, before the Princess Mary's birth the queen had brought forth four sons in all, none of whom survived longer than a few weeks. But now, aided by her physician Dr Vittoria and providence too, perhaps, she delivered a new babe who was described by her glowing father as 'a right lusty princess'.

Nevertheless, only a year or so after his daughter's birth, Henry's infidelities began to make their mark. There had been earlier rumours of dalliance, but these seem to have been consistent by and large with the rather cloying and impotently flirtatious gallantries typical of the time. The king had, for instance, apparently shown an interest in one of Queen Catherine's ladies-in-waiting, Lady Anne Hastings, as early as 1510, though after a whiff of scandal it came to nothing. Then in Flanders, in 1513, it was noticed how gaily the 22-year-old king had danced with Margaret of Savoy. A year later, a young lady from Margaret's court called Etienette La Baume, whom Henry had met on campaign, wrote and reminded him of their encounter at Lille where the king had spoken 'beaucoup de belles choses' ('many beautiful things'). All this denoted little of significance, however, and for almost the entire first decade of his marriage Henry appears to have been rather unique among his princely counterparts in terms of faithfulness to his spouse. In comparison to Henry's nil score up to 1519, the Emperor Maximilian, for instance, had sired eleven bastards.

Sometime before this, though, 'coeur loyall' had already begun a tiptoeing but inexorable descent into husbandly contempt, and at the sumptuous fêting of the French ambassadors during Michaelmas 1518, Elizabeth Blount, a lady-in-waiting to Queen Catherine, had caught his eye. Moreover, when on 18 November the queen gave birth to a dead princess, she did so in the cruel knowledge that Mistress Blount had just become pregnant by Henry. To add salt to the wound, the latter's healthy son was born in June 1519 and, as the years unfolded, he would be officially acknowledged and treated to a spate of high honours. While Henry's legitimate daughter, Mary, was eventually packed off to the Marches as Princess of Wales, his bastard son would be made Earl of Nottingham, Warden of the Cinque Ports, Warden of the Scottish Marches, Lord High Admiral and Lord Lieutenant of Ireland. Most significantly of all, he was created Duke of Richmond and Somerset – two combined titles that were of old and significant association among the Tudors. At the same time, he was also given his own household, which, at a cost of £4,000 per year, was markedly more substantial than that of his half-sister. And when the queen protested, Henry took no more notice than to dismiss three of her Spanish ladies as a lesson in wifely obedience. Worse still, he soon began to discuss with the council an altogether more startling project – that of entailing the crown upon his bastard son.

By the shaky sexual standards of the age, of course, the king might still be reckoned comparatively abstemious even after this first lapse, since he appears to have confined his adulterous exploits to the times when Catherine was either pregnant or recovering from childbirth. Nevertheless, the first bite of the extra-marital apple is almost invariably an hors d'oeuvre, and after Mistress Blount came Mary Boleyn, wife of William Carey since 1521 and sister of Anne. There was, moreover, a special piquancy about this particular liaison, for if Henry had already nibbled at temptation, then Mary herself had surely gorged and laid bare the orchard. Having been loosed at a susceptible age in the French court, she had succumbed too avidly to the gallant atmosphere pertaining there and emerged 'as a very great wanton with a most infamous reputation'. Francis I himself, indeed, was among her lovers and described this 'English mare' with typical sensitivity as 'a great whore, the most infamous of all'.

But then, after earlier dips, came Henry's fateful plunge. For at some point during 1525 or 1526 what began as a light flirtation with a less-than-ravishing raven-haired woman in her mid-twenties grew into something altogether more momentous. The offspring of a clan of avaricious social climbers, Anne Boleyn had joined her sister at the French court in August 1513 to learn the subtleties of deportment, dancing, polite conversation, high fashion and etiquette. Yet the ladies awaiting her there sought new freedoms and displayed new audacities, and though she would become in due course a committed advocate of the new religious thinking, she would also learn to shun austerity. Indeed, while Anne Boleyn and her French counterparts were attending to their prayer books, they were no less keen to apply their thoughts to the altogether less edifying pages of Margerite of Navarre's *Heptameron*. And having fully gauged the ways of the world, they could titillate and captivate accordingly, so that when, eventually, Mistress Boleyn finally encountered the man with whom her destiny lay, she was more than fully equipped to laugh and dance her way into England's history.

Yet if truth be told, the underlying reasons for Henry's decision to put paid to his marriage are rather more murky than is sometimes recognised and all too often the fears of dynastic insecurity that appear to have haunted him have also deceived historians. There is no doubt, of course, that there was a serious political dimension to the king's perplexity concerning the succession issue. Compared with France, where there were prolific lines of princes and princesses of the royal blood, the families of both Henry VII and Henry VIII were tiny. In England, the problem of rival claimants to the throne had been greatly eased by the early deaths or infertility of those descended from the Yorkist line. Apart from Henry VIII's own mother, who had in any case been bound to the Tudor cause by marriage, only one of Edward IV's six other daughters had produced a son, the future Marquess of Exeter, and nor, in spite of the attention they attracted, were Edward's two nephews ever serious contenders for the throne. Edmund de la Pole, after all, was already captive at the time of Henry's accession, only to be quietly executed in 1513. And although his exiled brother Richard had grandiosely styled himself the 'White Rose' and been proclaimed King of England by Louis XII of France in 1512, support for his claim was abruptly withdrawn only two years later when the French booted him unceremoniously from their country after peace had been made with Henry. Ultimately, he would end his exile only by being killed at the side of Francis I at the Battle of Pavia in 1525 – an event that caused Henry to declare confidently at the time that 'all the enemies of England are gone'. And in the meantime the grandchildren of Edward IV's hapless brother, the Duke of Clarence – Lord Henry Montague, Reginald Pole and Sir Geoffrey Pole – were always to remain irritants rather than genuine threats.

In reality, then, this was a comparatively flaccid brood to inconvenience the Tudor dynasty, particularly when the Poles continued to confine themselves to nothing more than armchair plotting and pungent comments – to the extent, indeed, that even by the late 1530s their sole threat seemed to progress along the lines that Henry 'will one day die suddenly; his leg will kill him and then we shall have jolly stirring'. Such was the measure of their subtle strategy. And while the Stafford line may ultimately have produced the most substantial potential rival to Henry VIII in the form of Edward Stafford, Duke of Buckingham, even he would be trapped neatly by his own indiscreet murmurings in 1521, leaving what can at very best be considered fringe claimants, such as Thomas Howard, Duke of Norfolk, who could trace his descent from Edward I, and Henry Brandon, the young Earl of Lincoln. Moreover, the consistent submissiveness of characters like Norfolk, not to mention the desultory nature of the so-called 'Exeter Conspiracy' of 1538, served simply as further proof, if any were needed, of the essential security of the second Tudor's throne.

So at that very point when Henry VIII was, in all likelihood, beginning to ponder the annulment of his marriage to Catherine of Aragon, the threat of rival dynastic contenders was diminishing almost beyond trace, though there was also, of course, the far from insignificant matter of the royal conscience to complicate matters. For time and again, as events unfolded, Henry made frequent references to 'the tranquillity of consciences and the health of his soul', in connection with Pope Julius II's dispensation of 1503 that had sanctioned his marriage to his brother's widow in the first place, and in particular its apparent breach of the biblical Book of Leviticus (20:21), which not only declared that 'if a man shall take his brother's wife, it is an unclean thing' but warned, too, that any resulting marriage 'shall be childless'. In 1529, he would write to Charles V, explaining that he could not 'quiet or appease his conscience remaining longer with the queen, whom, for her nobleness of blood and other virtues, he had loved entirely as his wife, until he saw in Scripture that God had forbidden their union'. Yet his growing conviction since at least 1522 that he was a victim of God's punishment as a result of his effectively incestuous marriage was essentially insubstantial. Indeed, the so-called 'Levitical seed' that supposedly tormented him, was, in reality, more pip than acorn, as John Fisher, whom Henry had once described as the most learned theologian he had ever known, would readily prove in a series of antidotes to Henry's scriptural headache delivered in the Long Gallery at Windsor in the late summer of 1527. For in contradistinction to Leviticus, the Book of Deuteronomy (25:5) actually contained a direct invocation for a man to marry his deceased brother's wife when that brother had died without children. And there was also, of course, the hardly insignificant consideration that, notwithstanding the threat of the 'Levitical curse', Henry's union with his wife was not in any case actually childless.

Yet although the birth of Princess Mary offered an apparently safe haven in the midst of this theological minefield, the king's conscience continued to serve as the lubricant that allowed him to force square pegs into round holes, and his response was simply to appoint another scholar to give him the answers he wanted. At which point, Robert Wakefield, a gifted young scholar of Hebrew with no eye for either professional or any other kind of martyrdom, duly emerged to oblige his sovereign by conveniently contending that the 'childless' reference in Leviticus referred exclusively to male offspring and that Deuteronomy was using the word 'brother' in the wider sense of male relatives in general. Nor was this all. For, having been readily convinced, Henry was now rocked on every side by portents of God's displeasure, which multiplied as they reverberated. His tomb, a towering marble structure, had been commissioned in 1519, and in 1521 he had been struck down by fever and begun to complain of severe sinus troubles. But if the creeping onset of middle age and infirmity had already begun to assail him by his mid-thirties in a century where a man's forties offered old age and his fifties held out only the release of the grave, Henry's preoccupation with Leviticus was now to be further fuelled by other events, including the worst plague in a decade, which seemed to descend straight from heaven in July 1525 to chastise the kingdom for his sinful union. At the contagion's peak, fifty people a day died in London and, as Henry was reminded in January 1526 when two gentlemen of his own household died, not even the protection of the royal court was a guarantee of safety.

Always susceptible to morbid presentiments of any kind, it was during the 1528 epidemic of the 'sweating sickness' that Henry's fears would reach truly exceptional heights. The mere name of 'the sweat', Bishop Gardiner wrote, 'is so terrible to his highness' ears that he dare in no wise approach where it is noised to have been'. Immured in Wolsey's residence at Tittenhanger, it now became his practice to shut himself away for long periods – sometimes in a high tower where he often took his supper alone or consulted with his physician Dr Chambers. At times like these, indeed, he feared to sleep alone and ordered Sir Francis Bryan to attend him in his privy chamber through-out the night, at which time his earlier scrapes with death will only have served to compound his fears. For in March 1524, he had entered the lists with the visor of his helmet open while jousting with the Duke of Suffolk. And although, according to *Hall's Chronicle*, the horrified spectators shouted to the duke to hold, he could neither hear nor see, so that his lance struck and shattered against the king's helmet less than an inch from his exposed face. A year later too, while hawking, Henry had vaulted a ditch, only to break his jumping-pole and fall head-first into the water, lodging his face firmly in the mud before panting attendants arrived in the nick of time to save their master from the kind of earthy earthly exit that would have led to merry banqueting barbs throughout the courts of Europe.

Yet the next challenge to the king's peace of mind would come from an even less likely quarter. For just as his existing anxieties and impatience were progressively overwhelming him, so some good distance from the royal court – at Aldington in Kent – the stirrings that would bring his misgivings to a critical pitch were about to be unleashed, with the launch of Archbishop Warham's episcopal commission to investigate the case of Elizabeth Barton. At the time of Barton's promised cure at Court-at-Street, the archbishop was, it seems, away from Canterbury, but in answer to an alert, presumably from Richard Master, he wasted no time in dispatching his registrar back to his cathedral city with a list of suggested participants, which left no doubt about either the urgency or gravity of the matter they would be examining, since this was no haphazard group of ignorant or light-minded persons. On the contrary, all seven nominees were men of excellent standing and known worth. Three were Benedictine monks under the jurisdiction of the Prior of Christ Church, Canterbury, of which the archbishop himself was titular head. Two more were friars of the reformed order of Franciscan Observants, who had recently established a house in Canterbury. And alongside these five members of the regular clergy were to sit also: Barton's confessor and spiritual mentor, Richard Master, who as local parish priest had an *ex officio* right to be involved, and a certain Thomas Wall, who was to act as secretary to the commission.

Certainly, the Priory of Christ Church itself, formally known as Holy Trinity, was one of the kingdom's most notable foundations, lying in the heart of Canterbury, and exceeding by some way even the prestige of the city's other great Benedictine house, the abbey of St Augustine's, which lay just outside the walls. And if its prior, 49-year-old Thomas Goldwell, may ultimately have lacked the fibre to resist pressure from without, even he, as a Doctor of Divinity and former Warden of Canterbury College, who had ruled the cathedral monastery for eleven years, was a figure of considerable substance. Indeed, in the event of the archbishop's death, it was upon the Prior and Chapter of Christ Church that the powers of the Primate of All England would devolve until a successor was found, making Goldwell one of the senior figures within the entire English Church. And at a time when the good name of monks was under common assault, he had also played no small part in ensuring that the reputation of Christ Church held largely firm by attracting the highest calibre of monks to its cloisters. As such, it was hardly surprising, perhaps, that the core of the nominees for Archbishop Warham's commission should indeed have been drawn from there. For all three were men of mature character, holding very senior and responsible positions within the monastery, and two were prestigious graduates of the University of Oxford. Indeed, Dom Edward Bocking, DD, and Dom William Hadleigh – whose names suggest that their forebears may possibly have hailed from manors belonging to the Priory of Christ Church in Essex and Suffolk respectively – had, like the prior himself, received their education at a house of studies founded in 1363 by Archbishop Islip for the monks of Christ Church, which was later incorporated into Cardinal Wolsey's new foundation of Christ Church College. And both had distinguished themselves not only by their exceptional scholarship but by the merits of their subsequent careers.

Bocking, some five years senior to Hadleigh, had been born around 1483, and although it is not known whether he was brought up within the monastery school itself or had entered the Benedictine Order in his teens, there is little doubt about his brilliance. For in 1504, at the age of 21 or thereabouts, he was already an established member of the University of Oxford. Only six years later, moreover, he had become warden of his college, holding this office for the next eight years, before receiving the degree of Bachelor of Divinity in June 1513, as a reward for his study of logic, philosophy and theology over the nine proceeding years. Nor was this the sum of his achievements. For in June 1518 he was granted his doctorate in divinity, after which he almost immediately applied to be dispensed from the normal term of regency, since he had just been 'appointed to rule his own monastery' – or, in other words, been recalled to his mother house of Christ Church, Canterbury, to join the governing body there as 'cellarer', one of the four principal offices of any monastic community, responsible for its housekeeping and internal management. Controlling a staff of twenty-eight monks, Bocking was conducting his administrative duties with his usual diligence and efficiency, when in 1526, at the age of around 44, he was nominated to serve on the episcopal commission that would change the course of his life.

Ultimately, too, it would render him the butt of the same kind of propaganda slurs as the woman who would now come to dominate his affairs. 'That he was a doctor I don't deny,' the Protestant controversialist Richard Morison wrote in 1537, 'though he never taught anyone anything,' and the doctorate itself was also dismissed with appropriate derision. 'The years he had spent, rather than studied, at the University,' cracked Morison without any further elaboration, 'had procured him a doctorate,' notwithstanding Bocking's other considerable achievements, both intellectual and administrative. Certainly, he was not an easy man. On the contrary, he was known to superiors like Prior Goldwell for his 'temerity, furious zeal and malicious blind affection'. But his peers were eventually forced to admit to Henry VIII that he had exercised considerable influence over certain monks, 'and especially such as were brought into our religion [i.e. Order] by Dr Bocking, being of the younger sort'. Significantly, these young monks were all university men themselves, attracted by Dom Edward's intellectual gifts and spirituality, and less inclined than their elders to resent his pig-headedness. Strong convictions forcefully expressed, something so irksome at times to the old, are, after all, occasionally more admired in the young. And neither should we forget to balance Morison's sniping against the judgement of John Fisher's anonymous biographer, who considered Dom Edward 'a learned and virtuous man'.

The same, moreover, could be said with equal confidence of the second of Archbishop Warham's appointees from Christ Church. Though quieter and more self-effacing, Dom William Hadleigh's career to date had been almost as distinguished, and he, unlike Bocking perhaps, also fell more clearly into both categories of the two sorts of model monk later specified by Prior Goldwell in 1538, i.e. not only 'witty' (intelligent) but 'a good man' (obedient) to boot. He had been born in 1488, received his degree of Bachelor of Divinity at Canterbury College, Oxford, in the same year as Dom Edward gained his doctorate, and succeeded him as warden of the college when Dom Edward went back to Canterbury in 1518. Remaining at Oxford, until 1524, Dom William, too, then returned to Christ Church, Canterbury, taking up, like Bocking before him, a post of significant responsibility – in his case, the role of penitentiary, which he was still holding two years later, at the age of 39, when the summons to join Archbishop Warham's ecclesiastical commission arrived and sucked him into a political vortex for which he, unlike Prior Goldwell, had neither the necessary guile nor instinct for survival. For while Goldwell was before long covering his tracks and distancing himself from the affair, bemoaning the doubtful reputation of the Maid and claiming in retrospect that he should have selected none of the men enlisted from his monastery to judge her, Hadleigh would go about his duties all too sincerely and naïvely – in much the same way, it seems, as the second of his colleagues from Christ Church: a certain Fr Barnes, about whom little is known beyond the fact that on a list of late 1533, he is described as master of the monastery's eleemosynary, or almoner.

Of the two Franciscan Observants appointed to the commission, meanwhile, little is known. The name of one, indeed, went entirely unrecorded, while the other, Father Lewis Wilkinson, is hardly less elusive, since his details fail to appear even on any university list for the period. Yet their Order was anything but unknown and would emerge before long not only as one of the most outspoken sources of opposition to the royal divorce, but among the very vanguard of those elements most feared by the government. Standing, as their name implies, for a strict maintenance of the Franciscan Rule, the Observants, unlike their so-called Conventual counterparts, held no property in common, and had renounced all vested incomes and accumulated goods, so that by the early part of the fourteenth century their reputation was secure. And though when the

time of trial eventually arrived, neither they nor similar groups like the
Bridgettines of Syon would endure the carnage accepted so readily by the
Carthusians, they would certainly adopt a bolder stance than many of their
more suppliant peers: ministering throughout to Queen Catherine from
their Greenwich friary, which fronted the Thames and adjoined the royal
palace; stridently criticising the king from the pulpit of the chapel in the
same palace's west wing; and ultimately refusing to comply with Thomas
Cromwell's commissioners for enforcing the oath of supremacy, on the
grounds 'that they had professed St Francis's religion and in the observance thereof they would live and die'.

Significantly, the Observants had already established a long-standing
association with royalty and were intimately tied not only to the everyday environment of life at Greenwich in particular, but also at Richmond,
where their foundation once again enjoyed easy access to a nearby royal
palace. Since they possessed no library in their own buildings at Greenwich,
they had been allowed complete use of the palace library, which they actually referred to as 'our library' and which added to their ongoing visibility in
the midst of the royal occupants. Furthermore, Henry VII had maintained
close and amicable relations with them throughout his life, and had chosen
his own confessor from among their number, while his wife, Elizabeth, had
also made the Greenwich friary an annual grant, and selected its chapel for
the baptism of her children. All six of England's Observant houses would,
in fact, receive legacies in the first Tudor's will, and nor was the future
Henry VIII lacking in gifts and affection for the Observants, informing
Pope Leo X how he could not sufficiently express his admiration for their
rigorous adherence to St Francis's rule of poverty and the sincerity of their
devotion to the poor. No religious order, claimed Henry, battled against
vice with more perseverance – and few, ironically enough, would prove
more attentive in their endeavour to keep Christ's fold intact.

But if the second Tudor's pronouncements in their favour were typically lavish, so his wife's actions on behalf of the Observants spoke much
more eloquently still of her own devotion, which dated back to her
acquaintance with, arguably, the most illustrious of all their number:
the celebrated canon and civil lawyer, Archbishop Ximenez of Toledo,
who was confessor to her mother. Such was the calibre of Ximenez's
zeal, in fact, that he had at first refused his archbishopric to preserve

his vow of poverty, only agreeing subsequently to don prelatical robes
at all on condition that his friar's habit was plainly visible underneath.
Thereafter, he would give a great part of the very considerable revenues
of his see for the relief of the poor and the ransoming of captives, and,
like Queen Catherine herself, he would also become a great patron of
learning, founding the University of Alcalá in 1504. Nor, after her arrival
in England three years earlier, did the queen's devotion to her Franciscan
friends waver. On the contrary, before the birth of her first child, she
vowed, while in labour, to present 'to St Peter the Martyr' one of her
richest headdresses, and duly dispatched it to Spain soon afterwards
by one of her maids. Surely enough, the saint concerned was Peter of
Sassoferrato, who had been sent to Spain by St Francis to preach the
Gospel, only to be martyred by the Moors at Valencia in 1231. And when
the queen's own life came to an end, it was little surprise either that her
final request would be for her burial in a church of the Observants –
curiously forgetting, or perhaps somehow unaware, that by that time the
whole Order had been suppressed.

Plainly, then, the selection by Archbishop Warham a decade earlier of
Father Wilkinson and his unknown colleague for the episcopal commission into Elizabeth Barton's case had added considerable weight to that
commission's credibility, since the Observant's reputation for integrity
was impeccable. Moreover, as the archbishop well knew, the presence of
this brace of Observants would help counterbalance the more distinctly
intellectual orientation of their three Benedictine colleagues, since they
were representative of what might be considered the new wave of mod-
ern-minded clergy. Emerging originally as what amounted to a protest
movement against the loose interpretation of the Franciscan Rule, they
had only been established by papal decree as an independent Order of
St Francis – that is to say, an Order entirely separate from their Conventual
counterparts – in 1517. But thereafter their experience of life outside
the cloister made them, quite literally, men of the world, and their resulting everyday contact with members of the laity, and particularly with
women, made them invaluable additions to Warham's panel – not, it must
be said, that the appointed Benedictines knew nothing of human nature
themselves. For to be head of an Oxford college, however clerical its con-
stitution, was hardly to live in a cloister, while to be cellarer, penitentiary

or almoner of a major monastery was certainly to know a tall story from a true one. In short, if Elizabeth Barton were deceiving or deceived, it would be made manifest soon enough.

But upon the commissioners' arrival in Aldington, their young subject's credibility could not, it seems, be impugned, for, notwithstanding the Protestant colouring of William Lambarde's redaction, the resulting account of Edward Thwaites makes amply clear that:

> These men opposed her in the chief points of Popish [*sic*] belief and, finding her sound therein, not only waded no further in the discovery of the fraud, but gave favourable countenance and joined with her in setting forth of the same.

Clearly, she had not only been vindicated by her inquisitors' 'oppositions', but won them comprehensively to her cause, so much so, indeed, that they attended a Mass of thanksgiving at a date of the now undoubtedly 'holy' Maid's own choosing in the chapel of Court-at-Street where her henceforth officially endorsed encounter with the Blessed Virgin had occurred. And the resulting event was not only a public and well-publicised occasion, with the commissioners themselves present, but remarkably well attended into the bargain. For, as even Nicholas Heath's hostile *Sermon* was to acknowledge:

> When the said day appointed by her came, Dr Bocking and this Parson of Aldington … with other clerks and religious men, accompanied with two thousand and more of the King's Grace's people, went in procession with [Elizabeth Barton] from her said master's house to the said chapel at Court-at-Street, singing the litany and saying divers psalms and orations [prayers] by the way.

If Thwaites is the better guide, moreover – as well he may be, since Heath's *Sermon*, just like the account in the Act of Attainder which followed it, is blatantly propagandistic in nature – the numbers present were actually considerably higher still, since spring, after all, was in the air, and as Thwaites takes up the story again, with the procession completing its 2.5-mile journey by descending the wooded way to the little plateau where the chapel stood, it is clear that the event had not merely attracted the low-born and credulous. On the contrary, according to Thwaites's account, Barton:

> Entered the chapel with *Ave regina caelorum* in prick-song [i.e. from printed sheet music, produced by the organisers, presumably at no small expense], accompanied with these Commissioners, many ladies, gentlemen and gentlewomen of the best degree, and three thousand persons besides of the common sort of the country.

Even if exaggerated, therefore, it is hard to deny that that the numbers involved must surely have created a remarkable spectacle, particularly when it is remembered that both *The Sermon* and the government's subsequent Act of Attainder could only venture to reduce them by a third. And the anthem they sang on their way marked not only their reverence for the Maid's celestial advocate, the Virgin Mary, but the season of the year – sometime between Candlemas Day and the Wednesday in Holy Week – which was also of special significance in the Church's calendar:

> Hail, Queen of the heavens,
> hail, Mistress of the angels,
> hail, Root: hail Gate
> through which the Light dawns on the world!
>
> Rejoice, glorious Virgin,
> loveliest of all creatures!
> And so farewell, fairest of all:
> pray for us to Christ.

Indeed, since Easter Day fell on 1 April in 1526, we can surmise that the procession occurred between 2 February and 28 March, perhaps on the feast of the Annunciation on 25 March. And if the account of Thomas Cranmer, produced in a letter to Nicholas Hawkins, Archdeacon of Ely, is any guide, it was conducted with Barton herself still in a state of considerable physical debility – even carried, perhaps, in a litter. For Cranmer's letter, dated 20 December 1533, tells how she was 'laid before the image of our Lady', before going on to relate how she emerged from her trance state 'perfectly whole', i.e. cured, after a remarkable disfigurement of her face and a 'voice heard speaking within her belly', sometimes 'sweet', sometimes 'horrible', according to whether it described heaven or hell. Thereafter, he tells us, she had 'lain there a long time before she came to herself again', and, in the meantime during her trance, she had related 'many things for the confirmation of pilgrimages and trentals, hearing of masses, and confessions, and many other such things'.

Yet what might at first be thought an invaluable account of an extraordinary episode is, in fact, anything but, since Cranmer's description is actually no more than a private, and initially light-hearted, treatment of a 'miracle', about which he always remained sceptical. His letter too, it should be remembered, is written by a committed reformer to a friend of similar outlook abroad. And although he had by that time twice examined Barton and also vetted Nicholas Heath's government-approved *Sermon* on the Maid's deceptions, it contains no new material beyond what Thwaites had produced in his *Marvellous Work*, even preserving some passages, including the cure itself that Lambarde once more saw fit to suppress later. That Cranmer should have so neglected any new material is noteworthy enough. But that his description should also have followed, virtually word for word, an account of the physical transformations experienced by another contemporary prophetess, the so-called 'Maid of Ipswich', described by Sir Thomas More five years earlier, casts grave doubt on this aspect of his narrative in particular. For if More was not himself imitating a lost passage of *A Marvellous Work*, Cranmer was merely working up second-hand material – most probably with his tongue set firmly in his cheek, as an exercise in comic hagiography solely intended to mock and undermine the central participant and those who were taken in by her antics.

So what, then, did happen within the walls of the little chapel at Court-at-Street on 25 March 1526, as thousands waited outside, unable to squeeze into its narrow confines? Here too, it seems, our most reliable source is necessarily Thwaites, whose eyewitness recollection tells us that:

There fell she eftsoons into a marvellous passion [i.e. suffering] before the image of our Lady, much like a body diseased of the falling evil [i.e. epilepsy].

In the which she uttered sundry metrical and rhyming speeches, tending to the worship of our Lady of Court-of-Street (whose chapel there she wished to be better maintained, and to be furnished with a daily singing priest);

Tending also to her own bestowing in some religious house, for such (said she) was our Lady's pleasure;

and tending finally and fully to the advancement of the credit of such feigned [i.e. alleged] miracles as that author [Thwaites] doth report.

Not altogether surprisingly, perhaps, Lambarde, as a dutiful Elizabethan Protestant, had seen fit to omit what was actually the whole point of Thwaite's story: namely, that Barton was ultimately cured. But in all other respects at least, he seems to have faithfully summarised the oracles, as recorded by Thwaites originally – and all of which, incidentally, were eventually realised. For a chaplain was indeed appointed to sing Mass daily in the old chapel; Elizabeth Barton did in fact become a nun; while Court-at Street went on, as predicted, to become not only a place of pilgrimage but a site, allegedly, for further miraculous happenings after Barton had finally gone away to her appointed Benedictine convent of St Sepulchre's at Canterbury.

Within a year of its publication by Robert Redman in 1527, moreover, Thwaites's *Marvellous Work* was so widely diffused that William Tyndale almost certainly had a copy of it on the Continent when writing *The Obedience of a Christian Man*, and if so, the scale of Elizabeth Barton's impact – as well as the magnitude of her potential threat – is apparent. Archbishop Warham's commissioners, after all, had only just confirmed the Maid's legitimacy when Our Lady of Court-at-Street had appeared to endorse their judgement, by virtue of a miraculous healing in full public view. All of which was potent stuff indeed, and more than sufficient grounds in a contemporary context for the generation of a cult that was soon becoming influential among all classes, notwithstanding the ongoing caution of Warham himself. For, as *The Sermon* confirms:

Dr Bocking rode up to the said Archbishop of Canterbury, and showed him that a great miracle had been done upon her at Court-at-Street by the mightiful power of God and his blessedful Mother Mary and desired him to declare the same for a miracle, and that it might please him to sequester that elected person of God to the nunnery of St Sepulchre's at Canterbury.

To whom the archbishop answered, that he would not be hasty therein [i.e. about proclaiming the miracle], but would counsel thereupon with the prelates and clergy of his diocese and with his Learned Council. And that he was contented that the said Elizabeth should be in the meantime in the nunnery of St Sepulchre's, if the prioress would take her.

Sensibly enough, then, Warham had remained circumspect, though without casting doubt of any kind upon the sincerity of either Bocking's judgement or intentions. And the Benedictine was indeed now central to events. For if the Act of Attainder of 1534 is to be relied upon, among the many 'wondrous words' uttered by the Maid at Court-at-Street was a declaration that it was the 'pleasure of God' that 'Edward Bocking should be her ghostly father [i.e. spiritual director]'. Nor did the archbishop make any appreciable effort to curb Bocking's role. On the contrary, he not only consulted his diocesan clergy and 'Learned Council' on the strength of the Benedictine's testimony, but thereafter submitted the written evidence to the king himself, who duly passed it on to Sir Thomas More, then High Steward of Cambridge University and Chancellor of the Duchy of Lancaster.

Later, in February 1534, by which time Barton's case was threatening to shake the entire kingdom, More described his response in a letter to Thomas Cromwell, in which he was characteristically evasive about his own responsibility for decisions any subsequent developments:

It is, I suppose, about eight or nine years ago, since I heard of that housewife [Elizabeth Barton] first. At which time, the Bishop of Canterbury that then was – God assoil his soul – sent unto the King's Grace a roll of paper in which were written certain words of hers as she had, as report was then made, at sundry times spoken in her trances. Whereupon it pleased the King's Grace to deliver me the roll, commanding me to look thereon and afterward show him what I thought therein. Whereunto, at another time, when his Highness asked me, I told him that in good faith I found nothing in these words that I could anything regard or esteem, for, saving that some part fell in rhyme, and that – God wot – full rude, else for any reason – God wot – that I saw therein, a right simple woman might, in my mind, speak it of her own wit well enough. Howbeit, I said, that because it was constantly reported for a truth that God wrought in her and that a miracle was showed upon her, I durst not, nor would not, be bold in judging the matter. And the King's Grace, as methought, esteemed the matter as light [unimportant] as it after proved lewd [silly].

But if More was, indeed, as condescendingly unconcerned as his letter suggests, his conjecture about the king's response is altogether less convincing. For although lazy-minded enough to pass the burdensome task of weighing the evidence to the man who would eventually become the most famous of all his martyrs, Henry VIII remained intensely susceptible to the wonder-workings and supernatural interventions so closely associated with pre-Reformation religion. And it was with his approval, therefore, that Archbishop Warham not only ratified Barton's miraculous cure but sanctioned the ringing of bells throughout the diocese and cathedral city of Canterbury in thanksgiving for the divine intervention on her behalf. It was Thomas Cranmer himself, moreover, who not only confirmed this in his letter to Nicholas Hawkins of 1533, but provided further evidence of the Holy Maid's impact, as demonstrated by the popularity of Thwaites's book:

> And so [he recorded] this miracle was finished and solemnly rung, and a book written of all the whole story thereof and put into print; which, ever since that time, hath been commonly sold and gone abroad among all the people.

For Cranmer, of course, the entire episode betokened the wellspring of ignorance and superstition against which he was so determined to direct his evangelical energies, and by December 1533, when his letter was written, he could clearly afford a degree of dismissiveness in recounting the episode, as the Maid and her main confederates mouldered in the Tower. But seven years earlier, as she sat in a cell of another kind within the convent of St Sepulchre's, she was anything but contained. On the contrary, she had swiftly acquired thousands of new admirers now encompassing far more than the common people of Kent – whom Richard Morison nevertheless considered more uneducated and susceptible to a religious hoax than those in other parts of England – along with a spiritual director of uncommon tenacity and boldness in Dom Edward Bocking, who was to shape her future and act, in effect, as her agent and impresario.

For, in compliance with the Elizabeth Barton's declaration at Court-at-Street, Archbishop Warham had indeed 'caused and given license to the cellarer to be this woman's ghostly father', though much to the disapproval, it must be said, of the prior of his own monastery who had obviously found Bocking's conduct throughout their relationship hard to handle – not least because he was mainifestly a man of considerable obduracy and therefore one whom an individual like Thomas Goldwell, in continual search of an uncomplicated life, could never warm to. All of which the prior made clear in a letter to Thomas Cromwell, dated 12 November 1533, in which he reflected upon his cellarer's new role in relation to Elizabeth Barton: 'And so he hath continued ever since, as far as I know, and resorted unto her at times convenient when he would himself; and that by my Lord of Canterbury's license and not mine.' Yet with Bocking's tenacious assistance, as the 1534 Act of Attainder confirms, 'the said Elizabeth' was indeed to be 'brought into a marvellous fame, credit and good opinion of a great multitude of the people of his realm' – which was well enough for now, perhaps, but only while she confined her pronouncements to their current limits.

And the prospect of such restraint seemed increasingly remote as the king's whims regarding his marriage assumed ever more menacing forms over the coming months. For by the spring of 1527, he had committed himself irrevocably to a series of frontal assaults on both his wife's word and papal authority. First, with utter insensitivity to Catherine's vehement denials and against Thomas Wolsey's express advice, Henry duly protested that his wife's marriage to his brother, Arthur, had indeed been consummated, therefore his marriage to Catherine was, as such, contrary to God's law. After which, having been adulterously bypassed, Catherine was left with no other choice than to acknowledge the loss of her honour in favour of a woman of no substance or reputation. Naturally enough, for a Trastámara princess such as she, this was utterly intolerable, and in response to her husband's secrecy, contempt and bullying, Catherine would ultimately throw away for good the keys to her co-operation. Equally damagingly, the king's chosen course also ignited the whole issue of papal authority by implying that no pope had the capability to dispense with God's law as laid down in the Bible. In short, Henry was determined to challenge his wife's honesty, to lecture the doctors of the Church on divinity and biblical exegesis, and to tell the pope his job. And as the price for his attempt to unpick the complex legal knots binding him to his wife, he would now find himself provoking not only Elizabeth Barton, but the even more formidable opposition of Bishop John Fisher.

That the king's intention henceforth was to annul his marriage once and for all first became certain in mid-May 1527 when a bizarre transaction was staged at York Place, Wolsey's mansion at Westminster. Acting in his capacity as legate *a latere*, the cardinal had duly decided to summon his royal master before a secretly convened court to answer a 'charge' that, for the last seventeen years, he had been living in 'open sin' with his brother's widow. The assessors were to be Wolsey himself along with Archbishop Warham, who had long harboured doubts over the papal dispensation of 1503, which had underpinned Henry's marriage to Catherine in the first place, while the queen was to be neither informed nor represented. And in the meantime, the king, suitably cast in the role of defendant rather than petitioner, was to appear before the court not so much as the instigator of a treacherous act but as the unwitting victim of a misconceived dispensation framed more than twenty years earlier. Explaining to Henry that, as legate, he was duty bound to investigate the validity of his marriage, Wolsey, too, could neatly sanitise his own role, posing as no more than the righteous executant of canon law and noble guardian of his sovereign's spiritual welfare. Warham, meanwhile, was to be deftly presented as the final arbiter of the marriage's validity, in the hope of expunging any charge of partiality or self-interest on Wolsey's part.

But even this was not the sum of the deception. For as the whole elaborate ruse unfolded and the Archbishop of Canterbury settled into his all-too-familiar role of exalted irrelevance in the cardinal's shadow, Henry, too, excelled himself as actor and master-deceiver – not only concealing from Wolsey his longer-term wish to marry Anne Boleyn, but showing no hesitation either in daring to present a feigned protest to the effect that he was indeed legally married to his wife. In the process, with cold-blooded gall, the king duly produced Pope Julius's dispensation on cue and then employed Dr John Bell, his proctor, to defend its validity, leaving

Wolsey's court to pore over the legality of Henry's union with Catherine for all of two weeks, during which time Bell's arguments were conveniently dismantled by the prosecutor, Dr Richard Wolman, and witnesses produced to challenge their soundness. There were concerns, it is true, over the queen's eventual reaction, and the likelihood that she would insist upon appealing her case to the pope and the emperor, thus transforming into an international crisis what Wolsey was hoping to present as a merely domestic matter. But the court itself seemed neatly insulated from all such external interference, and therefore appeared to be performing its function precisely as intended. Over its four sessions, indeed, it appeared to be proceeding inexorably to its preordained conclusion.

Yet by the time that the court adjourned abruptly for its last session on 31 May, a thunderbolt from Italy had robbed Wolsey once and for all of any illusion that this most delicate of tasks could be settled so neatly. For Rome, he now learned, had been captured by Spanish and Imperial troops more than a fortnight earlier, even before his legatine court had convened, and to increase the irony the capture had been effected by none other than England's former confederate, the Duke of Bourbon. Though Bourbon himself had been shot in the thigh during the onslaught and eventually died in the Sistine Chapel, his famished and unpaid troops had nevertheless taken a fearful toll upon the Holy City, killing up to a quarter of its population in the process. 'Never', wrote one commentator, 'was Rome so pilled neither by Goths nor Vandals.' Holy relics and sacred shrines were destroyed, virgins spoiled and wives ravished, while rampaging soldiers 'punished citizens by the privy members to cause them to confess their treasure'. Pope Clement, in the meantime, had fled in fear of his life to the Castle of San Angelo and was now under siege, leaving him, in effect, a captive of Queen Catherine's devoted nephew, Emperor Charles V – and with the most fateful consequences. For henceforth, it would be impossible for the pontiff to make even the slightest move without the emperor's permission, and Wolsey would be left to cobble together a thankless policy of bringing to bear whatever pressure he might muster against a wholly immovable obstacle to his royal master's plans.

At a stroke, therefore, Wolsey's legatine court had been rendered utterly impotent, since a pope at the emperor's mercy was a pope incapable of sanctioning any action intolerable to the emperor's aunt. And while

Clement cowered before her nephew, Catherine herself was no longer to be so lightly circumvented, let alone casually discarded. Indeed, in the brief time it had taken a breathless messenger to deliver his tale of disaster, Wolsey's task had gone from difficult to desperate, and he reacted accordingly. Ruling that it could not provide an authoritative decision on so intricate a point of canon law as the king's marriage, the legatine court – of which so much had been expected – now confined itself to a finding that the dispensation of 1503 was no more than 'open to doubt'. Only two days later, moreover, the beleaguered cardinal was expressing to his royal master the full gravity of the new situation:

> And surely sire [he wrote], if the Pope's Holiness fortune either to be slain or taken, as God forbid, it shall not a little hinder your Grace's affairs, which I now have in hand; wherein such good and substantial order and process hath hitherto been made and used.

Yet within those same two days Wolsey had conceived another grand enterprise – perhaps his grandest to date – shot full with complex crossing threads and diverse linking outcomes, all of which, he vainly contended, might rescue an all but hopeless situation and redound once more to both his sovereign's and his own greater glory.

For Henry, of course, the news of Rome's fall could hardly have been more frustrating. And though exhorted on all sides to rescue the pope, he remained, nonetheless, at a total loss as to how this might be achieved. 'What should I do?' he complained to Wolsey. 'My person nor my people cannot him rescue, but if my treasure may help him, take that which to you seemeth most convenient.' Certainly, the 'treasure' offered by the king, were it to be forthcoming, would indeed be convenient, since the first plank of Wolsey's proposed solution involved consolidating an existing alliance with the French. But something much more sweeping still was also required, for, with the pope subservient to a secular power, the Church itself was now in urgent need of a rescuer. And with that in mind, the cardinal therefore contrived to visit France in person, where Louise of Savoy was already suggesting that the princes of Christendom should withdraw their allegiance to the Bishop of Rome until his release. Once there, or so he hoped, he would duly proceed, in all his pomp and glory, to take over the government of Christendom on Pope Clement's behalf.

Though Wolsey's extraordinary objective was probably born of nothing more than utter desperation, the charge of megalomania is, of course, easy enough to level. For this, it should be remembered, was a man who wished to be buried, like the king, at Windsor and whose tomb was to match in splendour that of Henry VII. A black marble sarcophagus was to hold a carved bronze representation of the cardinal lying in repose, while kneeling angels bearing the symbols of Wolsey's dignities – his cross and cardinal's hat – were to guard his head and feet, as four more angels bearing candlesticks perched atop thick bronze pillars 9ft high. This too, likewise, was an individual used to the most extravagant deference. It had long been customary, in fact, for visitors at the English court to kiss the cardinal's hand before kissing the king's – an acknowledgement of the higher respect due to the divine office, but in practice as much a bow to Wolsey the person as to his rank within the Church. Yet if Wolsey's very name had already become for ego and ambition, he had not attained his current status without good reason And as both the leading churchman of the West not under Imperial sway and a figure whom the pope claimed to regard not merely as a brother but as a colleague, there were still slender grounds, perhaps, for hope of a kind, since his plan, as always, was not without an elegant logic. To resolve the crisis he would travel to France in person, win the allegiance of its king, and convoke an assembly of cardinals at Avignon, which was to oversee the administration of papal affairs during the pope's captivity. Then, by deft diplomacy he would secure Pope Clement's freedom and thereby guarantee the Church's compliance in the annulment of King Henry's marriage.

There could be no question, of course, that the king's sledgehammer tendencies would have to be carefully circumvented in such a delicate situation. Henry's preferred approach to his predicament was, after all, to contend that Catherine's previous marriage to his brother had indeed been consummated, in spite of her resolute denials, and to insist that the pope had not the authority to grant a dispensation that challenged divine law as laid down in Scripture. To argue thus, as Wolsey well knew, cast doubt not only on the queen's integrity, but upon papal authority in general, and was therefore bound both to inflame and complicate matters considerably.

The cardinal's own solution, by contrast, was therefore to accept the non-consummation of the marriage, and thereby invalidate the dispensation on much less provocative, but wholly effective, technical grounds. For if, as Wolsey reasoned, the marriage had not been consummated in the first place, then the dispensation had dealt with a non-existent impediment and was therefore without authority. As a further flourish, it might also be pointed out that Julius II's measure had not dealt with the issue of 'public honesty' or, in other words, the fact that Arthur and Catherine had indeed been formally married in a Church ceremony. In addressing a non-existent impediment, the original dispensation had on this basis also neglected a real one. And if the king could be persuaded, therefore, to leave well alone and allow his minister a free hand to execute his plans across the Channel, all, it seemed, might yet be executed with surgical precision and minimal collateral damage.

So when Wolsey left for France on 22 July, amid the usual outstanding pomp, he did so with some measure of his characteristic resilience, set fair, or so he hoped, for another master-stroke on the basis of a grand plan that appeared a triumph of vision and creativity – both sweeping in concept and bold in content, a masterpiece of intricacy and simplicity combined. Beforehand, he had drawn up a communication for the pope to sign, bestowing upon his own person absolute power as if he were indeed pope – power 'even to relax, limit or moderate divine law' – which meant that Clement would be undertaking to ratify all Wolsey's actions upon regaining his freedom. The cardinal had troubled, too, to consult with his astrologer about the most favourable date for his departure, and on the appointed day his splendid retinue duly formed ranks and set off for Dover, spreading out along the narrow road for over three-quarters of a mile. Hundreds of gentlemen and yeomen in black and tawny liveries rode in the vanguard, along with closely guarded carts and carriages loaded down with 'barrels of gold' and Wolsey's travel furnishings. While the cardinal travelled as always on muleback, his rich robes blending with the red velvet trappings of his mount, seven attendants rode before him bearing the usual paraphernalia of his office:

And before him [recorded his gentleman usher, George Cavendish, as the great procession made its way over London Bridge] he had his two great crosses of silver, two great pieces of silver, the great seal of England, his cardinal's hat, and a gentleman that carried his valaunce, otherwise called a cloakbag, which was made altogether of fine scarlet cloth, embroidered over and over with cloth of gold very richly, having in it a cloak of fine scarlet.

But it was Wolsey's stopping places en route to the coast and embarkation for Calais – and one in particular – that makes Cavendish's account so intriguing. For, as the gentleman usher noted in passing: 'The next day he rode to Rochester and lodged in the bishop's palace there; and the rest of his train in the city, and in Strood on this side the bridge.'

True, there were other errands to perform beforehand, not to mention prayers to recite, as the would-be man of the hour passed on his way. At Canterbury, for instance, he paused to join a special litany for the captive pope. 'Saint Mary, pray for our Pope Clement', intoned the monks, while Wolsey knelt and 'wept very tenderly'. There was time, too, to visit Archbishop Warham, whom the cardinal feared might be inclined to Catherine's side in any impending struggle, though the aged bishop's words were reassuring. 'However displeasant it may be to the queen,' he declared, 'truth and law must prevail.' But it was the meeting with John Fisher at Rochester that carried altogether greater significance, since the bishop had already expressed his opinions on the divorce in a cogent tract – making clear that he considered Pope Julius's dispensation valid and further inquiry needless – which Wolsey had forwarded to the king on 2 June, along with a lame observation, intended to assuage his master's anger, that Fisher's 'said opinion proceedeth rather of affection than of sincerity, of his learning or scripture'.

In fact, Fisher's views could hardly have been more unequivocal or less indicative of gut feelings based on personal prejudice. On the contrary, they were framed with characteristically rigorous logic and delivered with a frankness that both Wolsey and the king doubtless found withering. 'Having consulted all those silent masters [i.e. learned authorities] I have by me,' Fisher wrote:

And diligently discussed their opinions and weighed their reasons, I find there is a great disgreement among them, a great many asserting that it [i.e. a marriage to a deceased brother's widow] is prohibited by the divine law, whilst others on the contrary confirm that it is by no means repugnant to it; and having truly weighed the reasons on both sides in an even scale I think I see it easy to unravel all the arguments which they produce who deny it to be lawful by the divine law, but not so easy to answer the others; so I am fully persuaded that it cannot be proved by any solid reason that it is prohibited by the divine law now in force that the brother of a brother deceased without children shall take his wife; which, if true, as I do not doubt of its being most certain, who is there now that considers the plenitude of power which Christ has conferred on the pope, who can deny that the pope may dispense for some great cause with a brother of a brother deceased without issue taking his wife? But that granting the reasons on both sides equal and that neither weighed down the other, yet would that oblige me to be more inclined and yielding to the pope's side; I know it is allowed by both parties as part of the amplitude of the pope's power that it is lawful for him on hearing the opinions of divines and lawyers concerning the matter to interpret ambiguous places of Scripture, for that otherwise in vain had Christ said to him, *Whatsoever thou shalt loose on earth shall be loosed in heaven, and whatsoever thou shalt bind on earth shall be bound in heaven.*

'With no scruple remaining', therefore, John Fisher had in fact embarked upon the long road to Tower Hill and an appointment with his executioner, though it was a destiny that was anything but obvious as yet, particularly when Wolsey's visit to his residence on 4 July still appeared to hold out hope that at least the bishop's active opposition was by no means yet assured.

Certainly, the meeting could not have been anything other than intense, as the cardinal's letter to the king, dated four days later, confirms. For the validity of the royal marriage was now no longer presented as a purely academic question but as a matter of policy, as Wolsey explained how Henry's conscience had been sorely troubled by doubts about his marriage, expressed by the Bishop of Tarbes on his recent embassy to negotiate a marriage between the King of France and the Princess Mary. Nor, significantly, was this Fisher's first intimation of the whole affair, since his brother Robert had reported rumours of the York Place inquiry soon after it began, and the queen herself, it seems, had already sent him a message enlisting his advice on 'certain matters' between herself and the king, after she had heard of the inquiry on 18 May, thanks to the alertness of the Spanish ambassador. Henceforth, the pressure would be mounting on all sides, and the support of Fisher, whose reputation extended far beyond English shores, as a result of his writings against Luther, would be invaluable, making Wolsey's visit to Rochester anything but coincidental. Yet with regard at least to the validity of Julius II's dispensation, Fisher still harboured certain technical reservations, if Wolsey's account is to be trusted, and though this was hardly an unalloyed victory for the king's cause, it did at least proffer hope of less than all-out opposition from the man whose opinion at this stage was clearly considered paramount.

Even more encouraging, at the same time, was Fisher's response to word of the queen's apparent recalcitrance, though Wolsey's silence on how she had actually heard of the matter from the king himself is carefully avoided.

And I assure your grace [the cardinal's letter continues], my lord of Rochester, hearing the process of the matter after this sort, did greatly blame the queen, as well for giving so light credence in so weighty a matter as also when she heard it to handle the same in such fashion as rumour and bruit should spread thereof.

[The bishop] doubted not, but that if he might speak with her and disclose unto her all the circumstances of the matter as afore, he should cause her greatly to repent, humble and submit herself unto your highness; considering that the thing done by your grace was so necessary and expedient and the queen's act so perilous. Howbeit I have persuaded him that he will nothing speak or do therein, or anything counsel her, but as shall stand with your pleasure; for he saith, although she be queen of this realm, yet he acknowledgeth you for his high sovereign lord and king, and will not therefore otherwise behave himself, in all matters, concerning or touching your person, than as shall be by your grace expressly commanded.

Whether Wolsey had knowledge of Catherine's earlier request to Fisher is uncertain, but it is not hard to believe his description of the latter's response. For in light of Fisher's doubts about the dispensation, the York

Place inquiry was not of itself an inherently unreasonable expedient, rendering Catherine's 'very displeasant manner' unacceptable, particularly if, as was falsely suggested, she had merely heard of it 'as rumour and bruit should spread thereof'. As such, it is wholly likely, too, that the bishop would have accepted Wolsey's further request that he should 'nothing speak or do therein, or anything counsel her, but as shall stand with your pleasure' – particularly when the king's intentions regarding Anne Boleyn were still unknown and the prospect of an outright breach with the Holy See still, to all intents and purposes, inconceivable.

As far as the technical weaknesses of the original bull of dispensation were concerned, moreover, Fisher's reservations were equally consistent with his overall defence of papal authority. The document was, after all, shot through with flaws, which Fisher could hardly have sought to deny, and while he continued to maintain that the apparent impediment based on Leviticus was not, in fact, 'of divine law', he did not seek to hide his other misgivings, as Wolsey, no doubt with some residual relish, was keen to emphasise to Henry. For although the bishop 'said it was not his faculty anything to judge in this matter':

> Nevertheless he misliked it much ... and greatly lamented the negligence of them that so handled that thing in the beginning being of so high importance and great weight, whereupon might insurge doubt or question about the succession of your highness ... He noted the matter to be more and more doubtful and the bull diminute [lessened], marvelling that none other bull was purchased than that, being so slenderly couched and against which so many things might be objected. He would not reason the matter, but noted great difficulty.

Plainly, for starving men, even crumbs may offer comfort of a kind, and Wolsey was keen to gloss Fisher's responses in the most favourable possible light to his master – the more so, of course, at a time when so little else of encouragement appeared to be on offer. But the bishop had in fact remained non-commital, refusing to 'reason the matter' even on the subject of the dispensation, while studiously saying nothing to challenge the overall status of papal authority in any way shape or form, i.e. in the manner that was the king's own preference. And this, of course, was something of which Wolsey himself was fully aware – so much so, it seems, that he now urged the king to apply direct personal pressure.

For if Fisher's anonymous first biographer is to be believed, the bishop was subsequently summoned to Windsor, so that Henry might 'by fair means work him to incline his mind'. 'Wherefore,' we are told:

> The king on a day sent for him, and when he came, the king, using him very courteously, gave him many reverend and good words and at last took him into the long gallery at Windsor. And there, walking awhile with him, after divers words of great praise given him for his worthy learning and virtue, he at last break with him of this matter in the presence of the dukes of Norfolk and Suffolk and certain bishops alleging there how sore his conscience was tormented and how for that cause he had secretly consulted with his ghostly father [i.e. his confessor, John Longland, Bishop of Lincoln] and divers other learned men by whom he was not yet satisfied. And therefore said that upon special confidence in his great learning he had now made choice of him to use of his advice above all others, praying him to declare his opinion freely, so as with hearing thereof he might sufficiently be instructed in his conscience and remain no longer in this scruple wherewith he was so much unquieted.

But if the king's entreaties that Fisher 'declare his opinion freely', and assurances that his advice would be valued 'above all areas' were indeed genuine, he could hardly have been more disappointed by what followed, since the bishop, it seems, 'hearing all this case proposed by the king never stuck long in answering the matter, which he both knew and thought to be good and true'. On the contrary, speaking with what the anonymous first biographer describes as 'a reverend gravity after this or the like sort', Fisher told the king unequivovally that his fears were baseless:

> I beseech your grace in God's name to be of good cheer and no further to dismay yourself with this matter, neither to unquiet or trouble your conscience for the same. For there is no heed to be taken to these men that account themselves so wise and do arrogate themselves more cunning and knowledge in divinity than had all the learned fathers and divines both of Spain and of this realm in your late father's time, neither

yet so much credit to be given unto them as is to the see apostolic by whose authority was confirmed, dispensed and approved for good and lawful ... And as for any peril or danger to your soul that may ensue thereby, I am not afraid in giving you this counsel to take upon my soul all the danger, and will not refuse to answer against all men in your behalf either privately or openly that can anything object against this matter, nothing doubting but there are many right worthy and learned persons within this your realm that be of this mind with me and think it a very perilous unseemly thing that any divorce should be spoken of.

Under the circumstances, the message could hardly have been more forthright, even if the anonymous first biographer chose Fisher's words for him on this occasion, to outline the position that the bishop would henceforth advance unwaveringly. That Fisher was indeed so outspoken, moreover, reflects not only his natural bluntness, but his ongoing conviction at this stage that the king was in fact an honest man, acting earnestly under the influence of genuine moral scruples. For in a letter to an unidentified correspondent, probably written in the latter part of 1527, he declared his confidence not only that Henry would do nothing against the law of God, but that he would be quite justified in submitting his difficulties to the pope, to obtain, no doubt, final peace of mind.

Yet the same letter also notes in passing how kings, from the fullness of their powers, are apt to think that right which suits their pleasure, and in doing so reflects Fisher's appreciation, even now perhaps, that his sovereign's concerns might not be easily assuaged – especially when other influential voices were less inclined to express their misgivings. For in September 1527, in the wake of his encounter with Fisher, Henry had also opened his 'Great Matter' with Sir Thomas More for the first time, no doubt seeking affirmation of his preferred position after a response from the bishop, which had clearly failed to satisfy him. Once more, the king highlighted the crucial text in Leviticus and asked his councillor's opinion, but More was altogether more circumspect, begging for time to study the relevant passages in the works of the early Fathers, and consult, too, the learned theologian Dr Nicholas Wilson. At no point did he either reassure him, like Fisher, that his fears were groundless, let alone warn him of the potential dangers involved in any attempt to unravel his marriage. Instead, he merely suggested that St Jerome and St Augustine and other 'old holy doctors' would be the king's best councillors, and stated his preference not to be drawn into the discussions – a decision which, for the time being at least, the king would deign to accept, however reluctantly.

In the meantime, while the prolonged and confused negotiations with Rome ground out their weary course, Fisher turned his mind to a renewed study of the relevant problems in Scripture and canon law, observing later on how:

> The matter was so serious, both on account of the people concerned, and on account of the injunction given me by the king, that I devoted more attention to examining the truth of it, lest I should deceive myself and others, than to anything else in my life.

Nor, in conformity with his promise to Wolsey at Rochester and a further letter warning him not to interfere, did he consult with Catherine until his appointment as her counsellor in 1529. In consequence, he too like More would be left in comparative peace before the storm broke. For with his usual gift for self-deception, Henry had, it seems, convinced himself that he had indeed prevailed upon Fisher in their meeting at Windsor, suggesting as much in a letter dispatched to Wolsey as the cardinal wound his way to France. But the Bishop of Rochester was not Sir Thomas More, and even the bishop's learned counsel could not hope to still a self-serving conscience in a matter on which that conscience was already set firm. From the outset, the king was seeking not judges but partisans, and when Wolsey's schemes in France collapsed about his ears, the result, as the anonymous early biographer makes clear, were in effect a forgone conclusion. Indeed, from the very time that Fisher departed Windsor, we are told, the king, 'with his sick mind, perversely bent', had 'never looked on him with merry countenance as the good bishop did well perceive for that his grudge daily increased against him'.

5

GATHERING STORM

Prophesy not unto us the truth, but speak only pleasant words.

Isaiah 30:10

By the time that Thomas Wolsey reached Calais on the most crucial of all his missions, he had been given some further grounds for optimism. Already, in April, he had induced Henry to write to his French counterpart as his 'brother and perfect friend', thanking him 'for some birds you have sent me for the pursuit of the heron'. But now, according to a Hungarian envoy, the King of France was at a clear disadvantage in the coming negotiations. He was, Wolsey heard, 'destitute of good captains and money', and this was not all, since 'the said French king considering the captivity of the pope, the detention of his children with the emperor', and the likelihood of Imperial generals 'attaining Italy' was 'marvellous perplexed, not knowing what to do'. As such, the sealing of the Anglo-French treaties agreed to in England three months earlier and the arrangement of a marriage between Henry and a French princess, such as Renée, Francis I's sister-in-law, seemed a matter of course. Nor was Wolsey disheartened when he finally arrived at Amiens in August to conclude business, since the French king – surrounded by Greek and Albanian mercenaries, 'drawn up in a great piece of oats, all in harness, upon light horses' – was swift to agree a full alliance. And though Renée, somewhat to Wolsey's regret, was eventually spared a marriage contract with Henry, there was at least the considerable consolation of the Princess Mary's engagement to Francis's younger son.

For all its early success, however, Wolsey's time in France was punctuated with petty frustrations and apparent ill omens. At Boulogne he had been greeted by pageants at the city gate, one depicting 'a nun called Holy

Church whom the Spaniards and Almayns had violated, but whom the cardinal had rescued and set up again', and another of the pope 'lying under the emperor sitting in majesty, whom the cardinal pulled down'. Yet the mule that Wolsey was riding shied at the sound of cannon fire and nearly threw him to the ground. Furthermore, insulting graffiti were found in his lodgings. In one place, a cardinal's hat was carved into a stone windowsill, with a gallows over it, and to compound his problems he was subject to repeated thefts from his chamber, which included a valuable silver dish and other items kept for his personal use. Perhaps the worst loss of all came at Compiègne, however, when the truly indispensable silver and gilt inkpot, with which he composed his dispatches to Henry, went missing. The culprit, it emerged, was the protégé of a professional thief in Paris – a 12-year-old 'ruffian's page' – who was found hiding under a stairwell when the alarm was raised, and who subsequently confessed, prior to being placed in the pillory, how he had not only taken the precious inkpot, but everything else pilfered from the cardinal in recent days.

To add to Wolsey's vexation, moreover, an even more curious incident marred the banqueting that followed the meeting with Francis, for accompanying the cardinal as part of his travelling household was a group of highly skilled musicians, including a particularly gifted, but ill-fated, shalm-player. So impressed was the French king by their virtuosity that he subsequently borrowed the entire ensemble for a visit to the house of a nobleman, where they played on throughout the night and so captivated their audience that they were said to have thoroughly surpassed even the king's own players – none more so, indeed, than the celebrated shalm-player himself. Yet two days later, Wolsey's most revered musician was left breathless in the most literal sense of the term – a stone cold corpse who had died, it was said, 'either with extreme labour of blowing or with poisoning'. For the hapless cardinal, it seems, there was simply no escape on earth from envy.

Much more importantly, however, there was to be no respite either from the King of England's misjudgement and indiscretion. In London, the angry talk was that Wolsey was 'all French', and the commercial interests of the City were scarcely concealing their concerns about the threat to trade with the Low Countries posed by any new alliance with France. When Wolsey defended it, wrote Edward Hall, 'some knocked the other on the

elbow and said softly "he lieth"'. But now Sir Thomas More was reporting to the cardinal how the king, too, was restive about the same thing.
Pointing out 'how loath the Low Countries were to have any war with
him', Henry had also commanded Lord Sandys to 'hold back his troops
at Guisnes', lest his reluctant enemies 'reaped the goods of the English
merchants' and began 'some business upon the English Pale'. As Wolsey
proceeded to build bridges with the French, then, their foundations were
being steadily undermined by stirrings at home.

But these particular developments did not remotely match the much
more troublesome – and ominous – events that had also begun to unfold
in the cardinal's absence. For in spite of his appeals that Henry should proceed 'both gently and doucely' with the queen – at least 'till it were known
what should succeed of the pope' – the king had continued to bluster and
bully. Indeed, a month before the cardinal's departure, he had impulsively
confronted Catherine with his doubts about their marriage, which, he
declared, must make their separation inevitable. And in the aftermath of this
shockwave, she had somehow managed to obtain a passport for her trusted
servant of thirty years, Francisco Felipez, whom she now dispatched to her
nephew in Spain. Though Henry had informed the French of Felipez's
mission in the hope that he would be captured en route, the Spaniard nevertheless evaded his pursuers and duly reached Valladolid to inform the
emperor of his aunt's predicament. Now, therefore, Charles V was not only
apprised of what he termed 'this ugly affair', but became irrevocably committed to Catherine's cause. 'Nothing shall be omitted on my part to help
you in your present tribulation,' he told her, and to confirm his promise
he followed her suggestion and urged the pope to revoke Wolsey's legatine
power, which would leave him powerless in the matter of the marriage.

Meanwhile, the cardinal's enemies at the English court had also been
making hay. Much to his dismay, Wolsey learned, for instance, that the king
had enjoyed supper in his privy chamber with the Dukes of Norfolk and
Suffolk, the Marquess of Exeter and Sir Thomas Boleyn. Given Henry's
susceptibility to influence and proneness to whim, the possibilities were
obvious and with this in mind, John Clerk was therefore returned at once
to England to emphasise Wolsey's progress and explain his plans for the
future. He returned, too, with a personal letter from the cardinal, couched
in the most obsequious terms, assuring the king that it was his unstinting

desire to bring to pass 'your secret matter' with the pope. The letter was written, Wolsey assured Henry, 'with the rude and shaking hand of your must humble subject and chaplain'.

But the cardinal's hands would not be steadied by the bad news that next came his way, since he now learned that his royal master was actually intending to bypass him with a direct appeal of his own to the pope. William Knight, the special envoy appointed for the task, was ostensibly to convey the king's condolences for Clement's captivity and to assist Wolsey's current efforts to oversee papal affairs. He was instructed, further, to meet Wolsey at Compiègne, pretending all the while that his journey to Italy had nothing to do with the divorce and making every effort to conceal his true objectives from 'any craft that the Cardinal … can find'. In reality, however, Knight was to carry two draft bulls for the pope to consider – one permitting the king to marry any woman he chose once freed from Catherine, the other looking ahead to the possibility that the pope might not be able to declare Henry's marriage invalid. In the latter eventuality, the pope was to permit the King of England to enjoy a second, simultaneous, marriage with Anne Boleyn.

When Wolsey learned of these plans from a member of the king's household, the impact was nothing short of seismic. He had left England on his greatest and most critical enterprise to date, and now he had been decisively undermined by the master he was striving to serve against all odds. And not only was that master now courting disaster, he was also, it seemed, mistrustful of the only man who could help him. Without informing Wolsey, Henry had, for good measure, foolishly resolved to propose a marriage – and a bigamous one at that – to none other than Anne Boleyn, the very woman who, as an agent of her Howard relatives, could be guaranteed to seek his minister's destruction. It was, indeed, one of the cardinal's residing superstitions that his fall would be brought about by a woman, and now his worst fears were being realised. That the king should have sunk to such duplicity was the worst blow he had suffered so far, and for the first time in Wolsey's long career the threat to his pre-eminence stood out starkly. For not only had his master struck out independently and in the process left him both stranded and exposed, he was now expected to feign ignorance of the king's subterfuge, and, worse still, connive in a scheme that was as ominous for him personally as it was ill-conceived.

To compound an already dire situation, moreover, the projected meeting of cardinals at Avignon was already foundering hopelessly. With the King of France's half-hearted persuasion, six cardinals eventually answered the appeal to protest the imprisonment of Clement VII and pledge their refusal to any act he might make under compulsion. But in other quarters no further ripples of support were forthcoming. On the contrary, the College of Cardinals, in spite of lukewarm French pressure and Wolsey's bribes, stood icily aloof from the man whom they had already twice rejected for the papacy. Bad luck – in this case at least – was little in evidence. It was true that both English agents and Italian agents in English pay had experienced great difficulty in obtaining access to the pope now that news of the annulment had reached the emperor. But the simple truth was that Wolsey's motives had quite simply proven too transparent and fear of Imperial reprisals too strong. The pope, in any case, had rejected any delegation of power, and by December was enjoying a liberty of sorts at Orvieto after being allowed to escape his more blatant captivity at Rome. If ever Wolsey's conclave had been a viable option, now it was wholly superfluous.

After a desultory attempt to prevent Knight's passage to Rome on the quite legitimate grounds that he 'had no colour or acquaintance there', and a predictably futile appeal that the king 'take a little patience' and trust instead to the efforts of Girolamo Ghinucci, Bishop of Worcester, Wolsey was therefore squarely thwarted. Henry's reply had, it is true, been polite, expressing gratitude at his servant's efforts, 'which service cannot be by any kind master forgotten, of which fault I trust I shall never be accused, especially to youward, which so laboriously do serve me'. But it was clear that Wolsey would need to return, if he were to have any realistic chance of salvaging the imminent shipwreck. Knight's errand in Rome was bound for wholesale failure, and when king and minister were once together, there was still perhaps an outside possibility that Henry's thoughts might be guided as in earlier days. Above all, Wolsey must revive the crucial bond of trust, if not the old and easy familiarity, that had for so long held fast against all adversity.

On 13 September, therefore, the careworn traveller informed his master that he was making for home as speedily 'as mine old and cracked body may endure'. Predictably, the months of travel had worn him down as he rushed from city to city enduring French heat and French impudence, and, as summer gave way to autumn in more senses than one, so Wolsey gave way to self-pity, bemoaning 'the travails and pains which I daily and hourly sustain, without any regard to the continuance of my life or death'. In his absence, the slip of a girl whose love for Henry Percy he had once rudely quashed became exalted, indulging her passion for carp and shrimps at the king's high table, while he in turn expressed unbounded passion for her. 'For what joy in this world,' wrote Henry, 'can be greater than to have the company of her who is the most dearly loved, knowing likewise that she by her choice holds the same, the thought of which greatly delights me.' Though the king continued to maintain civilities with his wife and queen, Mistress Anne Boleyn was also firmly ensconced at Windsor, joining him when hawking or upon his afternoon walks in the surrounding parkland. 'Darling,' ran another of the king's letters, 'you and I shall [soon] have our desired end, which should be more to my heart's ease, and more quietness to my mind than any other thing in the world.'

Yet for all his many woes, Wolsey remained, it must be said, a formidable figure who had discharged a string of high offices and managed the affairs of princes far too long to be lightly discounted. Furthermore, he was still ostensibly the king's friend. Certainly, he knew his master's ways and whims, as well as his secret needs and wishes. He knew his weak points, too – his fears and insecurities, his volatility, his proneness to flattery and passing fancy. And though Wolsey's enemies continued to whisper against him, they did so mainly in corners. Nor did they offer any viable alternative to his primacy. And so it was, as the Dukes of Norfolk and Suffolk and Anne Boleyn continued to weave their webs around him, that the 'great panjandrum' duly played his final card, knowing full well that Pope Clement VII was, after all, a craven and muddle-headed procrastinator who had once been described as 'the most secretive man in the world'. For it was not only Charles V who could apply persuasive threats against the Holy Father, and in January 1528, therefore, notwithstanding the cries of those who sought his downfall, England joined the League of Cognac with France, delivering a formal declaration of war against the emperor on 28 January, though no hostilities followed, since Wolsey's plan was merely to bluff Clement into concessions.

Thereafter, Stephen Gardiner and Edward Fox were accordingly dispatched to Rome to apply the requisite pressure, and upon their arrival on 20 March they found Clement bearded and benighted. 'I cannot tell', observed Gardiner, 'how the pope should be described as being at liberty here, where hunger, scarcity, bad lodgings, and ill air keep him as much confined as he was in the Castle Angelo.' On the way to their audience, the Englishmen passed, it seems, through three rooms 'all naked and unhanged, the roofs fallen down, and, as we can guess 30 persons, riffraff and other, standing in the chamber for a garnishment'. When they met the Holy Father himself, furthermore, they found him, according to Gardiner, upon a couch covered with a rug not worth twenty shillings. As the meeting progressed, Pope Clement paced up and down his bedchamber in undisguised agitation, waving his arms like one distracted, sighing and wiping his eyes and bemoaning his fate. With the Spaniards at his doorstep, he found himself, he said, 'in the power of dogs'. But above all, he talked of the danger he would be in should he offend Charles, in response to which the envoys threatened him with the loss he would sustain if England and even perhaps France chose to sever their links with the Holy See. Indeed, true to their instructions, they displayed little sympathy and returned to the pope 'on the morrow', when they 'spoke roundly to him' and confirmed in no uncertain terms that their king would, if necessary, 'do without him'.

At the same time, it was impressed upon Clement that at this very moment French forces under Odet de Foix, Vicomte de Lautrec, were marching triumphantly through Italy to besiege Naples. How, in such circumstances, could he not comply, especially when, as Gardiner and Fox also emphasised, the King of England's motives were so honourable? For any suggestion that their sovereign's nullity suit was prompted by 'vain affection and undue love' for Anne Boleyn, or what the pope termed 'private reasons' was strenuously denied, along with swirling rumours at the papal court that the king's mistress was already pregnant. No doubt feeling the ink curdle upon his pen, Wolsey had, in fact, already instructed his men to speak up ardently in Anne's defence, emphasising the:

Excellent virtues [qualities] of the said gentlewoman, the purity of her life, her constant virginity, her maidenly and womanly pudicity, her soberness, chasteness, meekness, humility, wisdom, descent of right noble and high thorough regal blood, education in all good and laudable [qualities] and manners [and] apparent aptness to procreation of children.

Nor, of course, was it any coincidence that this particular encomium to the royal mistress had been prominently displayed in the recorded instructions to Fox and Gardiner, where it would be seen by the king himself. For if the cardinal's survival depended upon it, even he would have to worship at Anne's altar for the time being, just as he would not hesitate to cudgel his Holy Father in the way now chosen.

Even so, the discussions dragged on wearily day after day and often night after night as Gardiner answered all qualms and quibbles extempore in Latin. 'Discussed the matter warmly for five hours until one in the morning,' he informed Wolsey, 'when we departed with no other answer but that we should have a definite reply the next day before dinner.' But no reply came. On another occasion, the pope sent a canonist and his protonotary, Gambara, out to the houses of his cardinals for a speedy judgement, only to receive the answer that they would study the matter on the morrow. The pope, complained Gardiner, 'sees all that is spoken sooner and better than any other, but no man is so slow to give an answer'. 'Fearing a scorpion in every word', the pope's advisers were equally obstructive. Only the ongoing threat that the King of England might be forced to look elsewhere for a solution to his predicament – to 'live out of the laws of Holy Church', as it was said – seemed to afford any appreciable leverage.

But relentless pressure, combined with the advance of a French army in Northern Italy and the threat to Naples from Andrea Doria's galleys, did indeed give Clement the will to act at last. And with the emperor's troops increasingly demoralised and the prospect of a new and healthier balance of force in his homelands, the pope finally submitted on 7 April with a typical display of amateur dramatics. Walking frantically up and down the great audience chamber, with tears dripping down his copious beard and 'casting now and then his arms abroad', Clement duly agreed that the king's case could be heard at a legatine court in London headed by Wolsey and Lorenzo Campeggio, the Englishman's personal choice for co-adjudicator. There remained, it is true, the need for further clarification of certain details, which Wolsey was immediately alive to. Clement's initial agreement omitted, for instance, any reference to the binding authority of the court's decisions and did not preclude the possibility of revoking the case to Rome at a later date. But in a secret letter, dated 23 July 1528, the necessary assurances were delivered on all such scores. The pope's representative was, moreover, to travel to England, fully equipped with a decretal bull sanctioning an annulment of the king's marriage – something which Wolsey considered absolutely essential.

It was an outcome, not surprisingly, that Henry would hear of at Greenwich 'marvellously thankfully' and with 'marvellous demonstrations of joy and gladness'. And for Wolsey in particular the news that his co-legate to determine the 'Great Matter' would be none other than Cardinal Campeggio could not have been more heartening. 'One of the best and most learned men living', according to Erasmus, Campeggio was an expert in both canon and civil law, and a man of considerable worldly experience to boot. He had, after all, been married to one Francesca Guastevallani until her death in 1509 and had the unusual distinction of producing five sons before entering ecclesiastical service during the pontificate of Julius II. Thereafter, he had performed both diligently and effectively as cardinal-protector of the Holy Roman Empire, during which time he also became well acquainted with the English king and court as an expert cadger of English benefices and absentee Bishop of Salisbury. It was Campeggio, too, who visited England in 1518 to propose the launch of a new crusade against the Turk. Above all, however, the Italian appeared to be Wolsey's creature – a man, indeed, whom Wolsey had decisively upstaged, almost bullied, a decade earlier. And though he was bound to represent the pope and therefore avoid offence to the emperor, he was nevertheless known to be one of the more ambivalent supporters of Imperial interests – not least, perhaps, because his own house and possessions had been destroyed during the sack of Rome only a year earlier.

Yet the double game, of course, was still afoot and Wolsey now found himself the victim of what would amount to slow diplomatic strangula-tion – more drawn out, more frustrating, more ingenious, more inexorable and more excruciating than even he might have devised for an unwitting quarry of his own. It was Wolsey, in fact, who had kept Campeggio wait-ing interminably in Calais in 1518, as he applied pressure for his own appointment as a papal legate at that time. Now, however, the roles were reversed, as the Italian exploited every opportunity to loiter and obstruct. Acting under strict instructions from Clement, even his martyrdom to gout became from this time forth an invaluable asset. Unable either to walk or ride, it was all he could do, it seems, to sit confined in his litter, enduring the purgatory of unpaved roads and stifling summer heat as he trundled across Europe. Such, indeed, was his discomfort that curious villagers who caught sight of him along the way to his destination in London saw only a shrunken figure hunched in pain with a long untrimmed beard – a sign, they thought, of mourning for the English Church. But every shock and jar of his journey meant further delay and further opportunity for some unforeseen development that might somehow release the pope from the Gordian knot currently binding him.

By August, however, Campeggio's agonising odyssey was at last nearing completion. And as a nod to discretion in anticipation of his arrival, the king's mistress had even been encouraged to take up new apartments at Greenwich, specially prepared for her by Wolsey, to separate her from her lover. Even so, the apartments still allowed easy access, and while briefly absent on a hunting trip, Henry now informed her of the Italian's approach. Writing at 11 p.m. after a hard day's chase and 'the killing of a hart', the message to 'mine own darling' was encouraging. 'The legate which we most desire arrived at Paris on Sunday or Monday last past,' wrote the king, 'so that I trust by the next Monday to hear of his arrival in Calais; and then I trust within a while to enjoy that which I have so longed for, to God's pleasure, and our both comforts.' The 'while', however, would still be a long one. For it was not until 28 October that the Italian finally reached London – accompanied by much booing, since the divorce was already unpopular – to be housed, first, in the Duke of Suffolk's residence and then the Bishop of Bath's palace. And if Henry was expecting rapid results thereafter, he would be bitterly disappointed, since even by now the international situation had shifted fatefully. For while the Vicomte de Lautrec had been killed and the emperor's cause in Italy bolstered by the defection of Andrea Doria's galleys, there had also been a regrouping of the Italian states, and Florence had once more declared itself a republic. Only by coming to terms with the emperor, therefore, could the Medici pope now save his own family, and accordingly, in December he would write to Campeggio ordering him to burn the decretal commission and consign Henry's hopes and Wolsey's fortunes to ashes.

But as if all this were not enough, there remained one other looming storm cloud upon Cardinal Campeggio's arrival in England. And on 1 October, as he passed through Canterbury on his way to a meeting with Archbishop Warham, the Italian duly passed the very gates of the place where its source now resided. For the Benedictine convent of St Sepulchre, where Elizabeth Barton had already taken her place among the 'choir nuns' after swearing her solemn vows that midsummer, lay directly along the cardinal's route – nestled inconspicuously in the eastern suburbs of Canterbury, about a quarter of a mile from the city walls and almost adjoining Watling Street, the ancient Roman road running straight from London to Dover. With an income estimated variously as £381 19s 7d and £291 12s 5d at the time of its dissolution, there was little, in fact, to distinguish Barton's new home very visibly from the multitude of so-called 'lesser' religious houses, later specified by Thomas Cromwell as boasting an income of barely more than half that sum. And at the time of her arrival, the tiny community did indeed consist of no more than a prioress and five black-veiled nuns, all immured within an unpretentious building whose former existence may only be discerned today from scraps of old walls, the Gothic-sounding names of some surrounding properties, and a street sign pointing to Nunnery Fields.

Yet in this case especially, appearances were deceptive, since St Sepulchre's had sustained itself both effectively and honourably across the centuries after its foundation by Canterbury's second-ever archbishop, St Anselm of Bec. And long before the advent of its most famous resident, the convent already ranked as a corporation, boasting not only its own seal but all the other characteristics of a thriving nunnery, including, not least, the special favour and protection of the archbishop himself, as a result of which its nuns continued to enjoy an advantage even when dealing with their gigantic neighbours, the Priory of Christ Church and the Abbey of St Augustine. Remaining on good terms with both throughout their frequent rivalries – which on one occasion had resulted in nothing less than a pitched battle for the relics of their founding saint – the nuns had in fact avoided all scandal and, more importantly still, maintained their independence skilfully. For although located within the boundaries of the fee of the Abbey of St Augustine, St Sepulchre's had stayed quite independent of the abbot's jurisdiction, while receiving the patronage of a parish church from the abbey, as well as advantageous wooding rights to the north of the city in the forest of Blean, which belonged to the Priory of Christ Church. Even today, the name Minchen Wood – from the Saxon *mynecena* and Latin *monacha*, 'belonging to the nuns' – is a residing trace not only of their presence but the goodwill accorded them. And there had been royal patronage too, particularly from King Henry III, who in his fortieth year granted various liberties to the convent's prioress.

Later, in fact, Cardinal Morton had also bequeathed in perpetuity lands lying within the park at Maidstone called the Mote, along with a nearby mill. And during the time of Archbishop Whittesley (1368–74), John Bourn, Rector of Freckenham, had established a chantry chapel for the convent's upkeep. But generous patronage and the protection afforded by influential friends had been supplemented in St Sepulchre's case by that most distinctive gift of all: a largely spotless reputation. For its limited size had, it seems, played a significant part in preserving the sanctity of its hand-ful of residents under the leadership of Dame Philippa Jonys, the Mother Prioress, who, though sprung from comparatively humble stock within the serried ranks of the Canterbury bourgeoisie, had nevertheless acquired sig-nificant status within the city – not least as a result of Archbishop Warham's favour, and her own sterling efforts in consolidating St Sepulchre's worthy reputation. Certainly, her predecessor, Dame Mildred Hale, had done her job well, ensuring that the most recent 'visitation' of 1511 had uncovered no grounds for complaint beyond the fact that the nuns did not rise from matins in the middle of the night, but at dawn – an issue that the prior-ess had in any case actually raised herself and explained on the grounds that the doors of the cloister were being mended and the roof covered. But it was largely because of her successor's influence that the archbishop and Dom Edward Bocking had specifically chosen St Sepulchre's as a suitable residence for Elizabeth Barton, since the Benedictine rule had become so effectively observed under Dame Philippa's leadership that nuns from other convents – like one Dame Elizabeth Penny of Higham Priory – were sometimes transferred there for correction and rehabilita-tion. Diligent in prayer, modest in behaviour, moderate in lifestyle, the nuns displayed none of the excesses or shortcomings so characteristic of hostile propaganda, and if the inventory of Elizabeth Barton's possessions, taken at the time of her arrest, is any guide, she too had readily embraced the austerity of the community. For even when professed and at the height of her fame, the Holy Maid's total wardrobe consisted of nothing more – apart from the habit she stood up in – than one coat, two mantles (one of them old), two kirtles (one of them old), a collar and two stoles. Nor were the accoutrements of her cell any less rudimentary: a piece of plank for a table, two large chests and one small one, three candlesticks, five cushions, two mats, one of them cut in pieces, an old mattress, seven coarse sheets, two coverlets, two pillows, a bolster, three pillow-cases and an old diaper towel. Beyond these exiguities, there were merely two plates, two dishes, two saucers and a little metal basin.

In this modest setting, Barton's novitiate had proceeded to its end without hint of reproach, for in spite of her growing celebrity, which was attested to by the ongoing attacks of William Tyndale abroad, Barton herself appears to have remained entirely unspoilt. Widely admired, on the one hand, for what John Fisher's anonymous first biographer considered 'her virtues and austere life', she had continued, we are told, to receive her 'many revelations of Almighty God and his holy saints' without boast or affectation. According to the Act of Attainder that finally condemned her, she had seen 'heavenly lights', heard 'heavenly voices, heavenly melodies and joys', and made the convent's chapel of St Giles her place of special resort – 'and specially by night, saying that the dorter door was made open unto her by God's power'. Indeed, the visions begun at Goldwell and Court-at-Street's ancient chapel had, it seems, continued with almost weekly frequency, as she now found herself transported in trance state to the chapel and what she claimed to be miraculous encounters with Our Lady. But in spite of the increasingly reverential treatment that this attracted, and notwithstanding frequent recurrences of her illness, which are cited in Thwaites's *Marvellous Work*, she had nevertheless kept her convent's rule studiously and even earned Archbishop Warham's discerning praise as 'a very well-disposed and virtuous woman'.

Now a figure of nationwide repute, the Holy Maid's utterances had, in fact, also ensured that the chapel at Court-at-Street was no longer the damp and dreary ruin it had once been. On the contrary, it already boasted not only its own chaplain but a ceiling of lime and plaster that was considered sufficiently elegant for it to be copied on a larger scale at nearby Great Chart. And in the meantime, numerous bequests from far and wide continued to flow in from the likes of Thomas Stubbs of Borden, who wrote the chapel into his will, though he lived halfway across the country, as well as more exalted figures like Isabel Lady Poynings of Smeeth, who left the chapel's resident hermit a legacy of 6s 8d, along with 'a yard and two nails and a half of cloth of gold, for a vestment' for the chapel itself, and a baldachino for the altar. The number of pilgrims had steadily increased, some leaving silver thread the length of their bodies, as was the custom among wealthier invalids in payment for their cure, and, as word of miraculous healings mounted, so the upward spiral of fame escalated both for the shrine – for such it now was – and the young woman responsible for its renown. By this point no longer simply Elizabeth Barton but rather the Reverend Dame Elizabeth Barton, her life had been drastically transformed in less than two years. And there was every reason to believe that this process still had far to run, leaving her ideally placed, if she so chose, to settle for a life of religious distinction amid the tranquil glow of her many awed admirers.

But it was equally clear at such a crucial political juncture for the entire kingdom that the Maid's pronouncements, if unrestrained, might yet take on a new and altogether greater significance, which is, indeed, precisely what had started to happen by the time of Cardinal Campeggio's visit. For, as the 1534 Act of Attainder later put it, she had by now begun 'to be told by the Holy Spirit of God many things that should follow to the world for punishment of the sins of the princes and the people'. And nor, it seems, was this all, since 'by reason of the great perfection that was thought to be in her', she had also attracted the 'great confidence' of 'divers and great men of the realm, as [well as] mean men, and especially divers and religious men' who 'often resorted to her and communed with her'. Even on the very day that Cardinal Campeggio entered Canterbury, indeed, Archbishop Warham found himself penning the following message to none other than Thomas Wolsey, which presaged, in effect, the Maid's first entry into the very highest reaches of national politics.

Please it your Grace, so it is that Elizabeth Barton, being a religious woman professed at St Sepulchre's in Canterbury, who had all the visions at Our Lady of Court-of-Street, a very well-disposed and virtuous woman (as I am informed by her sisters), is very desirous to speak with your Grace personally.

What she hath to say, or whether it be good or ill, I do not know; but she hath desired me to write unto your Grace and to desire the same (as

I do), that she may come into your Grace's presence. Whom, when your Grace have heard, ye may order as shall please the same. For I assure your Grace she hath made very importunate suit to me to be a mean to your Grace that she may speak with you.

Expressed with considerable caution, the letter is significant from at least one other perspective, too. Certainly, there had never been any love lost between Warham and the man to whom he now wrote. They belonged, on the one hand, to different generations: the archbishop was in his late seventies, the cardinal in his mid-fifties. Likewise, Warham was a former chancellor, Wolsey the current one, and while Warham was *legatus natus*, his one-time junior now held the higher rank of *legatus a latere*, with the result that within both Church and State, the younger man held the whip hand, which he was sometimes all too ready to employ, even threatening at one point to have his older colleague deprived. For if Warham was by training a lawyer and by profession a diplomat of the Crown – some-one whose archbishopric had arrived, in effect, as a retirement pension – Wolsey remained a thrusting individualist and go-getter, whose own archbishopric and cardinal's hat had been earned by undisguised ambi-tion. As such, some circumspection on Warham's part was only to be expected, perhaps. But its extremity remains curious, since he vouches in his letter for nothing whatsoever beyond the fact that Elizabeth Barton is a renowned visionary, while the onus for recommending her as a pious and virtuous woman is shifted to the nuns of her community. Similarly, he effectively disavows, by his silence on the matter, any knowledge of what she wants to say. And although she is his own ecclesiastical subject, he gives the cardinal free license to do what he wishes with her afterwards.

Even more curious, perhaps, is the means by which Barton gained direct access to Warham in the first place, since no nun enjoyed freedom of movement from her convent without explicit permission – leaving us to assume with some confidence an initial introduction from Dom Edward Bocking, 'whose counsel', according to the 1534 Act of Attainder, she had 'used and evermore followed in her goings', and who must have given some advance notice of her business. Yet even with this, there is the added puzzle of how Barton, who had made such 'importunate suit' to Warham, had nevertheless failed to divulge to him any aspect of the nature of her message to Wolsey. Could she, moreover, have persuaded such a seasoned and cautious old diplomat to grant her wish in the course of a single interview, or is the implication that she had effectively laid siege to him, launching appeal after appeal over interview after interview until he finally conceded? Such a possibility is certainly consistent with the later deposition of Prior Goldwell of Christ Church, who contended that she was with the archbishop 'many times'. And this is not all, since the whole point of her persistence, according to Goldwell, was to deliver her 'revelations' not only regarding Wolsey but 'touching my Lord of Canterbury' himself. If so, then Warham emerges on this occasion as a very model of duplicity – particularly when he ascribed such authority to what he heard. For, according to the prior's testimony, Bocking 'showed unto me at divers seasons' how 'he [the archbishop] gave much credence unto her words in such things as she knew and surmised [claimed by inspiration] to know, that she did show unto him'.

So impressed was Warham by what Barton said, and so alarmed by the crisis precipitated by the arrival of the new legate to institute the next phase of the divorce, that he seems to have taken the risk – when his own character naturally inclined him to utmost caution – of sending her on to his rival, Wolsey, with a revelation that would prove no less disconcerting than the one she had in all likelihood delivered to him.

By writing on 1 October, furthermore, the archbishop knew that his letter would be delivered to the cardinal in London, long before the enfeebled Campeggio could get there, since the Italian was now unable to stand and in any case under instructions from the pope to delay at every opportunity the opening of the legatine court over which he was to preside. In consequence, Barton would be able to travel to Kent, probably in the company of one or two of her fellow nuns and, above all, her prioress, who was to effect the necessary introductions at court before Campeggio's arrival in the capital – something that did not in fact occur until 9 October, by which time he was so ill that he remained confined to his bed for almost a fortnight. Indeed, it was not until 22 October that he became well enough to attend an official reception given in his honour, and only on the 23rd did his first formal discussion with the king occur. As such, the first three weeks of October 1528 would prove an ideal time for the Maid to deliver her message, though Wolsey's distractions remained as intense as ever, as he pressurised Campeggio in his sickbed, and harassed the pope with importunities of his own:

> And there I was [complained the gout-ridden Italian in his dispatches] in bed all the time, and still am for that matter; and he has been to visit me three or four times since, arguing with me for three or four hours at a stretch.

The themes, moreover, were as unrelenting as the pressure itself: that if Henry were thwarted, the kingdom would be thrown into confusion by his fury and ruined for lack of a sure successor to the throne; that the Church would be defamed and persecuted; and that Wolsey himself would be disgraced, dismissed and probably put to death.

Under such circumstances, Campeggio was clearly not the only cardinal in agonies at that time, since his English counterpart was as troubled in mind as the Italian was in body, making Elizabeth Barton's message, when finally delivered, all the harder to bear. For she now imparted to him, just as she seems to have done to Warham only a little earlier, the time-honoured message that had been delivered to sinful rulers and their servants from the time of the Prophet Nathan and King David: namely, that unless they repented, death awaited. According to the *Sermon* preached by Nicholas Heath at St Paul's Cross early in 1534, which is likely to have been based on the Maid's own depositions four years after Wolsey's death in 1530:

> She said that God commanded her to say to the late Cardinal and also the said Archbishop of Canterbury that, if they furthered the King's Grace to be married to the Queen's Grace that now is [i.e. Anne Boleyn], they both should be utterly destroyed.

If, moreover, an anonymous document dating to November 1533 is to be believed, Barton had also been 'charged' by an angel – most probably the Archangel Michael of her earlier Aldington visions – to speak to the cardinal 'of three swords that he had in his hand: one of the spirituality [relating to his cardinalate], another of the temporality [concerning his lord chancellorship], and the other of the king's marriage'. The source involved was the testimony, it seems, of a certain John Wolff, a prisoner in the Tower of

London turned government informer, who later pumped one of Barton's associates – his cellmate, the Observant Franciscan Hugh Rich – for information. A merchant of the Steelyard, whose name also suggests Germanic origins, Wolff was in fact an international swindler, who had been imprisoned at the request of the Hanse merchants. But his account is confirmed by a similar letter of Sir Thomas More describing a conversation of his own held with another of the Maid's associates, Friar Richard Risby, at Christmas 1532, on this very topic:

> [Father Risby] told me that she had been with my Lord Legate in his life and with the King's Grace too; and that she had told my Lord Legate a revelation of hers; of three swords that God hath put in my Lord Legate's hand, which, if he ordered not well, God would lay it sore to his charge. The first, he said, was the ordering of the spirituality under the Pope, as Legate; the second, the rule that he bore in order of the temporality under the King, as his Chancellor; and the third, she said, was the meddling [involvement] he was put in trust with by the King, concerning the great matter of his marriage.

In effect, then, Barton had delivered a threat of divine retribution at the very time when its recipient was looking increasingly unable to avoid it, though how much effective influence she subsequently acquired over both Wolsey and Warham is not easy to say. Certainly, the Prior of Christ Church was of the opinion that she held the latter in her pocket, and Nicholas Heath's *Sermon* suggests further that her sway over the old archbishop was actually responsible for his apparently remarkable change of attitude over the divorce:

> For the said archbishop had, afore her coming to him, provoked [appealed] from the Pope to the General Council, intending to proceed in the King's Grace's said cause of matrimony and divorce, saying his Grace should have no indifferent justice shown him in other places.

Like other supporters of the divorce, Warham had, in fact, been prepared initially to endorse Wolsey's plan to circumvent papal authority by the summons of a general ecclesiastical council of the kind that the cardinal had envisaged on his mission to Avignon. After the Maid's intervention, however, his position altered radically. And this interpretation of the reason was consistent, too, with the opinion of the archbishop's successor, Thomas Cranmer, who, as an intimate friend of the Boleyn family, was almost certain to have known something of the inside story – albeit not at first hand, since in 1528–29 he was still a comparatively obscure Cambridge don. Significantly, in his private correspondence of 1533, there is the following observation about Elizabeth Barton's impact:

> And truly, I think, she did marvellously stop the going forward of the King's marriage by reason of her visions, which, she said, were of God … She also had communication with my Lord Cardinal and with my Lord of Canterbury in the matter; and in mine opinion, with her feigned and godly threatenings, she stayed them very much.

If true – and Cranmer was as good a judge as any available to us – the humble servant girl of Aldington had already achieved a truly astonishing, indeed pivotal, status, which even the Act of Attainder condemning her did not ultimately seek to hide, in spite of its more general efforts to discredit and belittle her. For as the act made clear:

> The late Cardinal of England and the late Bishop of Canterbury, being so well minded to further and to set at an end [achieve] the marriage which the King now enjoyeth, according to their spiritual duty, were prevented by the false revelations of the said Nun. And that the Bishop of Canterbury was so minded, it may be proved by divers which knew his towardness, and also by his provocation which he made from the Pope, in case he [the Pope] would make any process against him from meddling in the matter.

Although Warham was already dead by 1534, therefore, and as such a convenient scapegoat for the act's chief architect, Thomas Cromwell, the collective evidence explaining Warham's change of heart at Barton's urging remains compelling, particularly when Bishop John Fisher himself repeatedly asserted the identical conclusion to Cromwell, the House of Lords and indeed the king himself, freely acknowledging how:

My Lord of Canterbury, that then was both her Ordinary [diocesan bishop] and a man reputed of high wisdom and learning, told me that she had many great visions; and of him I learned greater things than ever I heard of the nun herself.

By the time that Fisher made these statements in 1534, of course, he too had been gravely compromised and was fighting for his life. But in the unlikely event that he, like Prior Goldwell, was happy to shift the burden of complicity on to a dead man's shoulders, the general picture still emerges that from 1528 onwards, the Archbishop of Canterbury – hitherto loyal executant of the royal will – had become a proponent of the Maid's visions and tacit supporter of her mission. Indeed, as the story unfolded, he would, at the very last, emerge as a gallant opponent of the royal will in a way that he had never remotely contemplated previously. Whether it was the Maid's transparent sincerity or some unsettling detail in her revelations that shook the archbishop from a lifetime's subservience remains unknown. Perhaps it was fear magnified by extreme old age and the imminence of death that worked its effect, or alternatively the honourable parting flourish of a disillusioned conscience freed at last from the world of dishonesty and double-dealing it had inhabited for so long. Certainly, Warham by his weakness, like Wolsey by his assurances of success, had allowed an emotional impulse on behalf of their king to attain unimagined proportions and to assume unimaginable ramifications. But what both men were now seeking, it seems, was nothing less than a heaven-sent intermediary who might somehow achieve at this late hour what they themselves could not hope to: a change of royal heart.

For in spite of certain appearances to the contrary, Wolsey, too, was not unmoved by the encounter with the Maid that had been engineered by Warham. The cardinal's first and most famous biographer, George Cavendish, makes no mention of her at all in his *Life and Death of Cardinal Wolsey*, and since Cavendish was his gentleman usher, who knew all his master's coming and goings, this might be considered significant. Yet a seemingly insignificant phrase in the *Sermon*, italicised in the extract below, may not only provide confirmation of the date of her first meeting with him, but also help explain precisely how the Maid affected the cardinal's outlook:

The said Cardinal was as well minded and bent to go forth in the King's
Grace's said cause of matrimony and divorce as any man living *according
to the law of God* and the law of nature, till he was perverted by this nun
and induced to believe that, if he proceeded in the same, God would
sore strike him.

At first sight, of course, this might simply seem to mean that Wolsey was
keen to pursue the king's cause until the appearance of Barton quelled
his ardour. Yet the cardinal continued desperately and unwaveringly to
achieve an annulment of the royal marriage up to the very moment of his
fall from power in October 1529. What did change in the meantime, however, was the strategy he employed in pursuit of his master's 'cause'. For
until October 1528 – the time of his meeting with the Maid – he was prepared to entertain the king's arguments about the law of God, as intimated
in Leviticus, but thereafter would not even pretend to justify the divorce
on these high grounds, opting instead for arguments founded purely upon
political necessity and technical flaws in the original dispensation granted
by Julius II.

And if Elizabeth Barton was indeed the catalyst for such a change of
tactics, then her influence upon the premier mover and shaper of English
affairs at this time, other than the king himself, was nothing less than
momentous, explaining not only the ultimate reaction of the government to her personally but, in part at least, the fate of Wolsey, too. For
to a king who prided himself upon the sensitivity of his conscience, not
to mention his grasp of theology, which had already encouraged him to
produce a defence of the Church's entire sacramental system, and earn, or
so he believed, the plaudits of all Europe, his minister's choice of altogether
baser ground on which to wage his fight amounted in effect to little less
than an act of treason against the royal genius: an act of treachery so gro-
tesque, in fact, as to suggest that the man concerned had been perverted or
bewitched. True, the Maid had not determined the cardinal's new tactics,
but in bidding him desist from his existing course on peril of his soul,
she appears to have persuaded him, in effect, to abandon the use of religious arguments for political ends – a new course that must have accorded
well with his own experience in negotiations to date. For with every religious justification he advanced, Wolsey was contradicted by an equally

convincing religious counter, and for every Father of the Church he cited, not to mention every General Council, papal brief or pontifical letter, there were invariably other citations, General Councils, papal briefs and pontifical letters to support the contrary position.

The king, meanwhile, remained tied to Leviticus like a bull to the ring in his nose, and, as Campeggio soon discovered, was in no mood to compromise one jot on the issue of his marriage. His desire for an annulment, Campeggio wrote a week after his arrival, was 'most ardent'; and the Italian did not exaggerate, since ego and self-righteousness, not to mention the remorseless application of flawed reasoning – all reinforced by a typically selective show of hard learning – left Henry in no doubt about the virtue of his cause. 'His Majesty has so diligently studied this matter,' observed Campeggio, 'that I believe in this case he knows more than a great theologian or jurist.' But if the king was well acquainted with what he considered the letter of the law, he was less familiar with the true scholar's preference for patience, balance and, above all, listening, while his supposed erudition remained, to all intents and purposes, as self-serving as his conscience. For four hours on one occasion he had held forth as Campeggio played the role of sponge and nodding student. But the real lesson emerging from the interview was neither legal nor theological. Reflecting on the king's intransigence, Campeggio drew the only possible conclusion. 'I believe that an angel descending from heaven would be unable to persuade him otherwise,' he noted wistfully. And on the following Sunday, like the supremely artful dodger he undoubtedly was, the Italian was persuaded to reveal the decretal bull, which appeared to sanction all that the king desired.

What Campeggio did not reveal, however, was the elaborate ruse that centred upon this document. For, in spite of previous assurances to the contrary, the pope had finally left him in no doubt that the bull should be shown only to Henry and Wolsey, and could not be produced in court. More importantly still, its terms were on no account to be executed. As such, its unveiling was nothing more than a sop to starving men – an appetiser for a non-existent meal and a prelude to further delay as Campeggio now took to his sickbed whenever convenient. Neither hero nor genius, the Italian knew at least how to lose slowly and to save what could be saved from a no-win situation, since Wolsey, too, had proved

unbending. 'I have no more success in persuading the cardinal,' wrote
Campeggio, 'than if I had spoken to a rock.' Thus, with king and cardinal alike insisting that they would 'endure no procrastination' since 'the
affairs of the kingdom are at a standstill', the Italian duly procrastinated,
fighting hot air with a steady cooling stream of paltry excuses and chill
indifference. Only when Campeggio suggested that Catherine might opt
for convenient seclusion within a nunnery had Henry's impatience temporarily abated. But she, too, remained another immovable object in the
stone wall maze confronting Wolsey.

As his options receded on every front, therefore, the cardinal who had
once carried all before him was reduced to increasingly futile stratagems.
Ever desperate to probe any and every avenue, he had met in August with
Robert Shorton, the queen's almoner, to debate her case, but was told
once more that Catherine had never known Prince Arthur as her husband. Worse still, Wolsey also learned of her conviction that no court in
England could offer her justice and of her determination to make use of
certain papal bulls existing in Spain that allegedly removed all impedi-
ments to her present marriage. When, therefore, Wolsey claimed to have
proof of consummation, centring on rumours that Catherine had been
pregnant at the time of Arthur's death, he was already clutching at straws.
Nor was the queen any more convinced by the cardinal's even lamer assertion that the current impasse cast a stigma upon all the learned men of
England who had found the marriage invalid. For, although she had been
left to hammer out her defence alone, she was nevertheless secure in conscience, convinced of her cause and raring by now to fight. If grounds of
expediency, therefore, or indeed any other grounds on offer had achieved
so little with the pope, was not the only answer at this point, to change the
mind of the king by the most desperate and unlikely option of all, which
had recently, as if by providence, come to hand: namely, the agency of a
humble young woman, apparently inspired from heaven, whose charisma
had already swayed an archbishop and the cardinal himself? Henry's piety,
after all, went hand in glove with superstition, and there was little doubting either that his intrinsic loyalty lay always with the papacy. Had not
his very badgering of Clement VII demonstrated, indeed, his underlying
commitment to the Holy Father as the supreme arbiter in matters of faith
and Christian morals? So as a devotee of Our Lady of Walsingham, patron

of the Friars Observant and would-be crusader against the Turk, might he not yet be persuaded to listen to a message, however unwelcome, delivered by a young and virtuous nun?

It was during these critical weeks of October 1528, therefore, that Wolsey arranged Elizabeth Barton's first encounter with the king, which, according to the testimony of John Wolff, gathered from his conversations with Friar Hugh Rich, had originated with a message delivered 'of an angel' that had bade her:

> Go unto the king, that infidel Prince of England, and say that I commend him to amend his life; and that he leave three things which he loveth and purposeth upon; that is
>> that he [ceases to] take off the pope's right and patrimony from him;
>> the second, that he destroy all these new folks of opinion, and the words of their new learning;
>> the third, that, if he married and took Anne to wife, the vengeance of God would plague him.

Quite where the first of Barton's three interviews with Henry took place is unknown. But such forthrightness certainly involved an act of considerable courage on the nun's part, even though the king himself appears to have remained surprisingly unmoved by the meeting. On the contrary, he appears, in fact, to have taken neither heed of her advice nor, more surprisingly still perhaps, offence at her audacity, still clinging in all likelihood to pipedreams that Campeggio's investigations would produce the desired result and free him from any burden of sin or heavenly retribution. Such, indeed, was Henry's apparent indifference that Wolsey saw no need afterwards to retain the Maid in London, where she could be consulted or produced as occasion demanded. Though Warham had recommended that she be transferred to Wolsey's episcopal jurisdiction, even this did not occur. Instead, she was merely dismissed and sent back to Canterbury.

From the silence of the Tudor chroniclers about this first interview, it might never have occurred at all, perhaps, were it not for a letter of Sir Thomas More to Thomas Cromwell in February 1534 in which he tells how he:

Had heard some times in my Lord Cardinal's days, that she had been both with his Lordship and with the King's Grace, but what she said either to the one or to the other, upon my faith, I had never heard any one word.

Typically canny in his efforts not to incriminate himself, More knew full well, of course, that his accusers at that critical time could not hope to prove whether he had previously heard the Maid's political revelations or not. And neither could they confirm that he knew for sure of her visits to the king and the cardinal in the first place, placing him under no compulsion to mention them at all. Instead he volunteered this information freely, which can only suggest that the meetings did actually occur. That More knew nothing of their content is also wholly plausible, since Barton's oracles to the king only became common knowledge after the preaching campaign of the Observant Franciscans against the divorce began in 1532. In the meantime, a security screen had enveloped the whole affair, it seems, which might also explain George Cavendish's silence on the matter.

It is curious too, perhaps, that no mention of the Maid occurs in Campeggio's dispatches to the Holy See, particularly when she represented such an outspoken potential ally, for by this time, the legate's task had been rendered even more intractable by events. He had tried, on the one hand, to call upon the good offices of the queen, to solve his quandary. If she could indeed be persuaded to enter a nunnery, for instance, there would be an adequate canonical case to allow her husband to remarry on the grounds that entry into a convent entailed a form of physical death for the person involved. This idea, first formulated by St Bonaventure three centuries earlier, doubtless had much to recommend it, since such an arrangement had already been employed when Jeanne de Valois, sometime wife of Louis XII, had humbly retreated to a nunnery at her husband's wish. Moreover, even John Fisher, the queen's staunchest supporter, was said by Campeggio to have warmed to the proposal when it was put to him. Catherine's religiosity was known, after all, to be sufficiently ardent for such an option to be plausible, and she might still have enjoyed all the comforts and privileges of her royal station, since Henry, typically enthused by such a convenient solution, had hastened to asssure Campeggio how Catherine would lose only 'the use of his person', and be accorded due honour and privilege in all other respects. Most important of all from the queen's point of view, her beloved daughter's legitimacy and birthright would remain intact.

Yet no sooner had Catherine declined Campeggio's initial proposal on 26 October, than another intemperate outburst by her husband put paid once and for all to any hope of breakthrough. For in a fit of rage the king had, it seems, insisted that the queen should accept Campeggio's proposal without delay, and in October, too, he complained to the Privy Council about her behaviour in general. She was, he grumbled, too light-hearted and dressed too richly, and should be prayerful for justice rather than presenting herself in public. He even implied, at one point, that she was involved in a mysterious plot to kill him, all of which prompted a letter from the Privy Council in which Catherine was told with cudgel bluntness that she was 'a fool to resist the King's will'. Henceforth, therefore, the main barrier to divorce was no longer international power politics, but simply a slighted woman's pride in the face of a torrid husband's mistreatment and bluster, as both Wolsey and Campeggio would swiftly discover. For on one of their three subsequent visits to the queen, she listened patiently over the space of two hours to the inducements offered her: the beauties of a life of religious contemplation; the guarantee that she would retain her dowry; the promise that she would retain the guardianship of her daughter. But her only response was to request legal counsel. And at the end of discussion, it was to Campeggio rather than Wolsey that she chose to make her confession. What Catherine subsequently revealed, moreover, she urged him to communicate to the pope, even though it was rendered under the sacred seal of the confessional. Covering the whole of her life from the time of her arrival in England, she made it clear that she had not slept in the same bed with Arthur 'more than seven nights' and 'that he had left her as he had found her – a virgin'. She affirmed, too, that 'she intended to live and die in the estate of matrimony, to which God had called her' and that 'she would always remain of that opinion and never change it'.

On their next visit to the queen, meanwhile, Wolsey and Campeggio found her flanked by advisers, and as adamant as ever that she would do nothing either to condemn her soul or violate God's laws, so that as Wolsey raised himself from his knees after one final flourish in which he pleaded that she listen to the voice of the Church, the course before him was at last clear. For, with the queen's assent out of the question once and for all, the scene was now irrevocably set for all the high and public drama of his legatine court – though not, predictably, before a further series of random obstacles and painful twists and turns had run their weary course. In mid-November, for example, Catherine produced a copy of a further dispensation, hitherto unknown in England and dating from 1505, which appeared to undermine the whole case upon which Campeggio's decretal bull was based. But then, as Sir Francis Bryan headed for Rome at Wolsey's behest to prove the document spurious, other news arrived that the pope was mortally ill and that 'another lapse will finish him' – though Wolsey's desperate fantasies of one further personal bid for the papacy and subsequent plans for hefty bribes proved fleeting, since Clement survived, and neither Stephen Gardiner's ongoing pressure at Rome throughout the spring of 1529 nor Bryan's best efforts yielded any progress. By Easter, indeed, Bryan had concluded that Henry's cause was hopeless and, unlike Gardiner – who had been manfully gnawing at granite for all of fifteen months – he was prepared to say as much. 'Neither fair means nor foul' could at this point prevail upon the pope, he reported to Henry, and 'if the cardinal feels aggrieved at the truth', the message concluded, then 'let him'.

Queen Catherine, of course, was not without her supporters, not least among the common people of London who were well accustomed to saying what they liked, and were already – according to both the French ambassador, du Bellay, and the devotedly loyal chronicler, Edward Hall – making their feelings known by booing cardinals as they passed, and cheering passionately on those occasions when Catherine ventured forth in public. And while it would be inaccurate to speak of anything approaching a 'Queen's party' in more exalted circles at this time, there was nevertheless ample reason for the king to proceed with some caution towards the next and ultimate step. For besides the Spanish members of her suite – which included Jorge de Atheca, Bishop of Llandaff, her physicians, de la Sà and Fernando Vitoria, her sewer, Francisco Felipez, her apothecary, Miguel de Soto, and her favourite old lady-in-waiting, Maria de Salinas – there was also the support of Catherine's long-standing personal friends like Mary, the king's sister, for her to depend upon, as well as the good offices of other Englishwomen of high status like the Duchess of Norfolk, the ever-resourceful Marchioness of Exeter, and Margaret Pole, Countess of Salisbury, who was still Princess Mary's governess. Richard Fetherston, the princess's tutor, the dauntless Dr Robert Ridley and the gifted Welsh scholar and preacher Dr Edward Powell were also equally unswerving in their loyalty, as were the Observant Franciscan friars, among whom numbered the queen's confessor, Dr John Forest, another to suffer martyrdom later in the reign.

More significantly still, perhaps, there was Thomas Abell, Catherine's chaplain, who would prove particularly outspoken in her defence and earn in consequence not only an entirely groundless citation in the Act of Attainder eventually employed against Elizabeth Barton but a martyr's laurel of his own more than half a decade later. For the queen herself, notwithstanding strenuous efforts to implicate her, had studiously avoided all association with the Holy Maid, and her chaplain's involvement, likewise, had never been more than marginal. Later, when the dust finally began to settle, Thomas Cromwell freely confessed to Eustace Chapuys, the Imperial ambassador, how he had used every trick he knew to extort evidence linking Catherine to the Maid, only to be thwarted at every turn, despite the fact that Barton had indeed been very insistent at various points in her desire to speak with her and to console her in her affliction. But Catherine had remained perfectly firm throughout in her personal loyalty to her husband – so much so, indeed, that Chapuys was to observe how her restraint and good sense in avoiding any action that might provoke suspicion seemed divinely inspired. And Thomas Abell too, in spite of his naturally combative nature, had been hardly less discreet in his dealings with Barton, though this would not spare him a charge of guilt by the most tenuous of links founded upon nothing more than the credence he had allegedly given to the nun's 'feigned revelations and miracles' – which had inspired him, it was said, to set forth 'divers' books in England to the slander of the king, and thereby 'animate' the queen 'to persist in her wilful opinion against the same divorce and separation'.

In fact, only one book would ever issue from Abell's pen, though he had ultimately needed no inspiration from the Holy Maid to take up his mistress's cause. Born around 1497 and educated at Oxford, where in 1516 he took the degree of Master of Arts, and subsequently acquired a doctorate in theology, he was in fact a shy, reserved, even cold and self-centred man, who apparently became the queen's chaplain sometime before the beginning of 1528, since in that year the king made him a New Year's gift in common with other members of her suite. But initially at least, there was certainly no discernible hint of any future disloyalty to the government as he proceeded to teach Catherine modern languages and music, and tended his everyday tasks dutifully. On the contrary, when the queen eventually dispatched him to Spain in quest of the original papal brief supporting the validity of her marriage, she actually appears – albeit through no fault of his – to have placed less than absolute confidence in his sympathies, partially concealing her motives for his mission and opting to send her faithful Spanish servant, Juan de Montoya, along with him. For only a little earlier she had expressed fear lest the brief should fall into her enemies' hands, as the king's agents were certain to spare no effort in obtaining it when there was no record of it in Rome, and there were in any case, as she well knew, informers all round her. Such, in fact, was her predicament that when the Imperial ambassador suggested she send a power of attorney to Rome, his advice, too, was refused on the simple grounds that she was surrounded by spies in her chamber and allowed so little freedom.

Under such circumstances, therefore, the queen's anxiety was almost certainly so acute by this point that she felt unable to place faith in anyone whose absolute loyalty had not been tested already in some vital matter – a principle that applied in practice even to a chaplain who had given no grounds for distrust. Yet in spite of the queen's apparent reservations and notwithstanding an arduous journey across the turbulent Bay of Biscay in the grim winter month of January, Abell had gone on to conduct his mission with commendable prudence and discretion, assuming direction of affairs over Montoya after their arrival, and setting forth in an interview with Charles V at Saragossa the reasons why the original brief should be kept in Spain and an attested copy brought back to England instead. For his services on this and other occasions, moreover, Abell would receive not only the award of the parochial benefice of Bradwell in Essex from Catherine upon his return, but something altogether more significant still: the unyielding animosity of her husband, as his defence of the queen's interests became more tenacious than ever and, most significant of all, more and more overt. For once his teeth were set, Abell was unyielding, and by 1532 he had published his *Invicta veritas. An answere, That by no manner of law, it may be lawfull for the most noble King of England, King Henry the eight to be divorced from the queens grace, his lawfull and very wife* – a treatise printed by Merten de Keyser in Antwerp with the fictitious press-mark of Luneberge, to avoid suspicion. In it, moreover, Abell answered the numerous tracts supporting the king's ecclesiastical claims so effectively that Henry duly bought up copies of the book in order to destroy them, before according the author the hospitality of the Beauchamp Tower in the Tower of London.

And this was not the end of Abell's persecution. For after a year's lib-eration, he was again imprisoned – this time in December 1533 – on hollow charges of disseminating the prophecies of the Maid of Kent. Kept in close confinement for six years until his persecutors had tired of break-ing his spirit by any other means than the common executioner's knot and blade, the Act of Attainder condemning him would declare how he had 'most traitorously adhered himself unto the Bishop of Rome' and 'been a common enemy unto your Majesty and this your Realm, refusing your Highness to be our Supreme Head of this your Realm of England'. For which he was sentenced to be:

> Drawn on a hurdle to the place of execution, there to be hanged, cut down alive, your members to be cut off and cast in the fire, your bowels burnt before your eyes, your head smitten off, your body to be quartered at the King's will.

With supreme irony, the butchery would be conducted ultimately at Smithfield, only two days after the execution of Thomas Cromwell him-self, and on the very same occasion that three evangelical Protestants – Barnes, Garrett and Jerome – were not only burned alongside Abell and two other Catholics, but even tied on the same hurdles as their religious foes, prompting one foreigner, John Foxe tells us, to make the follow-ing memorable observation that could hardly have been more apt by that time: 'What a country England is to live in when they hang papists and burn Anabaptists.'

Even now, in fact, there is still to be seen on the wall of Abell's prison in the Tower of London a rebus consisting of the symbol of a bell with an 'A' upon it and the name Thomas above, which he carved during his confinement. There is also extant a very pious Latin letter written by him to a fellow martyr, and another to Cromwell, begging for some slight mitigation of his 'close prison', allowing him 'license to go to church and say Mass here within the Tower and for to lie in some house upon the Green'. The application is signed 'by your daily bedeman, Thomas Abell, priest', and, needless to say, was never granted.

Plainly, when Iñigo de Mendoza, the Spanish ambassador, commented bitterly that 'in matters of self-interest the English are without conscience of common honesty', he could not have been thinking of Queen Catherine's chaplain. Nor, as events would soon prove, could he have been referring to the most significant of all her supporters, who was once again stirring to assume centre stage after his earlier guarantee to Wolsey that he would not meddle in the queen's affairs. For John Fisher had in fact been true to his word and confined himself in recent months to the administration of his diocese and his duties at Cambridge, where a statute had recently been passed in his honour, acknowledging his many benefactions, not only as adviser to Lady Margaret Beaufort in her foundations and in his labours to carry out her wishes, but also as a generous patron of the university in his own right and especially of St John's College. All this, it was felt, numbered him among the college's founders, and such was his reputation that it was also decided to establish an annual requiem on the day of his death. The statute ends, in fact, by hailing him as 'the most learned father, head and glory of this republic of learning', leaving Fisher himself to reply how such an honour was more fitting for a king than a 'poor bishop' (*pauperculo pontifici*), since he had only, in his own estimation, been the minister or agent of the king's mother. As her confessor, he had advised her, for her soul's wealth, to bequeath part of her wealth to the training of young men in learning and virtue so that they could preach the Gospel of Christ more effectively. And as such, he assured the senate that he would be more than content if they would link his name in their prayers with that of the noble lady.

But the same Bishop of Rochester's modesty was nevertheless strikingly abandoned when the senate's initial decision was challenged by none other than Richard Croke, Fellow of St John's at Fisher's own recommendation and the outstanding Greek scholar of his day. Only through Fisher's influence, in fact, had Croke been retained at Cambridge at all instead of moving to Oxford as he had been urged to do by both Archbishop Warham and Sir Thomas More. Initially, indeed, Fisher had even paid the scholar's salary, and upon his appointment in 1519, Croke had not hidden his gratitude, asking in his inaugural lecture:

> What then is the message of my lord of Rochester? Why he exhorts them to apply themselves with all diligence to the study of Greek litera-ture … The exhortation of one who had never urged them to ought but what was most profitable, might alone suffice.

Yet this had not prevented Croke, just under a decade later, from pen-ning an ungracious letter to the senate objecting to the decision to name his benefactor as one of St John's founders on the grounds that he had enriched himself and his relatives out of the Lady Margaret's estates – a claim that Fisher not only firmly rejected, but which prompted a per-sonal attack of his own, demonstrating all too aptly the sterner side of his nature. As chancellor, he declared, he had striven 'by every means to ensure that that the glory of the Foundress shall shine, and her name be every-where renowned!', though this was only the prelude to a change of tack that smacked not only of righteous indignation but of a bristling loss of temper: 'I hear you neither lecture, nor go to the common table, and also that you entertain guests from among the fellows in your rooms, against the statutes of the College, which I will not tolerate.' Then, possibly recall-ing recent events, he not only pronounced that he would willingly lay down the chancellorship but included a remarkable full-frontal assault on Croke's alleged religious sympathies:

> Perhaps some other person will take it who likes the Lutheran doc-trines … I do not doubt that the fathers and seniors of the University are much opposed to heresy, although there are many of you who are suspect, and some whose names are already noted.

It was a spiteful riposte and a sign, perhaps, that Fisher was experiencing more and more acutely the pressure of the gathering storm. There was more than peevishness involved and not a little childishness, indeed, in the hurt he had taken and the nature of the response, particularly in his supposed preparedness to give up his role on behalf of another 'who likes the Lutheran doctrines'. But the letter remains a measure, too, of both Fisher's fibre and his potential threat to the king's plans in the struggle to come. For, like Thomas Abell, his teeth, once set, would not be gently released. On the contrary, he would grip and gnaw at an issue until the truth was discovered and justice vindicated, pursuing the logic of any argument with precisely the rigour and tenacity that one would expect from so gifted an academic. He had weighed the alternative cases, drawn his conclusions and was now poised for defence of those conclusions. In this, moreover, he was not alone. Others among his fellow bishops had also done precisely that. But they lacked the same pugnacious streak, and they lacked ultimately the curious combination of stubborn selflessness and egotism that makes so many martyrs. For the king, too, had weighed the alternative cases, drawn his conclusions, and was accordingly poised, not for defence but for attack. The storm had long been gathering. But now the heavens would open with a vengeance.

6

TRUTH ON TRIAL

I have asked counsel of the greatest clerks in Christendom, and for this cause I have sent for this legate as a man indifferent, only to know the truth and settle my conscience, and for no other cause as God can judge. And as touching the Queen, if it be adjudged by the law of God that she is my lawful wife, there were never thing more pleasant nor more acceptable to me in my life, both for the discharge and cheering of my conscience, and also for the good qualities and conditions, the which I know to be in her.

From a speech delivered by Henry VIII at Bridewell Palace on 5 November 1528.

When Henry VIII's trap for the papal brief he desired so badly to discredit was forestalled by Thomas Abell's intervention, any receding hopes for a speedy trial and resolution of the king's torments had vanished altogether. Thereafter, royal agents in Rome laboured in vain, on a dozen flimsy pretexts, to have the brief declared a forgery, while Pope Clement was only too happy for the added delay. Campeggio too, nursing his gout as well as his shrinking treasury beside the foggy Thames, was no less glad of a further excuse for impeding a process that was by now so certain to end in failure. Like Clement, as long as no action was taken he could comfort himself with the hope that something might turn up – 'that time would bring forth something' to yield a breakthrough – by which he meant that either one of the principals would die, that Henry would lose his head and commit bigamy, or that Anne would someday fail to fend him off, and that once she was at last his bedmate, the king would lose his appetite for legal sanctions. Yet if Wolsey's predicament could stir the Italian's sympathy, the king's agitated subterfuges aroused in him only sardonic amusement. The mighty ruler had, after all, hustled the object of his passion out of London before Campeggio's arrival, then ridden after her to soothe his pangs of separation, and finally brought her back with the most transparent lack of discretion. He could, moreover, have spared himself the trouble, since the legate had known throughout of the lady in the case, and found it not a little amusing, indeed, that although she gave herself the airs of an acknowledged *maîtresse en titre*, her royal admirer was still unable to proceed to 'the ultimate conjunction' without the pope's approval.

For Wolsey, of course, the situation was indeed now critical, since on 29 May the king had instructed him to proceed with Campeggio under the terms of Clement's original commission, with the result that two days later formal arrangements were drawn up for Henry and Catherine to appear at Blackfriars on 18 June. Dangling agonisingly 'betwixt hope and fear', Wolsey still wondered in fact whether Clement might well renege upon his earlier guarantee and revoke the case to Rome. Even more perplexingly, however, he had received further confirmation of his own increasingly brittle relationship with the king. For during the previous summer he had blocked the appointment of Eleanor Carey as Abbess of Wilton and in doing so denied the wishes of Anne Boleyn. The result was a wholly unfamiliar barb from his royal master. 'Ah! my lord', wrote Henry:

> It is a double offence, both to do ill and colour it, too; but with men that have wit it cannot be accepted so. Wherefore, good my lord, use no more that way with me, for there is no man living that more hateth it.

Nor was this all, for Henry then proceeded to twist the knife by questioning both Wolsey's closure of certain monasteries and subsequent decision to redistribute the resulting funds to his beloved colleges at Oxford and Ipswich.

Naturally enough, therefore, it was with no little trepidation that, on Friday, 18 June 1529, Wolsey finally made his way to the long-awaited legatine court at Blackfriars, which lay conveniently near to the new palace of Bridewell just across the Fleet River. He was faced with the critical moment of his career and, though he only feared as much as yet, neither he nor Campeggio could actually deliver the favourable outcome on which all hinged. For, as the two scarlet-robed princes of the Universal Church, hatted, gloved and ringed, moved majestically to their chairs of state behind a railed and carpeted table, both were hopelessly at odds. As such, the great hall of the Dominican priory at Blackfriars – decked out 'like a solemn court' with carpets and wall tapestries – which had been the meeting place for the Parliament of 1523, may already have seemed more like a place of judgement for Wolsey personally; the queen's eleven advocates (seven English, four foreign) more like his prosecutors than her defenders. And then, of course, there was Catherine herself to consider, by her own confession 'a poor ignorant woman' unversed in the law, but idolised nevertheless by the Londoners who thronged outside the building. She had wooed them, as Wolsey bitterly acknowledged, 'by beckoning with her head and smiling' – 'which she had not been accustomed to do in times past' – and now she was to have her moment.

Certainly, the queen's advisers were a commendable and not unformidable array. Soon after Campeggio's arrival in England, Henry had consulted her about the appointment of her counsellors in the coming trial, and she had stated at that time her clear preference for the assistance of Spanish advocates and proctors. Yet on grounds of the delay that this would involve, Catherine had been allowed only the services of two young lawyers from Flanders – de la Blekerie and Van Scoere – who, though excellent jurists, left soon after their arrival, since the time was not then ripe for action and there was little, in effect, for them to do. Thereafter, once Juan Luis Vives, her protégé, friend and pensioner, had deemed it unwise to represent her, the queen was dependent mainly upon English counsel. But two of these – John Fisher and Henry Standish, Bishop of St Asaph – were nevertheless major theologians, and the others, with the exception perhaps of Catherine's Spanish confessor, Jorge de Atheca, Bishop of Llandaff, were comparable in proven ability and distinguished attainments with any advocate ranged against them on the king's side. Four, including Dr Robert Ridley, were conspicuously able theologians, albeit of lesser repute than Fisher and Standish, while the civil and canon lawyers at the queen's disposal were also figures of considerable reputation. For they included not only Cuthbert Tunstall, Bishop of London, Nicholas West, Bishop of Ely, and John Clerk, Bishop of Bath and Wells, but Archbishop Warham of Canterbury himself. All, it is true, lacked the steel in their characters possessed by most of the theologians who would sit alongside them at Blackfriars. Wolsey, indeed, had already told the king of Warham that he had 'sufficiently instructed him how he shall order himself in case the Queen demands his counsel'. But their presence remained significant, to say the least, rendering the additional presence of the queen's foreign counsellors almost an irrelevance.

Of the lesser theologians at the queen's counsel bench, three, in fact, would ultimately suffer martyrdom. Thomas Abell went to Smithfield on 30 July 1540, and did so in the company of the other two – Richard Fetherston and Edward Powell – partially, no doubt, because he, like them, had first blackened his copybook at Blackfriars six years earlier, and not least either because all were simply too substantial to ignore. Fetherston was a graduate of Cambridge who, as Archdeacon of Brecon, had risen to become chaplain to Queen Catherine and tutor to her daughter, Princess Mary. And though there is actually no firm evidence that he had achieved the rank of Doctor of Theology at one of the English universities, he was nevertheless described by John Pits in his *De illustribus Angliae scriptoribus* as '*sacrae theologiae Doctor*'. No less a figure than Juan Luis Vives, moreover, described him as 'learned and honest' and deemed the cleric a worthy successor to himself as tutor to the princess:

> As for your writing in Latin [Vives observed to the young Lady Mary upon his return to Spain], I am glad that ye shall change from me to Master Fetherstone, for that shall do you much good, to learn by him to write right.

And if Fetherston's intellect was not in doubt, neither was his loyal advocacy of the queen's cause, for even before the Blackfriars proceedings were under way, he had taken part in the session of Convocation that began in April 1529, and was one of the few members who refused to sign the act declaring the king's marriage with Catherine to be illegal, *ab initio*, through the pope's inability to grant a dispensation in such a case. Later, too, he is said to have written a treatise, *Contra divortium Henrici et Catharinae, Liber unus*, condemning the divorce – though no copy of the work is still extant – while in 1534, when called upon to take the oath of supremacy, he would resolutely refuse, resulting in his incarceration in the Tower of London on 13 December 1534, where he seems to have remained until his execution in 1540.

Equally unyielding to the king's designs was the Welshman Dr Edward Powell, who had been born around 1478 and gone on to become a fellow of Oriel College at Oxford in 1495 before receiving the degree of

Doctor of Divinity on 26 June 1506. Rector of Bleadon, Somerset, and prebendary of Centum Solidorum in Lincoln, which he exchanged for Carlton-cum-Thurlby in 1505, and the latter for Sutton-in-Marisco in 1525, he also held the prebends of Lyme Regis, Calstock, Bedminster, and St Mary Redcliffe, Bristol, along with the living of St Edmond's, Salisbury. But it was as a court preacher in high favour with Henry VIII that he first made his name, helping the king to write his *Assertio Septem Sacramentorum* in response to Martin Luther, and then publishing his own work on the subject in December 1523. Whereafter, the University of Oxford not only commended Powell's work, but styled him 'the glory of the university' in a letter to the king, though Powell, too, became, in effect, a marked man from the time of his appointment to defend the legality of royal marriage, and particularly after his decision to write the *Tractatus de non dissolvendo Henrici Regis cum Catherina matrimonio* in its defence.

Nor was this the last or least of Powell's 'indiscretions'. For in March 1533, he was selected to answer Hugh Latimer at Bristol, and was alleged to have disparaged his opponent's moral character. In consequence, Latimer complained to Thomas Cromwell, and Powell fell into further disfavour by denouncing Henry's marriage with Anne Boleyn – after which his path to martyrdom followed the familiar course. Discharged from the proctorship of Salisbury in January 1534, he was attainted in November, together with John Fisher, for high treason in refusing to take the oath of succession, and deprived of his benefices, before being imprisoned in the Tower of London. Such was his perceived threat, moreover, that when his gaoler offered to allow both him and Thomas Abell to be freed temporarily on bail, the unfortunate man was sent to the Marshalsea Prison. Sadly, it was the last prospect of freedom that the dauntless doctor would ever be afforded. For, like Abell and Fetherstone, he too would be tied to a hurdle in the company of a Protestant fellow martyr en route to Smithfield in the summer of 1540. In Powell's case, his companion was the Lutheran Robert Barnes, a divine like him, who had also fallen foul of the royal will, and whose treatment prompted an imaginary dialogue in verse, detailing the two men's ordeal and highlighting its ironies – *The Metynge of Doctor Barnes and Dr. Powell at Paradise Gate and of theyre communicacion bothe drawen to Smithfylde fro the Towar* – which can still be found in the British Museum today.

But if some of the queen's counsellors more than a decade earlier had therefore been made for martyrdom, others would ultimately prove more malleable. Henry Standish, for example, was from the outset the most doubtful of Catherine's advocates at Blackriars, and inevitably perhaps, from the evidence of his earlier career, eventually chose to tie himself to the king's chariot. He had studied at both Oxford and Cambridge, joined the Conventual as opposed to the Observant Franciscans, and gone on to become not only Warden of the Grey Friars at Newgate in London but Provincial of his Order. Before this, however, he had already come under Henry VIII's favour and was for years a court preacher. Nor was it without significance that in the shockwaves resulting from the notorious 'Hunne case' of 1515, Standish should have seen fit to displease Convocation by opposing clerical immunity from secular courts, receiving the king's protection in the process and consequently escaping without punishment. Three years later he was made Bishop of St Asaph, though not, it must be said, without the disapproval of Richard Pace, the king's Latin secretary, who confided ironically to Wolsey that he was 'right sorry for the good service he was like to do the Church'. And whether through ambition, pragmatism or principle, or perhaps a combination of all three, Standish would ultimately embrace the impending change of religious course without demur, even becoming in 1533 one of the three bishops who consecrated Thomas Cranmer Archbishop of Canterbury.

Four years earlier, he was prepared to speak in muted tones on the queen's behalf, but not for long. And the same willingness to tow the new religious line was true eventually even of Robert Ridley, who also arrived at Blackfriars in the summer of 1529 to defend the queen's marriage. Altogether more outspoken in his support than Standish, he came of an old-established gentle family, which for some 300 years had had its seat in South Tyneside. The Ridleys, indeed, had been substantial figures in Northumbrian affairs for much of that time, and the well-known religious conservatism of the north had not been without effect on Robert Ridley's own Catholicism. At Cambridge and the Sorbonne he had proved an able scholar, and both at Cambridge and in London, where he served as Bishop Tunstall's chaplain, he would become a figure of some prominence in the trials of heretics, notwithstanding the fact that his own nephew, Nicholas – for whose education at Pembroke Hall and the Sorbonne he provided –

would be burned at the stake by Mary Tudor more than two decades later. Ordained either by John Fisher or Nicholas West of Ely, another of the queen's counsellors, the younger Ridley's fate was testament to the mounting tides that would sweep certain men on both sides of the religious divide from safety and conformity to the jagged rocks of moral defiance, though Robert Ridley's charted course would involve little more than the comparatively cosy exchange of one type of conformity for another, as he too, alongside his former patron Cuthbert Tunstall, came in due course to accept the royal supremacy without resistance.

In this particular respect, moreover, as well as in its more general features, Tunstall's career is of particular interest. For he was born at Hackforth near Bedale in North Yorkshire in 1474, an illegitimate son of Thomas Tunstall of Thurland Castle in Lancashire, and spent two years as a kitchen boy in the household of Sir Thomas Holland, perhaps at Lynn in Norfolk, before being admitted to Balliol College, Oxford, around 1491, where he studied mathematics, theology and law. Some five years later he became a scholar of the King's Hall, Cambridge, though he did not in fact receive a degree from either Oxford or Cambridge, graduating instead from the University of Padua in 1505 with doctorates in both civil and canon law, after studying under some of Europe's leading humanists and becoming proficient in both Greek and Hebrew. By this time Tunstall's reputation for learning was so exceptional that he would be singled out for particular praise by Erasmus and become William Warham's chancellor on 25 August 1511, shortly before his appointment as Rector of Harrow on the Hill, and subsequent appointment as a canon of Lincoln in 1514 and Archdeacon of Chester in 1515. And this, as it emerged, was only the end of the beginning, since he was frequently employed thereafter on diplomatic business: in 1515 at Flanders, where he established an intimate friendship with Erasmus and travelled alongside Sir Thomas More; in 1519 at Cologne; and during 1520–21 at Worms, which gave him a lasting sense of the significance held by the Lutheran movement and its literature. And in the meantime, he had been made Master of the Rolls in 1516, and subsequently Dean of Salisbury in 1521, after which he became Bishop of London by papal provision in 1522, and on 25 May 1523 Lord Keeper of the Privy Seal, in which capacity he negotiated with the Holy Roman Emperor Charles V after the Battle of Pavia, and helped to arrange the Peace of Cambrai in 1529.

By any standards, therefore, Tunstall's career had been a glittering one. But in spite of his presence as Catherine's advocate at Blackfriars, he too would join the king's ranks as the breach with Rome finally unfolded. He did so, it is true, with reservations and moderation, and without, as he saw it, any fundamental sacrifice of his Catholic principles. Yet during the reign of Edward VI, Tunstall would suffer, first, house arrest and then imprisonment in the Tower and deprivation of his bishopric at Durham – to which he had been appointed in February 1530 – for resisting the more radical religious policies of the new reign. And although reinstalled under Mary Tudor, he was prepared once again to resist a ruler on grounds of conscience, refusing on the one hand to take the oath of supremacy under Elizabeth I, or, like-wise, to participate in the consecration of the Anglican Matthew Parker as Archbishop of Canterbury. Indeed, though by then 85 years old, he suffered arrest, deprivation of his diocese in September 1559, and imprisonment at Lambeth Palace, where he died within a few weeks. As such, his moral fibre was never in doubt and, if circumstances had dictated otherwise, there seems little doubt that he, too, might have been prepared to face the rigours of the scaffold. But under Henry VIII his position had amounted only to passive obedience, in direct contrast to those others now ranged alongside him at Blackfriars who, on the self-same grounds of conscience, would ulti-mately wend their way to Tower Hill or Smithfield.

Tunstall's tight-lipped compliance would hold true for the vast major-ity of the episcopacy as the story of the breach with Rome unfolded with all its twists and turns, and its ripples and eddies carried people first one way and then another, sometimes washing them to shores that even they themselves could never have predicted. One-time keen conserva-tive Robert Ridley, for example, had actually been a significant influence upon Thomas Cranmer, who, in a letter of 1532 to the distinguished German theologian Johann Cochlaeus, freely acknowledged his debt. Cranmer regarded the conservative Ridley not only as his teacher but as a source of particular inspiration in philosophy, and this may explain why the man who eventually married Henry VIII to Anne Boleyn had himself, on some occasions, shown wavering degrees of loyalty both to the king and his schemes for the divorce. Certainly, this was the opinion of Granvelle, the Holy Roman Emperor's chancellor, who later declared how surprised he was at Cranmer's support for Anne Boleyn in 1533, since he had been at Ratisbon only the previous year and roundly criticised what the English king and his ministers were doing at the time. Plainly, in a situation of flux and turmoil individuals are apt to behave unpredictably, particularly when their own fortitude is less than guaranteed, and in such circumstances, the best safe haven is often the new consensus that finally emerges from pressure at the centre – in this case the remorseless influence of the king himself. Under such circumstances, Cranmer was perhaps only typical of a timid mind, lifted from the quietude of his Cambridge study to become, at a most crucial moment in his country's history, a man of affairs. At the defining period of his life, two reigns later, of course, he would pendulate much more widely still, only to find his mettle by the most roundabout of routes and emerge in his own right as a martyr to his persecutor's flames.

There was vacillation too for another member of Queen Catherine's legal team: John Clerk, Bishop of Bath and Wells, who had studied at Bologna, receiving a doctor's degree in law there, before becoming Dean of Windsor from 1519 to 1523. Certainly, there had been early hope at Blackfriars that he might display a forthrightness equal to John Fisher's, for on the day after Catherine's last appearance at the court he would come before it, intrepidly asserting, according to the Venetian ambassador, that to prevent the king from falling into mortal sin, both he and the Bishop of Rochester would defend the rights of the queen to the limit and demonstrate how she was his legitimate wife. Even more surprisingly, perhaps, both Clerk and Fisher would not only go on to present a writ of appeal against the tribunal itself, but reject its two judges as suspect. Yet only a few weeks after proceedings at Blackfriars had run their course, Clerk duly altered his tune, on the grounds that the revocation of the case to Rome had tied England's hands, and that, in consequence, the queen should not attempt to advance her claims further. While Fisher remained unwavering, both Clerk and Tunstall would try to dissuade her altogether from attempting to pursue her suit at Rome, after Wolsey had told the former of the danger to her were she to act thus. All this Clerk knew well, of course, just as he knew of the danger involved for him personally, as a result of which he declined to act further as Catherine's counsellor, opting instead for loyal service to her nemesis. Indeed, when the time came, he would not only keenly endorse the annulment but actually help Cranmer draft the 1534 Act of Supremacy.

Such, then, were the varied responses of Catherine's advisers to what would prove to be their failure in the fateful summer of 1529, though for one at least – Nicholas West, Bishop of Ely – the ultimate agonising choice would never in fact arrive, since his death at the age of 72 on 28 April 1533 came at a time before the king's claims to supremacy had hardened into relentless fact. Beforehand, however, he too had been no less torn than so many of his counterparts by the conflicting loyalties engendered by the royal divorce. Certainly, his pedigree of long service to the Crown was impeccable, for after his ordination and fellowship at Cambridge, which dated to 1486, he became chaplain to Henry VII and, from 1509, Dean of St George's Chapel, Windsor. Thereafter, as Bishop of Ely, which he became in 1515, he continued his long and successful association with the Crown as a diplomatist, which had had begun as early as 1502 through his friendship with Richard Foxe, Bishop of Durham, and encompassed among other things: visits to Emperor Maximilian I and George, Duke of Saxony; the negotiation of an important commercial treaty with Flanders in 1506; attempts to arrange marriages between Henry VIII's daughter Mary and the future Emperor Charles V, and between the king himself and Charles's sister Margaret; as well as numerous embassies to France and Scotland, relating most notably to the French peace treaties of 1518 and 1525 and the negotiations at the Field of Cloth of Gold in 1520. At other times too, equally significantly, he was employed on personal matters by Cardinal Wolsey, living like the cardinal himself, it seems, 'in greater splendour than any other prelate of his time, having more than a hundred servants' – though none of this would stop him ultimately from witnessing the queen's appeal to the pope when it was drawn up on 16 June 1529, and providing yet another example of the unpredictability of the allegiances now to unfold at Blackfriars.

For at least one of those present that summer, however, there was no hint of ambivalence or equivocation: a tall, fraily thin figure, of greatly dignified and scholarly bearing whom one probable eyewitness of the scene, George Cavendish, described as 'a very godly man who after suffered death … which was greatly lamented through all the universities of Christendom'. The individual cited by Cavendish was, of course, John Fisher, who, as we have seen, was to remark towards the end of his life that of all the controversies in which he had become embroiled – including his remorseless polemical battle with Martin Luther – none had cost him more effort than that involving the king's marriage. And those efforts would now not only reach their climax, but confirm in effect, once and for all, the full scale of both his opposition and the threat it represented: not least because his writings against Luther – as well as those refuting Jacques Lefèvre d'Étaples, in which he debunked the medieval cult of the Magdalene as unscriptural – had been extensive enough in their own right to establish him as one of the controversialists on the European scene in the 1520s. Between 1522 and 1527, when he indicated his intention to withdraw from such writings, he had expended well over half a million words on five volumes of Latin polemic: a tract against the humanist Velenius defending the historicity of the tradition associating the apostle Peter with Rome; three works against Luther himself, including the *Assertionis Lutheranae Confutatio* of 1523, which constituted the first comprehensive rebuttal of the German's teachings; and what can only be termed a blockbuster of some 220,000 words against the eucharistic doctrine of the Swiss reformer Oecolampadius, in 1527. And now, after two further pamphlets in English originating in keynote sermons at Paul's Cross – the first on the occasion of the burning of heretical books organised by Wolsey in 1521, the second, by royal command, on the abjuration of Robert Barnes in 1526 – he was set to supplement his leadership in English academic circles with what amounted, quite literally, to a 'life-or-death' mission on behalf of the sanctity of the royal marriage.

It was a measure of the moral stature already obtained by Fisher, of course, that when the king first began his quest for a divorce in the spring of 1527, almost his very first move had been to attempt to secure the support of the Bishop of Rochester, though as the controversy developed, Henry's early admiration for 'the saintliest bishop in Christendom' swiftly turned to venom, which, under the circumstances and in light of the man concerned, is hardly surprising. For when interrogated in the Tower in 1534, Fisher estimated that he had written no fewer than 'seven or eight' works in defence of the queen's cause, four of which are known to survive, along with the outline of a further two and broad hints about the content of another. Perhaps the most significant, *De Causa Matrimonii*, was in all likelihood smuggled out of England in the Spanish ambassador's diplomatic bag, and printed in Alcalá in 1530. And this book alone, along with a sheaf of letters that also still survives, leaves little doubt of a characteristically relentless campaign on their author's part. Certainly, Fisher's writings were praised by supporters of the queen as diverse as the Imperial ambassador, Chapuys, and theologians like Johann Cochlaeus and Heinrich Cornelius Agrippa. But perhaps the most telling indicator of both their quality and quantity is the simple fact that while the king's advisers expressed little but contempt for his contributions, they nevertheless wrote more refutations of his works than any other. Indeed, until the appearance in 1531 of *Gravissimae Censurae* – a book summarising the opinions of the European universities that had been prepared at the king's order in the latter part of the previous year – Fisher's output determined the entire direction of the controversy, and even as late as 1534, he would be regarded as the man to beat, with two refutations of his arguments published in that year alone, though by that time, as the *Gravissimae Censurae* had already effectively confirmed three years earlier, his adversaries had been reduced to the basest techniques of misrepresentation and special pleading. For on theoretical grounds at least – whether in the exegesis of the Hebrew, in the evaluation and collation of scriptural texts, in the interpretation of patristic and scholastic writers, or in the application of theological and philosophical concepts of law – there could be no doubt that the object of their attack had bested them on all fronts.

Yet the dilemmas of the summer of 1529 and the years that followed were not, of course, to be resolved by dispassionate discourse and impartial legal process, but by policy, self-interest and force. And when Fisher made his mark at Blackfriars, his brazen defiance could have only one long-term outcome. In any case, the proceedings of the legatine tribunal had been immediately and irretrievably marred by the queen's total refusal to co-operate, since she appeared in person only at the second and third sessions on 18 and 21 June, and only then to protest against the possibility of receiving a fair hearing in England and to lodge her appeal in Rome. Upon her first appearance, moreover, she protested vehemently against Wolsey's appointment as judge before withdrawing regally and declaring famously how 'I be no Englishwoman but a Spaniard born!', though it was for her second and final appearance that the plump figure, dressed in a gown of crimson velvet edged with sable, saved what was indubitably her most widely remembered performance. For with flagrant disregard for official procedure, she weaved her way with high drama through crowded benches and tables to fall on her knees before her husband, pleading to him not to dishonour her or disown their daughter, while he sat staring past her, making no comment when she had finished, or as she swept from the courtroom to the loud acclaim of the crowds outside.

After this Catherine made no further appearance. Nor was there any real need, however, for although proceedings had indeed been of dubious legality from the outset, John Fisher took up her cause – albeit unofficially in view of her appeal to Rome – with a boldness and eloquence that remains remarkable across the centuries. Certainly, Campeggio was shocked at the court's irregularities, consoling himself as best he might that 'in the house of a foreigner one cannot do all one wishes'. But the die was cast and the Bishop of Rochester, notwithstanding his own obsession with niceties, legal and otherwise, would not be reined in. For when the king saw fit, after his wife's departure, to refer to Wolsey's secret tribunal of May 1527 and to the support he had received from the episcopacy at that time, the scene was set for an explosive exchange recorded by George Cavendish:

> I moved you first my Lord of Canterbury [Henry declared], asking your licence, forasmuch as you were our metropolitan, to put this matter in question; and so I did of all you my lords [bishops] to the which ye have all granted by writing under all your seals, the which I have here to be showed.

But when Warham confirmed the king's claim, Fisher strenuously denied it, as Cavendish makes all too abundantly clear in his description of the archbishop's affirmation and the extraordinary exchange that resulted, in which the Bishop of Rochester not only stood firm against both his monarch and his ecclesiastical superior, but boldly implied that they were all but liars, reducing even the king himself to the lamest possible final word on the issue. Such is the significance of the altercation as, arguably, one of the most noteworthy in the entire history of England's breach with Rome that it is worth repeating in full:

> 'That is truth if it please your highmess,' quoth the Bishop of Canterbury,
> 'I doubt not but all my brethren here present here will affirm the same.'
>   'No, sir, not I,' quoth the Bishop of Rochester, 'ye have not my consent thereto.'

'No hath,' quoth the king, 'look here upon this, is not this your hand and seal?' And showed him the instrument with seals.

'No, forsooth, sire,' quoth the Bishop of Rochester, 'it is not my hand nor seal?'

'Yes, sir,' quoth he [i.e. Warham].

'That is not so,' quoth the Bishop of Rochester, 'for indeed you were in hand with me to have my hand and seal, as other of my lords had already done; but then I said to you, that I would never consent to no such act, for it were much against my conscience; nor my hand and seal should never be seen at any such instrument, God willing, with much more matter touching the same communication between us.'

'You say truth,' quoth the Bishop of Canterbury, 'such words ye said unto me; but at the last ye were fully persuaded that I should for you subscribe your name and put-to a seal myself, and ye would allow the same.'

'All which words and matter,' quoth the Bishop of Rochester, 'under your correction, my lord, and supportation of this noble audience, there is no thing more untrue.'

'Well, well,' quoth the king, 'it shall make no matter; we will not stand with you in argument herein, for you are but one man.'

Yet, to the king's infinite discomfort and displeasure, that one man was far from done. For on what is likely to have been only the following day, both Fisher and Dr Robert Ridley were this time sorely at odds with Wolsey over the alleged consummation of Catherine's marriage to Prince Arthur, and the cardinal's contention that 'no man could know the truth about the matter', which, according to Cavendish, Fisher rejected out of hand as follows:

'Yes,' quoth the Bishop of Rochester, '*Ego nosco veritatem* [I know the truth].'

'How know you the truth?' quoth my lord Cardinal.

'Forsooth my lord,' quoth he, '*Ego sum professor veritatis* [I myself am a professor of truth]; I know that God is truth itself, nor he never spake but truth; which said *quod deus coniunxit homo non separet* [whom God has joined together, let no man put asunder]. And forasmuch as this marriage was made and joined by God to a good intent, I say that I know the truth the which cannot be broken or loosed by the power of man upon no feigned occasion.'

The sting, of course, lay in the final phrase, 'upon no feigned occasion', confirming quite categorically that Fisher's recalcitrance the previous day was no fleeting aberration. On the contrary, this was only the beginning, as both the king and Wolsey no doubt fully appreciated, of an escalation of opposition that might lead they knew not where. For Dr Ridley too, emboldened no doubt by Fisher's example, took up the assault, focusing in his case upon the 'divers presumptions', i.e. depositions, cited by Wolsey, which were purported by the king's counsellors to demonstrate that his marriage had not been valid from the beginning. If so, the proponents of the divorce maintained, employing the semblance at least of a sound syllogism, the marriage was not joined by God and therefore unlawful, since God ordains nothing without 'just order'. But, as Ridley well knew, all depended upon the 'presumptions', which he proceeded to attack with a vigour not dissimilar to Fisher's own, declaring quite unapologetically how it was a shame, and greatly to the dishonour of everyone assembled, that any such presumptions should be alleged in open court, since they were to all good and honest men 'most detestable to be rehearsed'. Most reprehensible of all, of course, were those depositions collected by the government that concerned the details of what had occurred on the royal couple's wedding night. And though Ridley did not refer to them specifically, he left little doubt of his intentions after Wolsey vainly instructed him to treat these 'presumptions' with greater respect: 'No, no, my lord [declared the bishop], there belongeth no reverence to be given to these abominable presumptions, for an unrevent tale must be unreverently answered.'

The battle, then, had clearly been openly and fully joined in a way that raises a host of intriguing question marks against the power of Wolsey, and indeed the king himself, to intimidate unconditionally those they chose to target. Yet after the ringing crescendos of 21 and 22 June, there followed a subsequent six days of tedious technicalities and dull routine until Fisher once again breathed life into the faltering court. He was present at Blackfriars, in fact, on each session of which there is record, and on 28 June, at the fifth session, he delivered an impassioned oration, described by Campeggio's secretary, which struck like a thunderbolt and openly signalled his readiness from this point onwards for martyrdom. Nor was the date coincidental, since this was the eve of the nativity of John the Baptist, who had himself been put to death by King Herod.

Under the circumstances, the resulting speech could hardly have been more provocative, not only casting Henry in the role of one of the great biblical tyrants, but denying, at one and the same time, a frequently cited mainstay of the entire royal case: namely that the sin for which Herod had been upbraided by the Baptist was the identical offence of infringing Leviticus by marrying the wife (Herodias) of his own brother (Philip). On the contrary, Fisher maintained, there was a whole raft of technical reasons why the two cases were crucially different. And as a result, even five years before Fisher's arrival upon Tower Hill, it seems that he had crossed a Rubicon from which there could be no hope of return. Like many other martyrs of his kind, he had died, in effect, long before the moment of extinction actually arrived, achieving in the process, if his subsequent behaviour is any guide, a resignation and peace of mind that comes with acknowledgement of the inevitable and the certainty of ultimate victory and happiness beyond death. It was a state of being that brought with it too, of course, a profound sense of liberation and indeed exhilaration, representing a critical dilemma for a government not yet committed, or even aware of how to achieve, the wholesale eradication of dissent.

As Campeggio's secretary describes them, events at the fifth Blackfriars session unfolded as follows:

Yesterday the fifth audience was given. While the proceedings were going on as usual, owing to the queen's contumacy, the Bishop of Rochester made his appearance, and said, in an appropriate speech, that in a former audience he had heard the king's majesty discuss the cause, and testify before all that his only intention was to get justice done, and to relieve himself of the scruple that he had on his conscience, inviting both the judges and everyone else to throw some light on the investigation of the cause, because on this account he found his mind much distressed and perplexed. If on this offer and command of the king he [Fisher] did not come forward in public and manifest what he had discovered in this matter after two years most diligent study [he would be failing in his duty].

Therefore, both in order not to procure the damnation of his soul, and in order not to be unfaithful to the king, or to fail in doing the duty which he owed to the truth in a matter of such importance, he presented himself before their lordships to declare, to affirm, and with forcible reasons to demonstrate to them that this marriage of the king and the queen can be dissolved by no power, human or divine, and for this opinion he declared he would even lay down his life. He added that the Baptist in olden times regarded it as impossible to die more gloriously than in the cause of marriage, and that since it was not so holy at that time as it has now become by the shedding of Christ's blood, he could encourage himself more ardently, more effectually, and with greater confidence, to dare any great or extreme peril whatever. He used many other suitable words, and at the end presented a small book [*libellus*] which had been written by him.

Campeggio's secretary mentions, too, how Henry Standish then spoke, 'expressing nearly the same opinion, but with less polished eloquence and in briefer terms', as did another unnamed figure 'who alleged various arguments from the sacred canons, which were not very cogent'. Clearly, Fisher was already in a league of his own, and firmly established not only as the centrepiece of any further resistance but, more importantly still, as a loose cannon whose campaign against the divorce was barely under way.

This affair [the secretary concluded] was unexpected and unforeseen, and consequently has kept everyone in wonder. What he will do we shall see when the day comes. You already know what sort of man he is, and may imagine what is likely to happen.

Most worrying of all, however, was the simple inability of the Bishop of Rochester's protagonists to parry even partially the force of his arguments or the power of his rhetoric. For as the French ambassador, Du Bellay, who was also present, noted: 'A rather modest answer was made by the judges, that it was not his business to pronounce so decidedly in the matter as the cause was not committed to him.' And if Fisher's speeches could not be countered effectively, the small book he submitted at the time only added to the government's perplexity and the growing anger of the king himself.

Such *libelli* were not, in fact, uncommon. On the contrary, counsel on both sides regularly submitted statements of learned opinion to the legatine court – sometimes on points of canon law, and sometimes on the general issues – so that on 9 July, for example, eight such 'libels' would be presented on behalf of the king, and seven in support of the queen. Of these latter, two were from the Bishop of Ely (Nicholas West), two from the Bishop of London (Cuthbert Tunstall), one from Richard Gwent (a canonist and later Archdeacon of London) and two more from the Bishop of Rochester. But the treatise submitted by Fisher on 28 June carried with it particular potency. Consisting of about 16,000 words and entitled *Licitum fuisse*, it is divided into six axioms of unequal length, the first two of which alone are given detailed consideration in the surviving manuscript. The first and longest deals with the central question of whether or not marriage to a brother's widow was forbidden by divine law. The second encompasses the theory and practice of papal dispensations, while the remaining four briefly affirm that if the marriage was indeed dispensable and had in this case been dispensed appropriately, then Henry's union with Catherine had been properly arranged, contracted and sacramentally sealed, and was thus indissoluble. As might be expected, the document is framed in highly scholastic fashion, containing extensive biblical references, especially to the case of Thamar and the sons of Judah in Genesis 38, in which Judah had not only instructed his second son, Onan, to marry Thamar, the wife of his first son, Er, but also his third son, Shelah, after Onan had also died without offspring. But the upshot was another stinging broadside against the king's case, reducing the entire problem to a series of simple propositions and plain truths that sliced at a stroke through the mire of subtle distinctions and conflicting witness that had so far bedeviled the court – leaving the outraged king with but one alternative. For although he still clung vainly to the delusion that the court could not dare to reject his wishes ultimately, Fisher's resort to brass tacks would be fatal to the moral foundation of any favourable outcome unless effectively and immediately rebutted.

The man chosen for this unenviable task was Stephen Gardiner. Fifteen years younger than the man he was instructed to attack, Gardiner nevertheless boasted a brilliant career at Cambridge where he had distinguished himself in civil and canon law, becoming Master of Trinity Hall in 1525, before being entrusted with the ill-fated embassy to Rome of 1528, where, in the company of Edward Fox, he set out to browbeat the pope with an arrogance and insolence that few envoys have dared to emulate. Certainly, he was a man of razor tongue, and although we have no knowledge of his previous relations with John Fisher as chancellor of his university, the personal animosity with which he conducted his current errand on behalf of the king is striking. By now in Wolsey's service and soon to be the king's secretary, Gardiner had, no doubt, been fully briefed by Henry concerning the lines upon which the attack should proceed, but the result was a work that, while beginning reasonably enough perhaps, would amount overall to a diatribe of remarkable bitterness, written as if delivered by Henry himself, which Fisher was handed in manuscript form and duly annotated with margin notes, highlighted in italics in the lengthy opening passage from the introduction provided below.

Since in this matrimonial cause now to be investigated, or in the controversy now to be determined, we have attempted or designed nothing, on our own authority, which were unsuited to the office of a true Christian prince; but on the contrary have always had regard before everything to equity, justice and truth, and have everywhere held that the judgement of the Church was to be deferred to with great respect; relying upon our consciousness of this our innocence, we hoped, O judges, that we should have all the best men as supporters of our honour, our efforts and our purposes, and hardly thought that there might come forth anyone to disgrace such a dutiful mind as ours, show enmity to our virtue, and jealousy of our fame. If this was to be (and we are not ignorant how many things have deceived the wisest, even in regard to their own concerns, and to public affairs), yet we never supposed, O Judges, that the bishop of Rochester would take up before your tribunal that accusation against ourselves, which would rather befit the hatred, or better still the fury, of bad citizens, and a multitude seditiously roused, than his own virtue and dignity. Of a certainty, O Judges, we did unfold to this Rochester, and this already some months ago [**Fisher**: *nearly a year ago*], and more than once, how far we had been from purposely seeking out or rashly devising those reasons, which long before had engendered us in scruples of conscience, in regard to this illegitimate and incestuous marriage. Which reasons this very Rochester thus far then approved, and deemed so weighty and powerful, that unless we applied to the oracle of our most serene Lord [the pope], which he then thought it necessary to consult upon those matters, he did not believe that our former peace of mind could be restored to us. [**Fisher**: *I did not say so, but the cardinal would have been glad if I had said so*]. Now when this same our most holy Lord [the pope] (yet not without the advice and opinion of some of the most reverend cardinals of the apostolic see, and of other members of the Roman court, most eminent for their worthiness and erudition) had judged that these same reasons made the cause of our marriage so intricate and ambiguous, that only through the ruling of the best chosen and most discreet judges could it be treated and set forth according to its dignity and magnitude; and when he has, most in accordance with your deserts, entrusted it to you, O Judges, and to your scrupulousness to be wholly determined; and has sent thee here, O most reverend Campegius, for no other reason, to the great charges indeed of his Holiness, and to thy huge peril and travail through the dangers of so many things and ways; what shall we believe, O judges, to have come into the mind of this Rochester, or by what spirit shall we think he has been led, to come here so impudently and so much out of season [**Fisher**: *I was obliged to this by the protestation of the king and cardinal*], in order to declare his own personal view of the matter, now at length after so many months, and even here before such a great and illustrious assembly as that of your court.

It had been of constancy on his part, not to ascribe now at last in public those scruples of conscience, which he had once thought we were right in harbouring, to mere commonplaces (as he calls them), to subtleties only probable in appearance, and other gilded persuasions of rhetoricians. It had been of Christian piety (if indeed by study of many opinions he had succeeded in ascertaining thoroughly what in this cause was just, what true, what lawful), to have reminded us of it again and again in private, and not to proclaim with such huge self-confidence, to the great blemishing of our conscience; it had been of his duty, of his faith and of his loyalty (which every good citizen owes to his king) to protect and vindicate our conscience from the calumnies of evil men; and since he saw, by tokens in no wise obscure, our conscience labour and fluctuate, to hasten to its help by all possible means; it had been of pious reverence and observance which he owes to the supreme Pontiff, when the latter had decreed that this cause was exceedingly intricate, and especially necessary to the preservation of this our realm, so that he could weigh everything by yourselves judging supremely, to acquiesce in his decision, rather than publicly to charge his Holiness with levity, as if the truth of the cause he had committed to you for investigation, and was so obvious, easy, plain, and open, that it would be foolish to call into question. [**Fisher**: *It is not obvious to all, but only to those who are compelled to study it*].

Lastly it had been of wisdom and modesty, when you had commenced in the cause assigned to you according to the most ample authority of your jurisdiction, to allow to you a free order of trial, and not to prescribe to you a so to say new formula for judging, and to bring forward of his own authority before your sentence.

Significantly, of course, the fulsome reference to 'pious reverence and observance' owed to the pope is a telling reflection of the king's ongoing allegiance to the Holy See, just as his unwavering respect for the legatine court itself leaves little doubt, at this stage, of his continued confidence in the likelihood of a favourable judgement. Nor, of course, is it any less plain from the surprisingly clumsy reference to 'this illegitimate and incestuous marriage', that the king had already pre-judged the outcome of the tribunal, notwithstanding the implied subservience of his supposedly 'dutiful mind' to the eventual verdict of its judges. But in a number of respects the points made against Fisher up to this point do indeed appear to carry a certain degree of force. For he had indeed, it might well be argued, exceeded his rightful brief at a number of levels, and in doing so behaved with an outspoken belligerence that not only transgressed, but actually shattered conventional standards of respect, both to the Crown and the pope. He had succumbed, it seems, to the kind of rush of blood that had overcome him in his dealings with Richard Croke, but now he had done so with both Wolsey, and far more importantly still, the king himself, rendering the references to his 'loyalty' and 'the preservation of this our realm' especially noteworthy. If, moreover, Henry had indeed pre-judged the case, the argument that Fisher had also preempted proceedings was far from groundless either, since the pronouncement of a verdict remained, of course, the judges' prerogative. Even Fisher's margin comments, for that matter, exhibit a characteristic testiness that serves, arguably, to reinforce the very claims against him.

Yet from this point onwards, the quickness and depth of the king's anger would dwarf even Fisher's own. For, after a comparatively moderate beginning, Gardiner's invective against Fisher on the king's behalf assumed the following far more vitriolic turn:

> But it is in vain that we require those things of this bishop, O Judges, whose breast and heart are so filled and stirred up by two most evil advisers, namely a certain immoderate arrogance, and a too self-confident temerity. (**Fisher**: *Arrogance – temerity*). For else whence did these words proceed, O Judges, that he would by sound and unanswerable arguments, at once place before your eyes, and those of all men, the naked truth of this cause; and that indeed he would defend it constantly, and defend it indeed as far as the stake (**Fisher**: *I said nothing of that*); and that he had now a juster cause, in withstanding the dissolution of this marriage than Saint John the Baptist had once had against Herod. O voice devoid of all modesty and gravity! (**Fisher**: *What more did I attest than the cardinal who* [affirmed] *he would be burnt or torn limb from limb rather than act contrary to justice?*) As if indeed, alone of all men, Rochester was gifted with discernment, and alone had investigated and illuminated the truth of this case.
>
> And what need was there for him to declare himself ready to endure fire and flame for that reason, when such manifest tokens gave him evident proof of our clemency and our zeal to protect, and not oppress, truth. And lastly how unjust is that comparison, by which he labours to couple together his cause and that of the holy Baptist. Unless perhaps he has conceived that opinion of ourselves, that apparently we were somehow playing the Herod, or daring some crime akin to the crime of Herod. To be sure, O Judges, never did Herod's impiety bear a pleasing aspect for us; and certainly we did learn from the rule of the Gospel and the voice of the Baptist that this in him was to be condemned, that he had taken to his wife the sister of his brother. But whichever of the two things Rochester may think in regard to us, we were always far removed from Herod's cruelty. If ever we proceeded with any severity against those who appeared to look upon this divorce with little favour, and did not rather lovingly draw them to ourselves with the highest favours, in proportion to their virtues, let Rochester come, and justly cast Herod's tyranny in our teeth. But let this man's evil-speaking against us his prince, be his own punishment. Yet, O Judges, lest you might be steeped in darkness, and lest your judgement might be hindered by his

assertion, uttered with great haughtiness, that he has now at last found the very truth, and plucked it out of darkness, it behoves us to examine this bragging and more than thrasonical pomposity of words.

Even in light of the stylistic conventions of the time, which, particularly in polemical works, could often exhibit a level of personal insult jarring to modern readers, Gardiner's onslaught was strong medicine, especially when it was composed to be passed off as the king's own. Certainly, Henry approved it and may even have edited it, which would explain not only the careless reference to his 'illegitmate and incestuous marriage' but also the technically unsound reference to Herod's marriage, since the issue there had actually been the prior divorce of Herod's wife, Herodias, from his half-brother Philip, which was deemed contrary to Jewish law. In any event, the danger for Fisher was now manifest and, if anything, heightened not only by his own unwillingness to retreat or compromise on theoretical grounds, but by his apparent inability to consider how his objections might have been expressed less challengingly. How, for example, he could suggest in his margin notes that he 'did not understand' why the king might interpret his comments as an attempt to place him on the same plain as Herod, is as hard to understand as some of his other quibbles concerning certain of Gardiner's slips elsewhere. The Bishop of Rochester's comments smack at times, indeed, of the schoolmaster with his pupil, and, ironically enough, confirm in part what was actually the most telling of all the criticisms directed against him, namely, that in pursuing the truth, he could lose sight of the sensibilities of those with whom he was dealing and slip into the very kind of 'thrasonical pomposity of words' cited so pompously by Gardiner himself. It was, of course, the perennial pitfall of the academic. But, if harmless enough in the lecture hall, at the centre of a budding political crisis, it could hardly have been more provocative, especially when the arguments put forward were, indeed, infuriatingly 'sound and unanswerable'.

For when Gardiner turned to a defence of the king's case, he could only rehearse the old justifications that were as familiar as they were flawed. Once more the validity of the dispensation was questioned on the grounds that the pope had been misled, since there was, in fact, no danger of war between England and Spain to justify the marriage in the way that had been proposed at the time. Likewise, the tired old contentions that

Henry had been too young to make a responsible decision when first betrothed were merely rehashed and the relevant texts in Leviticus and Deuteronomy pored over yet again with no fresh insights. Nor were the king's other counsellors able to stage even remotely convincing minor hits upon Fisher's position, as his mastery of biblical exegesis allowed him not only to counter their every move, but even to engage in what appears, on occasion, to have come very close to outright mockery, as the desperation of his adversaries became more apparent. When they argued, for example, that the marriage forbidden by Leviticus must have been intrinsically immoral, since it was described by Moses as an 'abomination', Fisher proceeded to point out that many things proscribed in Leviticus were nevertheless widely practised among Christians, including transvestism, which was permitted in plays, and the eating of eels. And this was not all. For Fisher also went so far as to examine the genealogy of Christ himself, alluding to the discrepancy between Matthew and Luke over the identity of Joseph's father, and concluding that it could be resolved if his mother had married two brothers under the injunction of Deuteronomy, making one his natural, and the other his legal, father.

Several months before the commencement of the tribunal, however, rumours had reached Fisher that the scholar who had actually taught him the rudiments of Hebrew had discovered something new in that language that might render invaluable assistance to the king's case. According to Robert Wakefield himself, he had indeed instructed Fisher 'about eighteen years ago', and we learn of his 'discovery' from a letter written by the bishop to a certain correspondent named 'Paul', who had been shaken, it seems, by a report that Wakefield's revelation was so crucial that it had caused all the bishops previously opposed to the king's wishes to change course and swing into line behind him. For Wakefield had simply denied, as we have seen, that the Hebrew text of Deuteronomy actually prescribed marriage between a widow and the brother of her first husband at all. Instead, he maintained, the true signification of the relevant Hebrew word was any near, male relative, i.e. 'cousin' in the sixteenth-century sense. As such, both the Septuagint and Vulgate versions of the Bible were in error and, if so, the doubt thrown on the Levitical prohibition to the king's marriage was at once lifted, since the prohibition in Leviticus now became a qualification on the text of Deuteronomy, rather than the latter an exception to the former. Clearly, this was a line of reasoning that Fisher could not ignore, though he assured 'Paul' at the time that he could see nothing of substance in the Hebrew to support the king's case, before rapidly extemporising a reply to Wakefield, which was eventually written up and expanded for presentation at Blackfriars in what became a verbal scholastic disputation before the court.

Once again, therefore, the bishop would foil his opponents convincingly, taking issue with Wakefield on several points, not the least of which was the tactlessness of his suggestion, especially when delivered before a gathering containing laymen, that the Vulgate contained errors. Might this not, he argued, undermine their faith in it, and thus the very Church that had endorsed it? But if indiscretion and, by implication, arrogance on Wakefield's part would seem a weak card to be played by a man soon to be accused of those very weaknesses himself, at this point at least, and in these particular circumstances, the ploy was undoubtedly an effective one when the two legates sitting in judgement were all too painfully aware themselves of the chaos likely to ensue within the Church should the reliability of the Vulgate be thus undermined. And Fisher, in any case, had other, far more effective tricks to play. He was hampered, of course, by the fact that Wakefield had taught him Hebrew initially and was not averse to reminding him of that fact. But in consequence, he steered clear of philology, and pointed out with no less effectiveness that the true meaning of Deuteronomy 25:5 was to be determined by interpreting it in the light of scriptural references elsewhere, all of which appeared to endorse it, as indeed did the writings of the various patristic authorities on the subject. It was unimaginable, after all, that the genealogies of Christ given by Matthew and Luke could not be reconciled on the issue of Joseph's parentage, and there was, in any case, the added consideration that the custom codified in Deuteronomy had actually been prevalent before the time of Moses: a consideration that he had gleaned from his own extensive knowledge of the Cabbala.

If not a killing blow in its own right to Wakefield's contention, therefore, Fisher had clearly done enough to trump the one potential ace available to his enemies and to carry the day in a way that he would continue to do throughout the summer of 1529, as the proceedings at Blackfriars ground out their hugely frustrating course for the king. Yet with every victory came further charges of arrogance, so that in little over a year, senior churchmen other than Gardiner were also shuffling uneasily at their colleague's behaviour. By December 1530, indeed, Archbishop Warham, Bishop Edward Lee of York, John Stokesley, Bishop of London, and Richard Fox, Bishop of Winchester, would all be urging Fisher to withdraw his writings in support of the queen, and objecting when told that the matter was too clear to warrant such action. Only one month later, the Imperial ambassador, Chapuys, would note how Fisher had finished revising a further book – probably an expanded version of his opinions stated earlier in court – which by August had been published in Spain, albeit, as Chapuys duly noted, without the permission of the author himself. Many thought, wrote the ambassador, that the bishop would go in fear of the king's displeasure, but in fact he seemed indifferent to what Henry might think or plan – so much so, indeed, that when questioned in the Tower, he could not, as we have seen, even remember how many books or tracts he had written in the queen's defence.

Nor, when questioned at that time, did he have any apparent notion of either the number of copies involved or the whereabouts of their circulation:

> I do not know, nor was I very careful about them except for the last two, which went to the heart of the matter ... I never sent them or any copies of them out of the country, nor consented to this being done.

Though no doubt truthful, this was nevertheless naivety of a truly staggering order. For Chapuys had certainly gained access to them and was steadily forwarding the results to Dr Pierre Ortiz, the emperor's representative in Rome, adding a whole new layer of significance and danger to their content, both for the king and, for that matter, Fisher himself. For from the time of his arrival in England in October 1529, Chapuys had in fact quickly assumed an organising role in opposition to the divorce that Fisher himself never sought. One of the bishop's main problems, indeed – and one of the reasons for the scale of the threat he presented, ironically enough – was that he never thought sufficiently politically. On the contrary, the divorce was from his perspective purely a matter of principle founded on strict logic, its broader, more practical ramifications a matter wholly for others: all of which compounded his status as a disconcertingly loose cannon and the most convenient of tools for those, especially abroad, who sought to exploit his talents and status for their own purposes.

Early in 1530, therefore, Chapuys was reporting to his Imperial master, Charles V, how he had dispatched a treatise by Fisher, and that the bishop had recently completed another, which Queen Catherine had ordered him to pass on. The two works concerned can probably be identified with *Licitum Fuisse* and *De Causa Matrimonii*, and significantly enough, Chapuys also confided how Fisher was afraid to be identified as the latter's author, though by December, the ambassador had nevertheless sent forward a further volume, *Brevis Apologia*, which had been written in response to the government's own *Gravissimae Censurae*. Consisting of some 60,000 words, the *Brevis Apologia* was, moreover, in at least one respect, arguably the most significant of all Fisher's treatises on the subject. For although it was never published, it represented a hardening of the bishop's position by contending, in accordance with Hesychias, that the Levitical prohibition was directed not so much against unlawful marriage as illicit sexual intercourse. If so, the validity of the king's marriage was beyond all further question. Equally significant, moreover, is the tone of the *Apologia*, since there is a very specific failure to remark upon the supposed good faith underlying Henry's concerns. For hitherto, Fisher's writings had been written on the clear assumption that both the king and his advocates were engaging in a dispassionate quest for truth, but now there are no such concessions on the bishop's part. On the contrary, the persistent use of the term *hi doctissimi* – 'these most learned doctors' – to describe the authors of the *Censurae* smacks of sarcasm, and, as he exposes one blatant misrepresentation after another, he now declares himself astonished at their outright dishonesty:

> Blessed Jesus, what sort of conscience do these learned fellows have, who so grievously mutilate and distort the sayings of so weighty an author [Hesychius] in a matter of such importance, in order to establish [i.e. support] their error – to use no stronger term for it – any way they can.

More portentously still, there was also the following statement: 'These most learned fellows do not seem to care how narrowly they restrict papal authority as long as they can secure a divorce.'

Even by this point, therefore, Fisher's defence of the marriage was already merging into the stand for the papal primacy that was eventually to bring him to the scaffold. And it was small wonder, of course, that not only Henry's government, but that of his successor too, would progressively come to perceive Fisher's writings with such concern. In April 1531, Dr Ortiz wrote that he had received two manuscripts different from the version of *De Causa Matrimonii* published in Spain, indicating the scale of the book's proliferation, and the records of Fisher's eventual interrogations in the Tower leave no doubt at all of the grave suspicions engendered by his close association with Chapuys. By that time, indeed, Fisher's notoriety in government circles, and especially with Thomas Cromwell, was such that almost any 'seditious' work might be attributed by him, including the so-called *Parasæve*, whose author claimed to have spent time studying in Paris, and which could only have been written at a time when the bishop was actually under house arrest at Lambeth.

Nor was it any coincidence that Fisher's early biographer should have related how:

> It was once told me by a reverend father that was Dean of Rochester many years together, named Mr Phillips, that on a time in the days of King Edward VI when certain commissioners were coming towards him to search his house for books, he for fear burned a large volume which this holy bishop [i.e. Fisher] had compiled containing in it the whole story and matter of the divorce; which volume he gave him with his own hand a little before his trouble.

Plainly, the bishop's influence was to last well beyond the grave, and it was a testament to his lasting influence, too, that in the reign of Queen Mary, Nicholas Harpsfield would employ Fisher's reply to the universities in his *Treatise on the Pretended Divorce of King Henry VIII from Catherine of Aragon*. Yet the fruits of his tenacity still amounted to little more than a relentless beating of the air in the summer of 1529 when he was staging his bravest and most remarkably overt resistance of all. For even as his scathing broadsides continued to hit home at Blackfriars, far-off developments in Europe of which he knew nothing had already been assuming a decisive significance all of their own.

As early as 27 July the struggles at the legatine court had become bogged down in technicalities, but by that time events in London were in any case irrelevant. For in June, Imperial forces had crushed the French at Landriano and, on 13 July, the pope duly agreed to the Treaty of Barcelona, which pledged him for the foreseeable future to side with Charles. Unbeknown to the participants at Blackfriars, moreover, the pope had also, in yielding to the emperor's pressure, annulled the legatine commission and summoned Henry to appear before the Rota in Rome. And though news did not reach England for some time, the situation was already dire enough even without such a thunderbolt, since on 31 July, only ten days before the final decision that Henry expected, Campeggio declared that the court would follow the Roman calendar and adjourn for the vacation, which meant that there would be no further proceedings until October.

With this announcement, not surprisingly, there was outrage and tumult in the court. 'By the mass,' thundered the beetle-browed Duke of Suffolk, 'it was never merry in England whilst we had cardinals amongst us,' whereupon Wolsey smartly reminded the fuming peer of the help that he had been given at the time of his marriage to the king's sister. 'If I, a simple cardinal, had not been,' retorted Wolsey loudly, 'you should have had at this present time no head upon your shoulders wherein you should have had a tongue to make any such report in despite of us!' Yet the power of the cardinal's language was not matched by the strength of his position, since the king had suffered a shattering blow and duly retired to Waltham Abbey to nurse his wrath and ponder all the hard things that Anne Boleyn and her grasping tribe of relatives would now be sure to utter against his minister. For although Henry's personal interventions had continually undermined Wolsey's efforts, it was, of course, the latter who would inevitably carry the blame.

By the time that the Franco-Imperial Peace of Cambrai was signed on 3 August, Henry's patience was already terminally exhausted and so, in effect, was the cardinal's primacy. Within a month, indeed, this great potentate of Church and State, the once unchallenged master of all he surveyed, whom Cavendish would call 'the haughtiest man alive', was teetering on the brink and Anne Boleyn and the faction around her were exercising all their influence to lever him over the edge. And surely enough, on 9 October 1529, Wolsey was finally charged under the Statute of Praemunire of 1393 on the grounds that he had used his ecclesiastical authority to impinge upon the legal jurisdiction of the Crown. The charge, of course, was purely a pretext and a smokescreen, since Wolsey's only real offence was failure to satisfy the caprice of his sovereign. But one week later he was nonetheless stripped of his Lord Chancellor's office and made to deliver up the Great Seal, before surrendering York Place and most of his other property in a desperate last attempt to placate the king, who had relied so heavily for so long on his chief minister's resourcefulness, only to scupper his stratagems and then proceed to spurn him for failure.

For a Bill of Attainder was indeed brought against the stricken cardinal on 3 November, and thereafter, with one of those rich ironies that are so common in history, York Place was swiftly renamed Whitehall and handed over to Anne Boleyn by an elated Henry for use as her personal residence. Soon after the former occupant had made his exit, moreover, Anne was brought in secret to view the fine tapestries and plate of her new dwelling. Thrilled by the splendour of it all, now she would have her own court and truly be queen in all but name. Accordingly, great changes were put in hand to enlarge the palace and satisfy her fastidious requirements, as neighbouring houses were compulsorily acquired to extend the site and make room for gardens. 'All this has been done,' reported the Imperial ambassador, 'to please the lady, who likes better that the king should stay in Whitehall than anywhere else, as there is no lodging in it for the Queen.' And in the meantime, the queen herself, by contrast, had been cast once and for all into marital and political limbo.

7

ANGER, PORTENTS, POTIONS, GUNFIRE

And therefore considering the manner of this dealing, it putteth me in remembrance of a fable, how the axe that lacked a handle came on a time to a wood and making his moan to the great trees how that for lack of a handle to work withal he was fain to sit idle, he therefore desired of them to grant him a young small tree whereof he shaped himself a handle, and being made at last a perfect axe in all parts, he fell to work and so laboured in the wood that in the process of time he left neither great tree nor small standing.

Words attributed to John Fisher at the meeting of Convocation in November 1529.

Not long before the Duke of Suffolk's brawny fist had smitten the table at Blackfriars in a despairing act of brute frustration at the legatine court's outcome, Elizabeth Barton delivered an oracle that not only mentioned him by name but incorporated part of the very expression he had bellowed at the time while delivering his final verdict on the cardinal whom he had always despised. Preserved in the Act of Attainder that was to condemn her, Barton's pronouncement was allegedly gleaned from the writings of Dom Edward Bocking and another Benedictine monk, Dom John Dering, and told of how 'it should never be merry in England' until a root with three branches was plucked up and destroyed. The first branch, unsurprisingly enough, was Wolsey, but the other two were none other than the Dukes of Norfolk and Suffolk who, along with Anne Boleyn's father, the Earl of Wiltshire, now took up the reins of government, wholly devoid of fresh approaches, let alone novel solutions, to their royal master's marital dilemma. In the background lay the new Lord Chancellor, Sir Thomas More, a man of altogether more prodigious talents, but one who had taken office only on the condition that, as the king himself put it, he should not be placed in either 'ruffle or trouble' of his conscience regarding the divorce. And the result was an administration that for the next two years drifted aimlessly between random acts of intimidation against the clergy, largely engineered by the king himself, and equally forlorn attempts at moral and political pressure upon the papacy. As all hopes of progress faltered, moreover, so the king's anger increasingly consumed him. 'Wolsey was a better man than any of you,' he was soon reminding his new right-hand men, as their policies proved no more watertight than the leaky roof of the shabby dwelling at York where the cardinal himself now resided, 'wrapped', as he put it, 'in misery and need on every side, not knowing where to be succoured or relieved'.

Now largely thrown back upon his own resources, therefore, the king's main concern initially extended little further than the mere semblance of action, and since he could not be seen to be idle, Parliament was promptly summoned to give vent, as he hoped, to what the London lawyer, anticler-ical MP and chronicler Edward Hall described as 'the griefs wherewith the spirituality had before time grievously oppressed them'. But if England's aggrieved ruler was wishing to unleash a slavering parliamentary hound in pursuit of the clergy and thereby intimidate the Bishop of Rome into submission, then all that he had to hand, for the present at least, was a largely toothless puppy, since the much-vaunted raging anticlericalism of what would become known as the 'Reformation Parliament' was far from evident in its first session. And the reason was apparent. For unlike the later sessions that ran on ultimately until 1536, the 310 MPs arriving in November 1529 had been largely elected without exceptional inter-ference from the Crown, with the consequence that, in spite of strong language and a measure of intemperate bluster, only three of the twenty-six acts passed in the subsequent six weeks actually involved criticism of ecclesiastical abuses, and even then as no more than a comparatively low priority, so that when the Mercers' Company of London complained of probate and mortuary fees exacted by the clergy, it did so only as the fifth of a five-point programme otherwise concerned with trade. The other item of legislation, meanwhile, addressed the problem of clerical non-residence and pluralism, but even here, for many MPs, the target is likely to have been not to so much the clergy in general as Thomas Wolsey in particular. For Parliament had been called, after all, with the express intention of killing two birds with one stone – the largest of which was the fallen cardinal, who was now to be stripped of his former glory by Act of Attainder, on grounds of forty-four charges, which were deemed, nevertheless, to be 'but a few in comparison of all his enormities, excuses and trespasses against Your Grace's laws'.

Only an hour or so before Parliament opened on 3 November Henry read a pleading letter that Wolsey had written with his 'rude and trembling hand', and then stood by impassively as his subjects tore into the cardinal's flesh with all the pent-up fury of almost two decades' dissatisfaction. Even the elegance of Sir Thomas More's opening oration did little to lessen its cutting impact. Presenting a travesty of the parable of the Good Shepherd, the normally accommodating Lord Chancellor now displayed his own set of finely filed teeth. The king, he said, like a good shepherd had seen the need for reform and just as any great flock contained creatures that were 'rotten or faulty', so he had rightly seen fit to cast out the 'great wether which is of late fallen, as you all know'. Wolsey, the new chancellor continued, had 'so craftily, so scabbedly, yea, and so untruly juggled with the King' that men must surely think he was either unable to see his wrongdoing or had counted on his master's ignorance. But, More concluded, 'he was deceived, for his Grace's sight was so quick and penetrable that he saw him, yea and saw through him'. Not only saw through him, moreover, but now looked on blankly into the deep blue horizon – much as he had done at Blackfriars when his wife confronted him – as his former favourite was systematically accused of making wrongful appointments to benefices, pillaging monastic foundations, depriving them of free elections and impeding bishops in their attempts to stamp out heresy.

Nor was there any flicker of defence when the king's sometime confidant was accused of embezzling the goods of his predecessors in the archbishopric of York as well as the sees of Lincoln, Durham and Winchester. He had, it was said, concluded treaties with both the pope and the King of France, as well as the Duke of Ferrara, without Henry's authority, and in his correspondence with foreigners he had used the expression the 'King and I', demonstrating that 'he used himself more like a fellow to Your Highness than like a subject' – something that was also confirmed by the appearance of a cardinal's hat on the coinage of the realm. He had even, it seems, endangered the king's health. For, knowing that he had 'the foul and contagious disease of the great pox broken out upon him in divers places of his body', he nevertheless 'came daily to Your Grace, rowning in your ear and blowing upon your most noble Grace with his perilous and infective breath'. And while the charges mounted, the king continued to lift not a finger to save the man who, with supreme irony, was now becoming, from some appearances, the very first martyr of the royal divorce. Accused of withholding ambassadorial letters to his sovereign, of granting himself licences to export grain for personal profit, of stifling debate on the king's council, and of interfering with the decisions of Common Law judges, he received no glimmer of sympathy. Equally, when spiteful reference was made to his former mistress, Joan Lark – 'which woman the said lord cardinal kept, and had with her two children' – there was no attempt to mitigate the onslaught. On the contrary, the articles were presented to the king on 1 December 1529 and thereafter sent, without amendment, directly to the Commons.

Wolsey had therefore, it seems, exploited and extorted on all fronts, and now he would be left to face the music almost wholly alone, though not entirely. For at least his rising servant, Thomas Cromwell, was prepared to offer sustained defence on his master's behalf as the newly elected MP for Taunton. Indeed, to every charge levelled, said George Cavendish, Cromwell 'was ever ready furnished with a sufficient answer, so that at length, for his honest behaviour in his master's cause, he grew into such estimation in every man's opinion' and 'was of all men greatly commended'. Even this, however, was little more than cupboard love. For, as Cavendish recognised, such a show of loyalty, when applied with the correct balance of professed loyalty and carefully crafted moderation, could at least be guaranteed to raise a principled profile among his peers without risking a rather less self-sacrificing head. Besides which, there was the far more pressing worry still that were the cardinal to fall, the prospects for his retainers were far from certain. So when Cavendish eventually found Cromwell weeping copious tears at Esher with a prayer book in his hands – 'which', said Cavendish, 'had been a strange sight in him afore' – the truth was soon forthcoming. 'Why Mr Cromwell,' said the gentleman usher, 'what meaneth this dole. Is my lord in any danger?' But Cromwell's main concern remained Cromwell, and the future ramifications of his employer's fall for him personally, especially within those more elite circles he had already set his eye upon. 'I am like to lose all that I have ever laboured for,' he confessed, since, he feared, he was already 'disdained for his master's sake' among the high and mighty, and an 'evil name, once gotten', was not to be 'lightly put away'.

Yet while Wolsey's former minion feared for his future prospects, John Fisher, by contrast, seemed further intent upon flagrantly wrecking his own. He had been summoned to both Parliament and Convocation in August 1529, and was now intent from the outset, it seems, to take up where he had left off at Blackfriars, notwithstanding the comparative moderation of the anticlerical legislation put forward by the House of Commons. For while limited in scope, Fisher appreciated all too acutely that the bills dealing with pluralism, non-residence, and probate and mortuary fees nevertheless represented an encroachment upon what had hitherto been exclusively ecclesiastical territory, and, true to character, he duly delivered a speech to the Upper House, which, according to the account of his anonymous early biographer, took no prisoners, as he now 'stepped up among the other lords and said in effect the followeth':

> My lords, I pray you for God's sake, consider what bills are here daily preferred from the Commons. What the same may sound in some of your ears I cannot tell, but in my ears they sound all to this effect, that our holy mother the Church being left unto us by the great liberality and diligence of our forefathers in most perfect and peaceable freedom, shall now by us be brought into servile thraldom like a bondmaid, or rather by little and little to be clean banished and driven out of our confines and dwelling places. For else to what end should all this importunate and injurious language from the Commons tend? What strange words be here uttered, not to be heard of any Christian ears and unworthy to be spoken in the hearing of Christian princes? For they say that bishops and their officials, abbots, priests and others of the clergy are covetous, ravenous, insatiable, idle, cruel, and so forth. What? Are all of this sort, or is there any of these abuses that the clergy seek not to extirpate and destroy? Be there not laws already provided by them against such and many more disasters? Are not books full of them to be read of

such as list to read them if they were executed? But, my lords, beware of yourselves and your country, nay, beware the liberty of our mother the Church. Luther, one of the most cruel enemies to the faith that ever was, is at hand, and the common people study for novelties and with good will hear what can be said in favour of heresy. What success is there to be hoped for in these attempts other than such as our neighbours have already tasted, whose harms may be a good warning to us? Remember with yourselves what these sects and divisions have wrought among the Bohemians and Germans, who, besides an innumerable number of mischiefs fallen among them, have almost lost their ancient and catholic faith. And what by the snares of John Huss and after him of Martin Luther (whom they reverence like a prophet) they have almost excluded themselves from – the unity of Christ's Holy Church. These men now among us seem to reprove the life and doings of the clergy, but after such a sort as they endeavour to bring them into contempt and hatred of the laity. And so finding fault with other men's manners, whom they have no authority to correct, omit and forget their own, which is far worse and much more out of order than the other … Wherefore I will tell you, my lords, plainly what I think. Except ye resist manfully by your authorities this violent heap of mischief offered by the Commons, ye shall shortly see all obedience withdrawn from the clergy and after from yourselves. Whereupon will ensue the utter ruin and danger of the Christian faith, and in place of it (that which is likely to follow) the most wicked and tyrannical government of the Turks. For ye shall find that all these mischiefs among them riseth only through lack of faith.

Once again, Fisher had excelled himself, both in bravery and insensitivity, as well as foresight and folly. Rigorously uncovering the logic of events, much of what he predicted would indeed come to pass. But the reproof of the Duke of Norfolk that followed, 'half merrily and half angrily', nevertheless, went to the root not only of the bishop's greatness but also his human weakness: 'I wis [know], my lord, it is many times seen that the greatest clerks be not always the greatest men.' And almost in confirmation of his adversary's point, Fisher could not, of course, resist the final word. For to Norfolk's rebuke, we are told, 'he answered merrily again and said that he could not remember any fools in his time that had proved great clerks'.

Nor was it only Norfolk that Fisher had stirred. On the contrary, as the chronicler Edward Hall makes abundantly clear, the MPs that had been the butt of the bishop's comments were, if anything, far more outraged still. And Hall, of course, as an eyewitness to events, was not only in the finest of positions to tell, but spared no detail in describing the response of his peers to the bishop's words. For, as he relates:

> When these words were reported to the Commons of the nether house, that the bishop should say that their doings were for lack of faith, they took the matter grievously, for they imagined that the bishop esteemed them as heretics, and so by his slanderous words would have persuaded the temporal lords to have restrained their consent from the said two bills which they before had passed as you have heard before.
>
> Wherefore the Commons after long debate determined to send the speaker of the Parliament to the king's highness with grievous complaint against the Bishop of Rochester, and so on a day when the king was at leisure, Thomas Audley the speaker for the Commons and thirty of the chief of the Common House came to the king's presence in his palace at Westminster, which before was called York Place, and there very eloquently declared what a dishonour to the king and the realm it was to say that they which were elected for the wisest men of all the shires, cities and boroughs within the realm of England should be declared in so noble and open presence to lack faith, which was equivalent to say that they were infidels and no Christians, as ill as Turks or Saracens, so that what pain or study soever they took for the commonwealth, or what acts or laws soever they made or established, should be taken as laws made by paynims and heathen people, and not worthy to be kept by Christian men: wherefore he most humbly sought the king's highness to call the said bishop before him and to cause him to speak more discreetly of such a number as was in the Common House.

Under the circumstances, the call for greater discretion was hardly misplaced, and nor was it surprising, as Hall makes clear, that the king 'was not well contented with the saying of the bishop'. Rather more curious, however, was the fact that on this occasion Henry 'gently answered the speaker', informing him that Fisher would indeed be sent for, and that

ultimately the bishop's explanation of his action, corroborated by six other
bishops in attendance, was eventually accepted so readily, since Fisher's
sole defence consisted of the claim that he had 'meant the doings of the
Bohemians was for lack of faith, and not the doings of them that were
in the Common House'. As such, the king's subsequent leniency was far
from welcome to the complainants. Indeed, the bishop's 'blind excuse', we
are told, 'pleased the Commons nothing at all'. For if Fisher was already
an identikit saint and martyr – a hair-shirted, hard-praying ascetic and
man of unwavering principle – he was continuing to exhibit a seemingly
indestructible ego, which, while fit perhaps to match the undoubted gran-
deur of his principles, was equally capable of magnifying issues and stirring
storms. Plainly, the line between prescience and overreaction is a fine one,
and perhaps it was for this reason that his fellow bishops declined to follow
his course from this point onwards – not so much out of cowardice in the
face of a coming tidal wave that might sweep them away, but rather from
a prudent inclination to ride out what they saw, at this stage, as more of a
troublesome squall than typhoon.

Yet if the Bishop of Rochester consequently stood largely alone among
the episcopacy, other stirrings elsewhere, and especially at Canterbury,
were merely serving to echo his own misgivings about the royal divorce.
For at Conceptiontide in the midwinter of 1529–30, as the king created
his intended father-in-law Earl of Wiltshire and Ormonde in an elaborate
investiture ceremony held at York Place – followed by a grand celebration at Whitehall over which Anne herself presided at the king's side amid
the winter blazes – Elizabeth Barton was labouring in pangs and ecsta-
sies, 'three or four days without meat or drink', at the distant convent of
St Sepulchre. And it was now, according to John Wolff's later account, that
she received a second prompting, this time delivered by an angel, 'to go
again unto the king':

> And say that, since her last being with his Grace, he hath more highly
> studied to bring his purpose to pass; and that she saw in spirit the King,
> the Queen [Anne Boleyn] and the Earl of Wiltshire, standing in a garden
> together; and that they did devise how to bring this matter to pass. And
> by no means it would not be.

Thereafter, according to the information gleaned by Wolff from his cell-mate, Fr Hugh Rich, the Guardian of the Friars Observant of Richmond:

> A little devil stood beside the Queen and put it into her mind to say this: 'You shall send my father unto the Emperor, and let him show your mind and conscience, and give him these many thousand ducats to have his good will; and that it shall be brought to pass.'

Whereupon, the angel delivered the following command to Barton: 'Go and fear not to show the King this tale and privy token, and bid him take his old wife again, or else … etc.'

As a man imprisoned in the Tower and intent upon escaping a death sentence of his own, Wolff's decision to avoid more specific detail about the nature of the Maid's oracle and to opt instead for an altogether blander 'etc.' is hardly surprising, particularly when the whole episode, as he timorously confessed at the time, was 'so naughty a matter that my hand shaketh to write it, and something better unwritten than unwritten'. But it was none other than John Fisher who, in a later attempt to justify his own association with Barton, saw fit to reveal how she had related the content of her recent prophecy to the king upon their first meeting, which occurred, as the bishop was keen to make clear, after she had already shared it with the king himself and then 'came unto my house, unsent for on my part'. Nor was Fisher eventually in any position to beat about the bush with what he had been told, for, as he related in a letter to his royal master, dated 27 February 1534, she had informed him that 'if your Grace went forth with the purpose ye intended, ye should not be King of England seven months after'.

By the time that this oracle had first been delivered, moreover, Henry's intended purpose could not have been more apparent. For although his relations with Queen Catherine would be maintained at formal occasions for around a year and a half after Blackfriars, and although they continued to meet 'every few days' for appearances' sake, the upper hand was already entirely Anne Boleyn's. And nor was she failing to employ it, since she was now in her late twenties and increasingly impatient at her own predicament:

Did I not tell you [she railed at her royal suitor in early November 1529] that when you disputed with the queen she was sure to have the upper hand … I have been waiting long and might in the meantime have contracted some advantageous marriage … But alas! Farewell to my time and youth spent to no purpose at all!

Yet even such outbursts failed to cool the king's ardour, it seems, for as Chapuys observed, his love was invariably 'greater than before' after such spats, and resulted in nothing more than a continual string of expensive peace offerings that included ornate French saddles and harnesses, fine linen for night clothes, as well as gold embellishment for Anne's desk. In December 1529, £180 was spent on purple velvet for Anne's gowns, and large sums of £100 or more also followed as New Year's gifts, along with expensive furs, diamonds and pearls in abundance, while Catherine of Aragon confined herself to mending her husband's shirts at Greenwich, regally contemptuous of her upstart rival and stoically resigned to her chosen path of fruitless resistance. For her rival was now not only snugly installed within her own apartments at the same palace but kept, we are told, 'an estate more like a Queen than a simple maid'.

No one, it is true, even at court, pretended to like the turn that events were taking. The Duchess of Norfolk, for example, had to be packed off home at Anne's request 'because she spoke too freely and declared herself more than was liked for the Queen'. And even her husband, the duke, who as Anne's uncle probably knew too much already of his niece's temper to be truly glad at her advancement, was heard to have complained that 'it was the devil and nobody else who was the inventor of this accursed dispute'. In Parliament, the Speaker had to rebuke those who suggested that 'the King pursued this divorce out of love for some lady and not out of any scruple of conscience'. And while common folk continued to cheer the queen and the princess, the women of Oxford would soon be hurling stones at the university's vice-chancellor when he sought to set its seal upon the document declaring the king's first marriage incestuous. By that time Catherine had already been ordered to vacate her apartments and move to Wolsey's former house at the More before beginning a further dreary and humiliating exodus, encompassing a series of distant royal manors at Ampthill, Buckden and finally Kimbolton. Forbidden ultimately either to write to the king or to see her daughter, her household was also progressively whittled away until it became a paltry embarrassment to all concerned, consisting of little more than a confessor, a physician, an apothecary, and three women, including the ever-loyal Lady Willoughby: a retinue even more inadequate than in Catherine's days of hardship at Durham House twenty-five years earlier.

That the king's Gordian knot was all but cut even before the end of 1529 seemed manifestly clear to most outside observers and especially Eustace Chapuys, the 40-year-old Imperial ambassador, who was in that year newly arrived at the English court. By now, indeed, as the queen's little court became increasingly 'scantily visited by courtiers', it appeared little more than a home for lost causes. Yet the precise means for effecting the divorce remained as elusive as ever, and all the more so when Henry's own attempts at independent diplomatic initiatives continued to backfire so manifestly. His appeal to Europe's universities, recommended by Thomas Cranmer, would prove indecisive, while plans for the Earl of Wiltshire's projected visit to the pope – the genesis of which had already been witnessed by Elizabeth Barton by means of angelic assistance, as the king, his mistress and the earl paced up and down in their furs under the wintry trees of York Place – were, in effect, merely indicative of the depth of the prevailing impasse. Indeed, the visit would provide the Holy Father with a priceless opportunity for gleeful disrespect, as he served the dumbstruck earl with a writ citing his master to appear before him at Rome, before issuing a series of bulls threatening excommunication if Henry should proceed with his intended marriage.

In the meantime, moreover, while Anne Boleyn's father floundered abroad, so his would-be son-in-law found himself further encumbered at home by other inconveniences, the most pressing of which by now was the re-emergence of the Maid of Kent from her cloister in Canterbury with a heavenly message so pressing that she was prepared to venture once more into the royal presence to deliver it. Not altogether surprisingly, perhaps, official sources preserve a discreet silence over this particular encounter, as they do over the first. But whatever transpired in 1528, the meeting in either December 1529 or January 1530 was altogether more significant, not least because the Maid's prestige had continued to increase considerably. From no less a source than John Fisher himself, indeed, we learn that she travelled once more with her prioress, Dame Philippa Jonys, and an escort of convent servants from St Sepulchre's, and we know, too, that this expedition was again made with the permission, if not the active encouragement, of the Archbishop of Canterbury. But it is John Fisher's earliest biographer who informs us that the Maid and her entourage finally caught up with the king at Hanworth – a royal manor in Middlesex, within easy distance of London and very near Richmond Palace – where she delivered an oracle declaring that:

> The King had an ill intent and purpose in him, especially in that he minded to separate himself and the good Queen Catherine asunder, and minded for his voluptuousness and carnal appetite to marry another; which by no means he could do without the great displeasure of Almighty God, for it was directly against his holy laws … saying that by her revelation she perceived that, if the King desisted not from his purpose in this great case of divorce but would needs prosecute the same and marry again, then after such marriage he should not long be king of his realm, and in the reputation of God, he should not be king thereof one day, nor one hour after, and that he should die a shameful and miserable death.

Largely in keeping with John Wolff's account of the same episode, Fisher's earliest biographer was probably present at Rochester when the Maid spoke of it during her unscheduled visit to the bishop shortly afterwards. And we can confirm, too, that the king was spending lavishly upon the renewal of Hanworth at this very time in preparation for granting it to Anne for life in the following year. So it was with the builders at work around them that the king's kneeling visitor:

> Opened all her mind as freely as she was able to utter it, desiring him therefore in God's name, as well for the safety of his own soul as for the preservation of this noble realm, to take good heed what he did and to proceed no further in this business.

When the interview took place, furthermore, it was not a private one, since Henry's reactions, as John Fisher's correspondence shows, were reported in Rochester by other witnesses as well, which may explain in part the otherwise surprising royal restraint. For the king, we are told:

All the while gave her quiet hearing, seeming to all men that were there present not only content with her words but also dismayed to hear them at the mouth of so simple a woman. And so dismissed her peaceably enough at that time to her house of Canterbury, where she remained not long quiet after.

Certainly, Henry's no more than temporary dismay accords well enough with the frequent oscillations between self-willed bravado and traditional piety that were so much a part of his make-up. But if a government informer, whose handwriting identifies him as the Observant Friar Fr John Lawrence of Greenwich, is to be believed, the meeting did not conclude without at least one further twist. For Lawrence suggests that, before dismissing her, the king introduced her to the circle of his adopted family, where he and Anne Boleyn and the Countess of Wiltshire attempted to enlist her support by means of various enticements. In Lawrence's own words: 'The said Nun did show to me being with her at Canterbury, that the King did offer to make her Abbess of … [left blank by Lawrence], which she did refuse to; for which the King was with her greatly displeased.' And the Boleyn ladies too, it seems, offered inducements of their own: 'The Queen [Anne Boleyn] would have had her to remain at the court. And my lady her mother [the Countess of Wiltshire] did desire her to wait upon her daughter.' If true, and there is no inherent reason to believe otherwise, Elizabeth Barton was now clearly established as a figure of considerable political importance even at the royal court – an individual whose good offices were crucial enough, indeed, to merit subornment at the highest possible level. And this was not all. For she was now gaining an international reputation to boot, as Charles V was swiftly apprised – some time before the Earl of Wiltshire visited him in Bologna – how a young Benedictine nun had 'reproved the King for his sins', snubbed his mistress and refused a handsome bribe.

When she knocked at the door of John Fisher's episcopal palace in Rochester, however, on her homeward journey to Canterbury, fresh from her royal encounter, she showed nothing more than an intense desire to share her prophecy with the most renowned ecclesiastic in the kingdom, in the hope that he at last might have some bearing upon the king. As Fisher himself put it, 'I conceived not by these – I take it upon my soul – that any malice or evil was intended or meant unto your Highness by any mortal man, but only that they were the threats of God, as she then did affirm.' And that Fisher did indeed believe he was encountering a divinely inspired seeress is beyond all doubt. Lawrence, in fact, suggests that the stern old bishop 'wept for joy' when he heard of the Maid's revelations, 'saying that he did give to them the more credence because that she had been with the King divers times and reproved him for his sins'. The *Draft of Charges* eventually levelled against Barton also suggested how 'of likelihood, the obstinacy of mind of [the bishop of] Rochester hath been confirmed by the said Nun's revelations'. And nor, of course, should this have been surprising, since what the Maid told Fisher in early 1530 was exactly what the bishop himself had been saying since 1527. Indeed, when later interrogated in the Tower for concealing Barton's words about the king, it was this very reason he gave for believing her: namely, that she merely confirmed his most gloomy forebodings.

For good measure, however, Fisher also gave six other reasons at that time for having taken her seriously, and for having invited her on two subsequent occasions to visit him, all of which throw vivid light upon the Maid's standing with the public and with the clergy in general at the turn of the year 1529–30:

> *Whereof the first* is grounded upon the bruit [reputation] and fame of her;
>
> *the second*, upon her entering into religion after her trances and disfiguration;
>
> *the third*, upon rehearsal that her ghostly father [Dom Edward Bocking], being learned and religious, should testify that she was a maid of great holiness;
>
> *the fourth*, upon the report that divers other virtuous priests, men of good learning and reputation, should so testify to her;
>
> *the fifth*, upon the praise of my late Lord of Canterbury [Archbishop Warham] which showed … that she had many great visions;
>
> *the sixth*, upon the saying of the Prophet Amos: *Non faciet Dominus Deus verbum, nisi revelaverit secretum suum ad servos suos prophetas* – The Lord does nothing without first revealing his secrets to his servants.

To Fisher, then, with his taste for the miraculous and the occult, not to mention the wondrous secrets of numerology and the Cabbala, which had influenced his study of the Septuagint in particular, it seemed entirely plausible that God had at last spoken against the disorders of the English Samaria – against the English Ahab and the English Jezebel. And since God had spoken, the Maid – being mystically united to the will of God, as all declared – had no choice but to prophesy and her hearers no choice but to listen. Since the voice of prophecy was now raised, moreover, wholesale change – conceivably for the better – was plainly at hand.

Yet in the wake of Barton's departure, the point of crisis actually seemed to be looming ever closer. For the king's first response was to remind the papal nuncio of the law of *praemunire*, which declared that those who brought or received papal bulls into England relating to 'our Lord the King, against him, his crown, and royalty of his realm' should be 'put out of the King's protection, and their lands, tenements, goods and chattels forfeited' to the Crown. Furthermore, in the summer of 1530, writs of *praemunire facias* were indeed issued against fifteen clergy, which included not only John Fisher but all of Catherine's supporters among the episcopacy, with the exception of Cuthbert Tunstall, on the specific charge that they had aided Wolsey in his offences by handing over part of their income to him. And even before a decision had been reached in this case the charge was extended in December to the entire English clergy. 'No one,' Chapuys said of the Statute of Praemunire, 'can fathom the mysteries of this law. Its interpretation depends wholly on the King, who limits or amplifies it according to his will, and applies it to anyone he pleases.' Nor were the penalties any less arbitrary, for in eventually surrendering, the provinces of Canterbury and York were required to pay fines of £100,000 and £18,840 respectively in return for a royal pardon, and were further forced to recognise Henry as their 'singular protector, only and supreme lord ... even Supreme Head' – an acknowledgement that clearly set a potentially handy precedent for the Crown if it chose at some future juncture to press its control of ecclesiastical affairs.

But the success of the king's attack had not been achieved without arduous effort and intense pressure, and nor in any case was his victory complete, since the Bishop of Rochester, who had for so long remained austerely apolitical in his earlier career, once again emerged as the lynch-pin of resistance to anticlerical bullying on behalf of the parliamentary Commons and the regime they were now unquestioningly buttressing. As Fisher's anonymous early biographer records it:

When this matter was come to scanning in the Convocation House, great hold [contention] and stir was made about it. For among them there wanted not some that stood ready to set forth the king's purpose; and for fear of them, many others durst not speak their minds freely. But when this holy father [Fisher] saw what was towards and how ready some of their own company were to help forward the king's purpose, he opened up before the bishops such and so many inconveniences by granting of this demand, that in conclusion all was rejected and the king's intent clean overthrown for that time.

There followed the predictable royal threats to all concerned, 'putting them in mind what danger and peril they stood in at this present time against his Majesty', since the law decreed that 'their bodies and goods were wholly at his highness' will and pleasure'. But while his colleagues faltered, Fisher as always remained unyielding, earnestly requesting Convocation 'to take good heed what mischiefs and inconveniences would ensue to the whole Church of Christ by this unreasonable and unseemly grant to a temporal prince'. And neither was he moved when the king's counsellors assured Convocation of their master's good intentions and 'fell into disputation among the bishops of a temporal prince's authority'. On the contrary, 'my lord of Rochester answered them so fully that they had not list to deal that way any further'. 'For they were indeed,' as the anonymous early biographer puts it, 'but simple smatterers in divinity to speak before such a divine as he was.'

Yet there was, of course, a further price to pay for a victory that remained no more than moral, since the king's representatives departed, we are told, 'in great anger', 'showing themselves openly in their own likeness and saying that, whosoever would refuse to condescend to the king's demand therein, was not worthy to be accounted a true and loving subject'. And as pressure mounted, so Fisher's fellow bishops, knowing the king to be 'cruelly bent against the clergy', once again slowly melted before the 'threatening persuasion' exerted against them, though not before 'sundry days' argument in great striving and contention', and not before one parting master-stroke and final indignant flourish from the man at the centre of the storm, which his anonymous biographer describes thus:

My Lord of Rochester, perceiving this sudden and hasty grant [i.e. payment for a royal pardon] only made for fear and not upon any other just
ground, stood up again all angry and rebuked them for their pusillanim-
ity in being so lightly changed and easily persuaded. And being very
loath that any such grant should pass from the clergy thus absolutely
and yet by no means able to stay it for the fear that was among them, he
then advised the Convocation that seeing the king by his own mouth
and also by the sundry speeches of his orators had faithfully promised
and solemnly sworn in the high word of a king that his meaning was to
require no further than *quantum per legem dei licet* [as far as the law of God
allows], and that by virtue thereof his purpose was not to intermeddle
with any spiritual laws, spiritual jurisdiction or government more than
all his predecessors had always done before, 'If so be that you are fully
determined to grant him this demand (which I rather wish you to deny
than grant), yet for a more true and plain exposition of your meaning
towards the king and all his posterity, let these conditional words be
expressed in your grant *quantum per legem dei licet*, which is no other wise
(as the king and his learned counsel say) than yourselves mean.'

With much ingenuity, therefore, and even greater effrontery, Fisher had
found his loophole and exploited it with all the artistry of the politician he
never usually was. Technically at least, he had partially negated the king's
claims to be 'only and supreme lord of the Church and the English clergy'
and 'also their supreme head' by appending the theoretical restriction 'as
far as the law of God allows' – a term first used, ironically enough, not
only by the king himself but by his own representatives in attempting
to demonstrate his honourable intentions. And in doing so Fisher had
stirred the bishops anew in defending this principle against the 'open and
continual clamour' of those same representatives 'to have the grant passed
absolutely'. Indeed, the early biographer tells us how the clergy had 'gotten
new courage by this good man's words', and that nothing thereafter 'could
prevail among them'.

Nor, given the power of Fisher's oratory, was its effect altogether surprising. For as the debate reached its climax, so the bishop's words appear
to have attained a new level of intensity:

> We cannot grant this [supremacy] unto the king but [unless] we must renounce our unity to the see of Rome; and, if there were further matter in it than a renouncing of Clement VII, Pope thereof, then the matter were not so great: but in this we do forsake the first four General Councils, which none ever forsook; we renounce all canonical and ecclesiastical laws of the Church of Christ; we renounce all other Christian princes; we renounce the unity of the Christian world; and so leap out of Peter's ship, to be drowned in the waves of all heresies, sects, schisms and divisions.

And as if this were not enough, Fisher once more made reference to Herod while adding a further allusion to Nero and yet another crushing application of logic to expose the flaws and contradictions in his opponents' reasoning, since by accepting the royal supremacy:

> We renounce the judgement of all other Christian princes, whether they be Protestants or Catholics, Jews or Gentiles, for, by this argument, Herod must have been head of the church of the Jews; Nero must have been head of the church of Christ; the Emperor [Charles] must be head of the Protestant countries in Germany; and the church of Christ must have had never a head till about three hundred years after Christ [when the Emperor Constantine became a Christian].

In a nutshell, the whole structure of organised religion in Western Europe hinged upon papal authority, and the failure to accept as much could only result in catastrophe, as Fisher made clear in his concluding comments:

> Then is the granting of the supremacy of the Church to the King a renouncing of this unity, a tearing of the seamless coat of Christ in sunder, a dividing of the mystical body of Christ's spouse, limb from limb, and tail to tail, like Samson's foxes, to set the field of Christ's Holy Church all on fire; and this is it which we are about.
>
> Wherefore let it be said unto you in time, and not too late: Look you to that!

North aspect of Cobb's Hall, Aldington, Kent. It was at this place, while engaged in the household of Thomas Cobb, that Elizabeth Barton, later known as the Holy Maid of Kent, first established her reputation as a prophetess that would carry her to international fame and, ultimately, a traitor's death at Tyburn.

St Mary's Church at Aldington, little changed since the sixteenth century when Elizabeth Barton worshipped there. The rector at that time was Richard Master, who had been directly appointed by Archbishop Warham of Canterbury to serve the parish, and who succeeded a series of distinguished incumbents, including the Dutch scholar Erasmus and Thomas Linacre, physician, humanist intellectual and Latin tutor to the future Queen Mary.

All that remains of the deserted chapel at Court-le-Street where in the spring of 1526 Elizabeth Barton was said to have been miraculously healed of an epileptiform ailment by the Virgin Mary, in the presence of numerous witnesses.

Although initially circumspect, Archbishop William Warham was eventually convinced of the authenticity of Elizabeth Barton's visions after her case was referred to him by Richard Master. A grave, devout, learned man, trained as a Wykehamist canon lawyer and one of the leading humanists of the day, Warham had been for most of his life a pliant servant of the Crown, but would ultimately declare himself ready to be 'rewarded by God with the great honour of martyrdom, which is the best death that can be'.

On 20 April 1534, Elizabeth Barton was executed at Tyburn with her fellow 'conspirators' for having prophesied the death of Henry VIII and, in the words of the parliamentary attainder against them, 'traterously attempted many notable actes intendyng therbye the disturbaunce of the pease and tranquyllytie of this Realm'. Today the site of the infamous Tyburn tree is marked by a stone on a traffic island at the junction of Edgware Road, Bayswater Road and Oxford Street.

Elizabeth Barton's execution occurred in the company of two Benedictine monks, two Franciscan friars and a former secretary to the Archbishop of Canterbury, all of whom had been among her leading advocates. The five men were hanged, drawn and quartered, though Barton, as a woman, was merely hanged, after which, according to John Stow, 'the Nun's head was set on London Bridge, and the other heads on gates of the City'.

Clockwise from top left: Born in 1469 and venerated by Roman Catholics as a saint, John Fisher was an English Catholic bishop, cardinal and theologian who also served as Chancellor of the University of Cambridge. He was executed by order of Henry VIII for refusing to accept the king as Supreme Head of the Church of England and for upholding the doctrine of papal supremacy. He shares his feast day with St Thomas More on 22 June in the Roman Catholic calendar of saints, and is commemorated by the Church of England on 6 July; Portrait of Henry VIII's grandmother, Lady Margaret Beaufort, who, under John Fisher's guidance, founded St John's and Christ's Colleges at Cambridge, and a Lady Margaret Professorship of Divinity at each of the two universities at Oxford and Cambridge, Fisher himself becoming the first occupant of the Cambridge chair. From 1505 to 1508 he was also the President of Queens' College; Located next to the Queen's House at the Tower of London, and dating to the end of the twelfth century, the Bell Tower, where John Fisher was imprisoned, derives its name from the small wooden turret situated at its summit which contained a 'curfew bell'. This was used to inform prisoners who were allowed to leave the confines of their quarters that it was time for them to return.

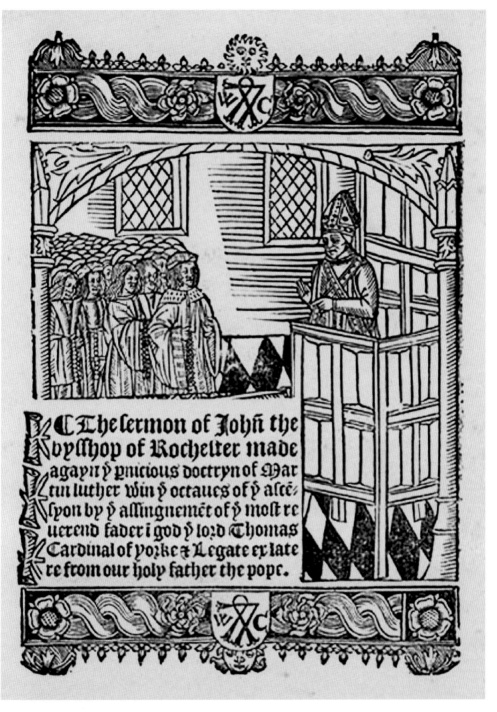

¶The sermon of John the bysshop of Rochelter made agayn ẏ pnicious doctryn of Martin luther wtin ẏ octaues of ẏ ascē lyon by ẏ assingnemēt of ẏ most reuerend fader i god ẏ lord Thomas Cardinal of york ⁊ Legate ex late re from our holy father the pope.

Title page of *The Sermon of Johan the Bysshop of Rochester made agayn the Pernicious Doctryn of Martin Luther, c.* 1521. The sermon concerned was preached 'on a Good Friday' at Paul's Cross, and by 1527, Fisher had produced well over half a million words of Latin polemic against the teachings of the man whom he perceived as the most dangerous of the Church's enemies.

Unlike some more fortunate prisoners, John Fisher was kept under close confinement in this cell, where he found himself raggedly clothed, deprived of his books and racked by the cold. 'I have neither shirt nor sheet,' he informed Thomas Cromwell in December 1534, 'nor yet other clothes that are necessary for me to wear, but that be ragged and rent so shamefully. Notwithstanding I might easily suffer that, if they would keep my body warm.'

A small brick pavement in Trinity Square Gardens now marks the site of the scaffold on Tower Hill where John Fisher was executed on 22 June 1535. We are told that his 'headless carcass' was left 'naked on the scaffold for the rest of the hot June day saving that one, for pity and humanity, cast a little straw upon it'.

The family of Sebastian Newdigate bore a long and intimate connection with the Church of St Mary the Virgin at their home of Harefield in Middlesex. Today it contains numerous fine memorials, including many dedicated to the Newdigates, who owned the local manor from the fourteenth century.

No likeness of Sebastian Newdigate remains, but this idealised image by Francisco Zurbarán depicts John Houghton, Prior of the London Charterhouse that Newdigate joined after withdrawing from service in Henry VIII's privy chamber. A man of exceptional spirituality, Houghton was a source of particular inspiration to those entrusted to his charge, many of whom were of wealthy or distinguished family. On 4 May 1535, he would precede Newdigate to a martyr's death.

This painting of the martyrdom of Humphrey Middlemore, William Exmew and Sebastian Newdigate by Vicente Carducho resides at the Monastery of El Paular in Spain. They were incarcerated at Marshalsea for at least a fortnight, during which time they were bound by 'great fetters fast ryved [riveted] on their legs with great iron boltts', as well as 'iron collors' and other chains loaded with lead. The three Carthusian monks were eventually hanged, drawn and quartered at Tyburn on 19 June 1535. Throughout their captivity at Marshalsea, they had never, we are told, been 'loosed for any naturall necessitie [nor] voiding of ordure or otherwise'.

For several years after the dissolution of the London Charterhouse, members of the Bassano family of instrument makers were amongst the tenants of the former monks' cells, whilst Henry VIII stored hunting equipment in the church. But in 1545 the entire site was bought by Sir Edward (later Lord) North (c. 1496–1564), who transformed the complex into a luxurious mansion house. North demolished the church and built the Great Hall and adjoining Great Chamber. In 1558, during North's occupancy, Queen Elizabeth I used the house during the preparations for her coronation.

Nor was this the only sting in the tail. For when Archbishop Warham subsequently put Fisher's suggested amendment to the king's title to Convocation on 11 February, he did so on the assumption that silence signified assent: *Qui tacet consentire*. And the deadly hush that followed was not only ringing, but enough, it seems, to drive Henry to further fury when news of the decision reached him from those of his representatives who had been present:

> Mother of God! You have played a pretty prank. I thought to have made fools of them; and now you have so ordered the business that they are more likely to make a fool of me, as they have done of you already.

Even so, Chapuys was to report to the Emperor on 21 February 1531 that Fisher was actually very ill with disappointment at the overall outcome regarding the supremacy. He had 'opposed it as much as he can', wrote the ambassador, 'but being threatened that he and his adherents should be thrown into the river, he was forced to consent to the king's will'. As might be expected for a man of the bishop's disposition, the consolation of the phrase *quam per legem dei licet* had been of small comfort amid the broader retreat, and the strain of resistance is indeed likely to have taken a temporary toll. More than twenty days, after all, had been spent in discussing the royal demand, and although the possibility exists that his anonymous biographer may have ascribed too dominant a role to Fisher himself, his account, which is the most detailed available, would certainly explain the delay of some twelve or thirteen sittings between the grant of money in return for a royal pardon and Convocation's final acceptance of the king's new title. But it was not merely bitter disappointment that had harmed the bishop's health. For his principled stand had also made him enemies who would now, it seems, stop at nothing to be rid of him, and on 20 February 1531, his cook, a man named Rouse, who was said by some to have been acting on the instructions of either Anne Boleyn or her father, had poisoned a cauldron of broth with a mysterious white powder, which was served to the bishop and his household.

According to Chapuys's account, which mistakenly suggests that Fisher had not tasted the broth and was only incapacitated from disappointment at Convocation's acceptance of the royal supremacy, the incident had unfolded as follows:

> There was in the bishop's house about ten days ago some pottage, of which all who tasted it, that is, nearly all the servants, were brought to the point of death, though only two of them died, and some poor people to whom they had given it. The good bishop, happily, did not taste it. The cook was immediately seized at the instance of the bishop's brother, and, it is said, confessed that he had thrown in a powder which, he had been given to understand, would only stupefy the servants without doing them any harm. I do not yet know whom he has accused of giving him this powder nor the issue of the affair. The king has done well to show dissatisfaction at this; nevertheless, he cannot wholly avoid some suspicion, if not against himself, whom I think too good to do such a thing, at least against the lady [Anne Boleyn] and her father.
>
> The said Bishop of Rochester is very ill, and has been so ever since the acknowledgement made by the clergy of which I wrote. But, notwithstanding his disposition, he has arranged to leave tomorrow by the king's leave. I know not why, being ill, he is anxious to go on a journey, especially as he will get better attendance of physicians here than elsewhere, unless it be that he will no longer be a witness of things done against the Church, or that he fears there is some more powder in reserve for him. If the king desired to treat of the affair of the queen, the absence of the said Bishop and of the Bishop of Durham [Cuthbert Tunstall] would be unfortunate.

In fact, Fisher had only been saved by eating so sparingly of the broth, which was his wont, and was left with excruciating abdominal pains for some time thereafter. But two men died at table and seventeen others – including some beggars who were unlucky enough to be treated to the leftovers – fell seriously ill, with the result that even Fisher seems to have deemed it unavoidable to beat a rapid exit thereafter, notwithstanding his condition and the potential consequences of his absence for the queen. Such was the publicity of the case, moreover, that in its aftermath Henry VIII went in person to the House of Lords and in a speech lasting one and a half hours declaimed upon the barbarity of poisoning.

In truth, the fuss raised by the king seems likely to have had much less to do with Fisher's plight or justice *per se* than with his own morbid terror of poison, which is well documented. But a law was nevertheless enacted making murder by poison high treason and punishable by boiling in oil. And the outcome for the bishop's hapless cook was a particularly ghastly one, for, as the following entry in the *Chronicle of the Grey Friars of London* records, he duly became the new law's first victim:

> This year was a cook boiled in a cauldron at Smithfield, for he would have poisoned the Bishop of Rochester with divers of his servants, and he was locked in a chain and pulled up and down with a gibbet at divers times till he was dead.

But even now Fisher remained in danger. For it was not long after his return to Lambeth that another, arguably even more dramatic incident, was recorded by his early biographer:

> Suddenly a gun was shot through the top of his house not far from his study where he accustomably used to sit. Which made such a terrible noise over his head and bruised the tiles and rafters of his house so sore, that both he and divers others of his servants were suddenly amazed thereat. Wherefore speedy search was made whence this shot should come and what it meant. Which at last was found to come from the other side of the Thames out of the Earl of Wiltshire's house who was father to the Lady Anne. Then he perceived that great malice was meant towards him and calling speedily unto him certain of his servants, said, 'Let us truss up our gear and be gone from hence, for here is no place for us to tarry any longer.'

Having narrowly escaped the deadly effects of poison from within, then, the Bishop of Rochester and his household were once again on the move after a near-fatal cannon shot from without, though whether Anne Boleyn and her relatives, as both the anonymous early biographer and Chapuys believed, were indeed responsible remains a matter for conjecture. The real significance in any event is that the extremity of Fisher's perceived threat to the king's designs was now undeniable. No other critic of the divorce among the kingdom's elites would, in fact, be more outspoken and no opponent of the looming breach with Rome would be treated to such levels of intimidation. For where Sir Thomas More opposed by silence, and only after prolonged attempts to preserve his position, the Bishop of Rochester's resistance was vigorous, forthright and prolonged. And if Eustace Chapuys was of a sanguine temperament and ofttimes inclined to see things as he would like them to be, he was nevertheless on sure ground when he wrote on 9 October 1531 of Anne Boleyn's fears of Fisher and the bishop's ongoing determination to oppose her marriage, irrespective of the personal risk involved:

> The lady fears no one here more than the Bishop of Rochester, for it is he who has always defended the queen's cause, and she has therefore sent to persuade the bishop to forbear coming to this Parliament that he may not catch any sickness as he did last year, but it is no use, for he is resolved to come and to speak more boldly than he has ever done should he die a hundred thousand times.

A veiled threat? Certainly, Fisher could not have been blamed for believing as much after the harrowing events of the previous months. But battle had been joined and the war itself was broadening, as the king's attitude towards the papacy hardened in the wake of the conflicting verdicts of Europe's universities and the Earl of Wiltshire's failed embassy to the pope. Not altogether surprisingly, of course, the 'intellectual' inclinations of the Continent's leading universities had ultimately borne a striking resemblance to the political priorities of their rulers. In England, France and Northern Italy, where anti-Habsburg feeling was strong, the universities duly found in favour of Henry. After Poitiers had supported Catherine, for instance, Francis intervened on behalf of his current ally and Paris was bullied into compliance. Orléans, Bourges and Toulouse followed suit. On the other hand, Alcalá and Salamanca did as they were bidden by Emperor Charles and found in favour of the pope, as did those German universities under the emperor's thumb. In Italy, not surprisingly, only Ferrara, Padua and Bologna were for the divorce, although Vicenza would also have supported Henry had its bishop not arrived, with a beefy gang of minders in attendance, to tear up the theses that nine learned doctors were ready to maintain. Most of the decisions were, in fact, paid for. But upon his return to England on 30 September 1530, the Earl of Wiltshire had reflected a new prevailing mood within government circles by confirming to Antonio de Pulleo that the king now considered himself 'absolute emperor and pope in his kingdom'.

In reality, of course, the English ruler's defiant posturing, spiteful threats and token gestures of confidence in the aftermath of Blackfriars were more indicative of growing frustration and deepening impasse than of any budding desire to break with Rome, since his attempts at irresistible force were continuing to founder upon the immovable position of a pope, hemmed in on all sides by circumstances beyond his control. Indeed, in the twelve months following the ending of the legatine court at Blackfriars, the king's policy was remarkable only in terms of its confusion. In June 1530, for instance, when his case was finally revoked by the pope to Rome, Henry summoned his leading subjects to court to give speedy judgement on his behalf, since informed opinion in England and Europe as a whole, or so he claimed, was in no doubt of the rectitude of his case. But at this very time, he was also urging his representative in Rome, William Bennet, to procrastinate at all costs in the vain hope that by some unforeseeable change of circumstance a breakthrough might yet be achieved. Clearly, if an overall plan existed at all, it was almost entirely camouflaged in a meandering stream of empty bluster and idle threats.

Yet in spite of his agonising twists and turns, like a sleepwalker in a maze, Henry did indeed appear during this time to stumble on at least the right direction, if not a precise route, to his desired ends. For although a severance with the underlying doctrinal principles of Roman Catholicism remained unthinkable for the defender of the faith, a juridical breach had its attractions both for his ego and, ultimately, of course, his purse. And throughout 1530 this realisation appeared to grow upon him. On Christmas Eve 1529, for instance, Henry had given notice to Catherine of Aragon that 'he prized and valued the Church of Canterbury as much as the people across the sea did the Roman', while in April 1530 he went on tell the French ambassador that he intended to settle the matter of his divorce within his own kingdom and without recourse to the pope 'whom he regards as ignorant and no good father'. By September 1530, indeed, he was prepared to declare with more stridency than ever that he had 'a pinnacle of dignity' and 'no superior on earth'. And nor were such pronouncements framed purely for foreign consumption, since his references to himself as Supreme Head of the Church in his letters to Bishop Tunstall further suggested a growing preparedness to contemplate the ultimate step. All of which might still be interpreted, of course, as little more than yet another fit of bellicose foot stamping, were it not for the fact that the first drafts of the treason laws, which were later used to crush opposition to the royal supremacy, are known to have been drawn up without advertisement as early as 1530.

In consequence, John Fisher would have to maintain the fight, as the king continued to prowl and probe for weaknesses in the Church's armour by increasingly desperate means. Just as Catherine of Aragon had denied the authority of the legatine court in 1529, so now it was the king's turn to deny the authority of the papal tribunal in Rome: to stall, to block, to challenge, to threaten appeal to even higher authority – if a General Council of the Church could indeed be considered such. And as Fisher's fellow bishops looked on in silent dismay, so the king pleaded an alternative justification for his claims: the fictitious immunity of England, whether derived from the Trojan kings who had supposedly colonised England after Troy's fall, or from the Emperor Constantine, whose mother's roots were English, or indeed from King Arthur, that imperial paladin of the Dark Ages. The more outlandish the claim, the more tortuous the reasoning, the more inclined the king became to seize upon it, as a great trawling of obscure chronicles began, comparable to that conducted in the theological libraries of Europe's universities earlier in the year. But now, instead of bulls and briefs and dispensations, new searchers turned up ancient traditions and prophetical material of origin so antique and nebulous as hopefully to pre-date St Peter and the papacy itself, or if not that, then at least to pre-date the coming of St Augustine and the introduction of a pretended papal jurisdiction into England.

Certainly, the researches of Edward Fox, Thomas Cranmer and John Stokesley were by now playing a major role in feeding Henry a diet of evidence that would help him fuel the rationalisations and self-justifications that he was always inclined to embrace so ardently. Working together, the three divines had indeed compiled for Henry's benefit by September 1530 a massive collection of legal and historical evidence, entitled *Collectanea satis copiosa*, supporting the judicial independence of the Crown from Rome. The pre-eminence of the king was confirmed, on the one hand, from Old Testament examples connected with Solomon and David, and on the other by medieval Catholic authorities, such as Ivo of Chartres. Likewise, the Council of Nicea of AD 325 and subsequent councils had, it was now argued, affirmed the principle that no legal case should be taken outside the ecclesiastical province of its origin. And for good measure, the *Collectanea* included a letter, written supposedly by Pope Eleutherius around AD 187, in which he addressed the mythical King Lucius I of Britain as 'vicar of God'. Last but not least, William Bennet and Sir Edward Carne were now accorded the impossible task in Rome of reading all the Vatican Registers to abstract entries that would support Henry's claim to 'authority imperial'.

And in the meantime, Henry turned, too, to British sources. The Constitutions of Clarendon of Henry II's reign, for instance, had enshrined England's jurisdictional privileges, while another favourite source for Henry's legal burrowers proved to be the largely mythical chronicle of Geoffrey of Monmouth, which favoured a version of English history based on the claim that Christianity had been brought across the Channel in biblical times by Joseph of Aramathea, and therefore wholly independently of the Roman Church. The king's archivists also tried to trace the descent of the kings of England back to the Roman Emperor Constantine via King Arthur, in spite of the fact that such myths had already been exposed by Polydore Vergil. Given, they argued too, that it was the so-called Donation of Constantine, which had first granted papal authority, and that this document had been proven a forgery, it followed in any case that England's rulers had always been independent of the papacy. And so, by such twisted logic and dubious scholarship of various kinds, Henry thus sought to press home his case that the Christian world had started as, and still should be, a federation of autonomous, local churches, each ruled over by a prince appointed by God and rejecting the fraudulent universal authority of the Bishop of Rome.

Predictably, of course, King Arthur continued to feature prominently in the new surge of propaganda in other ways as well. For as a previous vanquisher of Roman ambitions, it was only natural, perhaps, that prophecies derived from Arthurian legend should have been invoked so freely and circulated and expounded from one coast to another. The vaticinations of Merlin, as derived from Geoffrey of Monmouth's *History of the Kings of Britain*, were, indeed, an especial favourite, and one in particular that told how:

> A tree shall rise up above the Tower of London that, thrusting forth three branches only, shall overshadow all the face of the whole island with the spreading breadth of the leaves thereof. Against it shall come the Northwind as an adversary, and an evil blast shall tear away the third branch, but the two that remain shall occupy his place until the one shall bring to nought the other by the multitude of his leaves …
>
> London shall mourn the slaughter of twenty thousand, and the River Thames shall be turned into blood. They that wear the cowl shall be provoked into marriage, and their outcry shall be heard in the mountains of the Alps.

All these catastrophes, moreover, were to be heralded by a portent: the sign that the grimy, gloomy Tower of London would turn white – all of which had indeed begun to happen, in the wake of the cleaning operations enacted by the new king after he had taken up residence there upon his succession.

Here, then, it seemed, was something for everyone: an oracle for King Henry, if he understood himself to be the Northwind; a warning the clergy, whose vows of celibacy the reformers in Europe were already set upon abolishing; a fearsome prediction for Londoners, threatened by strife and massacre from an unspecified quarter; not to mention a prophecy for the king's detractors to ponder, including, of course, the Maid of Kent, whose own *Parable of the Three Branches* had already foretold the fall of Wolsey. According to the testimony of William Harlock, moreover, who was examined by the authorities in September 1530 for encouraging malicious rumours, some almanacs in ready circulation were emphasising three other alternative themes to those preferred by the government: namely, that there would be 'a great battle of priests'; that England would be invaded by foreign armies; and that King Henry's reign would be cut short. Clearly, during a period of such invasive uncertainty and tension, even the most agitated ramblings could attract the keen notice of the authorities. And in the process many simple people were said to have been 'greatly agitated' by another prediction, which had begun to circulate from around 1530 onwards, to the effect that the kingdom was to be destroyed by a woman. Equally alarmingly, a series of occult marvels and heavenly portents seemed to confirm the imminence of grave danger. A monstrous dead fish, said to be some 90ft in length, was beached on the northern coast and not long afterwards a freak tide flowed into the Thames for nine straight hours, causing the river to rise higher than ever before, to the very steps of the royal chapel at Greenwich. Even more ominously, there was talk of a ball of fire falling from the sky near the same place, and for some weeks a comet with a long tail 'in the form of a luminous silver beard' was visible before daybreak.

Most significantly of all, however, Thomas Wolsey's death at Leicester Abbey on 29 November 1530 had only served to heighten the profile of Elizabeth Barton. That summer, apparently broken in health and tormented with leeches, which he described as 'very hungry ones', he had taken to signing his correspondence with Stephen Gardiner as 'Thomas the miserable, Cardinal of York'. Yet in spite of his straitened circumstances, Wolsey had lost none of his appetite for status and power. Certainly, he continued to entertain and even to build lavishly – so much so that on 18 August Cromwell issued a word of warning. 'Sir,' he wrote, 'some there be that doth allege that Your Grace doth keep too great a house and family and that ye are continually building.' Therefore, suggested Cromwell, it was time to curtail any familiar excess and 'put to silence some persons that much speaketh of the same'. More importantly still, in May Cromwell had also advised his former master to be much more circumspect in what he said and wrote, since the king was aware of his wish to undermine the Duke of Norfolk in particular. This, Cromwell warned, was a risky enterprise. And it was not, to his great misfortune, the only gamble that Wolsey now undertook. On the contrary, too long accustomed to greatness, he could not resist the temptation to meddle and now attempted to enlist the favour of Catherine of Aragon, who, like him, had suffered so grievously at the hands of the Norfolk–Boleyn faction. In early June the Imperial ambassador received a letter from Wolsey's physician, Agostini, which seemed to imply that his patient was willing to supply information beneficial to the former queen. And before the end of the month, Wolsey had dispatched another letter, this time asking how the queen's divorce case was progressing and urging the ambassador that strong action – presumably by the emperor and the pope – should be taken on her behalf. By August, indeed, the cardinal was sending messages to Chapuys on an almost daily basis. 'He dislikes delay above all,' wrote the ambassador to his emperor, 'for he thinks that, this business settled, he has a good chance of returning to power.'

Not long since, Henry had, it seems, lost his temper in the council room and in a spiteful outburst berated his advisers, telling them once more that 'the Cardinal was a better man than any of them for managing matters'. 'Repeating this twice,' observed Chapuys, 'he flung himself out of the room,' since when 'the Duke [of Norfolk], the Lady Anne and her father have not ceased to plot against the Cardinal, especially the Lady.' But the king, in spite of his outburst, subsequently needed little persuasion, since a report had reached him on 23 October that a papal brief had already been issued forbidding him to marry while his divorce was still under litigation. More provocatively still, he had heard further rumours that Pope Clement intended to excommunicate him and banish Anne Boleyn from court. All this, coupled to Wolsey's summons of a northern convocation without royal permission, convinced him that his one-time favourite's long-overdue formal enthronement as Archbishop of York on 7 November might well become the occasion for the official publication of a bull of excommunication. Always more than capable of mistaking the smoke from smouldering ashes for forest fire, Henry therefore panicked and came to the conclusion that Wolsey must be guilty of 'presumptuous sinister practices made to the court of Rome'.

On All Souls' Eve, meanwhile, the cardinal is said to have received a premonition of his impending misfortune. Sitting at dinner with various members of his household – the great silver cross of York positioned at one end of the table – Wolsey received his warning just as the meal reached its end. Rising to take his leave, none other than Dr Agostini, wearing a 'boisterous black gown of velvet', seems to have swept against the cross, causing it to fall upon the head of Edmund Bonner, the cardinal's personal chaplain. 'Hath it drawn any blood?' asked Wolsey of George Cavendish after a moment's stunned silence. 'Yea, forsooth, my lord,' responded the gentleman usher, whereupon the cardinal looked long and sombrely at his servant. *Malum omen* – ill luck – came his final comment at last, as he made for his bedchamber, heavy, Cavendish tells us, with foreboding. And the following Friday, 4 November, again at the end of dinner, when Wolsey was 'at his fruites' in his private room, the young Earl of Northumberland, accompanied by a gaggle of eager gentry, duly entered the great hall at Cawood after taking the keys from the porter and sealing the gates with sentries. 'My Lord,' declared the cardinal's visitor, 'I arrest you of high treason', and laying his hand upon the victim's arm, rendered him dumbstruck.

On his subsequent journey south, Wolsey was taken 'with a thing about his stomach as cold as a whetstone', which turned before long into full-blown dysentery. In spite of medicinal powders administered to him by a physician at Shrewsbury – which he would only accept, for fear of poison, after Cavendish and the physician himself had tasted them – he showed no sign of improvement. Ominously, too, he was delivered at Sheffield Park into the custody of Sir William Kingston, Constable of the Tower, who arrived with twenty-four royal guards. At which point, we are told, his 'bloody flux' worsened markedly, 'in so much from the time that his disease took him unto the next day', Cavendish tells us, 'he had fifty stools, so that he was next day very weak'. 'The matter that he voided,' it seems, 'was wondrous black, the which physicians call *choler adustum*', and such was his weakness and fever that he could not resume his journey for twenty-four hours. Indeed, on the way from Hardwick Hall, we are told, 'he waxed so sick that he was divers times likely to have fallen from his mule'. Yet he continued his journey from Hardwick to Nottingham and from there to Leicester Abbey, which he reached on the evening of Saturday, 26 November. Propped up on both sides by yeomen and greeted with torches at the abbey gate by Abbot Pexall, it was plain to everyone, and especially him, that his condition was fatal. 'Father Abbot,' he told Pexall, 'I am come hither to leave my bones among you.'

And in this respect, at least, Wolsey would finally prove true to his word. For just before dawn, the mayor of Leicester and his aldermen were duly invited to view the mitred body, dressed in all its archiepiscopal robes within a coffin of boards. And thus identified, the Cardinal of York was then carried to the Lady Chapel where his body lay open and barefaced, 'that all men might see him there dead without feigning'. Throughout the night, too, the corpse lay on display amid wax tapers and mournful dirges before it was brought to its final resting place in the abbey's main aisle – not far, we are told, from the body of Richard III in what, according to the Imperial ambassador, was commonly called 'the tyrants' sepulchre'. His death, the Maid of Kent was soon revealing, had been premature, and for that reason he would not be judged by God until the further period of what should have been his natural life had elapsed. Or this at least was the suggestion in Dom Edward Bocking's 'great book', which was quoted in Nicolas Heath's *Sermon* some four years later:

> That my Lord Cardinal came to his death before God would have him by the space of fifteen years; and therefore Almighty God hath given no sentence upon him, but will defer it till those years he expired, which it was the will of God that he should have lived in the world.

Even now, however, the Maid's connection with Wolsey was not quite over. For, according to the testimony of John Wolff, she would subsequently witness 'the disputations of the devils for his soul … and was three times lifted up and could not see him, neither in heaven, hell nor purgatory'. In the process, she would witness – among other things of which she could not speak – many souls 'fly through purgatory', and she would tell, too, of her revelations concerning 'the going of the Earl of Wiltshire into Spain, with the receiving of the King's letter, and the answer of the Emperor', which proved a flat refusal to countenance in any way either the divorce or the summoning of a General Council to overrule the pope. But, for all her wondrous visions, the most significant of all for her Church, her kingdom and indeed her own personal fate had eluded her: namely, the identity of Wolsey's ultimate successor as her sovereign's right-hand man – the very individual, in fact, who would henceforth plot his master's course anew and thereby lead him to the longed-for promised land of his frustrated desires.

8

DEADLY PILOT

When the lion roars, who can help feeling afraid?
When God himself speaks, who dare refuse to prophesy?

Amos 3:8

If Henry VIII was in fact contemplating a new course in the early months of 1531, his tactics for achieving it remained hopelessly inadequate. For the attempt to smother the pope with a welter of archival evidence, like Cranmer's appeal to the universities before it, was never more than a powder puff effort. Like it or not, the pope remained diplomatically mana- cled and neither words nor sticks nor stones could force him to comply. So while the king finally began to ponder his only realistic alternative, he remained hopelessly unable, all the same, to strike upon the appropriate method for achieving it. As the new year dawned, indeed, both Henry's ministers and his strategies were proving nakedly unproductive. Eustace Chapuys, for his part, noted that, 'Parliament is prorogued from time to time as though they do not know their own minds about the measures proposed therein.' But if Henry was edging blindfold towards the notion of a national Church under his direct control, it would require somebody else to furnish the means for its achievement and the intellectual case upon which it might be founded – an outsider who might also drive the slug- gish Reformation Parliament by fair or foul persuasions towards a more 'constructive' goal. And though few, if any, knew it at this stage, precisely such a figure was now at hand.

Thomas Cromwell, whose origins may well have been rather less auspi- cious than is generally recognised these days, was born in the small village of Putney, which then lay some 4 miles from the capital. Though not, therefore, quite a Londoner, it is nevertheless certain that he will soon have felt the

irresistible pull of the many-spired and malodorous city in which his years
of power were to be passed. Appropriately enough, the year of his birth is
thought by some to have coincided with the Battle of Bosworth and the
triumph of the Tudor dynasty with whose fortunes he would be so closely
linked. And if Cromwell's arrival did indeed occur in 1485, he shared his
birth year with a cluster of famous figures, including Cortés, the conqueror
of Mexico, and Catherine of Aragon, whose marriage would greatly influence the minister's rise to eminence. Yet the chronological link between the
boy from Putney and such individuals would have seemed at the time to be
the likely limit of any connection, for when he entered the world wrapped
in anonymity and burdened with the dead weight of humble parentage,
none could have predicted for him so prominent a place in history. Bereft
of rank, connection or fortune, even the prospect of formal schooling was
to be denied him. And if, as some have suggested, he was descended from
the rich Nottinghamshire magnate Ralph Lord Cromwell, there was little
evidence of it in his upbringing. Indeed, his will of 1529 made more than
one reference to 'poor kinsfolk' still living and in later life he is known to
have shaken the hand of an old bell-ringer at Syon House before a crowd
of courtiers, confessing, according to one source, that during his childhood
'this man's father had given him many dinners in his necessities'.

Cromwell's own father, meanwhile, had been a man of many parts –
with few of them particularly worthy. Though often described as a brewer,
Walter Cromwell was primarily a blacksmith and fuller, who, as a sideline,
apparently brewed bad beer, for he was more than once condemned at the
assize of ale. Moreover, as well as being prone to dishonesty and occasional
bouts of drunkenness, he was also quarrelsome and known to the local
magistracy for assault and overgrazing the common pasture. But in spite
of the fact that he led a life of more than typical commotion, the elder
Cromwell was not without his fair share of native wit and it is highly probable that the influence of such an artful, devil-may-care fellow upon his
son was considerable. Certainly, young Thomas appears to have acquired a
patina of tough unconventionality, which he carried into adulthood, even
proudly. Never one to hide behind airs and affectation, he later confessed
to the ever-earnest Cranmer, doubtless with some glee, that 'he had been
a ruffian in his youth', and Chapuys would confirm that 'for some offence
he was thrown into prison and obliged afterwards to leave the country'.

Yet if this may sound an unpropitious start, it was not without benefit, too, for it set him upon a European odyssey lasting a decade, which would equip him most fittingly for the tasks ahead.

Although we cannot be sure if Chapuys was correct about the reasons for Cromwell's departure from England, we do know that in December 1503, at the age of 18, he was with the French army in Italy as either a soldier or page. We know, too, that after his military adventures ceased, he remained in Italy in the service of the Florentine banking family of Frescobaldi and travelled widely there, operating mainly in Florence, but also in Pisa and Venice. Significantly, it was during his Italian sojourn that he came into contact with a range of new ideas and approaches, and readily absorbed the emerging rationalistic ethos of the day, which would prove so important in equipping him for his later role. Not least of all, he was introduced to Marsiglio of Padua's seminal work, *Defensor Pacis*, which emphasised the primacy of the secular ruler in ecclesiastical affairs. But more importantly his considerable commercial experience reinforced his natural tendency to think in terms of efficiency and outcomes rather than hidebound traditions. On his travels, too, he encountered and was genuinely influenced by the writings of religious reformers, although contrary to what is still a widely held misapprehension, the impact of reforming ideas upon him at this stage may not necessarily have been quite as substantial as is often assumed. Curiously, the inventory of his London home for the year 1527 mentions numerous pious objects that were wholly in keeping with the devotion of the old religion, including two images in gilt leather of Our Lady and St Christopher, as well as a golden leather image of St Anthony tucked away under the stairs. Furthermore, the centrepiece of Cromwell's 'new chamber' appears to have been an ornate gilded altar of Our Lord's Nativity. Even his jewels, for that matter, included a golden *Agnus Dei* with an engraving of Our Lady and St George.

In truth, almost all aspects of Cromwell's early years are obscure, but what can be said with certainty is that upon his return to England he was a highly marketable commodity in his own right. This, after all, was the age when a quick-witted person with a practical knowledge of men and affairs and an eye for the main chance could vie with lords and dukes, provided that he doffed his cap with all due humility to those who held the keys to advancement. Then again, as one of the 'new men' brought to the fore by the increasingly flexible outlook of the sixteenth century, he had developed a cutting edge, based upon a simple knack for grasping the internal logic of policies and the momentum of events, which would prove invaluable in any position of impasse. Endowed with great energy and vision, Cromwell displayed, finally, an unerring determination to pursue to the bitter end all he attempted, and not altogether surprisingly, therefore, we next hear of him operating between 1520 and 1524 as a thriving solicitor whose expertise in the Common Law was bringing him important business from Wolsey himself. By 1525 he was established as one of the leading lights of the cardinal's household where he was employed – somewhat portentously – upon the task of suppressing twenty-nine monasteries.

It would be in Wolsey's service, in fact, that the really substantial opportunities for advancement materialised and, upon the cardinal's fall, Cromwell was fortunate to be able, at long odds, to sustain his rise. With the Duke of Norfolk's help he was duly elected to the first session of the Reformation Parliament as the new member for Taunton, and now, in addition to the talented beavering that had already carried him far, he demonstrated both an intuitive grasp of the epoch he would help to shape and what amounted to a sixth sense for timing. In particular, Cromwell's prominent role in the anticlerical debates that occupied Parliament during November and December 1529 happened to coincide perfectly with the king's mood and needs. At the same time, he was given ample opportunity, as we have seen, to engage in the kind of earnest posturing that is so vital for any aspiring public servant. Unlike others, such as Stephen Gardiner, for instance, who fled Wolsey's cause at the first hint of impending disaster, Cromwell chose to remain steadfast until the last possible moment. Indeed, while the vultures circled hungrily, he alone of Wolsey's household was prepared to speak up on his master's behalf, attempting to persuade the Commons to reject the Lords' Bill of Attainder against him and engineering ultimately a formal pardon for the beleaguered cardinal under the Great Seal.

In this way, the blacksmith's son fuelled his reputation for loyalty, and hereafter his rise was swift. For by the autumn of 1530, Cromwell had at last become personally known to his sovereign as a dependable man of service. Moreover, in helping Henry to replenish the treasury with the spoils from Wolsey's forfeited see of Winchester and abbacy of St Albans, this rising political star gave clear notice of his ability to deliver – something, of course, that seemed so sorely lacking in Henry's existing aristocratic advisers. He now also demonstrated that infinite capacity for taking pains, which would always be one of his outstanding characteristics. Whether drafting laws, overhauling the machinery of government or vigorously pursuing enemies of the State, Cromwell's meticulous eye for detail would never waver. Towards the end of 1530, therefore, he joined the king's council and, within a year, he belonged to its inner ring. In fact, as he wove his subtle magic in loosing Henry's bonds to Rome during the next few years, his ascent would prove unstoppable. By early 1533, he was the king's chief minister, while in 1534 came the really decisive consolidation of his influence when he was appointed Henry's principal secretary. His father, Walter, might well have been proud, though by now, some two decades after the old man's death in 1510, the son had altogether bigger thoughts to fill his head.

Throughout 1531 the government's blind and unavailing threshing had continued, as had the rancour it engendered, for the second session of the Reformation Parliament, which began in January, had yielded only resistance and altercation. On 30 March, Sir Brian Tuke had brought the House of Lords an unexpected and unwelcome message from his sovereign in the form of a long letter, exposing the troubled state of the king's conscience and reiterating the opinions of the universities against his marriage. The Bishop of Lincoln, Henry's confessor, also delivered a carefully prepared speech in favour of the royal divorce that was solemnly seconded by the Bishop of London. To the dismay of the government, however, two other bishops, Bath and St Asaph's, offered instant hot rebuttal and Sir Thomas More, when appealed to, also refused to support the divorce. Thereafter, it was left to George Talbot, Earl of Shrewsbury, to voice his displeasure in no uncertain terms, and the general hum of comment that accompanied his words left no doubt concerning the overall opposition of the peers. In a hasty and less than dexterous face-saving manoeuvre, the Duke of Norfolk rose awkwardly on the Crown's behalf in a vain attempt to reassure all present that the king's message was only for the information of the Lords rather than for their action. And at an uncomfortable signal from the duke, Tuke swiftly retreated, flanked by his supporting bishops, to try his luck in the Commons. There, once again, he read the king's long-winded message and again the two bishops spoke in turn, taking it upon their consciences that the king's marriage was null. But the MPs 'little edified, returned no answer'.

Even the Speaker, it seems, was silent, and Tuke and his bishops beat a second retreat before Henry abruptly prorogued Parliament until October.

Nor were Henry's continued assaults upon the queen's resolve any more fruitful, even though the pope's procrastination in opening the case in Rome was placing her under untold pressure. Having at last informed the emperor that the hearing was to begin not later than September 1530, Clement had still done nothing by June 1531, at which point Henry embarked upon another frontal attack upon his wife's determined stand. The tactic this time involved a mob-handed harangue, which was delivered as Catherine prepared for bed on the Tuesday evening after Whitsunday. Led by the Dukes of Norfolk and Suffolk and the Earl of Wiltshire, a party of some thirty privy councillors, reinforced by half a dozen bishops and a clutch of frowning canonists, attended upon the queen to convince her of her folly. It was Norfolk, in fact, who began proceedings by launching into a characteristically pompous and garbled prelection, which soon trailed off into a maze-like account of how her father's conquest of Navarre had been made possible only by English assistance. Eventually regaining a tenuous thread of sorts, Norfolk then emphasised the king's pain and surprise at his wife's continued insistence that her case should be opened at Rome. That the pope should have summoned Henry there in person was, said the duke, an unparalleled humiliation and if she was determined not to abandon her vain request for a legal judgement, she should at least be content with a neutral hearing in England conducted by impartial judges.

Predictably, perhaps, Catherine's response to this rambling attack upon her judgement was as unflinchingly resolute as her confidence in her cause. Though no living person, she said, could regret Henry's inconvenience more than she, it was, nevertheless, her husband who had first laid this case before the pope. Besides which, she added with scarcely concealed bitterness, she had no especial reason to expect favour at the hands of His Holiness, since he had so far offered her little succour and, if anything, caused her much injury by his persistent delay. Concerning the king's new title of Supreme Head of the Church of England, which Norfolk had touched upon, Catherine readily accepted that her husband was lord and master of the whole kingdom in things temporal, but as for spiritual matters it was the pope alone who 'has the power of Our Lord Jesus Christ on this earth, and is, in consequence, the mirror image of eternal truth'. On this principle she could never bend, and she prayed God that her husband would never think otherwise.

This, then, was the point at which Henry's rubicon was finally reached. Standing in her nightclothes, the embattled queen had seen off an assemblage of England's great and mighty with consummate ease and loosed the first pebble in a landslide of undreamed magnitude. Unquestionably, the costs of a breach with the papacy were difficult to estimate. If it did entail war with Charles V and a subsequent severing of commercial relations between England and Flanders, the government might well be thrown into the most serious danger. The projected marriage with Anne was, of course, already notoriously unpopular in its own right, and if it was to be accompanied by the burden of war taxation and a grievous disruption to trade, there was no telling where things might end. The events of the year had, after all, shown that public opinion was being violently stirred and when the *praemunire* fine was demanded of the London clergy, a riotous assault upon the bishop's palace ensued. Mutinous words had also been voiced in the House of Commons, when it was suspected that the laity might, too, be mulcted under the pretext of *praemunire*. 'The King,' it was said, 'had burdened and oppressed his kingdom with more imposts and exactions than any three or four of his predecessors and should consider that his strength lay in the affections of his people.' At the same time, the threat from without continued to loom, since the defences of the Scottish border were weak and in Ireland a Spanish envoy had appeared just at the time when the Earl of Desmond was throwing off his allegiance to Henry.

By the time that the third session of the Reformation Parliament and a fresh meeting of Convocation began in January 1532, therefore, there were ominous rumblings on all fronts. In Parliament itself there were soon unwelcome warnings from the lower chamber about attempts to extract further taxation, as well as a call for the king to restore his wife and daughter to favour. And the government's attempts to advance its case by a campaign of bribery and intimidation and an accompanying flood of propaganda in the country at large were clearly proving no more successful either. For when a priest inveighing against the divorce at St Paul's was arrested in full flow, and when Henry subsequently commanded every priest in the kingdom to preach in his favour, few dared to do so after one who did was hissed and torn from the pulpit at Salisbury. Even in the Commons, for that matter, an

MP named Temse took the occasion of a money bill to say that if the king
would take back his true wife, he would not have an enemy in Christendom
and would not need to oppress his people with exactions. More worryingly
still, the London merchants who traded with Flanders and feared war with
the emperor applauded this opinion, while among the lay peers Anne's insolence had alienated many of her earlier supporters. And though for a year
she fought back at them, forcing Sir Henry Guildford's dismissal from the
council and boasting always that a few months would see her married, she
could not cow or neutralise them all. Even the Duke of Norfolk, Chapuys
thought, was so disgusted with his niece, and so frightened by the popular
outcry, that he, too, would have opposed the king's divorce except that he
was 'one of those men who will do anything to cling to power'. Certainly,
his own wife, who by now had become estranged from him, was still among
the most forthright supporters of the queen, as were other noblewomen like
the Marchioness of Exeter and the Countess of Salisbury.

Never had the king's plans lay at such a critical juncture, and it was against
this background that Thomas Cromwell was finally set at the head at the
head of a rudderless and foundering cause. With the opening of the third
session of the Reformation Parliament, Cromwell soon emerged as the manager of government business, and now for the first time, as his sovereign's
frustration reached breaking point, he would be given the green light to
implement his more radical plans, and lock horns with any like the Bishop of
Rochester who might stand in his way. For now, more than ever, John Fisher
was a marked man, and Cromwell the designated troubleshooter to meet
him head on in a way that none of his predecessors had yet been capable of
doing. Already, as Chapuys's correspondence was making abundantly clear,
the bishop was seen not only in England but on the Continent, too, as the
lynchpin of resistance and prime target for retribution. Indeed, shortly before
the meeting of Parliament, the ambassador had reported to the emperor that:

> Respecting the Bishop of Rochester, I will inform him as soon as possi-
> ble of the paragraphs in your majesty's letter that concern him. This will
> be done in writing and through a third person, as there is no other means
> at present of communicating with that prelate, for he has lately sent me
> word that, should we meet anywhere in public, I must not approach him,
> or make any attempt whatever to speak.

Clearly, the Cambridge academic and dutiful diocesan bishop was finding himself sucked into a world of political subterfuge, both domestic and foreign, that was as unfamiliar and undesirable to him as any sphere of affairs possibly could be. But circumstances had brought him to this extraordinary pass, along, of course, with his own unbending temperament, which, once entrenched in the unassailable logic of a particular set of premises, could not be compromised.

Nor was it any coincidence that Fisher had not been summoned by the king to attend the House of Lords, though this, as Chapuys confirms, would not be enough to silence him. For on 22 January, the ambassador sent this further dispatch:

> The assembly (Parliament) is numerous, being attended by almost all the lords, temporal as well as spiritual. Only the Bishop of Durham [Tunstall], one of the queen's good champions has not been called in; no more has Rochester, as I have been informed, though this last has not failed to come, and is actually in town, intending to tell the king the plain truth about the divorce and speak without disguise. No sooner did the king hear of the bishop's arrival than he sent him word he was very glad at his coming, and had many important things to say to him. The bishop, fearing lest the communication which the king said he had to make should be for the purpose of begging him not to speak on the subject, seized the moment when the king was going to mass, attended by the gentlemen of his household, to make his reverence and present his respects, thus avoiding, if possible, the said communication. The king received him more graciously, and put on a better mien than ever he had done before, deferring the conversation till after the mass; but the good bishop, owing to the above fears, prudently retired before mass was over.

It was an extraordinary state of affairs and an extraordinarily revealing episode. For Henry was never more dangerous than when at his most affable, and Fisher had at last exhibited some of the acuity and finesse that might have been worthy of any practised courtier enmeshed in high affairs of State. Not only had he timed his entrances and exits, his silences and utterances with careful forethought, he was also communicating with the ambassador of a foreign power that at that very time was the primary obstacle to the successful operation of his own sovereign's policies. Plainly, his loyalties were already, at the very least, divided and in all likelihood fatally compromised. For if ever an individual could apprehend the overall direction of events and chart their inexorable course, it was John Fisher – just like the man who now opposed him and stood poised to guide the king at last through the tides and eddies that had so far thwarted his progress.

Irrespective of whether Thomas Cromwell did indeed utter the following words attributed to him by Reginald Pole in his *Apologia ad Carolum Quintum*, they could not have summarised his thinking more aptly, as the King of England now slipped all too readily into the new and fateful path laid down for him by his servant:

> Let the King, with the consent of Parliament, declare himself Head of the Church of England, and all his difficulties would vanish. England at present is a monster with two heads. If the King should take to himself the supreme power, religious as well as secular, every incongruity would cease; the clergy would immediately realise they were responsible to the King and not to the Pope, and forthwith become subservient to the royal will.

Given its complexities, not to mention the potential opposition involved, the process could not be rushed, but for Thomas Cromwell's tidy mind, there had been far too many untied threads to date. Accordingly, therefore, with the greatest possible craft, he now deliberately decided to stir the one issue that he knew still smarted with the swarms of common lawyers so influential in the Commons: the activities of the Church courts. Linking this with the legislative power of Convocation, which the Crown wished to control, he thus devised a powerful bait that even the most vacillating of MPs would find difficult to resist, and on 18 March 1532, Cromwell's 'Supplication of the Commons against the Ordinaries' was duly drawn up. It was a list of 'particular griefs' that incorporated a wide range of abuses associated with the episcopacy, but concentrated mainly on abuses associated with ecclesiastical courts and particularly those relating to the expense of litigation and the delays involved. In particular it attacked nepotism, the free use of excommunication, the number of secular posts held by clergy, and Convocation's independent power to frame canon law. And in the process the singularly potent demands for a single sovereignty and individual allegiance within the realm were inserted almost innocently – so innocently, in fact, that few, if any, of those who lent their names to the measure could have fully realised what they were now committing themselves to so irrevocably.

Fisher, ironically, had been stricken with illness and absent throughout at the critical moment when Convocation was presented with the Supplication, though he had been one of the bishops who had judged the heresy case involving Hugh Latimer in March. No doubt, he would have welcomed the opportunity to deliver another blistering onslaught on the measure that, according to Chapuys, now dictated that, 'Churchmen will be of less account than shoemakers who have the power of assembling and making their own statutes.' But any resistance, beyond the ultimate option of martyrdom itself, was by now vain, and even that was premature for the moment, since for now at least, the breach with Rome, however inevitable in the longer term, had not yet been sealed formally. Instead, on 11 May, the king, flanked by his chief councillors, merely ordered Convocation to submit all its legislation, past and present, for his consent, and five days later that august body duly submitted and presented the king with the so-called 'Submission of the Clergy', in which they acceded to all his demands. Beforehand, while John Fisher lay in his sickbed at Lambeth, Henry had told his 'well-beloved subjects' how, hitherto:

> We thought that the clergy of our realm had been our subjects wholly, but now we have well perceived that they be but half our subjects, yea, and scarce our subjects: for all the prelates at their consecration make an oath clean contrary to the oath that they make to us, so that they seem to be his [i.e. the pope's] subjects, and not ours.

In their alarm at these fresh attacks on their authority, the clergy had decided to send a deputation to Fisher. But without the Bishop of Rochester's steely resolve directly on hand to fortify them, and notwithstanding a 'great protest', reported by Chapuys, by the archdioceses of Canterbury and York and the diocese of Durham, Convocation duly crumbled before the king – who was nevertheless 'greatly displeased', irrespective of the fact that he himself had gone against all he had supported for most of his life.

At a single stroke, then, the English Church had been subordinated, Henry had been offered a way forward and Thomas Cromwell had found his niche. In the meantime, moreover, even Sir Thomas More found himself unable to shelter any longer in the moral undergrowth and duly resigned the chancellorship, though promising, nevertheless, to keep silent and never more 'to study nor meddle with any matter of this world', while John Fisher and a handful of Observant Franciscan friars, along with the most unlikely figure of the hitherto compliant William Warham, were left to assume the role of loan gladiators for their Church's cause. In his report to the emperor on 21 June 1532, Chapuys wrote:

> About twelve days ago the Bishop of Rochester preached in favour of the queen, and has been in danger of prison and other trouble. He has shut the mouths of those who spoke in the king's favour, but the treatment of the queen is not improved.

Yet while no action was in fact taken against Fisher, and he was back in his diocese by July, the same was not the case for the Archbishop of Canterbury, who now found himself, though over 80 and too ill to speak in his own defence, threatened with a writ of *praemunire* for having, in 1518, consecrated Henry Standish as Bishop of St Asaph's before royal consent had been given. Already, as early as 8 February, Warham had been facing prosecution, along with a number of senior clergy, concerning the right by which they exercised a number of manorial privileges – all of the most commonplace type, sanctioned by ancient custom, and inseparable from the administrative system obtaining in England from the days of the Norman Conquest. But the subsequent charge of *praemunire* now proved too much even for the man who had so far kowtowed to royal pressure so readily.

In truth, there had always been something intrinsically moth-eaten about England's primate: qualities aptly captured by Hans Holbein in the portrait preserved in the Royal Collection. And his part so far in the royal divorce had certainly been anything but heroic. This, after all, was the man who had been, as Wolsey assured the king, 'sufficiently instructed' on how 'to order himself in case the Queen demands his counsel'. And when called upon to defend Queen Catherine in 1529, the archbishop, with his lymphatic eyes, dewlap, and fusty fur collar, had offered her no more inspiring advice than that to anger a prince was to court death. Likewise, during the Blackfriars hearing, his only significant contribution had been to obstruct John Fisher, after which, in December 1530, he summoned Fisher to retract a book written in defence of the queen – a book so able that, as we have seen, it made headlines on the Continent after its publication. And in 1531, he let the royal title pass in the kind of lugubrious silence that had become his trademark. A grave, devout, learned man, trained as a Wykehamist canon lawyer and one of the leading humanists of the day, who had been elected to a fellowship of New College, Oxford, more than fifty years earlier, he had from the outset harboured doubts about Pope Julius's dispensation, which may also help to explain his previous reticence. But now at last, even this sickly elder statesman was prepared to fire up sufficiently to take his ebbing life in his hands and assert not only the jurisdiction of the pope but the privileges of the see founded by St Augustine long before the Crown of England existed.

In March 1532 the archbishop had spoken contrary to the king's wishes for the first time and been treated for his trouble to a burst of foul language and a declaration from Henry that were it not for his age, he should have been made to repent for his words. Yet the malice underlying the archbishop's prosecution for *praemunire* merely strengthened his defence of the Holy See and that of Canterbury to which he had been consecrated long ago in the previous reign. And in an extraordinary draft declaration prepared shortly before his death, he now emphasised in clear, incisive terms the importance with which he viewed the spiritual as compared with the temporal power. He did so, moreover, with a forthrightness and defiance worthy almost of John Fisher: 'I intend [declared the 82-year-old archbishop] to do only what I am bound to do by the laws of God and the Holy Church.'

And there was a potent reference, too, to Thomas Becket's struggle against Henry II for the freedom of the Church and, in particular, the saint's eventual martyrdom. For Becket, he said:

Was rewarded by God with the great honour of martyrdom, which is the best death that can be … which thing is the example and comfort of others to speak and do for the liberties of God's Church … I think it is better for me to suffer the same than in my conscience to confess this article to be a praemunire for which St Thomas died.

Long ago, Erasmus had lauded Warham's qualities of mind and character, even speaking of him in terms similar to those he had applied to Fisher, and at the very last the archbishop had indeed proved his mettle, becoming, in the process, perhaps the greatest 'martyr that never was' of the Henrician Reformation. For on 23 August 1532, before the ultimate sacrifice became an option, he died of natural causes.

But if Warham's death removed one more obstacle and opened the way for a more complaisant successor, in all other respects the year had remained an uncomfortable one for the king, even within the confines of his own home. For on Easter Sunday, which that year fell on 31 March, Henry and his court heard Mass in the chapel of Greenwich Palace, only to be exposed to a remarkable tirade from the pulpit by Father William Peto, one-time Fellow of Queen's College, Oxford, and in 1532 the Minister of the English Province of the Friars Observant. The subject of Peto's sermon was the life and death of King Ahab, the ruler who ruined his reign and his dynasty by marrying a heathen woman of no morals – an Old Testament theme, the topicality of which had early been recognised by John Fisher and other controversialists. And now it was hammered home, in the direct presence of Henry himself, with a force that left all present dumbfounded:

> Your Highness's preachers [Peto thundered] are too much like those of Ahab's days, in whose mouths were found a false and lying spirit. They flatter, and proclaim falsehoods, and are consequently unfaithful to your Highness. Theirs is a gospel of untruth. They dare to speak of peace when there is no peace, and are not afraid to tell of license and liberty for monarchs which no king should dare even to contemplate.

To say that with these comments the friar was sailing close to the wind would, of course, be an understatement of the most egregious kind. But Peto's most vigorous assault was still to come when, seized by the spirit of prophecy like Micaiah of old, he ended his sermon with this dire threat:

> I beseech your Grace to take good heed, lest if you will need follow Ahab in his doings, you will surely incur this unhappy end also, and that the dogs lick your blood as they licked Ahab's – which God avert and forbid!

These were words such as no man had ever used before the king. Certainly, Warham had never come close to such language even in his ultimate act of defiance, while for Sir Thomas More, of course, such boldness was simply inconceivable. When Fisher spoke to the king, moreover, he had done so mainly in fatherly tones, and if the Maid of Kent had spoken thus in her unrecorded interviews with her sovereign, her rebukes had at least been delivered in comparative privacy or within the closed circle of the king and Boleyns *en famille*. But Peto held forth for all in the Chapel Royal to hear, and in doing so he spoke, equally significantly, to London and to the kingdom at large.

Nor was this the end of the matter. For when Hugh Curwen, one of the royal chaplains – an Oxford doctor of civil law whose services to the Crown ultimately brought him the archbishopric of Dublin – delivered a refutation of Peto from the self-same pulpit the following Sunday, the results were no less explosive, as the penetrating voice of Father Henry Elstow, Guardian of the Greenwich Observants, suddenly rang out from the rood loft in Peto's defence:

> Good Sir, you know well that Father Peto, as he was commanded, is now gone to a Provincial Council being held at Canterbury, and never fled from fear of you [as Curwen had suggested in his sermon]; for tomorrow, God willing, he will be here again.
>
> In the meantime, I am another Micaiah. Even unto thee, Curwen, I say, who art thyself one of the four hundred lying prophets, into whom the spirit of lying is entered; thou seekest by proposing adultery to establish a succession. In this, thou art betraying the king to everlasting perdition, more for thine own vain-glory and hope of temporal gain by promotion, than for the discharge of the thing you call your conscience or for the King's eternal salvation.

Clearly, the situation was escalating, and to a degree that the above account by Father Thomas Bourchier, written almost half a century after the event, does not fully reveal. For Peto had not, in fact, gone to Canterbury during the previous week, as Elstow claimed, but to Toulouse – and not with the intention of attending a chapter meeting there, as he himself claimed, but for the express purpose of arranging the publication in the Low Countries of a treatise against the royal divorce, which rumour attributed to John Fisher.

Upon his return, moreover, Peto was immediately commanded to deprive Elstow of office, and the result was a further angry exchange within the royal council chamber itself, where Peto's interrogation took place. For when the Franciscan refused to comply, the Earl of Essex resorted to the following outright threat: 'You shameless friar! You shall be sewn up in a sack and thrown into the Thames, if you do not speedily hold your tongue.' To which the dauntless Peto is said to have retorted: 'Make those threats to your fellow-courtiers. As for us friars, we make little count of them indeed, knowing well that the way lieth as open to heaven by water as by land.'

Once again, the exchange could hardly have been more extraordinary, and a fortnight later the king was writing to Rome for a commission to try both Peto and Elstow, while Chapuys and the papal nuncio were submitting a counter-plea, which eventually achieved the friars' release after a few months' imprisonment. For even now, it seems, the king lacked the killer instinct towards the clergy that was soon to be stirred and satisfied so adeptly by the agency of Thomas Cromwell. In the autumn of 1532, indeed, Henry still saw fit to authorise alms of £6 13s 4d to the Observants in chapter in Richmond, leaving Peto and Elstow to pursue not the 'way to heaven' along the Tyburn road, as would soon be the case for their successors, but the route to Antwerp, where they continued their activities against the divorce and remained in frequent contact with their fellow Observants at Greenwich, who now found themselves led by a man of even more intransigent temper: Fr John Forest, Queen Catherine's confessor, who would himself be martyred on 22 May 1538.

Palpably, the resistance of the Greenwich Observants was to be no mere nine-days' wonder. For while Peto and Elstow were deprived the lasting publicity of martyrdom and headed instead for history's byways in exile, their action had nevertheless signalled the overt opposition of the most popular religious order in the country: an order enjoying considerable royal patronage and wielding great influence at court. As such, their defiance was, in some respects, altogether more far-reaching in its implications than Warham's protests that year about the rights of the pope and the see of Canterbury, or even, perhaps, John Fisher's speeches before the legatine court at Blackfriars or the House of Lords and Convocation. Certainly, it was more dangerous, potentially, than any number of learned treatises published in Latin on the Continent. For the friars were an order of preachers in close touch with every section of society, from princes and princesses to lepers and outcasts. They had seven houses spread throughout the kingdom and 200 members – the vast majority of whom were English, with a few French and Flemish additions – as well as a solid reputation for strict observance, uncompromising if uncultured orthodoxy, and a forthright bluntness of speech that was in stark contrast to the conventional outlook of the majority of England's other friars.

They were, in a word, most 'Catholic' in temper, resembling very nearly the Spanish and other Latin friars of the time, and when roused, they were not likely to be cowed by intimidation or ignored by the king's subjects. For unlike even the most zealous secular clergy, the Observant Franciscans, as we know, had foresworn worldly possessions and position, and in consequence had nothing to lose for Christ's sake but their very lives. Unlike monks, moreover, they were not confined to monasteries. On the contrary, they had a duty to be 'in the world', preaching the Gospel, relieving distress and correcting error wherever the need arose. And while one of their number, John Lawrence, would become an agent and informer for Thomas Cromwell after complaining of his ill-treatment at Greenwich for supporting the king, the majority followed the line taken by Peto, Elstow and Forest over the months and years to come. Indeed, when most others yielded, the Observants held firm, so that at Eastertide 1534 we hear how the warden of the Southampton house was 'wanted' by Cromwell for a sermon upholding papal supremacy delivered at Winchester on Passion Sunday, while two years later Cromwell's commissioners were still complaining how, in spite of extensive efforts to persuade the friars at Richmond to abandon their allegiance to Rome, 'all this reason could not sink into their obstinate heads'. Nor, it seems, had the Observants even by then exhausted their penchant for bold speaking – or daring action. For at precisely the same time that Cromwell's commissioners were foundering at Richmond, John Hilsey, commissioner to the friars as a whole, found himself chasing two Newark Observants from Bristol through Devon and Cornwall and back again to Cardiff whither they had shipped themselves in clerical attire. There they were arrested and taken off to Westminster – though their captor still felt danger in keeping the slippery pair 'so near the sanctuary' – and interrogated, among other things, about their apparently reluctant role as assistants at Princess Elizabeth's baptism, leading one to quip how she had been dipped in water that was hot, but 'not hot enough'.

Ultimately, despite their bravado, both men would eventually break during imprisonment and deny that they had spoken against the king. But well before then, another of their number would pay with his life, though for an offence far more grievous than impertinent banter: namely, his association with Elizabeth Barton, who in the summer of 1532 was once again about to assume her central role in resistance to the king's wishes and Thomas Cromwell's designs. The friar concerned was Fr Richard Risby who, at Dom Edward Bocking's request, had already introduced the Holy Maid to Thomas Goldwell, the Prior of Christ Church, Canterbury – a man, as we have seen, possessing years of administrative experience, and one, too, of great simplicity and little malice. Yet, for all his more admirable qualities as a gifted and learned cleric, not to mention his craft in avoiding political quicksand, Goldwell certainly remained unfit for the pressures that had devolved upon him with the death of Warham and his subsequent role of temporary stand-in until a replacement for the archbishop was appointed. Nor, as events would now prove, was he even equipped to remain entirely untouched by the overtures of the Maid of Kent who, in Warham's absence, now sought him out. Hitherto, quite wisely, he had studiously avoided all association with her on the grounds that he chose 'not to be familiarly acquainted with women'. But, under pressure from Bocking through the agency of Risby, Goldwell's splendid isolation from the growing clamour surrounding Barton was at last to be compromised.

Richard Risby himself, meanwhile, was beyond reproach in either background or spirituality. Born in 1490, he had been raised in Reading and educated at Winchester and New College, Oxford, graduating as a Bachelor of Arts in 1510, before entering the Franciscan Order in 1513. By 1531 he was a member of the small Observant community at Canterbury, of which he would become Guardian only eighteen months after his arrival. His acquaintances, as listed by John Wolff at the time of his imprisonment in the Tower, were in fact mainly clerical, and for the most part confined to his own order, while his contacts in the broader world were merely the fruit of introductions from his friend, Fr Hugh Rich, the fashionable evangelist and Guardian of the Observant house next door to Richmond Palace. Nor was this surprising, for if the charges eventually levelled against him are any guide, he was typical of a number of the clerical devotees of the Holy Maid, who, we are told, preached on her behalf and 'gave themselves to great fasting, watches [vigils], long prayers, wearing of shirts of hair and great chains about their middle'. Having heard and believed the prophecies uttered by the Maid, the charges tells, 'the said Risby, Friar Observant, was one of them that took upon him the high penance as is afore rehearsed'. And it was probably Risby's reputation for zeal and asceticism that finally encouraged Goldwell to accede to his pleas that a meeting with Barton should finally take place. 'I suppose,' wrote the prior in November 1533, 'an [if] his motion had not been I had never been acquainted with her.'

By the time Goldwell made this statement, moreover, he was indeed already regretting the acquaintance and distancing himself from Barton in the way that he had clearly attempted to do from the very outset of her activities. For as the momentum of the royal divorce increased, so too did the Maid's prominence, and Goldwell's stomach was never a martyr's. And by no means all her revelations at this time were political. On the contrary, some were comparatively mundane and others narrowly personal to the many visitors who sought her counsel. According to Sir Thomas More, for instance, Father Hugh Rich had told him of 'strange things as concerned such folks as had come unto her, to whom (as she said) she had told the causes of their coming ere themselves spake of'. On another occasion, meanwhile, according to the testimony of Richard Risby as related to John Wolff, she appears to have saved three monks from breaking their vows and of aggravating this sin by adultery:

> The angel warned her [according to *Item vii* of Wolff's testimony] that she should go unto an Abbot and warn him to take three of his brethren by name, for they were purposed to have run away, the night, with three men's wifes; and that God would, they should have better grace, etc.

At the same time, there were merciful interventions, too, on behalf of those in mental anguish, including 'a certain gentleman dwelling about Canterbury, that had long time been tempted to drown himself by the sprite of a woman that he had kept by his wife's days'. 'A long and strange matter,' Wolff adds, but one that is more significant, perhaps, for the light it throws on the social status of Barton's growing list of clients. For as Jonathan Strype relates in his *Memorials Ecclesiastical*, she was now known 'to ramble about the countries unto gentlemen's houses'.

Yet it was not so much these activities that rendered Goldwell so uneasy, nor even such claims, as related to Sir Thomas More by Richard Risby, that the soul of Thomas Wolsey 'was saved by her mediation'. For, much more worryingly still, the death of the archbishop had, in fact, marked the removal of an effective restraining hand, and opened the door for new, more energetic, capable and indeed full-time recruits to her ministry, which would further its transformation into something fast approaching an organised movement. Before long, as rumours of Princess Mary's bastardisation circulated amid growing outrage in the country at large and the prospect of foreign intervention, Barton's declarations would also assume an increasingly political, if not treasonous tone, as the *Draft of Charges* raised against her would eventually make abundantly clear:

> Where she surmised herself to have made a petition to God to know, when fearful war should come, whether men should take my Lady Mary's part or no, she feigned herself to have had answer from God by revelation, that no man should fear but she [i.e. the princess] should have succour and help enough, that no man should put her from her right that she was born unto.

Plainly, a whole new level of provocation had been reached and a whole new raft of dangers created. And now such declarations would have the more than capable talents not only of Richard Risby but men like Henry Gold, the unemployed chaplain of the late Archbishop Warham, to reinforce, sustain and propagate them.

Known to Barton and her friends as 'Harry', Gold was probably born at St Neots in Huntingdonshire between 1495 and 1498, graduating as Bachelor of Arts at Cambridge in 1514–15. Such were his intellectual accomplishments that John Fisher admitted him as one of the foundation fellows when St John's College first opened in 1516. Six years later, by which time he had become a Master of Arts, he was chosen as one of the designated preachers to the university, and it was in this capacity that he had attracted William Warham's attention, although it was not until 1525, while Elizabeth Barton was still living at Aldington, that the up-and-coming don was called from supervising undergraduates and the spare-time study of Greek, to join the archbishop's household. Leaving Cambridge for good, he was presented to the vicarage of Ospringe, a country parish on Watling Street in Kent, 10 miles west of Canterbury – a living worth £10 a year, and one to which Gold was instituted on 17 June, 1525 – whereupon he also assumed the role of secretary to the archbishop, and continued, it seems, to distinguish himself in that capacity too. For on 10 December 1526, he was further rewarded with a London living as well: the rectory of St Mary Aldermary, which, as its name indicates, was the oldest church dedicated in honour of the Blessed Virgin within the walled city.

While discharging his not inconsiderable secretarial duties, Gold also maintained a private correspondence with a number of Cambridge intellectuals, including William Gonell – a distinguished scholar, friend of Erasmus and sometime tutor to St Thomas More's children – as well as Nicholas Darington, fellow of St John's, who had by that time moved across the Channel to Louvain. Clearly no mere time-serving hack of the variety so common among parish priests of the time, Gold duly resigned the living of Ospringe in September 1527 to become vicar of Hayes in Middlesex fifteen months later. And from surviving drafts of his sermons delivered there, we can begin to gauge the temper of the man who was soon to become one of Elizabeth Barton's most ardent advocates. All are roughly written, much corrected and interlineated, and difficult to read, reflecting an intensity and restlessness, if not agitation, of thought that is reflected in their content, which rails against sinners and sinfulness to such a degree that his Hayes parishioners finally carried a case to Star Chamber refuting the charges that Gold had laid against them: that they did not pay their tithes properly; that they played unlawful games, such as bowls, football, dice and cards; and that they had committed riots. He had been overly free, it seems, in condemning those whose 'chief delight and felicity' lay 'in feeding their bodies', and had not hesitated to remind his congregation how 'the everlasting woe and sorrow of the pains of hell shall light upon all such'. Scorners of the word of God, Gold stigmatised as mad dogs and filthy stinking swine more damnable than Sodom and Gomorrah, and none more so than those hypocrites who 'do daily sing the holy psalms of the Psalter so solemnly that they think themselves to behave like clean vessels', though 'their bellies be filled with delicious wines and with swans, cranes and fat venison pasties'.

But if Gold was all too ready to chide his flock in the most intemperate language he could muster, there could be no doubting either the sincerity of his faith or his absolute conviction in the everyday intervention of God in human affairs, the second of which, in particular, guaranteed his unwavering loyalty to Elizabeth Barton and her circle, which now also included Dom John Dering, a Benedictine of Christ Church, Canterbury, whose family was connected by marriage to the St Legers of Leeds Castle. For by 1532, as he made clear in a gushing letter introducing himself to Dering, Gold was not only acquainted with the Maid – 'my spiritual sister' – but so captivated by her that anyone who had received her approval was to be embraced with equally 'vehement heart':

> For I know by experience [he told Dering], not of my own merit but only of the great mercy of God, that she do neither love nor accept as her familiars any but such as God loveth and accepteth cordially, or, at the less-wise, such as hath a great zeal to God and godliness.

'Commend me to your confessor, Father Risby, my Lady Prioress and to all other as you will,' the letter concludes, before adding how, 'I have sent you a little piece of figs *de horto* [from Gold's London garden], and another of raisins of the sun,' along with the following final message: 'My servant shall tarry with you at your pleasure [to await an answer]. Show nothing to him of the contents of my letter.'

And it was this very last sentence of all, of course, that reflected the temper of the times most tellingly. For even Gold had reason to be wary now, lest a servant's indiscretion should betray connections and activities best kept hidden, and thereby pre-empt the most flagrant assault on the royal divorce to date. For Dering was already compiling a book, *De duplici spiritu* (The Lying Spirit), which would be published in 1533 and was to be a vindication of the Maid's oracles against the king's divorce in the wake of Fr Peto's sermon at Greenwich. In all probability, Dom Edward Bocking had suggested the theme to him, then mediated his subsequent correspondence with the Maid. And since Gold acknowledges that he was present when she received letters from Dering – 'not with a little gladness' – it seems clear that he must have known, too, that the object of Dering's visit to Canterbury was to collect material from Barton's own lips at the very time that the friar was preparing his own counter-blast against the king in the form of an extraordinary sermon, entitled *Sanctificetur nomen tuum* (Blessed be thy name).

As Gold presents it, the Maid was now relishing the prospect of broadening her audience even further and of escalating her onslaught, and if the content of Gold's own sermon is any guide, he too was merely awaiting the right moment to take to another new pitch the struggle against a king 'wrapped over and over in stinking mire and dirt of obstinate rebellion against the preaching of the holy laws of God, like a stinking and filthy swine'.

For if desperate times require desperate measures, the progress of the divorce was once again achieving a fresh momentum, which left Barton and her circle with little choice but to stage one final all-out effort to rock the kingdom's ruler from his chosen course. Baulked by the emperor and the pope on all fronts, Henry had begun in 1531 to put out feelers for a rapprochement with the King of France, and one year later negotiations had evolved so effectively that the two monarchs had decided to meet for the first time since the chivalric extravaganza of the Field of Cloth of Gold twelve years earlier. Though there was now no Wolsey on hand to stage-manage every detail, the meeting of October 1532 was intended to be hardly less sumptuous or spectacular. Involving the transport of 2,000 persons or more across the Channel, the odyssey was to serve, too, as the ultimate confirmation of the newfound status of Anne Boleyn, who was to accompany her would-be husband, bathed in the afterglow of her creation as Marchioness of Pembroke – a rank second only to that of a royal duke and one intended to lend a sheen of sorts to the somewhat dowdy heraldic shield of her forebears, in preparation for her imminent marriage. Holding her new title in her own right and duly granted lands worth more than £1,000 a year in Hertfordshire, Somerset and Essex, Anne had worn her hair long at the splendid investiture ceremony conducted on 1 September in St George's Chapel, so that Henry might easily slip a coronet over her head. And now she was bound for France, once more in the lap of luxury, amid swirling rumours that the king was to make the most of his opportunity and marry her outside the country.

With no small irony, as events would prove, orders had been given for the expedition to muster at Canterbury on 27 September, and it was there, in the hurly-burly of the little walled city – with the bells ringing out their welcome to the king, and the funeral tapers barely quenched around the tomb of Archbishop Warham; with the inns packed with noblemen and gentlemen and their retinues; and the streets jammed with baggage waggons transporting

the royal bed and all the other paraphernalia entailed by the journey – that
Elizabeth Barton and her circle prepared to stage their most spectacular ges-
ture to date. Every Canterbury lane from the West Gate to the Riding Gate
and from the Castle to North Gate was blocked with dukes and marquesses
and viscounts and their retinues – not to mention the retinues of four bishops
and the household of the king's bastard son, the Duke of Richmond, as well
as the teeming staffs of the various royal departments, incorporating accounts,
kitchen, bakehouse, larder, pantry, buttery, chandlery, confectionery, laundry,
boiling-house, scullery, scalding-house, pastry, woodyard and picture-house.
Accordingly, in the midst of the turmoil the king and his loved one had seen
fit to disport themselves in the quiet and privacy of the enclosed garden of
the Abbot of St Augustine's. But their hoped-for seclusion was short lived.
For it was here, according to local tradition, that, with all the drama befit-
ting the tale of a kingdom at the crossroads, Elizabeth Barton duly burst in
upon them through a postern-gate; not to kneel and plead as she had done
previously at Hanworth, but to threaten and harangue like a female Elijah
pronouncing God's damning verdict in Naboth's vineyard.

In the account of the Act of Attainder that eventually condemned her,
the words of her pronouncement were as follows:

> That in case he [Henry] desisted from his proceedings in the said divorce
> and separation but pursued the same and married again, that then within
> one month after such marriage he should no longer be king of this
> realm, and in the reputation of God should not be a king one day nor
> one hour, and that he should die a villain's death.

And the significance this time was, of course, altogether different from any
prediction delivered by the Maid before. For when her personal warnings
to the king had been delivered in 1528 and again in 1529, his marriage
to Anne Boleyn had still hung in the balance and the tone of the Maid's
message had been moderated accordingly. But now in 1532, the obstacles
had largely fallen: Wolsey was gone, freeing Henry from what seemed to
many a twenty-five years' tutelage; Sir Thomas More, who made the king's
conscience uneasy, had betaken himself into obscure retirement; Warham's
potential last stand had been circumvented by his death; the Church was
tied in knots; and even John Fisher, increasingly sickly and accosted by

the wear and tear of his advancing years, seemed curiously quiet of late. At home, in a word, there seemed no effective opposition at all. And abroad, too, the horizon had brightened for the king, since his French counterpart was planning a marriage between his second son and Clement VII's niece, Catherine de Medici, and seemed willing to make the match dependent upon papal recognition of Henry's divorce – if only to spite his enemy, the Emperor Charles. The French, even more encouragingly, had two new cardinals who were willing, for a fee, to plead the English king's case in Rome, so that after five years of planning and manoeuvring in a political minuet of the most complex kind, Henry VIII's affairs had at last reached a point where the marriage, so long desired and almost despaired at, was finally in touching distance – possibly within a matter of weeks.

How Henry and Anne reacted to Barton's intervention at this point can only be guessed. But if it shocked and vexed them, as it undoubtedly must have, nor did it delay or deter them from their chosen destination. For, with plague raging in London as a further token of divine displeasure, the royal cavalcade nevertheless went riding past St Sepulchre's shortly afterwards on its way out of Canterbury to Dover, which it reached on 10 October. Soon after, the Maid was experiencing further visions of 'the blood of our Lord's side in a chalice'. And nor when Henry finally left England was he beyond the Maid's mystical interference, it seems, since, according to Thomas Goldwell, who had heard her account of the incident from her own lips: 'She also said that, when the King was at Calais, a priest being there at mass, the sacrament was taken from the altar and brought to her, and she received it.'

Such was the importance of this particular incident, moreover, that it was specifically cited in the Act of Attainder against her, which not only referred to her claim that the sacred Host had indeed been removed from the priest's chalice and divinely transferred to her, but also mentioned her explanation 'that God was so displeased with his King's Highness, that his Grace saw not that time at the mass the Blessed Sacrament in the form of bread'. And as if this was not worrying enough, Barton's gift of prophecy was apparently spreading, since she was now said to have prevailed upon her guardian angel to let the wife of Thomas Gold, her old master, experience a vision of her own concerning Queen Catherine, which confirmed another of the Maid's revelations, detailed in the Act of Attainder: 'That the said Lady Catherine should prosper and do well, and that her issue, the Lady Mary, the King's daughter, should prosper and reign in his kingdom and have many friends to sustain and maintain her.'

A large number of those 'friends', moreover, were now being actively cultivated by the Guardian of the Richmond Observants, Fr Hugh Rich – a somewhat shadowy figure whose activities were already sufficient for him to be mentioned on a list of suspects drawn up by Thomas Cromwell on 13 September 1532. Though little is known of him, including the date and circumstances of his first meeting with the Holy Maid, Rich is likely to have encountered her on one of her tours to either the Bridgettine convent of Syon Abbey, the Charterhouse at Sheen, or, most likely of all, the Observant house at Richmond, which occurred in 1531 or at the latest early 1532. And according to the testimony of John Wolff, the nun's impact upon her latest adherent was immediate:

'Father Rich,' she said, 'my Guardian Angel bids you believe in me.'
   'What sign can you give me that what you say is true?'
   'I can tell you the names and anniversaries of dead people written in your notebook, of people for whom you are bound to pray and of those for whose intentions you have agreed to offer the Holy Sacrifice.'
   'Indeed, and what are they?'
   'They are such-and-such; furthermore in the cell of Friar So-and-so there is a picture of St So-and-so, and in the refectory, where no woman has ever penetrated, there is a lectionary open at such-and-such a page.'
   'Extraordinary!' cried the Guardian. 'I believe'.

Such, then, was the power of the Holy Maid to win new disciples to her cause. And by the beginning of Lent, 1533, Rich, too, was informing Sir Thomas More how 'he had seen her lie in her trance in great pains, and that he had at other times taken great spiritual comfort in her communication'.

Nor, significantly, was the former Lord Chancellor of England the only individual of high status with whom Rich fostered links. For along with Henry Gold, according to statements extracted from both men in 1533, he now became the busiest of all the Maid's adherents, sowing her seed among both the royal and aristocratic and clerical and mercantile elites of the kingdom, including Queen Catherine herself; Princess Mary; Margaret Pole,

Countess of Salisbury and governor to Princess Mary; Gertrude Courtenay the Marchioness of Exeter and her husband, Marquess Henry Courtenay, who at that time remained heir presumptive to the throne; Dorothy Stanley, the Countess of Derby; Sir Edward Seymour and his family; John Lord Hussey, chamberlain to Princess Mary; Lady Anne Hussey; the Reverend Thomas Abell; and a number of prominent courtiers like Sir Thomas Arundell, Sheriff of Dorset, Sir John Arundell, Vice-Admiral of the West and Sheriff of Cornwall, and Sir John and Sir George Carey. Thomas White, Richard Daubney, Thomas Percy and a certain 'Mr & Mrs Nele' were among those contacts described as 'merchants of London', and John Baker, Recorder of London, was also listed, alongside Lady Kingston, wife of Sir William Kingston, Constable of the Tower and Captain of the Royal Body-Guard, and 'other unnamed ladies'.

While not exactly a comprehensive inventory of Tudor England's power elite, the list was nevertheless more than sufficient to convince Thomas Cromwell that the necessity for action was increasing drastically – and especially at a time when the culmination of his intended revolution was so close at hand. The Countess of Derby alone controlled through her husband vast territories and reserves of manpower throughout the north of England, while the Arundells wielded immense influence in the west. The Earls of Derby, by changing their allegiance in the past, had, moreover, already overthrown one dynasty, and a coalition of such magnates now, with the added influence of the Seymours and the Careys, and a little winking of the eye by the Captain of the Royal Body-Guard, was more than enough, conceivably, to end another reign overnight – especially when the mood of the more common breed of English men and women was also taken into account. For, according to a report reaching Venice from France, a furious mob of between 7,000 and 8,000 women had already gathered in London on the night of 24 November 1531 and marched to the riverside house where Anne Boleyn was dining in the company of only her host and a few attendants. The crowd, which was said to have included a number of men dressed as women, was apparently set upon lynching the king's mistress, and might well have succeeded had word not reached her of their approach.

Making her way to safety across the river, Anne escaped, it seems, in the very nick of time. But this was by no means the limit of the mounting groundswell of hostility, as a wave of suicides swept London 'foreboding future evil' and the final details of Cromwell's plans clicked neatly into place between May 1532, when Parliament was prorogued, and February 1533, when it reassembled. For on 23 August 1532, Henry's threats duly extracted the necessary bulls from the pope for Warham's replacement by the ever amenable Cranmer. And thereafter, with a suitably compliant archbishop properly consecrated and granted the authority of *legatus natus*, Henry was at last securely placed to have his previous marriage annulled in a way that satisfied his curious desire to abide by 'legality'. Only the formalities remained and accordingly in January 1533, after a stint as ambassador to the Imperial court, Thomas Cranmer did indeed become Archbishop of Canterbury, declaring openly at his consecration on 30 March that his oath to the pope could not bind him to violate England's laws or God's prerogative.

In consequence, Cromwell could now proceed unhampered to address the end game – and not before time. For, around September 1532, Anne had finally consented to share the king's bed with the result that in December 1532 or January 1533 she became pregnant, finally encouraging Henry to marry her in secret on 25 January, within his private chapel at Whitehall. In a hushed ceremony quite unlike the one she had wished for, only four or five witnesses were said to have been present, one of whom, ironically, was Henry Norris of the king's Privy Chamber, who would later be accused of adulterous dealings with the new bride. But if the marriage lacked lustre, it did at least allow Cromwell, by one deft magician's tug, to pull the carpet from Queen Catherine once and for all, as the Act in Restraint of Appeals to Rome became law that March. Henceforth, she would be denied legal recourse to the pope, and on 2 April a depleted Convocation speedily declared that it was unlawful for a man to marry his deceased brother's wife; that papal dispensations were void; and that the consummation of Catherine's marriage to Prince Arthur had been proven beyond doubt. Within a few days she was also told of her husband's new marriage, as a consequence of which she would revert to the status of Princess of Wales, leaving her bitter rival to be crowned queen on 1 June, amid festivities described by the Imperial ambassador as 'cold, meagre and uncomfortable and dissatisfying to everybody'.

'All the world is astonished at it,' wrote one contemporary of Henry's marriage to Anne, 'for it looks like a dream and even those who take her part know not whether to laugh or cry.' At best, the court had for years shown only feigned deference to the new queen for her royal lover's sake.

Indeed, during that time she had progressively alienated most leading men and women, including her own blood relatives. Anne's disapproving aunt, the Duchess of Norfolk, had, on the one hand, predictably refused to attend her niece's coronation, while the Duke of Norfolk, continued to consider his niece a 'she-devil' – and not without reason, it might be added, for she was said by now to have heaped more insults upon him 'than a dog'. At her Eastertide appearance in 1533, moreover, the king was reported to be 'very watchful' of his courtiers' reaction to his second wife, even begging them afterwards 'to go and visit and make their court to the new queen'. And if Henry's courtiers held Anne in low esteem, the commons would continue to hate her as roundly as ever. 'It is a thing to note that the common people always dislike her,' wrote the Spanish merchant, De Guaras, and even if this Spaniard's observation was not entirely impartial, it was confirmed by other reports. For as early as August 1530 the Venetian ambassador had been expecting a rebellion were the marriage to proceed, and in the same year, too, Chapuys was reporting 'the wishes of the whole country for the preservation of the marriage and the downfall of the Lady'. Royal representatives who came to Oxford to justify the annulment had been met by furious females armed with rocks; another preacher in Salisbury who supported the king's actions had to be rescued before he 'suffered much at the hands of women'; and at St Paul's in London, a woman responded to a sermon favouring the divorce by calling the preacher a liar and claiming that the king should be chastised for undermining the institution of marriage.

As the drama unfolded in Parliament, however, the lone voice raised in protest had once again been John Fisher's. 'No one,' wrote Chapuys, 'dared open his mouth to contradict except the Bishop of Rochester,' before adding how 'his single voice cannot avail against the majority'. And on 6 April, Fisher had been placed under house arrest in the care of Stephen Gardiner, Bishop of Winchester, while the new Archbishop of Canterbury neatly tied the remaining loose ends of the royal divorce. The excuse for Fisher's detainment was his claim that George Boleyn, Lord Rochford, had been guilty of bribery in securing adherents for Henry's cause in France, though he was allowed, it seems, to carry on diocesan business, and a fortnight after the coronation of Anne Boleyn he was allowed to return to Rochester, as rumours of war now added further tension to the prevailing mood of foreboding. For the Imperial ambassador had been continuing to urge direct intervention upon Emperor Charles for some months, and on 10 April duly dispatched another appeal to the same effect:

Considering the great injury done to Madame your aunt, you can hardly avoid making war now upon this king and kingdom … an undertaking which would be, in the opinion of many people here, the easiest thing in the world at present, for this king has neither horsemen nor captains and the affections of the people are entirely on the side of the queen and your majesty.

In fact, the proposal was wholly implausible, since Chapuys's talk of 'innumerable people' in England anxious to welcome Charles V as their saviour and deliverer was as wide of the mark as his underestimation of the emperor's pressing distractions in coping with the manifold problems of his own scattered dominions. Even more importantly, there was the dogged refusal of Queen Catherine herself to countenance any such action, since she had already made clear to her nephew that 'she would consider herself damned eternally were she to consent to anything that might provoke war'.

But the dispatch of the message was in this case, arguably, as significant as the practicality or otherwise of the proposal itself, since it reflected a further escalation of the stakes, and a further justification for swingeing action by a government now deprived of options for retreat – especially when John Fisher himself was now convinced that, in the words of Chapuys, 'strong action must be taken'. For the Act in Restraint of Appeals and the increasing evidence of Thomas Cromwell's guiding hand upon events had finally persuaded even Fisher that armed intervention was now the only option:

As that excellent and holy man, the Bishop of Rochester, told me some time ago [Chapuys informed Charles in September], the pope's weapons become very fragile when directed against the obdurate and pertinacious, and therefore, it is incumbent upon your majesty to interfere in this affair, and undertake a work which must be as pleasing in the eyes of God as war upon the Turk.

9

HOLY INNOCENTS?

And as for my part, I would that all such obstinate persons of them, who be willing to die for the advancement of the bishop of Rome's authority, were dead indeed by God's hand; that no man should run into obloquy for their just punishment. For the avoiding whereof, and for the charity that I owe to their bodies and souls, I have taken some pains to reduce them from their errors, and will take more if I be commanded, specially to the intent that my sovereign lord, the king's grace, should not be troubled or disquieted by their extreme folly.

Letter from Thomas Bedyll, commissioner for the enforcement of the Oath of supremacy, to Thomas Cromwell, August 1534.

As all England teetered on the brink of come what may during the spring of 1533, one place, at least, within the kingdom's capital, just outside the city wall and close to Smithfield, remained entirely untouched by the gathering storm: a 30-acre haven of peace, forming a parallelogram almost 300 by 600 yards in extent, bounded today on the east by Goswell Road, on the north by Clerkenwell Road, and on the west by gardens at the rear of the houses of modern St John's Street. Set five centuries ago in orchards and gardens running up among the town houses of the great and boasting its own hayfield, along with a wilderness to the north, which harboured at least the smaller species of game, the House of the Salutation of the Mother of God, better known as the London Charterhouse, could scarcely have failed, in view of its location, to be a centre of considerable religious influence. But particularly after the priorate of William Tynbygh from 1500 and the arrival in 1531 of his equally influential successor, John Houghton – a man of exceptional spiritual and leadership qualities – the small community of Carthusian monks, some twenty of whom were under the age of 35, had also established a universally acknowledged reputation for godliness and rigorous self-discipline, which distinguished their home as a shining beacon of sprituality.

'Short, with a graceful figure and dignified appearance, his actions modest, his voice gentle, chaste in body, in heart humble', Houghton was sprung of gentle family in Essex, and had taken a degree in laws at Cambridge from Christ's College before becoming, first, a secular priest and then taking the monastic habit in 1515. After this he had distinguished himself throughout the next sixteen years by the exceptional devotion and constancy that would prove so infectious for those eventually entrusted to his charge, many of whom were of wealthy or distinguished family, and some of whom, like Sebastian Newdigate, had arrived at the Charterhouse's gates consciously seeking shelter from all association with the activities of their monarch. For, according to a dispatch from Eustace Chapuys, dated January 1534, it was not only Newdigate, sometime member of the king's Privy Chamber, who had found his royal master's example intolerable, but at least one other high-ranking courtier in the shape of the king's vice-chamberlain, Sir John Gage, 'who is of the council, and one of the wisest and most experienced in war of the whole kingdom, and has renounced his office and gone to the Charterhouse, intending with the consent of his wife to become a Carthusian'.

Unlike their Observant Franciscan counterparts, or, of course, the Bishop of Rochester or the Holy Maid of Kent, all were content with the stillness of the cloister in preference to the white-hot heat of conflict and controversy. Seeking deliverance from the city's clamour and the worldliness of high politics by subjecting themselves to the austerity of a monastic Rule established by St Bruno some four centuries earlier, not one had been active in opposition to the king's new marriage and none had appeared conspicuously as a champion of Queen Catherine. Instead, each had stuck placidly to the solace of isolation and pursuit of spiritual perfection, sternly adhering, we are told, to the rules of fasting and silence, and forgoing fires in their cells save in extreme cold. Their night choirs in winter, when the lessons were long, began shortly after 10 p.m. and lasted until 3 a.m., and it was commonly remarked that if a man should wish to hear the divine service carried out to perfection, he need look no further than their Charterhouse, two of whose residents, Brothers Roger and John, were reputed by another of their colleagues, Dom Maurice Chauncy, to be frequently raised from the ground by divine agency while praying in ecstasy. And if Chauncy himself, with his excessive love of the wondrous and other shortcomings of temperament and judgement, was not always the most reliable of sources, it remained small wonder, nevertheless, that Sebastian Newdigate's departure from court and preference for the unquestionable challenges of the Carthusian way should have so surprised his sister Jane – to such an extent, indeed, that she would not be persuaded of the authenticity of his decision until she had spoken in person to Prior Tynbygh himself.

Yet for all their commitment to tradition and orthodoxy, the members of the Charterhouse had continued to distance themselves from the looming challenge to their way of life. On 3 June 1531 John Fisher had conferred the diaconate upon Newdigate, but there is no record of any association with the bishop thereafter. And unlike their Carthusian counterparts at Sheen – at least five of whom, along with the sexton, were in contact with Hugh Rich and Henry Gold – the London Carthusians had forged no significant connection with Elizabeth Barton. The Bridgettines of Syon Abbey, the Friars Observant at Richmond, and the Knights of St John of Jerusalem had all been hosts to Rich and Gold, but although the Maid visited Prior Houghton's community once, she had been treated to nothing more than the hospitality required by convention, as demonstrated by the charges eventually laid against her, which made no effort to mark the Carthusians out as her advisers or abettors. Early in 1533, she was claiming to have received a 'golden letter' from Mary Magdalene, a copy of which Dom Edward Bocking had preserved for display in Canterbury as 'a solemn relic'. And John Fisher, in particular, had been so impressed by her claim that he sent his own chaplain, Dr John Adeson, to St Sepulchre's for a definitive answer to his own researches into one of the knottiest problems of Christian textual criticism: the question of whether there were, in fact, three Mary Magdalenes or one. Fisher's *De Unica Magdalena* of 1519 had argued in favour of one, and when the Maid confirmed as much, in spite of what new-fangled students of Scripture were claiming, he not only concluded that she was every bit as orthodox as himself, but was more than ever disposed to believe her when she spoke on other topics – including the king's divorce – on her two subsequent visits to him.

Yet if the Bishop of Rochester was amenable, the residents of the London Charterhouse gave even less encouragement to the Maid and her advocates than Sir Thomas More, who had also been sought out by Father Rich over the golden letter, but remained characteristically circumspect, as he was very much at pains to make clear in a message penned to Cromwell in February 1534. Acknowledging that she was probably 'a good, virtuous woman', since he had heard 'so many good folk so report her', and thinking it 'well likely' on the same basis that 'God worketh some good and great things by her', the former Lord Chancellor nevertheless left no doubt that these 'strange tales' formed 'no part of our creed', warning Rich 'not to wed yourself so far forth to the credence of them as to report them very surely for true, lest that if they should hap that they were afterward proved false'. Ever the lawyer and still nurturing that instinct for survival that would so signally elude John Fisher, More had also thwarted Richard Risby when the friar visited him at his Chelsea home around Christmas 1532 during his pious – and increasingly impoverished – retirement from State affairs:

> I said unto him [Cromwell was told] that any revelation of the King's matters I would not hear of; I doubt not but the goodness of God should direct his Highness with his grace and wisdom, that the thing should take such end as God should be pleased with, to the king's honour and surety of the realm ... And he and I never talked any more of any such matter.

Such self-conscious prudence was, of course, understandable enough as the tide of events duly followed what had long been the only possible course. For in July, Pope Clement not only declared King Henry's marriage invalid, but gave him two months to put away his mistress or face excommunication. And this was not all, since on 7 September, with the pope's deadline passed, Anne Boleyn was delivered of a child: a healthy baby girl.

'God has forgotten him entirely,' observed Eustace Chapuys of the King of England, 'hardening him in his obstinacy to punish and ruin him.' And surely enough, six days before Easter, the papal diplomat Silvestrio Dario had arrived in England from Scotland, to confirm even further the growing scale of the task ahead. Native of Lucca and sub-collector of papal revenues in England since 1528, Dario was responsible for gathering and dispatching to Rome the annates, Peter's Pence and other ecclesiastical dues that Henry VIII and his House of Commons so bitterly resented. Yet he was a congenial man, whom the king had entrusted with diplomatic business of his own from time to time, not least because the pope had appointed his fellow countryman Apostolic Nuncio to Scotland, in recognition of his capability in dealing with far-off foreigners. Ever the shrewd and seasoned professional, he was, indeed, typical of his kind: watchful always, cautious continually, and unbendingly devoted to the furtherance of papal interests. And with his current mission duly completed in April 1533, Dario was accordingly set for his return journey to Rome – though not without a brief stop at Canterbury to visit the woman whose reputation, as a result of the scandal stirred by the English king's divorce, was now so firmly planted even within the Holy See itself.

On 21 April, in fact, Dario had been routinely issued with a passport to leave the country, but a day or two later duly spoke to Elizabeth Barton on his way to Dover, assisted by the elderly priest, Thomas Lawrence, Registrar to the Archdeacon at Canterbury, who at that time was transcribing the first volume of the Maid's revelations, and now acted as interpreter. According to Father Rich's subsequent words to John Wolff, Barton had foreseen the nuncio's arrival in Canterbury by means of an angel, who had also instructed her to warn him that the pope should be 'scourged of God', were he to 'give sentence against the Queen that then was', by whom she meant Queen Catherine. The nature of the message was confirmed, too, by Thomas Goldwell, who had it from the Maid herself, that she had informed Dario how, if Clement weakened, 'God would plague him from it.' And there was also, if Nicholas Heath's *Sermon* is to be trusted, a repetition for the Italian's benefit that, if the king should marry Anne Boleyn, he would not remain king for more than a month. For Henry's bigamous marriage in January still remained a close secret.

How Dario reacted is unknown. But as he rode away from St Sepulchre's with the pope's fees, fines and indemnities jingling in the saddle bags of his mules, he may well have suspected that, just as the woman he was leaving could not remain at liberty indefinitely, so these jinglings were to be the last. Less than one month later the Marchioness of Exeter, also deeply alarmed at the gathering pace of events, staged her own remarkable journey to consult the Kentish prophetess. Devoted intimate of Queen Catherine, daughter of the queen's old chamberlain Lord Mountjoy, friend

of the Imperial ambassador, and wife of the very man whom Barton saw as
Henry VIII's prospective replacement, the marchioness – 'lying at Kew' on
the other side of the Thames to Syon Abbey – had seen fit to disguise herself as the servant of her waiting-woman, Constance Bontayn, and ridden
over 60 miles to Canterbury on a mysterious mission kept secret even
from Bontayn herself. For, according to the waiting-woman's's later testimony to Thomas Cromwell's inquisitors:

> The Lady Marquess never showed her the cause of her going, neither
> what communication she had with the said nun, saving only that the
> said Nun had showed her that she, the said Nun, should come to a very
> shameful death.

In fact, the marchioness had travelled to receive a political oracle of
her own and, in doing so, discovered that Elizabeth Barton was already
resigned to her fate. For by June, of course, the king's marriage was no
longer secret, and the supposedly final month of his reign at hand, making
her an object of greater interest than ever.

In the final week of that month, meanwhile, the Maid was back at Syon
Abbey, where she met and talked not only to Sir Thomas Arundell, but
once more to Sir Thomas More, who informed her at once that:

> My coming to her was not of any curious mind, anything to know of
> such things, as folk talked, that it had pleased God to reveal and show
> unto her, but for the great virtue that I had heard for so many years
> every day and more spoken and reported of her.

The meeting occurred, it seems, in a 'little chapel' with only the two present, and related only, according to More, to 'herself and myself', with a
passing reference to the dealings of another contemporary visionary, Helen
of Tottenham, whom Barton considered deluded. Whereupon, claimed
More, 'after no long communication, came my time to go home. I gave her
a double ducat and prayed her to pray for me and mine, and so departed
from her and never spake with her again.' Yet the former Lord Chancellor's
visit at such an intensely sensitive moment leaves much to be explained, as
does his actual account of what transpired, which is directly contradicted

by the testimony of the Observant Friar, John Lawrence, who deposed that autumn that Barton had declared her revelation to More 'at divers times: which Sir Thomas at the first time did little regard the said revelations. But finally, he did greatly rejoice to hear them and he did give faith to them.'

Certainly, the significance of Syon as a clearing-house of Yorkist intelligence was well known, and More would not make the same error of meeting the Maid again, as the stakes continued to increase. For on Friday, 27 June, while Barton was still there and the prophecy concerning the king had only three days to run, she received an invitation from the Marchioness of Exeter to spend the weekend at her family's country mansion in Exeter, ostensibly to enlist her prayers during the marchioness's pregnancy, so that 'she might have issue and fruit that might live'. But there was talk too, according to Barton's later confession under interrogation, 'that we should have war', and confirmation that Lady Exeter's concern about her pregnancy sprang not only from the grief of frustrated motherhood, but from the keen awareness that her husband, as heir presumptive to the throne of England, had no son to succeed him. Moreover, when the marquess was himself finally arrested in 1538, the Maid's statement made five years earlier was pored over in minute detail and evidence relating to her visits recorded in a summary of testimony taken from members of the Exeter household, which, though torn, charred, soaked and half-obliterated, can still be identified unmistakably as Thomas Cromwell's own. Nor does the summary in Cromwell's distinctive hand make any mention of short-lived children or prayers for their survival. Instead, the emphasis, even at five years' distance, fell entirely upon the burning questions that high and low alike were asking in 1533: how much longer could King Henry's reign last, and who was the right man to succeed him?

Catherine Bontayn, the marchioness's waiting-woman, was also able to throw particular light on the Maid's weekend visit to Horsley, and what transpired there:

That after the Lady Marquess was come from Canterbury again, the said Nun came to Horsley and there fell into a trance … Also she heard that men of noble blood were put out and the king taketh in other at his pleasure [a reference to Cromwell]. She says also, she heard it spoken in my Lord Marquess's house and elsewhere, that the said Nun should say that the king should flee the realm one day.

Why Sir Thomas More, of all people, had therefore been sufficiently injudicious to leave the comparatively safe haven of his home on the bank of the Thames, to risk a meeting with a woman whose days, of her own admission, were now numbered, continues to puzzle across the centuries. And the explanation, perhaps, lies simply in the kind of naivety to which he was sometimes prone on other occasions – not least when he incriminated himself fatally in conversation with Richard Rich the following year. Certainly, he was not a natural martyr, and in the wake of his visit to Syon was determined to re-establish the distance from Barton that he had hitherto maintained so assiduously, issuing strict orders, according to a fragmentary deposition made by an unnamed female member of his household, that 'neither she … nor none of his household should speak to her'.

On 1 July, too, More was at pains to write to the Maid, not only distancing himself once more from all hint of political subterfuge and counselling her against disloyalty, but even making direct reference to the Duke of Buckingham's fate just under fifteen years earlier:

> Now, Madam, I consider well that many folk desire to speak with you, which are not peradventure of my mind on this point. But some hap to be curious and inquisitive of things that little pertain unto their parts; and some peradventure hap to talk of such things as might peradventure after turn to much harm: as I think you have heard how the late Duke of Buckingham [was] moved with the fame of one that was reported for a holy monk, and had such talking with him, as after was a great part of his destruction and disinheriting of his blood, and great slander and infamy of religion.
>
> It sufficeth me, good Madam, to put you in remembrance of such thing, as I nothing doubt your wisdom and the Spirit of God shall keep you from talking with any persons, especially with lay persons, of any such manner things as pertain to princes' affairs, or the state of the realm; but only to commune and talk with any person high and low of such manner things as may to the soul be profitable for you to show and them to know.

How readily Barton will have grasped the full import of such a complexly worded letter is itself by no means certain. But by More's own standards it was bluntness personified, and his message in any case was intended as much for Thomas Cromwell's consumption as for the woman to whom it was sent. For he had cannily copied the original and duly produced it when the time for his own interrogation came.

Neither was that time to be long in arriving after the final threads linking England to Rome were systematically severed during the fifth session of the Reformation Parliament, which would open in mid-January 1534 and last until March. One of the new laws, the Act for the Submission of the Clergy, put the clergy's submission after the Supplication Against the Ordinaries of 1532 into statutory form and imposed the penalty of fine or imprisonment on all who acted contrary to its provisions. Similarly, appeals to Rome, which the act of the previous year had prohibited only in certain cases, were now forbidden under all circumstances. But it was not until the Act of Succession in March that the political objective supposedly driving the king throughout the preceding years of trouble was at last obtained. For, aside from settling the succession to the throne upon the progeny of Henry's marriage to Anne Boleyn, the new law also embodied an oath to the succession, which any subject could be called upon to swear and which included in its preamble clear-cut recognition of the royal supremacy. Surely enough, it was within this oath rather than the outer casing of the act that the terrorist explosive was, in fact, subtly packed by Cromwell. And not surprisingly either, two of its primary targets were John Fisher and Thomas More, since neither would be able in conscience to subscribe to the preamble, which repudiated papal authority.

In the meantime, however, the government's initial priority was to move against the rogue female who was showing no signs of moderating her prophecies. On 4 July 1533 – curiously enough, only three days beyond the one-month period foretold by Elizabeth Barton as the limit of Henry's reign were he to marry Anne Boleyn – the pope had not only quashed Thomas Cranmer's judgement repudiating the king's former marriage, but conditionally excommunicated the king himself, rendering Barton's prophecy at least more-or-less defensible in terms of its accuracy. And when Antonio Pulleo, Apostolic Nuncio to England since September 1530, was subsequently withdrawn from England, he not only met Barton, but was once again charged, like Silvestro Dario before him, to deliver a further warning to the pope 'that if he did not his duty in reformation of kings', God would destroy him: an extraordinary effrontery on the Maid's part by any standards. Yet when the *Draft of Charges* was compiled against her, even Thomas Cromwell seems to have considered that her prognostications may actually have had some effect upon the pontiff's actions: 'By reason whereof, it is to be supposed that the Pope hath shown himself so double and so deceivable to the King's Grace in his great cause of marriage as he hath done.'

That Barton's discourse with another papal emissary should have occurred at all is, of course, remarkable enough, but that a claim like the one in Cromwell's *Draft of Charges* should have been considered sufficiently credible for inclusion in a document specifically designed to condemn her is perhaps the most compelling proof of all that she would now have to be silenced permanently.

Even so, the task was a delicate one, necessitating the appearance at least of due process, and accordingly that process was to be initiated by the newly appointed – and excommunicated – Archbishop of Canterbury, who had not yet ventured to his cathedral city, and was spending the summer at Otford, a few miles north of Sevenoaks, on an estate belonging to his archbishopric. Enjoying, perhaps, what would prove to be the last comparatively untroubled holiday of his life, Cranmer would observe to his archdeacon that December how 'about Midsummer last, I, hearing of these matters, sent for this holy maid to examine her'.

But the precise date of the meeting appears to have been Wednesday, 6 August 1533, for by Monday, 11 August Dr Richard Gwent, Dean of the Court of Arches, had drawn up his report of the archbishop's interrogation of the Maid for Thomas Cromwell, who was observing the conduct of Cranmer every bit as intently as that of the Maid herself. And not, perhaps, without good reason, since England's primate was noted neither for toughness nor his ability to intimidate, and duly allowed his visitor to ride back to Canterbury a free woman, in time for the greatest feast of the ecclesiastical calendar on Assumption Day, 15 August, and the near-certain announcement of another round of oracles.

According to Gwent, the Maid had declared 'many mad follies' to Cranmer during their meeting and requested a licence to travel to Court-at-Street, where she anticipated 'without fail' a further trance in which she would 'know perfectly' additional information concerning the king's marriage. And Cranmer had indeed granted her wish, on the grounds,

Gwent tells us, that he might then 'plainly perceive her foolish dissimu-
lation'. But such indulgence, though prudent for the man on the spot,
with a clear appreciation of the Maid's local popularity, was altogether less
acceptable to the government's prime mover in London, and Cromwell
duly followed up with a questionnaire to be used by the archbishop in a
further interview with the Maid, which had the desired effect of elicit-
ing answers bearing on the king's marriage. For by the end of September,
Barton had been 'had to Mr Cromwell in London', as Cranmer put it,
and Sir Christopher Hales, the Attorney-General, was at Canterbury preparing to round up the selected victims from Barton's circle. 'As I can
catch them, one after other,' he wrote Cromwell, 'I will send them to
you', before adding with no apparent sense of irony how 'the two religious men [Bocking and Dering] are of as good reputation as any in their
degree in these parts' – a fact that Hales, as the Member of Parliament for
Canterbury and a resident of the north-eastern suburbs of the city, could
be relied upon to know with confidence, though even his recognition of
the victims' good names was further glossed for Cromwell's consumption
with the qualification, 'wherefore they may the sooner deceive many persons, if indeed they be of evil disposition'.

And the evidence that Bocking, at least, was a man of ill intent was
already conveniently to hand, with the startling news that his great book
of the Maid's revelations was already in print and ready for distribution.
A list of things to be done by Cromwell, undated but written not later
than 23 September, is devoted almost entirely to the activities of the
Maid and her associates, and by the following day orders for the arrest of
Bocking, William Hadleigh, Richard Master and Thomas Lawrence, who
had transcribed Bocking's manuscript, were duly delivered to Hales at
Canterbury, where the Quarter Sessions over which he was presiding were
already under way. By the evening of 25 September, moreover, as Hales
informed Cromwell, Bocking and Hadleigh were already under arrest and
on their way to London, though Lawrence was 'yet forth in the country'
and awaiting apprehension, while the 'parson of Aldington' was due to be
taken next day. Along with a letter explaining his actions, the Attorney-
General had also sent Cromwell 'sundry writings' discovered in Bocking's
chamber and the burnt fragments of the Maid's veil that he had apparently
preserved for some reason as a memento. But there was a hint, too, in the

footnote to his letter that even Hales was now uneasy about the project he was assisting: 'Sir, I pray you, if no cause to the contrary shall appear unto you, help to dispatch these religious men homewards again as soon as conveniently it may be so.'

And when Master and Lawrence were duly packed off to the capital on the evening of 29 September, their treatment too had begun to prick the Attorney-General's conscience, though not enough, of course, to make him challenge the orchestrator's motives outright. For, as he made clear in the letter that accompanied the two new prisoners:

> I have no acquaintance of the parson but he is a good man. And if the Official [Lawrence] have not offended in the matter presupposed, I can speak largely for his honesty. I can find in his house no spot of matter to be signified unto you; nevertheless, your industry herein to make the matter open in God or Christ, as of truth it is, shall be most honourable in my mind before God and the world.

In truth, of course, there was little of honour in Hales's role and less still underlying the motives of Cromwell who, with his usual sense of purpose, had determined to seize the opportunity for what amounted to a show trial exposing the imposture of the king's excommunication in Rome on 4 July. For if the pope had been influenced in his action by the Maid, and the Maid herself was nothing more than a deluded criminal, encouraged and abetted by men of 'evil disposition', the conclusion was inescapable.

Yet the minister's task was, even now, still no less sensitive than ever, and Barton in particular would have to be carefully softened before the endgame ensued. Writing to Emperor Charles V on 20 November, there-fore, Chapuys noted that, upon her arrival in London, Barton had been treated 'all the while like a *grosse dame*', i.e. a lady of rank and consequence. Indeed, she may even have lived for some brief time in Cromwell's house in Fenchurch Street, a few minutes' walk from the Tower. But it was to the Tower, once suitably softened, that she was soon committed, and there, too, that she was swiftly broken down. Taken across the Thames to Lambeth Palace for periodic interrogation by a specially empanelled commission, comprising Cromwell, Cranmer and Hugh Latimer, Barton's treatment at once changed drastically, as she now encountered the kind of concentrated hostility to which she had never before been subjected and with which she was wholly ill-equipped to cope. Each of her inquisitors, ironically enough, would suffer violent deaths of their own at the hands of either the king or his daughter Mary. But they formed an irresistible trio for a young country woman from Kent, who, as the account of the Protestant controversialist Richard Morison makes clear, was soon yielding to the whirlwind, and conceding to the developing narrative that she had been moulded and manipulated by her clerical associates:

> The business [wrote Morison of Barton's interrogation] was handed over to men well-known for their great prudence and erudition, to ferret out whether her miracles were performed by the power of God or by the ingenuity of the monks. When she was asked now whether she could divine what people had done in the past, she found very little to say. When the commissioners insisted, she said it was necessary for the questioners to be in good faith and in a state of grace: and that perchance the time was no more, when God wished her to do that sort of thing.

Cast adrift on a melting ice floe, she was clearly floundering, and before long, if the account in Nicholas Heath's *Sermon* can be relied upon, had confessed 'without any fear of compulsion' that:

> She had never in her whole life any revelation from God, but that they were of her own feigning, wherein she had used much craft to make and devise them consonant and agreeable to the minds of them that were resorting to her.

The principal charge, predictably enough, was that Barton had influenced opinion against the king's divorce and second marriage, and particularly the opinions of Warham, Wolsey and the pope himself. And by 23 October, when Cromwell produced another revealing memorandum of things to be done concerning the Maid, an immense amount of hard information had emerged to ease the way for a double indictment of treason and heresy, much of it delivered with the assistance of Solicitor-General Richard Rich, who had already provided a detailed report on Edward Bocking's book. The origins of the copy of St Mary Magdalen's supposed letter had been tracked down to St Augustine's Abbey. Thomas More's letter to the Maid, with its reference to the Duke of Buckingham now offering an allegedly sinister clue to the objectives of her mission, was also known, while Edward Thwaites, author of *A Marvellous Work*, was also currently under arrest. And the net was closing, too, on a number of more marginal figures, such as John Dering, William Hawkhurst and an anchorite named Christopher Warriner of the Dominican Friary at Canterbury. Most important of all, however, it was tightening upon one prize individual whom Cromwell had long been stalking. For the minister ended his memorandum with a note to determine 'whether the king will have my Lord of Rochester sent for'.

Richard Risby, meanwhile, was 'taken' in early November and 'his readiness and promptness to confess the truth at his first examination' had also put Cromwell on the trail of Hugh Rich who, for the next week or so, assumed top priority on the list of targets until the king formally sanctioned the friar's arrest on the 12th. On the same day, too, a threat to Prior Thomas Goldwell, warning of imminent arrest were he not to provide a full and candid account of his connection to the Maid, provided what amounted to the final ammunition. For when suitably caged, the bird duly sang, beseeching Cromwell 'to continue good master to me and to my church here and to take no displeasure with me', while distancing himself from the misdemeanours of Bocking and his confederates, 'seeing that it is done against my will and knowledge'. The Maid's revelations against the king were confirmed, including the threat that if 'he married another woman, he should not reign one month thereafter', as were her dealings 'touching my Lord of Canterbury that was [i.e. Warham], and my Lord Cardinal [Wolsey]'. In sending 'such matters as I could call to mind concerning the matter of the Nun', moreover, Goldwell not only promised Cromwell his 'daily prayers' for the rest of his days but offered a further declaration of gratitude for his clemency, 'seeing that I am somewhat in age, and weak, and much disposed to a palsy'.

But according to Morison's account, it would take one last demeaning examination before the Privy Council to ensure, like Joan of Arc before and Edmund Campion after, the definitive confession from Barton herself:

Ordered several times to fall down, distort her face and distend her jaws in the presence of the Duke of Norfolk and other senior councillors, she fell down, distorted and distended as often as they pleased, after which she admitted that she had learnt men's sins from the priests and that the Roman nuncios had often promised her that Clement would do everything he could to deprive the king of his realm.

Next day, 17 November, Eleanor Lady Rutland wrote to her father, Sir William Paston, how she had just heard that the 'Holy Woman of Kent' had been examined by the Privy Council and confessed 'one of the most abonimablest matters that ever I heard of in my life, as shall be published openly to all people within these three or four days at the farthest'. And the climax duly arrived at a meeting described by the apostate Benedictine monk, Dr John Capon, as 'as greate an assembly and counsel of the lords of this realme as hath been seene many yeares heretofore out of a parliament': a gathering like none Barton had previously witnessed, including not only a nucleus of councillors but the principal judges in the land, a number of bishops and a throng of nobles from 'almost all the counties of the kingdom', who for three whole days together proceeded to debate, no doubt in the wider context of the threat from Rome, what Chapuys now saw fit to describe as 'the crimes, or rather the foolish superstitions of the nun and her adherents'.

At the height of proceedings, which were held in public session at the Palace of Westminster, Barton, Edward Bocking, John Dering, Hugh Rich, Richard Risby, Henry Gold, Richard Master, Thomas Lawrence, Edward Thwaites and Thomas Gold were all present, though William Hadleigh and others questioned had apparently been discharged. And it fell to Chancellor Thomas Audley to thank God for bringing to light the 'damnable and great wickedness of the said Nun and her adherents', as well as those 'accomplices' still at liberty at that time – a scarcely veiled allusion to John Fisher in particular. Naturally enough, there were references to 'a certain invalid sentence said to have been given by the pope against the king' and a declaration, too, that 'the most lawful marriage which the king had made with this Lady [Anne]' was not for his own gratification but to procure a lawful successor in the kingdom. Yet it remained 'the diabolical plot of the said Nun' that dominated, and especially her relationship with the pope, to whom she had written 'a thousand false persuasions', proffered 'in a spirit of prophecy and divine revelation in case he should not give sentence'. As such, Audley concluded, no credit should be accorded to those papal sentences induced by the nun's 'damnable and diabolic intrumentality' or to her prophecies that the king would shortly be faced with rebellion and dethronement, and ultimately the prospect of eternal damnation. At which point, Chapuys informs us, 'some people began to interrupt, shouting that she should be burnt alive'.

Throughout, it seems, Barton had been present 'without exhibiting the least fear or astonishment', though making no attempt at any stage to exonerate herself. And just as no defence was offered, so no witnesses were called and no sentence delivered, albeit contrary to the express wishes of the king who was keen to ensure that 'there is no one who will dare to contradict him, unless he wishes to be taken for a fool or a traitor'. For the Common Law, in fact, precluded such an option, since verbal treason was not yet criminal by statute, and no charge of misprision of treason could be levelled against those who had merely heard what Barton had actually told the king to his face. Nor, to add to Cromwell's frustration in particular, had any evidence been uncovered establishing Queen Catherine's complicity in the affair. Indeed, it was at this point, while conferring with Chapuys during the proceedings, that the minister openly confessed, as we have seen, how he 'had used all the devices possible to draw from the Nun whether the Queen had any intelligence with her, but he could find none' – for which the ambassador in turn 'praised the Queen greatly for not allowing the Nun to speak with her, saying that God must have given her her wit and senses'.

But where the law could not suffice, as Cromwell all too keenly appreciated, propaganda could, of course, be made to supply the deficit, even though the Maid herself was now a broken reed. After years of celebrity, she had been confined to the Tower, and not only repeatedly subjected to searching and pitiless interrogation by a trio of extremely able and tendentious commissioners, but almost certainly exposed to the kind of unrelenting moral pressure so vividly revealed in the later letters of Cromwell to Sir Thomas More and John Fisher, and in the reports of their trials. In the immediate aftermath of her initial 'confession', Barton had apparently encountered Thomas Gold, one of her associates in the Tower, and told him that her admission of guilt had been inspired by the visit of an angel who had informed her 'that the time is not come that God will put forth the work'. But now her credit was destroyed beyond hope of recall, and she had neither the inner reserves of heroism nor even, perhaps, the clarity of mind that would ultimately allow her more sophisticated successors to face their time of testing with greater fortitude. Though never likely to have been so entirely a tool or 'medium' of her clerical associates in the way suggested, she was nevertheless defenceless without them, and they without her, as Cromwell now decided to seal his victory by heaping contempt and ridicule upon one and all.

Working on the principle that the idea must necessarily be killed before the body, the means to this end was to be a public denunciation and open penance, first at St Paul's Cross in the City of London, and then in the graveyard of Canterbury Cathedral, centring upon the sermon composed by Nicholas Heath and Thomas Cranmer, and delivered by Dr John Capon, who would soon be forsaking his Benedictine cowl for the bishopric of Salisbury. And accordingly, on Friday and Saturday, 21 and 22 November, workmen were to be found erecting a 'high scaffold' opposite the great churchyard cross and open-air pulpit outside St Paul's Cathedral. They were busy, too, constructing the temporary staging intended to seat the more eminent of the many spectators expected. For this was to be a show of the first order, involving the barefoot arrival of the 'penitents' from the Tower, their 'vilification', as Chapuys described it, by means of a sermon dripping with scandal and innuendo, and a bill of confession 'to be openly read before the people'. There would be penitential psalms in plenty, ardent litanies, solemn tolling of bells and passionate cursings, resulting, or so it was hoped, in a final triumphant exorcism of the sympathies that had rendered the Maid's activities so unsettling in the first place. Equally, there would be a further – invisible – platform established for the subsequent extinction of John Fisher.

On the Sunday morning, according to the London cloth merchant Richard Hilles, there was consequently a larger throng of Londoners at St Paul's than any seen in 'forty winters', and Dr Capon did not disappoint. For in addition to 'deprecating and condemning with all the force of which he was master, the king's first marriage' and 'vehemently exhorting the people not to attach faith to those who maintained its lawfulness', the sometime monk lost no opportunity to pepper his speech with tales of 'stinking gums and powders', used by Barton to convince her fellow nuns of diabolic visitations, and night-time excursions, 'twice or three a week', at which she satisfied base urges 'when she perceived her sisters in deep sleep'. 'Then,' declared Capon, 'she went not about the saying of her Pater Noster!' Even without its introduction, which has been lost, the *Sermon* runs to approximately 5,000 words, and when delivered in the slow, histrionic manner required by the conventions of the time, it could certainly not have lasted less than an hour. But with pauses for laughter and cries of execration from the audience, and with the introduction of dramatic pauses, repetitions and intervals for refreshment, the entire spectacle is likely to have extended to double that time, as Barton, Bocking, Dering, Rich, Risby, Gold, Master, Lawrence and Thwaites stood lightly clad and barefoot in the late November chill.

Thereafter, with Capon finally seated after his exertions, came the confessions, as the king's officers stepped forward on cue and delivered each one a written confession that they duly handed to a presiding dignitary who read it aloud while the penitent concerned was displayed to the outraged and jeering crowd. Certainly manufactured by the government, the manuscript copy of Baton's declaration of guilt still exists today and is written in the same hand as the text of the *Sermon* – evidence that it was prepared in advance by Nicholas Heath. Nor is there any evidence to suggest that either Barton or her associates knew in advance the contents of their confessions, since none, it seems, were signed. Indeed, the confessions formed as routine an element of a public penance as the platform on which the penitents were displayed and the staging on which their accusers sat. Brief, formulaic and utterly unequivocal, Barton's declaration followed, in fact, the standard pattern in every detail:

> I, Dame Elizabeth Barton, do confess that I, most miserable and wretched person, have been the original of all this mischief, and by my falsehood have grievously deceived all these persons here and many more, whereby I have most grievously offended Almighty God and my most noble sovereign the King's Grace.
>
> Wherefore I humbly, and with heart most sorrowful, desire you to pray to Almighty God for my miserable sins and, ye that may do me good, to make supplication to my most noble Sovereign for me for his gracious mercy and pardon.

But there would be no pardon, of course, and when the ordeal of Barton and her adherents was finally over, 'they went', the *Chronicle of the Grey Friars of London* tells, 'to the Tower of London again' along with 'much people through all the streets of London'.

Chapuys, meanwhile, concluded his account of events as follows:

It is said that on the next two Sundays, the Nun and the above-mentioned persons will play their respective parts in this comedy – for it hardly deserves any other name. And that afterwards, they will be taken through all the principal towns of the kingdom to play out a similar charade, in order to efface the general impression that the Nun is a saint and prophet.

Though no believer himself, he would claim, nevertheless, that the people of England were still thirsting for 'prophecies and divinations of this kind'. But if so, no more would be had from the lips of Elizabeth Barton. On the contrary, she had been utterly tied and trussed, so that the only way forward for her and her circle now was along the path to Tyburn. For Henry Man, the Sheen Carthusian to whom Barton had been 'my good mother Elizabeth, in whom is my trust', she was a figure 'who has raised a fire in some hearts that you would think like unto the operation of the Holy Spirit in the primitive church'. But Sir Thomas More had been present at St Paul's Cross and was in no doubt that she had been 'proved nought' – 'a false, deceiving hypocrite'. And if More was unprepared to accept, as seems likely, that some at least of her self-deception was intrinsically sincere – or, in other words, that she was a type of mystic *manqué* who had been too readily exposed by Bocking in particular to the credulous adulation of her devotees – he was not, it must be said, alone. For her credit had been decisively undermined and the fire, not only of her credibility but also her threat, wholly extinguished, as her most influential supporters rapidly deserted her.

On 25 November, for example – a much luckier St Catherine's Day for one of her leading advocates than for the Maid herself – the king had granted a pardon to the Marchioness of Exeter, as an act of clemency to mark the marriage of his illegitimate son. Wondering whether her own secret visit to Canterbury had been revealed in the gloom of the Tower, and under the combined effects of pregnancy and raw terror, the marchioness had, in fact, initially taken to her bed at the prospect of what appeared to await her, before pulling herself together, under Thomas Cromwell's far from disinterested advice, and appealing for mercy on the grounds that she was 'a woman whose fragility and brittleness is such as most facilely, easily and lightly is seduced and brought into abusion and light belief'. At this the king had duly relented, though not without the severest of covering letters for the abject petitioner, and a dressing-down for her husband soon after Christmas, which included not only a warning that neither he nor any other of the king's vassals must 'put a foot wrong, or waver, on pain of losing their heads', but a further promise to put an end to Princess Mary's 'nonsense' in refusing to serve her infant half-sister as a waiting-woman.

Nor, with the king so firmly intent upon retribution, and Thomas Cromwell already set to become the master of killing entire flocks with a single stone, could the quiddities of the Common Law long prevent a final reckoning with either Elizabeth Barton and her intimates or, more importantly still perhaps, any other unhappy enough to persist in resistance. In the Star Chamber, Audley had loudly denounced Barton's crimes and misdeeds but declined nevertheless 'for many good reasons to specify what they were'. There was, after all, no evidence of any actual plot, and by the same token it was therefore impossible to establish the complicity of others in crimes that could not be proven to have been committed in the first place. A series of more wide-reaching open trials under the Common Law, moreover, might offer John Fisher, the government's primary target at this point, not only the right to defend himself, but to denounce the king's actions far more expertly than either the Maid herself or her devotees had ever been able to do, with the even more dreaded prospect of acquittal thereafter. Yet there was still no doubt that Henry and Cromwell were shaping for a broader and indeed definitive assault upon the final obstacles to their plans. For on 28 November, as Chapuys had predicted to the emperor earlier that week, 'the king sent for his judges and certain others that were servient to the law, and propounded the case unto them, acquainting them with that which every one [i.e. the existing prisoners and other suspects still at liberty] had done, desiring to know their opinions therein'.

Accordingly, with the king hectoring and bullying them to ignore the Common Law and convict on the royal will, the kingdom's leading judges opted for a compromise, by which the Maid and her immediate circle were, for reasons of State, to be condemned for treason by Act of Attainder – that is to say, by special Act of Parliament, without further legal process of any kind – and certain named sympathisers were to be attainted for misprision of treason, i.e. culpable complicity, which entailed lifetime imprisonment and forfeiture of all goods. Nor was there to be any delay in pressing forward. For on Sunday, 7 December, the eve of Our Lady's Conception, the Maid and her companions did public penance all over again, as laid down earlier at the Westminster hearing, 'in the churchyard of the monastery of the Holy Trinity [i.e. Christ Church at Canterbury] at the sermon time', and by January the requisite Bill of Attainder, which included the names of John Fisher, Sir Thomas More, John Adeson, Fisher's chaplain, and Thomas Abell had already been framed. Beforehand, Barton and her friends had stood in the biting wind of a December morning on a platform like the one erected at St Paul's Cross, 'grievously rebuked of their horrible fact'. And though Barton was described by the presiding preacher as 'fat and ruddy', Richard Master was already ill with pneumonia. But they, in any case, were now merely the hors d'oeuvres to the 3,000-word *Draft of Charges* currently being drawn up for the primary purpose of entrapping Fisher and those others still at liberty.

Upon learning of the Bill of Attainder, Sir Thomas More wrote at once to Cromwell, to establish how limited his association with the nun had been, enclosing the copy of the letter in which he had told her to avoid the king's affairs. But Cromwell also received a letter from Fisher, which, though no longer in existence, can be gauged in some degree from a further letter sent in response to the minister's own reply. For in it Fisher complained of the 'heavy words' and 'terrible threats' employed against him, plainly indicating that, unlike More, he had been anything but defensive about his dealings with the Maid. Yet if the bishop was still set for conflict, so too was his protagonist who duly claimed that he had sent him 'no heavy words, but words of great comfort' that had merely confirmed 'how benign and merciful' the king was, along with an invitation to seek pardon for his 'offences', which 'his Grace would not deny you now in your age and sickness'. Already assumed to be guilty, though no formal investigation had been conducted against him, Fisher was also treated to the claim, again unsubstantiated, that his own self-professed 'great opinion' of the holiness of the Maid was premised on no more than the fact that her sentiments were in agreement with his own:

> My lord, all these things moved you not to give credence unto her, but only the very matter whereupon she made her false prophecies; to which matters ye were so affected, as ye be in all matters which ye enter once into, that nothing could come amiss for that purpose. And here I appeal your conscience, and instantly desire you to answer, whether if she had showed you as many revelations for the confirmation of the king's grace's marriage, which he now enjoyeth, as she did to the contrary, ye would have given as much credence to her.

It was a simple, but ingenious tack on Cromwell's part, which may in its own condescending way have achieved no little depth in plumbing Fisher's personality and the common weakness of human reason in the midst of conflict. For the bishop was not a man, once committed, to be persuaded from his premises and conclusions, and was prone, perhaps, like others before and after to seize more readily upon evidence that supported those self-same conclusions than materially challenged and contradicted them.

In any event, Cromwell would not confine his approach to that of gentle father confessor. For while he assured Fisher once again that his royal master 'would benignly accept you into his gracious favour' were the bishop to acknowledge his 'negligence, oversight and offence', the undertone of subtly applied menace remained, as he added how 'men report that at the last convocation, ye spake things which ye could not well defend'. One year earlier, Stephen Vaughan, one of the leading members of Cromwell's elaborate spy system, had recommended from Antwerp that 'privy search be made' of Fisher's house for incriminating literature, and the minister had little, if any, reason now to believe that persuasion might yet avail. Instead, his correspondence at this point was little more than a nicety – perhaps no more, in fact, than a regrettable but nevertheless delectable first turn of the screw against, as he saw it, an unbending defender of an archaic, dysfunctional and soon-to-be-dismantled old order. For cling as the intended victim might to the claim that he had kept from the king nothing that the king had heard from the Maid directly, Cromwell was now set to sweep John Fisher away with the same kind of efficacy that he had applied to Elizabeth Barton herself.

When Parliament met on 15 January 1534, therefore, the words of the indictment summoning the old, sick prelate to appear were already formulated:

> And the said John Fisher, Bishop of Rochester ... having knowledge of the said false and feigned and dissembled Revelations, traitorously conspired against our said sovereign lord, did nevertheless make concealment thereof, and uttered not the same to our said sovereign, nor any of his honourable council, against their duties and allegiance in that behalf.

Nor, if his response of 28 January is any guide, was there much to suggest at first that Fisher had any more resources for further resistance than the Maid herself would exhibit when faced with the inevitable and overwhelming force of the impending final showdown. For the bishop sent little more than a sicknote, beseeching Cromwell 'to have some pity of me, considering the case and condition I am in':

> For in goodsooth, now almost this six weeks I have had a grievous cough, with a fever in the beginning thereof, as divers other here in this country have had, and divers have died thereof. And now the matter is fallen down into my legs and feet with such swelling and ache that I may neither ride nor go, for the which I beseech you eftsoons to have some pity upon me and to spare me for a season, to the end the swelling and aches of my feet may assuage and abate; and then by the grace of Our Lord, I shall with all speed obey your commandment.

Even though acutely aware of the tightening net around him, Fisher could offer only this. And while the weakness of his condition is not in doubt, a further letter, written three days later and asking Cromwell to trouble him with no further letters, confirms the impression that, with the inevitable in process, he wished merely to minimise his participation in the preliminaries. Already clearly convinced that anything he said would be wilfully misinterpreted, Fisher's message is a mixture of resignation and ongoing

weary defiance, tinged with an undertone of barely disguised contempt
for the man who was now openly his persecutor:

> After my right humble commendations, I most entirely beseech you that
> I no farther be moved to make answer unto your letters, for I see that
> mine answer must rather grow into a great book, or else be insufficient,
> so that ye shall still thereby take occasion to be offended, and I nothing
> profit. For I perceive that everything I write is ascribed either to craft, or
> to wilfulness, or to affection, or to unkindness towards my sovereign; so
> that my writing rather provoketh you to displeasure than it furthereth
> me in any point concerning your favour, which I most effectually covet.
> Nothing I read in all your letters that I take any comfort of, but the
> only subscription wherein it pleased you to call you my friend; which
> undoubtedly was a word of much consolation unto me, and therefore I
> beseech you so to continue, and so to show yourself unto me at this time.

There are, as might be expected, the customary courtesies, but the overall
import is never remotely in doubt, especially when Fisher makes subsequent reference to the clash of conscience involving himself and the king,
and his own reluctance to declare his inner feelings 'any more largely than
I have done' for fear of 'offending his grace in that behalf': 'Not that I condemn any other men's conscience. Their conscience may save them, and
mine must save me.'

Ignoring Cromwell's advice to write at once to the king, the bishop
would not, in fact, do so until 27 February, citing once again his weakness
from 'so many perilous diseases one after another which began with me
before Advent'. Nor did he frame his letter in the form of a plea for forgiveness as Cromwell had suggested. On the contrary, he insisted upon his
innocence concerning the 'Nun of Canterbury', emphasising that he 'conceived not by her words' that 'any malice or evil was intended or meant
unto your highness or any mortal man', and affirming that he had never
counselled her unto her 'feigning nor was privy thereunto nor to any
such purposes as it is now said they went about'. Significantly, too, there
was a further reference to the central premise of Fisher's defence, namely
that Barton had assured him that she had already delivered the self-same
revelation to the king. If so, of course, he could hardly be guilty of misprision,

and had risked even further displeasure at the prospect of delivering an unwelcome message of which Henry already had knowledge:

> But since she did assure me therewith that she had plainly told unto your grace the same thing I thought doubtless that your grace would have suspected me that I had come to renew her tale again unto you rather for the confirming of my opinion than for any other cause.

He wished, he said, to be 'delivered of this business, and only to prepare my soul to God, and to make it ready against the coming of death, and no more to come abroad in the world'.

But, as Fisher surely knew, none of these requests were feasible, and soon afterwards a lengthy unsigned letter 'from the Bishop of Rochester' – written, as a result of his infirmity, not in his own hand – was delivered to the House of Lords, reiterating his innocence concerning Barton and requesting that he should be tried according to the established law of the land, whereby 'I can declare myself to be guiltless herein', rather than by Bill of Attainder. Even now, however, he could not resist a biting sideswipe at the men expected to condemn him, warning them to 'look upon your own perils' lest the law of attainder should one day be turned on them, 'for there sitteth not one lord here but the same or other like may chance until himself that now is imputed unto me'. It was, of course, a prophetic statement, but, equally, one that could never stem the overwhelming tide of events. For on 12 March the intended Bill of Attainder was indeed agreed in the House of Lords, and sent on the 17th to the Commons where it was passed at once – 'per communes expedita'. According to Chapuys, 'the good Bishop of Rochester, who is a paragon of Christian prelates both for learning and holiness, has been condemned to confiscation of body and goods. All this injustice is in consequence of his support of the queen.'

But the penalty of confiscation was in fact remitted for a fine of one year's revenue from his bishopric, while Richard Master would ultimately be reprieved in July 1534. Clearly, a semblance of clemency and due process was still desirable, which would explain why Sir Thomas More escaped with nothing more at this stage than the loss of his pension, and why Fisher's chaplain, John Adeson, appears to have lost only his benefices rather than his life. Similarly, Thomas Gold, Thomas Lawrence and Edward

Thwaites were to suffer only imprisonment, while Thomas Abell was left to linger in the Tower until his martyrdom in 1540.

Yet if a few were to be spared for now, there was no residing shadow of doubt, as Lords and MPs prepared to consider the forthcoming bill, that their overriding function was not only to eradicate all traces of Elizabeth Barton and her circle, but 'to provide such remedy as, by fear of punishment, men shall not be so bold hereafter to attempt any such thing'. On 16 February, five days before her case was even presented to the House of Lords, the Maid's few belongings were inventoried and valued, and by the time that *An Act Concerning the Attainder of Elizabeth Barton* eventually passed through Parliament, she had already long been dead in all but dying. Consisting of some 6,700 words, the act had stipulated:

> That the said Elizabeth Barton, Richard Master, Edward Bocking, John Dering, Hugh Rich, Richard Risby and Henry Gold, for their several offences above rehearsed, by time recognised and confessed, shall be convict and attainted of High Treason, and shall suffer such execution and pains of death as in cases of High Treason hath been accustomed.

Nor was the time long in coming when the Lieutenant of the Tower, Sir Edmund Walsingham, would proceed to the cells of the convicted, with his turn-key before him, to announce in solemn tones the nature of their punishment and to lead them thence for its enactment. On 23 March, John Wolff's 'harlot' wife, Alice, had received a similar visitation prior to her own execution alongside her informant husband, who had failed to save himself by his treachery, and at that time Walsingham offered her words of consolation at her fate, bidding her 'take it well and thank God for it'. Whether similar comfort was offered to the one-time 'Holy Maid' as she prepared to leave the confines of her cell for the final occasion, a little less than one month later, is unknown.

Upon the scaffold at Tyburn, having made her required reverences to the officials and to the crowd, she spoke up, we are told, as follows:

> Hither am I come to die, and I have not been the cause only of mine own death, which most justly I have deserved, but also I am the cause of the death of all of these persons which at this time here suffer.

And yet, to say the truth, I am not so much to be blamed, considering it was well known to these learned men [Bocking *et al.*] that I was
a poor wench without learning; and therefore they might have easily
perceived that the things that were done by me could not proceed by no
such sort but their capacities and learning could right well judge from
whence they proceeded and that they were altogether feigned.

But because the things which I feigned were profitable unto them,
therefore they much praised me and bare me in hand that it was the
Holy Ghost and not I that did them.

And then I, being puffed up with their praises, fell into a certain pride
and foolish fantasy with myself, and thought I might feign what I would.

Which thing has brought me to this case; and for the which now I
cry God and the King's Highness most heartily mercy, and desire all you
good people to pray to God to have mercy on me and all them that here
suffer with me.

It was no small irony, of course, that one of those also awaiting the executioner's attention that day was Henry Gold, one of the early students
of St John's. For the college's founder had already been summoned to
Lambeth only one week earlier to take the oath of supremacy required
by the Act of Succession, that would mark the beginning of his own
final journey to the scaffold. According to Fisher's early biographer,
who apparently based his account on the recollections of members of
the bishop's household, the news of the summons 'cast such a fear and
terror among his servants and after among other of his friends abroad in
the country, that nothing was there to be heard of but lamentation and
mourning on all sides', though Fisher himself, it seems, was 'nothing at
all dismayed therewith', accepting his impending execution 'as a thing
he daily and hourly looked for before'. Certainly, he did not expect to
return, telling his 'family to be of good cheer' and informing them that
'being once gone, you may doubt of the time of my return hither to you
again'. Yet he was sure that what followed 'should be to the glory of God
and his own quietness', and set off next day, having made arrangements
for the disposition of his goods, and leaving just enough 'to defend his
necessity in prison whereof he counted himself sure as soon as he was
come before the commissioners'.

In his book *Pro ecclesticae unitatis defensione*, Reginald Pole records how he 'heard afterwards that when he [Fisher] was summoned to London to be imprisoned, on the journey he swooned away for some time for weakness', and though he 'dined openly in the air' along the way at Shooter's Hill – 'nigh twenty miles from Rochester, on the top whereof he rested himself and descended from his horse' – the bishop's early biographer also makes clear that 'he feared himself to be entered into a consumption'. As such, the prospect of interrogation must have been more daunting than ever, though his own weakness may even have been a consolation of sorts, since he had hardly the strength to perturb himself in the old familiar fashion, and his protagonists were unlikely to prolong an encounter that was already a *fait accompli*. Shortly before his arrival, Sir Thomas More had already refused the oath before Cromwell, Cranmer, Audley and William Benson, Abbot of Westminster, and been committed to the charge of the abbot in the vain hope that he might change his mind. But the process had been almost routine, and after his own unfussy refusal, Fisher, too, was 'granted space for four or five days' to reflect at his own house in Lambeth Marsh, albeit in the charge of Cranmer, whose archbishop's palace lay next door.

Not until 17 April, in fact, was the oath once again proffered to both More and Fisher, and only then were both men committed to the Tower – the latter, we are told by William Rastell, being 'closely imprisoned and locked up in a strong chamber from all company saving one of his servants, who, like a false knave, accused his master to Cromwell afterwards'. On the same day, moreover, Cranmer was still prepared to write to Cromwell in search of a compromise, whereby both the accused might be required merely to accept the Act of Succession without the offending preamble and its 'diminution of the authority of the Bishop of Rome'. If so, the archbishop reasoned, 'it should be a good quietation to many other within this realm', pacifying at a stroke all others of 'an indurate and invertible conscience'. But Cromwell's response was predictable and, under the circumstances, entirely logical:

> For, in case they be sworn to the succession, and not to the preamble, it is to be thought that it might be taken not only as a confirmation of the Bishop of Rome's authority, but also as a reprobation of the king's

second marriage. Wherefore, to the intent that no such things should be brought into the heads of the people by the example of the said Bishop of Rochester and Master More, the king's highness in no wise willeth but that they shall be sworn as well as to the preamble as to the Act. Wherefore, his grace specially trusteth that ye will in no wise attempt or move him to the contrary, for as his grace supposeth, that manner of swearing, if it shall be suffered, may be an utter destruction of his whole cause, and also to the effect of the law made for the same.

There could be no plainer proof, of course, of the paramount importance of both Fisher's and More's punishment for the government's plans. Cranmer had emphasised how their acceptance of the succession might guarantee that 'not one within this realm would once reclaim against it', and not only 'stop the mouths of the princess-dowager and the Lady Mary … but also of the emperor and other their friends'. But for Cromwell the solution to the agreed problem was not compromise but eradication, particularly at so critical a juncture. For, only the next month, the oath was refused by the king's first wife with an ominously strident riposte to the threats raised against her in the event of her non-co-operation: 'If one of you has a commission to execute this penalty upon me, I am ready. I ask only that I be allowed to die in the sight of the people.' And nor was this all. For on 4 May royal commissioners duly arrived at the gates of the London Charterhouse, to raise another whirlwind tending who knew where.

10

COLD STONE WALLS, HEAVY IRON CHAINS

I care nothing for the Church. Will you consent or not?
Words attributed to Thomas Cromwell during an interrogation in the
Tower of London in May 1534.
From Dom Maurice Chauncy, *Historia aliguot nostri sæculi Martyrum cum
pia, tum piicunda, nunquam antehac typis excusa* (1550).

By no means all the residents of the London Charterhouse were spiritual
athletes of the calibre of Prior John Houghton and Sebastian Newdigate
or the sixteen others who would ultimately suffer martyrdom at the
hands of a government bent upon their eradication. On the contrary,
some seventeen in all, including a certain Maurice Chauncy, would eventually accept the royal supremacy and surrender their possessions to the
Crown in return for modest pensions received of his majesty's 'mercy
and grace' when the Charterhouse finally succumbed to the fate of
England's other monasteries on 10 June 1537. Educated at Oxford, 'in an
ancient place of literature', before proceeding to Gray's Inn as a student
of the Common Law, Chauncy had subsequently assumed the habit of
a Carthusian monk after living a life of pleasure until censured by his
father. But unlike his martyred counterparts, he would fail to stand firm
when the supreme trial of conscience finally arrived, and became, as he
himself admitted in his own agonised confession some years afterwards, a
Saul among the prophets, a Judas among the apostles, a cowardly child of
Ephraim turning himself back in the day of battle. Haunted by his frailty
in taking the oath of supremacy, he would finally produce a history of the
Charterhouse's last years, which – for all its prolixity, superstitious embellishments and frequent inaccuracy in small matters of fact – stands alone

among the documents of the time as an intrigung eye-witness account of the extraordinary fortitude of a small community of men determined to stand united against the irresistible forces of political necessity ranged against them.

When the royal commissioner Thomas Bedyll first arrived at the London Charterhouse in the spring of 1534 to obtain the oath of succession from Prior John Houghton, it had come as no surprise. Late the previous year, Chauncy tells us, Houghton had left the choir one morning to pray in the cemetery where his dead brethren lay, and beheld a terrifying portent: a blood-red globe suspended in mid-air above the Charterhouse. But, upon their meeting, Bedyll found his quarry initially evasive. For, when asked his opinion about the king's marriage, the prior replied how 'it pertained not to his vocation and calling nor to that of his subjects to meddle in or discuss the king's business'. He maintained, indeed, that 'it did not concern him whom the king wished to divorce or marry, so long as he was not asked for any opinion'. Yet when instructed to summon his brethren in chapter for the purpose of extracting the oath from all concerned, Houghton's hand was at once forced, notwithstanding the heavy consequences that were certain to ensue. And in response to the question whether the king's first marriage was indeed invalid, and whether the monks would obey the heir of the second marriage in the event of the king's demise, Houghton became more forthright, declaring plainly that 'he could not understand how it was possible that a marriage ratified by the Church and so long unquestioned should now be undone': a viewpoint endorsed by the entire community – Sebastian Newdigate among them – and in particular the convent's procurator, Humphrey Middlemore, who at once found himself dispatched to the Tower along with Houghton himself. By the law, as it stood, neither Bedyll nor his fellow agents were in fact empowered to make inquisition of a man's opinion on the king's marriage to Catherine of Aragon. Nor, for that matter, had Houghton's response actually entailed an explicit rejection of the king's prospective heirs by Anne Boleyn. But as England prepared to enter its season of bloodshed and one humble Berkshire man reflected ruefully how 'thy father's father never saw such a world', this was manifestly no time for niceties.

Accordingly, for the next month, Houghton and Middlemore found themselves subject to persuasion by Edward Lee, Archbishop of York,

and John Stokesley, Bishop of London, to the effect that the question of
the succession was not a cause for which they should sacrifice their lives
on grounds of conscience. But if the testimony of Maurice Chauncy
and the treatment meted out to a certain 'Mr Legge', chaplain of the
confessor of Syon Convent, who was also imprisoned in the Tower at
this time, are any guide, the blandishments to the two Carthusians' consciences are sure to have consisted of altogether more than words alone.
For in addition to the dirt and pestilential atmosphere of the dungeon
in which they were confined, there was also the prospect of an absolute
want of food, should their limited funds run out. Legge, indeed, had
been confined with only three shillings in his purse, and his relatives
had been informed by Cromwell in person that 'if he lacks money he
will have neither meat, drink nor bread'. And if this was not enough to
depress the prisoner's spirits, he could expect neither fire to warm his
bones nor the comfort of restful sleep to console him, since there would
have been 'no bed but the boards for him', we are told, were it not for
the kindness of the gaoler's wife who saw fit to bring him a mattress
and clothes to lie upon.

Marginally better perhaps, but far from pampered, was the treatment
offered to John Fisher and Sir Thomas More, who were also by this stage
under strict confinement close by: Fisher in the Bell Tower and More, it
is usually contended, in the Beauchamp Tower – both kept strictly apart
as they had been on the two days when they appeared before the king's
commissioners at Lambeth, and likewise refused access, initially at least,
to books, writing materials and visitors. Each was allowed one servant
– in Fisher's case, Richard Wilson, and in More's, John à Wood – but,
as with humble 'Mr Legge', the cost of all necessities was borne by the
prisoners themselves. Upon More's arrival in the Tower the porter, in the
presence of the lieutenant, had demanded of him his upper garment as
a down payment for expenses, and when the former Lord Chancellor
feigned to misunderstand him and offered his cap with the quip, 'I am
very sorry it is no better for thee,' the response was unsmiling: 'No, sir, I
must have your gown.' Since bishops, as lords, were charged on a higher
scale than commoners, moreover, Fisher would have to pay £1 a week
for himself and his servant, in comparison to More's 15s – a sum that
had already, when he appealed to Cromwell in December, exhausted his

limited funds and reduced him to abject misery. For, as he made clear at that time:

> I have neither shirt nor sheet, nor yet other clothes that are necessary for me to wear, but that be ragged and rent so shamefully. Notwithstanding I might easily suffer that, if they would keep my body warm. But my diet also, God knoweth how slender it is at many times, and now in mine age my stomach may not away but with a few kinds of meats, which if I want I decay forthwith and fall into coughs and diseases of my body, and can not keep myself in health. And as our Lord knoweth, I have nothing left unto me to provide any better, but as my brother [Robert] of his own purse layeth out for me to his great hindrance.

The bishop's well-wishers were, it is true, allowed to offer him some minimal assistance, not least because of fears that he might die in incarceration – with all the attendant suspicions that might raise – and more importantly still escape trial and conviction, so that when Robert Fisher died in the spring of 1535, some help was provided by a certain William Thornton and another whose name is now illegible in the relevant documents. George Gold, the lieutenant's servant, mentions how he visited Thornton's house in Thames Street for the bishop's diet, which was supplemented too, it seems, by the good offices of a Florentine merchant long resident in London, named Antonio Bonvisi, who had been an intimate friend of Sir Thomas More, and subsequently undertook to supply Fisher with a quart of French wine every day and three or four dishes of jelly after his health had worsened considerably from February 1535 onwards.

Around that time, too, Bonvisi seems to have consulted medical opinion about the nature of the bishop's physical deterioration. For, according to the deposition of John Pennoll, who had been Fisher's falconer, a letter from his former master had been carried by him to the Italian, who then contacted the physician Mr Clement, another of More's friends and one of his household. In response, Clement sent word that Fisher's liver was wasted and that he should take goat's milk to help, while, according to the evidence of twenty-one mutilated papers containing the depositions of other witnesses, there was further contact concerning appropriate medicine involving another doctor, as well as letters to Edward White, Fisher's brother-in-law, asking him to seek help. According to one testimony provided by a doctor named Hall, the king himself sent 'divers physicians' to the bishop at one point, 'to give him preservatives' and 'spent upon him in charge of the physic the sum of forty or fifty pounds' – though only, it seems, with the intention, that the patient 'might the rather be able to come to his public trial and cruel punishment, which the king above all things desired'.

Yet, notwithstanding the ongoing determination to pursue him to the bitter end, by the latter months of the bishop's incarceration the restrictions on his contact with the outside world had slackened somewhat, and in a deposition delivered shortly before his death, Sir Thomas More acknowledged that, while neither man ever met, both had been able to send each other little presents of meat and drink received from their friends. Unlike Fisher, in fact, More had actually been allowed initially to attend Mass and to roam occasionally under guard in the Tower's precincts, receiving, into the bargain, occasional visits from his family, at least one of which occurred in an enclosed garden. Both men too were eventually given limited access to books and writing materials. But such meagre privileges could scarcely conceal the much starker realities of their incarceration in what More's daughter, Margaret, described as 'a close, filthy prison' where her father was 'shut up among mice and rats'. Nor did both men's proximity to the lieutenant's lodgings imply either warmth from his fires or dainties from his own table. And when Rowland Lee, the new Bishop of Coventry and Lichfield, consecrated by Cranmer in the same month as the imprisonment of Houghton and Middlemore, visited Fisher in another vain attempt to persuade him to concede, he, too, left no doubt about the captive's condition: 'Surely the man is nigh gone and doubtless cannot stand [survive] unless the king and his council be merciful to him, for the body cannot bear the clothes on his back.'

Doubtless, Fisher was treated more harshly than More, as a consequence of the unrelenting opposition he had exhibited both in his writings and in Parliament, as well as from the pulpit. And as he faced the rough stone whitewashed walls of his cell and slowly paced the same flagged floor that has changed little to this day, peering through the same windows, which were then rough glazed, and the narrow shuttered apertures, out on to

Tower Hill to the west and the church of All Hallows, he found himself denied, above all, the consolations of his religion. For he had pleaded with Cromwell that, 'I may take some priest within the Tower by the assignment of master lieutenant to hear my confession against this holy time,' but the request was denied and his ban from Mass in one of the Tower's chapels was ongoing. Indeed, even in the final hours before their executions, neither Fisher nor More would be allowed the ministrations of a priest and the all-important consolations of a last communion.

Before then, however, some fourteen long months would have to pass, as the cumbersome machinery of due Tudor process ground out its familiar arduous course. Naturally enough, no time had been lost in ensuring initially that the bishop's papers and goods were secured in accordance with the Act of Attainder by which he had been convicted. Indeed, the lists of his possessions at Rochester and Halling are dated 27 April 1534, only ten days after he had been sent to the Tower and before he had been formally arraigned. But if the commissioners appointed for the task were expecting rich pickings they were to be sorely disappointed, as the following extract from the detailed inventory of his Rochester belongings make clear:

In his own bedchamber. A bedstead and mattress, a counter-pane of red cloth lined with canvas. A tester of old red velvet nothing worth. A leather chair with a cushion. An altar with a hanging of white and green satin of Bruges with Our Lord embroidered on it. Two blue silk curtains. A cupboard with a cloth. A little chair covered with leather and a cushion. A close stool with an old cushion upon it. An andiron, a fire-pan, and a fire shovel.

In the great study within the same chamber. A long spruce table and other tables. Three leather chairs. Fire irons. Eight round desks and shelves for books.

In the north study. Divers glasses with waters and syrups and boxes of marmalade. A table, four round desks and bookshelves.

In the south gallery. Fifty glasses of sorts with a curtain of green and red say.

In the chapel in the end of the south gallery. A cushion in the seat of the chapel, the altar cloths, two pieces of old velvet and an altar stone. Four gilt images with a crucifix.

In the broad gallery. Old hangings of green say. Old carpets of tapestry. An altar cloth painted with green velvet and yellow damask. A St John's head standing at the end of the altar. A pontifical book. A painted cloth of the image of Jesus taken down from the Cross.

In the old gallery. Certain old books pertaining to divers monasteries.

In the wardrobe. A tunic of stamnel [coarse woollen cloth], a Spanish blanket, an alembic to distil *aquae vitae*, with divers old trash. A trestle bedstead, a pair of sheets, six boards, two pair of trestles.

In the great chapel. The altar hung with red silk crosses, and under it two hangings of yellow silk of Bruges and blue damask; eight gilt images upon the altar; two latten [a type of brass] candlesticks … An old carpet on the ground before the altar. Hangings of painted red say. An altar beneath in the same chapel hung with old dornick, and a painted cloth of the three kings of Cologne. Five images of timber …

In the little chapel next the great chapel. Hangings of old painted cloths, a great looking glass broken. An old folding bed.

Plainly, the royal agents were nothing if not thorough, but their findings strike a curiously melancholy note, as they went about their humdrum business noting numerous 'old' items and other tired paraphernalia, all reflecting in their own way a dowdy otherworldliness on behalf of the owner, which stands in such contrast to similar lists drawn up for Thomas Wolsey's possessions at the time of his attainder. The residing impression is of a 'bachelor bedsit' rather than an episcopal palace, and though there is an accompanying inventory of plate, this too suggests a notable lack of ostentation. 'Cruets, altar basins, &c, with the port-cullis upon them' had almost certainly been the gift of Lady Margaret Beaufort, but the total weight of plate in Fisher's possession was only just over 2,000oz Troy weight – a very modest amount by comparison to his peers – and half of this in any case was gilt, with much of the remainder so-called 'white silver'.

All, however, was duly dispatched to 'my master Cromwell to the king's use', along with the bishop's letters and papers, among which were several addressed to Queen Catherine by an unknown writer whose name Fisher would claim during his first lengthy interrogation in the Tower to have forgotten. Nor did he admit at that time to any complicity

in the dispatch overseas of a book written by him that one correspondent – a representative of 'a German prince' – claimed to have received,
or to any other wrongdoing implied by his inquisitors as they pressed
home their investigation of his dealings with Warham, More, Thomas
Abell and a range of more obscure figures. The possibility of linking
Fisher to a foreign ruler was, of course, a particularly tempting prospect even at this stage, since it would have provided grounds at once
for a charge of treason, and this indeed may well have been the aim.
For there was no mention as yet, significantly, of the oath of succession,
which remained, ostensibly, the reason for Fisher's imprisonment, and
a heavy emphasis instead upon other potentially incriminating correspondence, including that with Ralph Baynes, fellow of St John's and a
leading Hebrew scholar, who had sent letters, it was claimed, 'in which
the king's cause was defamed'. There is the possibility, too, that the ques-
tioners were seeking some new disclosure against the former queen
herself, since it was widely rumoured that a further Bill of Attainder was
to be brought before Parliament against both her and the Princess Mary.
But in all respects the search proved barren, as Fisher, sickly though he
was, watched his words and held his ground. His responses, it is true,
were weary rather than challenging, displaying little of the belligerence
that had characterised his more notable performances in Parliament and
Convocation and at Blackfriars. Nor did he employ the craft and coun-
ter-play of Thomas More under similar interrogation. Yet if the fire in his
belly seemed to have waned with the strength of his body, the impression was deceptive, since his spirit was as resilient as ever.

   And the same was no less true of John Fisher's Carthusian counterparts,
notwithstanding the fact that within a month of their initial imprisonment, both had taken the oath of succession and been subsequently placed
at liberty. For Cromwell, unlike his royal master, had already realised that
terror is never more potent than when suitably rationed, and was equally
aware by now that the two Carthusians had been confined wholly illegally,
since the words of the requisite oath had been included only within the
preamble to the Act of Succession rather than the act itself – a technical
blunder of the kind not usually associated with its architect, though one
of which a sharp legal mind like Thomas More's had been immediately
aware. 'I may tell thee, Meg,' More told his daughter at the time of his

own imprisonment, 'they that have committed me hither for refusing this oath not agreeable with the statute are not by their own law able to justify my imprisonment.' Indeed, the error concerned would actually necessitate a second Act of Succession when Parliament reassembled in November 1534, though such technicalities are unlikely to have featured in the thinking of Houghton and Middlemore who may, in all likelihood, have been kept ignorant of the offending preamble with its implicit repudiation of papal authority. In any event, they were careful to accept the oath only insofar 'as it might be lawful', though this was enough to secure their release, on the assumption, no doubt, that, as altogether smaller fry than More and Fisher, they could be consumed at leisure thereafter, when time and opportunity afforded.

In consequence, both arrived home at the Charterhouse as yet unharmed, albeit to a reception that was by no means unequivocal, since even now, it seems, they had moved too far and fast for the rest of their community, most of whom were still intent upon refusing the oath altogether. Indeed, when royal commissioners returned to administer it, they received no adhesions at all, while at a second attempt no more than half a dozen swore. Only on the third occasion, in fact, did the entire community submit – and only then when surrounded by men-at-arms and under express orders from their prior who was still determined, if at all possible, to avoid the sacrifice of his entire community by incurring the brunt of royal displeasure himself. Though the lord mayor had been present, the sullen reluctance of a determined hard core ensured, in fact, that the swearing itself occupied two separate days, since even Prior Houghton's entreaties did not yield the desired effect at once. Instead, on 24 May, when the commissioners were Bedyll and Edward Lee, only fourteen subscribed, among whom were Houghton and Middlemore, and not until the second day, 6 June, did the rest of the community finally conform in the presence of Lee and another visitor, Thomas Kitson.

But if the submission might nevertheless have implied acceptance of the new status quo, appearances were deceptive, even though for Chauncy, it is true, the danger appeared to have passed:

We all swore as we were required, making one condition, that we submitted only so far as it was lawful for us so to do. Thus like Jonah, we were delivered from the belly of this monster, this *immanis ceta* [vast fish], and began again to rejoice, like him, under the shadow of the gourd of our home.

Yet even he would appreciate with hindsight that 'it is better to trust in the Lord than in princes, in whom is no salvation'. 'God,' he added, 'had prepared a worm that smote our gourd and made it perish.' And the reason was simple, since the Carthusians' initial opposition to the king was based wholly upon a strong disapproval of his actions rather than a clear appreciation of the more fundamental principles at stake that had already been grasped so readily by Fisher and More alike. As such, the monks could submit at this stage without wholly compromising their consciences upon a matter of faith, though this, as their prior already fully appreciated, could not last indefinitely. Upon his release from the Tower, indeed, Houghton had not only informed his brethren of his submission, but added how he was convinced that his yielding would not protect him long from the destruction he foresaw:

> Our hour, dear brethren [he declared in the monastery's chapter house], is not yet come. In the same night in which we [himself and Middlemore] were set free I had a dream that I should not escape thus. Within a year I shall be brought again to that place, and then I shall finish my course.

Far from being a solution, then, the oaths of May and June were nothing more than a prelude and a final parting point between those monks made for martyrdom and others less stalwart, one of whom subsequently wrote to Cromwell imploring his aid and relating how he had furnished Bedyll with important information about his brethren in the chapter house 'on Friday after Corpus Christi' – for which, he complained, the prior had subsequently kept him 'like an infidel out of sight and speech of all friends'.

In light of what was now to follow, of course, the anonymous informant might well be forgiven his weakness, since the seventh session of the Reformation Parliament, which met from 3 November to 18 December 1534, provided the government with all the requisite tools to crush its opponents definitively. Initially, the government's policy of religious nationalisation was effectively completed by the Act of Supremacy, which not only granted the king control of clerical discipline, but accorded him the right to try heresy cases and, as such, confirmed his ultimate control of all religious teaching. Much more ominously still for the London Carthusians, however, and especially John Fisher and Sir Thomas More, Thomas Cromwell also seized the opportunity for silencing all opposition by means of a Treason Act, passed simultaneously with the Act of Supremacy, which entailed an unprecedented broadening of the concept of treason to encompass all types of 'malicious' attack upon the king, Queen Anne or the succession, including those made even orally or in writing. Designed to root out the seditious 'imps of the said bishop of Rome', this so-called 'law of words' both legalised the imprisonment of Fisher and More retrospectively and left few, if any, hiding places within the legal foliage. Henceforth, it would be treasonable to call the king a heretic, schismatic, tyrant, infidel or usurper, and although it was not made an offence to refuse to answer questions relating to the supremacy until 1536 with the Act Extinguishing the Authority of the Bishop of Rome, there was now little refuge to be had even in honourable silence, as Sir Thomas More would find to his cost.

'It was,' said Lord Montague at the time, 'a strange world as words were made treason,' and it was a measure of the Treason Act's stringency that it would be repealed in the very first Parliament of the next reign on the grounds that it was likely to 'appear to men of exterior realms and many of the king's majesty's subjects very strait, sore, extreme and terrible'. It was undeniable that men had been executed for words rather than actions well before 1534 when their utterances had been 'constructed' as treason. And dubious evidence, likewise, had always been a feature of political trials: the cases of the Duke of Clarence in 1478 and of the Earl of Warwick in 1499 are striking examples of such miscarriages. Nor, it must be said, were all those arraigned under the new law of treason necessarily subjected to its full rigours. On the contrary, only one in every three prosecutions led to condemnation. When Cromwell heard, for instance, that an absent-minded canon nearing his eightieth year had mistakenly offered prayers for 'Catherine the Queen' instead of Anne, he did not press for punishment. Similarly, a drunken servant of the Duchess of Northumberland who had been 'in danger of his limbs' for criticising the king was eventually released from prison when his mistress interceded for him on the grounds that he had been insensible at the time and now had no memory of his offence.

Yet the arrest or interrogation of the king's subjects for such ill-considered remarks undeniably served to create what would become by degrees a pervasive culture of suspicion and denunciation. And even if some two-thirds of those accused of treason were acquitted, pardoned or had their cases dropped, up to 130 people had still lost their lives for 'treasonable words' before the decade was out. Certainly, Fisher and More were now brought nearer to the block than ever, though attempts to persuade them of their error remained ongoing. In Fisher's case, we are told, he was visited 'several times' by Bishop Stokesley of London, Stephen Gardiner of Winchester and Cuthbert Tunstall of Durham who acted, the early biographer suggests, 'against their stomachs, and rather for fear of the king's displeasure in whom they knew was no mercy'. On another occasion, moreover, a further panel of some 'six or seven bishops' came 'by the king's commandment' in hope of prevailing upon Fisher, only to be rebuked by the prisoner for their own inconstancy. 'The fort is betrayed even of them that should have defended it,' Fisher is said to have uttered, before telling his audience how he was an 'old man and looked not long to live'. And when Richard Wilson, his attendant, asked him why he should 'stick' more than the rest of the bishops had done, Fisher remained adamant:

> Tush, tush, thou art but a fool and knowest little what this matter meaneth but hereafter thou may knowest more. But I tell thee it is not for the supremacy only that I am thus tossed and troubled, but also for an oath, which if I would have sworn, I doubt whether I should ever have been questioned for the supremacy or no.

Gleaned no doubt from Wilson himself, the early biographer's account leaves little doubt of the pressure to which Fisher was subject as even those close to him enticed him to submit. And there was trickery too, it seems, as both the bishop and Sir Thomas More were assured that the other had actually taken the oath. Fisher, indeed, seems to have accepted this as fact, 'because he mistrusted not the false trains [deceits] of the councillors'.

Yet this, likewise, 'could not move him' and even now in his isolation, cut off from the sacraments of the Church, there were consolations of a kind, not the least of which was a message sent up to him on behalf of the fellows of St John's College by 'two of their company, Mr Seton and Mr Brandesby', which was intended 'partly to salute him and visit him in the name of the whole house and partly to desire of him the confirmation of their statutes under his seal, which he himself had long before made and drawn in writing but never yet confirmed'. Under the circumstances, perhaps, it was small beer, but though the letter that Seton and Brandesby carried may not have been seen by him directly, it reaffirmed his standing within the institution that had always featured so prominently in his thoughts, and, like a similar letter sent around the same time by Erasmus, was written with deepest warmth and reverence. Referring to 'the bitter and troublesome cares which of late' had overtaken him, the writers admitted how they were contacting the prisoner 'more because they are ashamed to be silent than because they know what is fit for them to say' and declared that 'when all others who bear the Christian name, or love their country, lament at this time his troubles and distress, they should be very ungrateful did they not feel a still greater grief'.

> You [the letter continues] are our father, our teacher, our preceptor and lawgiver, and above all our pattern of virtue and holiness. To you indeed we owe our sustenance and learning, and whatever we have or know that is good. We have no way of showing our gratitude or of repaying these benefits save by the prayers we continually offer to God on your behalf.

There was an offer, too, of whatever material assistance the college could offer during his stay in the Tower, and above all a reminder that 'if he pleased men, he would not be the servant of Christ'.

But even such limited consolations were swiftly outpaced by further events. For Fisher would learn only a few weeks later how those same Cambridge colleagues had nevertheless, out of sheer fear, both taken the oath of supremacy and renounced all allegiance to Rome. And as his own university finally deserted his cause, so he found himself cut off, too, before long from the beloved diocese that he had served so devotedly for thirty years. For although the *congé d élire* to the chapter at Rochester is dated 8 August 1535, Fisher's removal had actually occurred more than eight months earlier, on 2 January, as a result of an early deployment of the king's new ecclesiastical authority, and represented in effect the final act of punishment on the Crown's behalf, short of the executioner's axe itself. No protest on Fisher's behalf was forthcoming, no stirring of dissent was even remotely visible, though the irony of the king's choice of replacement was particularly wounding, since the man concerned was selected from the very Dominican Order whose name was usually synonymous with orthodoxy. For some time, in fact, John Hilsey, the new Bishop of Rochester, had regarded Cromwell as his patron and had actually spent much of the summer of 1534 administering the oath of succession to friaries throughout England. But this was not all. For in claiming poverty upon his appointment, Hilsey would even deign to beg Cromwell for Fisher's mitre, staff and seal, and be granted his wish – though not without a sneering observation from his benefactor that he was guilty of 'covetousness' – before preaching at Catherine of Aragon's funeral in January 1536, and producing, as a further token of his integrity, a wholly implausible allegation that, in the hour of death, she had acknowledged how she had never been Queen of England.

Plainly, there were healthy pickings to be gleaned from compliance with the new status quo, and Hilsey was not the only figure – whether from self-interest, conviction or a curious mixture of both – to seek them, since the world was changing helter-skelter and, in such circumstances, it was easy enough for those in its midst to be swept along by events and settle for the wisdom and comforts of the herd. For others immured from the world and its ways, however, and therefore more inclined to seek guidance from within than without, absolutes and 'truth' were, of course, always likely to be more compelling, so that even Sir Thomas More had by now closed the shutters of his cell, to sit all day in contemplation of the joys of heaven after his correspondence with John Fisher had been discovered and his books removed. When the Tower's lieutenant had remarked the closed shutters, More had jestingly replied how the shop may be shut when the goods are gone. But Fisher too, it seems, having long since accepted his own fate, if not his kingdom's, had by this time opted for a similar resort to prayer and devotion. 'I came to my master while he was saying evensong,' recorded his servant Richard Wilson in May 1535, confirming that in spite of his abject condition, Fisher was continuing to cling faithfully to the consolations of the only book now in his possession – his breviary.

During his solitary hours, More had already written his *Dialogue of Comfort Against Tribulation*, and Fisher, likewise, had been busy with his quill before its final removal. Three short books, in fact, were produced by him during his captivity, the most enduring of which are *A Spiritual Consolation* and *The Ways of Perfect Religion*, written to his half-sister Elizabeth White, by then a Dominican nun at Dartford in Kent, who was said, at the time of the books' publication in the reign of Queen Mary, to be 'so like the said Bishop of Rochester in person' that the queen herself revered her. Though no match for More's masterpiece, perhaps, which for wit, pathos and eloquence has, arguably, few equals among literature of its kind, *The Ways of Perfect Religion*, in particular, is nevertheless a testament to the fruits of a lifetime's meditation – the summing up, in some respects, of a man's entire goals – and an inspiring *entrée* into the thoughts of an individual faced with the ultimate sacrifice for principles that it was now beyond him to forsake. Though Fisher's treatment of the vanity of life and the need for repentance, not to mention his preoccupation with death, judgement and the wrath to come, may sit uneasily with modern readers, he was no less constant in reminding sinners of the infinite mercy of God and the eternal joys of those who learn to love him. And his final writings show him, in fact, at his rounded, most humane best: more keenly aware than ever that spiritual gain, powered by love, is, in effect, unattainable without physical sacrifice – a point that he makes most famously by reiterating his favourite comparison between the life of the true Christian and that of a hunter:

> What life is more painful and laborious of itself than is the life of hunters which most early in the morning break their sleep and rise when others do take their rest and ease, and in his labours he may use no highways and soft grass, but he must tread upon the fallows, run over the hedges, and creep through the thick bushes, and cry all the day long upon his dogs, and so continue without meat or drink until the very night drive him home; these labours be unto him pleasant and joyous, for the desire and love that he hath to see the poor hare chased with dogs. Verily, verily, if he were compelled to take upon him such labours, and not for this cause, he would soon be weary of them, thinking them full tedious unto him. Neither would be rise out of bed so soon, nor fast so long, nor endure these other labours unless he had a very love therein. And

therefore I may well say that love is the principal thing that maketh any work easy, though the work be right painful of itself and that without love no labour can be comfortable to the doer.

Though never a sociable or, for that matter, easy man, Fisher's physical weakness and final incarceration had, from the evidence of his final writings, largely rid him of the pugnacity and irascibility that had, from some perspectives, brought him to this final pass in the first place – leaving, much more visibly than ever, the inner ardour that had driven him all along. Always more a man of the spirit than a man of affairs, his impending martyrdom was indeed his life's realisation and, as he himself undoubtedly saw it, an essentially welcome release from the vanities that had always sat so uncomfortably with him. As such, it was only fitting, of course, that his final little work should conclude as it did with eight 'considerations' or meditations upon the main theme:

> O blessed Jesu, make me to love thee entirely.
> O blessed Jesu I would fain, but without thy help I can not.
> O blessed Jesu, let me deeply consider the greatness of thy love towards me.
> O blessed Jesu, give unto me grace heartily to thank thee for thy benefits.
> O blessed Jesu, give me good will to serve thee, and to suffer.
> O sweet Jesu, give me a natural remembrance of thy passion.
> O sweet Jesu possess my heart, hold and keep it only to thee.

The literary tropes and flourishes of scholarship that are so characteristic of Fisher's earlier works are gone, and we are left with what may be the only true expression of his inner life laid bare, other than a five-page fragment among his miscellaneous papers, tattered and badly mutilated, which contains the following prayer, likely to have been written during the final term of his stay within the Tower: 'Rescue me from these manifold perils that I am in, for unless thou wilt of thine goodness relieve me, I am but a lost creature.'

How Fisher's papers were removed from the Tower, we know not. Perhaps Robert Fisher or Richard Wilson smuggled them out, just as the manuscript of Thomas More's *Dialogue of Comfort* escaped the authorities, most probably by the skill of his daughter Margaret. Certainly, not all their gaolers were insensitive to both men's bravery and sufferings. But if lone sympathisers were still inclined to acts of compassion, and the surrounding ring of security remained less than watertight, there was nevertheless no question of ultimate mercy or hesitation on behalf of a government set on sealing what already amounted to a revolution.

As the wheels of State continued to turn, furthermore, it was only to be expected that any brief respite for Carthusian community of the London Charterhouse would be woefully short lived. Indeed, the efforts to bring the monks to compliance with the royal will had been continued throughout the period after their initial acceptance of the oath of supremacy. And since the prior of the Bridgettines of Syon was considered by Cromwell to be particularly zealous in the king's service, several Carthusians had already been sent to him for advice in the hope of peeling away those of more compliant temperament. Needless to say, Sebastian Newdigate and his fellow future martyrs were spared the effort, but two, William Broke and Bartholomew Burgoyn, both of whom were priests and professed monks, eventually changed sides after long argument, and subsequently thanked the prior for the 'great pains' he had taken to win over two others as well, albeit in vain. Maurice Chauncy, too, seems to have forsaken his martyr's mantle by the same means, since he, along with another Carthusian, was sent to Syon at the end of August 1534, bearing a letter signed by an agent of the government, entreating the prior to reason with them and 'show charity to them as you have done to others'. They are scrupulous, the writer says, 'about the bishop of Rome', but are not 'obstinate', and each has a 'book of authorities' that must be answered.

But by the time that the term 'Supreme Head' was formally incorporated into the king's title by decree of council on 15 January 1535, it was abundantly clear both to Cromwell and the king himself that whatever the few weaker spirits among the Charterhouse community might do, the Carthusians as a body would resist to the death any further demand for the rejection of papal authority. And now, therefore – with an authority 'to visit, repress, redress, reform, order, correct, restrain, and amend heresies, errors, abuses, offences, contempts and enormities, whatsoever they be' – royal commissioners would indeed descend once more upon Prior Houghton's monks, and not only submit them to an interrogation intended to lay bare at last their secret hostility to the king's second marriage and ongoing allegiance to Rome, but administer the retribution laid down in law by the new Treason Act, which came into force officially on 1 February. Though no oath was attached to the act, all religious houses in the kingdom were to find themselves forced to swear upon the Gospels their acceptance of the royal supremacy, while any refusal to accept the 'dignities or titles' of the king was now to be considered a 'malicious' offence, since all loopholes had been closed and any room for manoeuvre finally excluded. As a result, the monks of the Charterhouse, like John Fisher and Sir Thomas More, would have to risk what they considered their eternal salvation or face instead the daunting road to Tyburn.

According to Chancy's account of what followed, Prior Houghton's chief concern was for the many younger members of his community whose vocations he had carefully fostered and whose professions he had received. But initially at least, his fears were not so much for their lives as for their religious perseverance if the Charterhouse were suppressed and they found themselves at large once more in the wider world:

> When we were all in great consternation [writes Chauncy], he said to us: 'Very sorry am I, and my heart is heavy, especially for you, my younger friends, of whom I see so many round me. Here you are living in your innocence. The yoke will not be laid upon your necks, nor the rod of persecution. But if you are taken hence and mingle among the Gentiles, you may learn the works of them, and, having begun in the spirit, you may be consumed in the flesh.'

Hoping even now that some accommodation might yet be found, he once again intended to save his monastery and its residents by taking responsibility on behalf of all, and swearing alone to the supremacy, with some words of reservation. But the response, if Chauncy is to be believed, was unanimous: 'Then all who were present burst into tears, and cried with one voice, "Let us die together in our integrity, and heaven and earth shall witness for us how unjustly we are cut off."' And at this, Houghton moderated his position accordingly, still maintaining that the government sought only the elder monks as quarry, yet accepting now that all should die, were he to be wrong:

The prior answered sadly – 'Would, indeed, that it might be so; that so dying we might live, as living we die. But they will not do to us so great a kindness, nor to themselves so great an injury. Many of you are of noble blood; and what I think they will do is this: Me and the elder brethren they will kill; and they will dismiss you that are young into a world which is not for you. If, therefore, it depend on me alone – if my oath will suffice for the house – I will throw myself for your sakes on the mercy of God. I will make myself anathema; and to preserve you from these dangers I will consent to the king's will. If, however, they have determined otherwise – if they choose to have the consent of us all – the will of God be done. If one death will not avail, we will all die.'

At this point, Chauncy tells us, Houghton's voice faltered and he became extremely troubled, as a result of the struggle between his love of God, which made his fear of offending Him intolerable, and, on the other hand, the fear of losing the souls committed to his charge. But he recovered himself sufficiently to set aside three days of preparation within the community for the ordeal ahead: on the first all were to make a general confession of their sins; on the second, led by Houghton himself, all would ask pardon from each of his brethren in turn for any offence caused during their stay together; and on the third, the entire community would attend Mass, sung by the prior himself, in quest of guidance from the Holy Spirit.

No specific mention at this stage is made in Chauncy's account of the role or reaction of Sebastian Newdigate or any other of the 'many' monks 'of noble blood' within the Charterhouse. But they, like others, were swept up, it seems, in what Chauncy suggests was the indescribable fervour accompanying the ensuing sung Mass of the third day. For when the moment came for the elevation of the consecrated Host, we are told:

There came, as it were, a soft whisper of the air, faint indeed to outward hearing, but of mighty power within the soul. Some perceived it with their bodily senses; all felt it as it thrilled into their hearts. And there came a sound of melody most sweet, whereat the venerable prior was so much moved, God being thus abundantly manifested, that he melted into a flood of tears, and could not for a space continue the offering of the Mass. The community meanwhile remained stupefied, hearing the melody and feeling its marvellous and sweet effects upon their spirits, but not knowing whence it came nor whither it went. Yet their hearts rejoiced as they perceived that God was with them indeed.

Whether Chauncy, with his characteristic love of the supernatural, had merely embellished the episode or altogether invented it, there is nevertheless little doubt that the Charterhouse's residents were suitably galvanised as events now gathered pace. For while Houghton awaited the summons from Cromwell, his fellow priors of Beauvale and Axholme visited him. The former, Robert Laurence, was in origin a monk of London; the latter, Augustine Webster, had professed at Sheen. And together all three men now decided to forestall the arrival of Cromwell's commissioners by seeking an interview with him in which to seek exemption from the obligation of the oath.

Unsurprisingly, however, the quest was in vain, and after a series of three interrogations conducted by the minister in person, they found themselves locked in the Tower on 13 April or thereabouts. When subsequently examined by the members of the king's council, moreover, Houghton took careful notes, and these – after being somehow read by Fisher – were, it seems, conveyed to the Charterhouse where Chauncy claimed, not altogether implausibly, to have seen them, before they were apparently destroyed. If true, Cromwell roughly brushed aside all qualifications when the three monks professed their willingness to consent to the oath 'so far as the law of God might allow'. Likewise, when they asserted that the Church had always held otherwise, and that St Augustine had set the authority of the Church above that of Scripture, the minister replied that he cared naught for the Church and that St Augustine might hold as he pleased. His only wish was to know whether they would swear a direct oath or no. At this point the monks refused absolutely – Laurence and Webster both declaring how they could 'not take our sovereign lord to be supreme head of the Church, but him that is by God the head of the Church, that is the bishop of Rome, as Ambrose, Jerome and Augustine teach'.

Not long before, Houghton and his two colleagues had been joined in the Tower by Father Richard Reynolds, a Bridgettine monk of Syon, and he too was equally adamant, boldly declaring that though 'he would spend his blood for the king', the pope's status remained sacrosanct, and that in stating as much he was merely maintaining what 'a thousand thousand that are dead' had maintained before. In all cases, the monks were influenced solely, it seems, by their conviction that a matter of divine faith was at stake. Certainly, the Carthusian Order was in no direct dependence upon the papacy, nor did the pope figure in their statutes. Nor, for that matter, had Houghton and his companions any concern, like Sir Thomas More, with the unity of Christian nations. All that Chauncy suggests, and all that can be extracted from the fragments of Houghton's notes and recorded sources, confirms that the Carthusian priors, along with Sebastian Newdigate and the other monks of the Charterhouse still awaiting their own ordeal to come, stood purely and simply by the traditional axioms of their Church in the divine commission delivered to St Peter – which made them in the most literal sense of the term, 'martyrs of the faith'.

Realising as he had no doubt done from the outset that their constancy was unassailable, Thomas Cromwell therefore lost no time in appointing a special commission to try all four men for treason under the Act of Succession. On 24 April 1535 the grand jury was returned, and the trial appointed for Wednesday 28th, on the grounds that the accused 'did on 26 April, at the Tower of London, in the county of Middlesex, openly declare and say, "the king our sovereign lord, is not supreme head in earth of the Church of England"' – an offence of verbal treason under the terms of the new Treason Act. The venue for the trial, which occurred over two days, was to be Westminster Hall, though, if both Chauncy and the following account contained in the so-called 'Arundel Manuscripts' of the British Library are to be relied upon, the monks' ultimate conviction was not obtained without considerable browbeating of the jurors:

The jury could not agree to condemn these four religious persons, because their consciences proved them they did not it maliciously. The judges hereupon resolved them, that whosoever denied the supremacy denied it maliciously, and the expressing of the word maliciously in the act was a void limit and restraint of the construction of the words and intention of the offence [i.e. any denial was by definition malicious]. The jury, for all this, could not agree to condemn them, whereupon Crumwell, in a rage, went unto the jury and threatened them if they condemned them not. And so being overcome by his threats found them guilty, and had great thanks, but they were afterwards ashamed to show their faces, and some of them took great [harm] for it.

Thereafter, Archbishop Cranmer made one of his characteristically cautious attempts to save the condemned men, but his offer was unacceptable to Cromwell, and the sentence was duly carried out at Tyburn on Tuesday, 4 May. By royal command, the victims were executed in their monastic habits, with the hair shirts of their Rule beneath, after each in turn had received a further offer of pardon beforehand that was duly spurned. Houghton, the first to die, embraced his executioner and addressed the vast crowd thus:

> I call Almighty God to witness, and all good people, and I beseech all here present to bear witness for me in the day of judgement, that being here to die, I declare that it is from no obstinate rebellious spirit that I do not obey the king, but because I fear to offend the majesty of God. Our holy mother the Church has decreed otherwise than the king and parliament have decreed, and therefore, rather than disobey the Church I am ready to suffer. Pray for me and have mercy on my brethren, of whom I have been the unworthy prior.

Whereupon, kneeling down, he recited a few verses of Psalm 31 and resigned himself to the hands of the executioner. Like the other men that followed him – including not only the other Carthusian priors of Axholme and Beauvale but also the Bridgettine, Reynolds, and John Hale, Vicar of Isleworth – Houghton bore the subsequent barbarity, aggravated by the tough hair shirt, with what seemed a more than human patience, invoking the Lord he loved and had followed to the Cross at the age of 48.

That morning, Sir Thomas More's daughter had been allowed to visit him, and as both watched the beginning of the martyrs' dreadful journey, More had coined another of his most memorable observations: 'Lo dost thou not see, Meg, that these blessed fathers be now as cheerfully going to their deaths as bridegrooms to their marriage.' Whether John Fisher had witnessed the same scene from the Bell Tower is unknown. Certainly, it may have been arranged for him to do so, since the presence of Margaret Roper with her father had probably been specifically intended to weaken her father's own resolve. Yet, if so, any attempt to influence Fisher was no more effective than in More's case, as Richard Wilson makes clear in his record of the bishop's single comment after the execution:

> They be gone. God have mercy on their souls.

During the monks' examination, Wilson recalled, Fisher had prayed only that 'no vanity subvert them', though his final remark on their butchery was reserved for George Gold, the lieutenant's servant, two days after the deed had been done, when he remarked upon the Treason Act how 'he saw not so great peril in the statute, unless it were done or spoken maliciously, and he marvelled much that the monks were put to execution, saying that they did nothing maliciously nor obstinately'. But if Fisher did indeed remain somehow credulous about his oppressors' regard for due process, the victims themselves, of course, were already beyond all such qualms and quiddities. Indeed, in the wake of Houghton's slaughter, and as a fitting token of the king's wrath, one of his quartered arms had been hung over the archway of the Charterhouse to awe the remaining brothers into submission – albeit in vain, since the ordeal of Sebastian Newdigate, as well as Humphrey Middlemore and another Carthusian, William Exmew, was about to be played out with greater brutality still.

Even while Houghton lay mouldering in prison, government agents were still busy among the residents of the London Charterhouse, endeavouring to secure their compliance, and one of Cromwell's men, John Whalley, who appears to have been specially appointed to guard the monastery, had written revealingly to his master not only of the resistance he encountered but of what he considered the most appropriate response:

> It is of no use for one Mr Rastall [Cromwell's commissioner] to come there. He pleads, indeed, that you wished him daily to resort hither [but the monks] laugh and jest at all things he speaketh. No question of it, they be exceedingly superstitious, ceremonious, and pharasaical, and wonderfully addict to their old *mumpsimus*; nevertheless, better and more charitable it were to convert them, than to put them to the extremity of the law.

But if humble John Whalley was hoping somehow to prevail upon his master in the interests of lenity, he was sorely mistaken, and he was no less misguided either in thinking that the resistance now centring upon Middlemore, Exmew and Newdigate could be realistically extinguished by the arguments of 'some honest, learned' preachers. For only two days after Houghton's execution, the ever-dutiful Thomas Bedyll, commissioner for the enforcement of the oath of supremacy, wrote to Cromwell how these three monks in particular were beyond all persuasion. On the very day of the martyrdom of their prior, indeed, he had gone to the Charterhouse, bearing:

> Divers books and annotations both of mine own and others against the primacy of the bishop of Rome and also of St Peter, declaring evidently the equality of the apostles by the law of God. And after long communication of more than an hour and a half with the vicar [Middlemore] and procurator of the house [Exmew], I left those books and annotations with them, that they should see the Holy Scriptures and doctors thereupon concerning the said matters, and thereupon conform themselves. And yesterday they sent me the said books and annotations again home to my house by a servant of theirs without any word or writing. Wherefore, I sent to the procurator to come and speak with me, seeing I kept my bed by reason of sickness and could not come to him; and at his coming I demanded of him whether he and the vicar and other of the seniors had seen or heard the said annotations, or perused the titles of the books making the most for the said matters. And he answered that the vicar and he and Newdigate had spent time upon them till nine or ten of the clock at night, and that they saw nothing in them whereby they were moved to alter their opinion. I then declared to him the danger of this opinion, which was like to be the destruction of them and their house forever; and as far as I could perceive by my communication with the vicar and procurator on Tuesday, and with the procurator yesterday, they be obstinately determined to suffer all extremities rather than to alter their opinion, regarding no more the death of their father [Houghton] in word or countenance than [if] he were living and conversing among them.

That Newdigate was mentioned without further elaboration is proof enough that Cromwell was already familiar with his name, and the acquaintance can only be explained, it would seem, by the king's particular interest in him. Until now, after all, the monk had avoided any degree of prominence, but his resistance at this point was plainly of special personal concern to the king who had known him as both courtier and intimate within his most private circle. If Houghton, therefore, might be dismissed and dispatched as a largely faceless obstacle to the king's wishes, the same was hardly true of this new figurehead of resistance to the royal will.

Yet far from evoking compassion, the result of the two men's previous intimacy, as so often with Henry, was merely an increase in outrage and vengefulness on his part, ensuring that Newdigate's treatment would be even more barbaric. For on 25 May, Newdigate, Middlemore and Exmew were – in the words of Henry Clifford, biographer of Newdigate's great-niece Jane Dormer, Duchess of Feria – 'drawn out of the cloister with inhuman violence' and lodged in Marshalsea Prison. Just over two weeks earlier, two of the Charterhouse's lay brethren had been standing by the gate where Houghton's severed arm was nailed, when the gory relic supposedly fell down at their feet. Already in possession of the blood-stained hair shirt in which the prior had been martyred, the monks of the monastery then not only removed it, but proceeded to revere it, so that more than a decade later, John Stow would record how on:

> July 1 1547, two priests were arraigned and condemned in the Guildhall for keeping of certain Reliques, amongst the which there was a left arme and shoulder of a monke of the Charterhouse, on the which arme was written: 'It was the arme of such a monke which suffered martirdome under King Henry the Eight.'

And now, in full knowledge of what had occurred and with full awareness of its deathly significance for what lay ahead in his own case, Newdigate no doubt contemplated the relic from the darkness of his Marshalsea dungeon where he and Middlemore and Exmew – men 'not very aged in years' yet 'ancient and reverent in deportment' – were, according to Clifford, kept 'fourteen days bound to pillars, standing upright with iron rings about their necks, hands and feet'. Another account, contained in the Arundel Manuscripts, speaks also of a seventeen-day period of confinement, in which the men were bound by 'great fetters fast ryved [riveted] on their legs with great iron boltts', as well as 'iron collors' and other chains loaded with lead. Unable throughout to sit, 'never loosed for any naturall necessitie [nor] voiding of ordure or otherwise', they ate, according to this description, only bread, since the 'fleshe' that was offered to them was 'contrary to ther rule and profession'.

Before their confinement, we are told, the monks had first been brought to Cromwell – 'to his howse at Stebunheyth [Stepney] a myle frome London' – where they had persisted in 'refusing constantlie to acknowledge the Kyng's supremacie'. But even by the standards of the time, the subsequent harshness of their treatment was exceptional – so exceptional, indeed, that the king himself appears to have momentarily wavered. For on 8 June 1535, the Bishop of Faenza recorded not only how Newdigate and his fellows were 'in prison with chains around their necks' but that the king had tried in person to persuade them to recognise his supremacy. Only three days into his confinement at Marshalsea, Newdigate had, it seems, been visited again by Henry, who, according to Clifford's account, pleaded with him thus:

> See how sincerely I love you, Sebastian, and how deep an interest I take in your welfare! Think what kind of return my affection deserves. Return loving obedience for loving condescension, and submit to my laws before it is too late.

Already, the Bishop of Faenza believed, the Carthusians were certain to be condemned – 'but perhaps not publicly, for fear of the displeasure of the people, which was shown at the death of the others'. Yet this had not prevented a further effort by the king to ease his nagging conscience, which he concluded, characteristically enough, by a reminder to Newdigate of all the graces and favours he had received by royal gift and the subsequent ingratitude he had now displayed in siding with the tiny handful of recalcitrants still resisting. If he were to submit even at the very last, Henry told him – or so, at least, Clifford suggests in his account – the former courtier need not remain a Carthusian at all, and would be loaded instead with riches and honours.

It was, said Clifford, 'a mighty temptation and a great encounter!' and one not inconsistent with what we know of the king's pendulations on other occasions between gusts of fury, remorse, mawkish sentimentality and, of course, shameless self-pity. Clifford, it should be remembered, was an intimate of the granddaughter of Newdigate's sister, and someone who had resided for many years in her household, witnessing her death and assisting at her funeral. And while he doubtless embellished Newdigate's subsequent response no less than his description of Henry's initial pleas, there is little reason to question either the encounter between the king and monk itself, or that he captured the essence of what remains a wholly plausible exchange. For in acknowledging the 'special and great honour' that the king had accorded him in visting 'so undecent a lodging' and while offering to pray for the king's 'health, prosperity and happiness', Newdigate is said to have remained adamant that, as 'a religious man', he was all 'the more obliged sincerely to speak the truth'. He had retired from court in the first place to protect his soul from 'the hazards and dangers of the world', and could not now forsake it when Christ himself had redeemed it 'with so great cost as the price of His life and the shedding of His most precious blood'. Never, Newdigate concluded, had he been guilty of 'contempt or obstinacy' – 'nor discontent, nor intent of gainsaying, nor counsel of any that hath power to withdraw my submission to the law' – but had acted only according to 'the doctrine of the holy Church and law of God, the offence whereof I may not incur'.

Within a fortnight, Newdigate, Middlemore and Exmew were brought before selected members of the Privy Council, examined separately and again questioned about the new Act of Supremacy, which they were told had banished all foreign authority. But, according to Henry Clifford, they remained constant in the face of all interrogations, threats and promises, maintaining throughout that 'the authority of the Church was not foreign in any Christian country; and that in no sort could they yield to anything not agreeable to the law of God or contrary to the doctrine of our holy Mother the Church'. Nor, it seems, did they waver when subsequently dispatched to the Tower, where Clifford suggests that Newdigate received a further visit from the king, which this time involved more menaces than persuasion. 'Art thou wiser and holier than all the ecclesiastics and seculars of my kingdom?' Henry asked, and followed the monk's denial with a harangue to the effect that just as Newdigate had sought to emulate his former prior in life, so he should now do so in death. For on 1 June a special commission of Oyer and Terminer, including among others the new chancellor, Sir Thomas Audley, Anne Boleyn's father, the Earl of Wiltshire, the Duke of Suffolk, and Thomas Cromwell as its secretary, was empanelled to try the case, along with a jury, including, as we have seen, a certain John Newdigate Esquire – in all probability the brother of the accused monk.

Finally brought to the bar on Friday, 11 June by Sir Edmund Walsingham, Deputy Lieutenant of the Tower, all three men pleaded their innocence to the charge of treason, and proceeded to defend themselves by 'citing and alleging divers authorities of the divine Scripture, of the ancient Fathers and of the sacred Canons'. Dressed in their Carthusian habits, they boldly maintained that they were 'commanded by the word of God', which 'it were temerity and sin to opugn', and confirmed once more their unbending conviction that 'no temporal prince can arrogate to himself the Church's government, which the King of kings and supreme Lord Christ Jesus gave and granted to St Peter and his successors'. At which point, according to the following description by Clifford, Sebastian Newdigate was singled out for special attention just as the trial reached its climax:

But before the judge would pronounce sentence of death, he used many reasons and persuasions now at last to yield and conform themselves; assuring them, upon submission, of the king's mercy, and withal wishing them to consider the loss of so many good parts which might be serviceable to God and beneficial to their country. He spoke of the hastening of their end with an infamous death; the grief of their friends; the scandal of their kindred. In particular he addressed himself to Father Sebastian, repeating to him the nobility of his blood, the honourable allies [links] he had in the kingdom, the duty he owed to His Majesty, having been his servant; the many favours he had received from him; which if they would consider and be submissive, he did assure them that there was place for mercy and pardon.

Once again, however, neither Newdigate nor the others made any reckoning, we are told, 'of these vain and worldy considerations'. Nor did they react, Clifford suggests, when told of the fate awaiting them. On the contrary:

The Reverend good Fathers heard and received this cruel sentence, answering with alacrity of countenance, *Deo Gratias*, giving praise to our Saviour Jesus Christ for His gracious favour to make them worthy to suffer for His Faith and the defence of His Church.

Not all were so fulsome in their praise of the monks' conduct. Writing from the perspective of a convinced Protestant, the MP and chronicler Edward Hall, for instance, described their behaviour thus:

These men, when they were arraigned at Westminster, behaved themselves very stiffly and stubbornly; for, hearing their indictment read, how traitorously they had spoken against the king's majesty, his crown and dignity, they neither blushed nor bashed at it, but very foolishly and hypocritically acknowledged their treason, which maliciously they avouched, having no learning for their defence: but rather, being asked divers questions, they used a malicious silence, thinking as by their examinations afterwards in the Tower of London it did appear, for so they said, that they thought these men, which was the Lord Cromwell and others that sat upon them in judgement, to be heretics, and not of the Church of God, and therefore not worthy to be answered or spoken unto. And therefore as they deserved, they … were hanged, drawn and quartered at Tyborne, and their quarters set up about London, for denying the king to be supreme head of the Church.

Doubtless, too, there were others of Hall's persuasion as Newdigate, Middlemore and Exmew made their final, wretched journey to the great triangular gibbet upon which their final agonies were to be played out, though Chauncy tells us how 'they went to death as to a banquet, receiving it with the greatest alacrity of body and gladness of visage, in the hope of life everlasting'.

The date was 19 June 1535, and 'being arrived at the place of execution', Clifford relates, 'they praised almighty God'. Whereupon:

They untied Father Sebastian from the hurdle with the rope about his neck and put him in a cart; there he commended himself to the prayers of the good assistants; prayed for the king that God almighty would give him long life and health, and His grace to have care of his salvation and of the good of his kingdom that had flourished so long in the Christian religion and in the unity and obedience of Christ's Catholic Church. He intimated his own innocence both to the king and all the world, and that his death was only for the testimony and defence of the Catholic Church, as their judges could do no less than testify. And so preparing himself to die said in Latin the psalm: 'In Thee, O Lord, have I hoped, let me never be confounded,' to the verse, 'Into Thy hands I commend my spirit: Thou hast redeemed me, O Lord, Thou God of truth.'

Then, Clifford continues:

The cart being drawn away, he remained hanging a very little or no space; or both he and the two other Fathers were cut down, being yet alive; presently bowelled; their bowels cast into the fire, their heads cut off, their bodies quartered, and their quarters set up in the high ways and upon the gates of London.

And so the deed was done, bringing about what Clifford described as the 'violent death but most happy end of Father Sebastian, an approved valorous gentleman, a perfect religious, and a glorious martyr of Christ Jesus'. 'Somewhat tall of stature, his body well-proportioned and comely, his aspect lively and settled', Newdigate had also been blessed, it seems, not only with 'great courage' but a pleasing demeanour, 'carrying with it a natural honesty and remarkable modesty', all of which, we are told, were 'much magnified' by his retirement to the Charterhouse as a young man. His great-niece, meanwhile, would eventually spend the last twelve years of her life at Louvain, becoming 'a foot to the lame, an eye to the blind, a staff to the weak, a true mother of orphans, and a patroness of widows', sheltering in her house many of the exiled priests who eventually followed in her great-uncle's footsteps in the reign of Elizabeth I. And in doing so, she would also keep alive her forebear's memory by means of her retainer and biographer, relating to him the recollections handed down to her before her death in 1591 and subsequent burial, appropriately enough, in the church of the Louvain Charterhouse – in the midst of the choir, just before the high altar.

By that time too, of course, John Fisher was already long cold in his grave – another casualty of the religious revolution that had driven Lady Jane Dormer and numerous others like her into permanent exile. For three days after Sebastian Newdigate's execution, Thomas Cromwell and other members of the council, along with Thomas Bedyll, visited the bishop in his cell, in an effort – described in the following account of a subsequent interrogation of Richard Wilson – to extract a definitive incriminating declaration from him that the king could never be Supreme Head:

> On Friday [7 May] after Ascension Day last, Mr Secretary [Cromwell] and others of the Council, came to examine Fisher on the Act of the Supreme Head, and this respondent [Wilson] standing in the chamber without the partition, heard some part of the examination. Mr Secretary said they were sent for two things touching the Act of Supremacy; the second point respondent did not hear. Mr Secretary read the Act, and Fisher replied he could not consent to take the king as Supreme Head. The Act was also read to him making it treason to deny the king to be Supreme Head. After supper respondent told his master that he thought Mr Bedyll's reason weak when he said the king was head of his people, and the people was the Church, with some further observations. The bishop asked if he had been too quick with Mr Bedyll, and respondent said no.

If accurate, it would seem from this that Cromwell now already had what he required: an explicit denial from Fisher of the royal supremacy. But the waters are muddied by a later statement from Wilson affirming that two days after his interrogation, the bishop himself could remember 'no such thing', and by the fact that Wilson would subsequently affirm, at one point at least, that he too was unable recall any direct denial of the supremacy on Fisher's behalf. Worried, nevertheless, that he may unwittingly have uttered the fatal words to Bedyll, Fisher had therefore checked his memory of the encounter against Wilson's recollection of events, and been assured by his servant that no slip had been made. Moreover, the fact that Wilson was interrogated at such length both initially and subsequently suggests that Fisher had not provided his inquisitors with any clear-cut statement, and that the servant was being pressed for precisely the kind of damning evidence that the bishop himself had failed to provide.

Ultimately, however, Wilson went on to testify how he had visited Fisher later the same day, while he was saying evensong, to tell the bishop that he had indeed told his interrogators 'that he did not think the king might be Supreme Head'. But Wilson's evidence, of course, now remained partially tainted by the contradictory nature of his statements – making a further, altogether less ambivalent, declaration necessary to achieve the required outcome in court. Wilson's evidence had, moreover, been gleaned from the other side of a partition, making his deployment in court even less ideal still. As such, another tack was required, and, if the account of one contemporary, William Rastell, is to be relied upon, the fateful decision was now taken to incriminate Fisher by stealth and deception rather than direct attack. For, according to Rastell, who was a student at Lincoln's Inn at the time and later a judge during the reign of Mary Tudor, the government secretly dispatched at this point 'a crafty caitiff' to tell Fisher that the king required an honest answer regarding the supremacy, on the assurance that 'no manner of hurt nor harm should come to him', even were he to suggest that it was 'directly against the laws of God'.

The message, it seems, was accompanied by a guarantee of good faith upon 'the word of a prince', which proved enough, in Rastell's opinion, to bring forth from Fisher an open declaration that:

He believed directly in his conscience and knew by his learning precisely that it was very plain by the holy scripture, the laws of the Church, the general council, and the whole faith and practice of Christ's Catholic Church from Christ's ascension hitherto, that the king was not, nor could be, by the law of God, supreme head of the church of England.

Whereupon, Rastell continues:

When the king was by this messenger ascertained that the bishop had thus plainly declared his opinion against his supremacy, then he was very glad thereof, because he had thereby some plain matter to lay to the bishop's charge, to arraign him and condemn him for speaking against

his supremacy, where before this time by no means any such advantage
could be caught against the bishop.

Nor was this particular explanation of Fisher's final downfall put forward by Rastell alone. For it is also cited by the bishop's anonymous early
biographer, who goes on to name the man responsible for delivering the
deception as none other than Richard Rich: the very man who would
ensnare Sir Thomas More by similar means, and the only person to provide testimony at Fisher's trial.

Deception had, of course, already been used against both prisoners
when each was told that the other had agreed to the supremacy, in an
attempt to break their resistance, and there is no reason to doubt the
general opinion, handed down across the centuries, that Rich was more
than capable of compromising his conscience in the lucrative service
of his master, Thomas Cromwell. Appointed Solicitor-General in 1533,
as a direct result of Cromwell's patronage, Rich had formerly served
in Sir Thomas More's household, but been held in low esteem, 'always
reputed light of his tongue, a great dicer and gamester, and not of any
commendable fame'. But both the king and Cromwell were now, with
good reason, anxious to conclude matters, especially after news reached
England at the end of May that the new pope, Paul III, had taken the
offensive in the most drastic fashion possible by appointing Fisher
'Cardinal-Priest' of San Vitale. His ostensible motive, as expressed to
Gregory Casale, Henry's agent in Rome, was to gain Fisher's release for
a forthcoming General Council of the Church, since 'the writings of
Rochester were held in great esteem, especially in Germany and Italy'.
But his real desire, it appears, was to stage a final attempt to save Fisher's
life, since no cardinal had ever been executed previously, and, at the same
time, to throw down a direct challenge to the King of England, presenting him with a Rubicon beyond which there could be no further hope
of reconciliation, and trusting that he would blink at last when faced
with the precipice.

Certainly it was a bold, and arguably long overdue, step. But it was also
one that would effectively ensure the prisoner's execution. For, as Casale
told the pope directly upon hearing the news, 'no greater blunder had ever
been committed', and it was a view shared, it seems, by the King of France,

who was also enlisted by Rome to do what he could for the endangered bishop, but told the papal nuncio in Paris how 'this [cardinal's] hat' was likely to bring only harm. 'Strange measures', as he put it, had already been used against the Carthusians, and Henry 'was the hardest friend to bear in the world: at one time unstable, and at another obstinate and proud, so that it was almost impossible to bear with him'. 'Sometimes,' the French king continued, 'he treats me like a subject. In effect, he is the strangest man in the world, and I fear I can do no good with him.' And if further proof of Francis I's contention was required, it was rapidly furnished by Henry's actual reaction, which was described in a letter from Chapuys to the Holy Roman Emperor, dated 16 June:

> As soon as the king heard that the Bishop of Rochester had been created a cardinal, he declared in anger several times that he would give him another hat, and send the head afterwards to Rome for the cardinal's hat. He sent immediately to the Tower those of his council to summon again the said bishop and Master More to swear to the king as head of the Church, otherwise before St John's day [24 June] they should be executed as traitors.

Fisher, meanwhile, had heard the rumour of his elevation to the cardinalate from George Gold, servant to the Tower's Lieutenant, and greeted the news with comparative indifference:

> Then said Mr Fisher, 'A cardinal! Then I perceive it was not for nought that my Lord Chancellor [Thomas Audley] did ask me when I heard from my master the pope, and said there was never a man that had exalted the pope as I had.'

Indeed, according to an official report of Fisher's own response under interrogation, he had declared, before both Gold and Richard Wilson, that 'if the cardinal's hat were laid at his feet, he would not stoop to pick it up', though that eventuality would never arise, since the hat was blocked at Calais, and all haste was now made to make good the king's subsequent quip to Thomas Cromwell that 'whensoever it cometh, he [Fisher] shall wear it on his shoulders, for head shall he have none to see it on'.

On 11 June the interrogation turned to more marginal figures –
Richard Wilson, servant to 'Mr Fisher, doctor of divinity, late bishop of
Rochester'; John à Wood, More's servant; as well as George Gold, John
Pewnoll, falconer at Rochester, William Thorneton of Thames Street
who supplied the bishop's food, and Edward White, brother-in-law to
Fisher – with the intention of establishing that the prisoner had been in
correspondence with Rome regarding his promotion. If so, such letters
would have come under the terms of the new laws, and Wilson, in particular, was therefore subjected to especially intense pressure, being 'very
closely shut up also and terribly threatened to be hanged'. Yet neither he
nor any of the others produced anything of value, and subsequent interrogations of both Fisher and More bore out the substantial truth of the
servant's answers. Indeed, even when Fisher admitted under examination
by Thomas Bedyll on 12 June that letters – 'four or thereabouts' – had
been passed by Gold between himself and More, nothing treasonous
could be established about their content, though all had been 'burned as
soon as he read them'.

Plainly, the semblance, if not the spirit, of due legal process was still intact.
But if the government could not convict by guesswork and imputation,
it could nevertheless condemn by suspect laws and crudely contrived
evidence, as was demonstrated all too forcefully when 'one John Fisher,
late of the city of Rochester, otherwise called "Dominus" John Fisher,
late Bishop of Rochester', finally faced his accusers in Westminster Hall
on 17 June, charged with 'falsely, maliciously and traitorously' declaring on
7 May that 'the king our Sovereign Lord is not Supreme Head in earth of
the Church of England'. 'Not having God before his eyes', the indictment
declared, the accused had been 'seduced by diabolical instigation' and
traitorously imagined, invented, practised, and attempted to deprive the
king of his full and rightful dignity, 'contrary to the form of another act
passed the twenty-sixth year of the King's reign', i.e. the Treason Act. As
with all State trials of the period, Fisher was to be allowed no counsel,
nor could his witnesses, if the court allowed them to be called, be heard
on oath. And in consequence, the hearing, true to type, amounted to little
more than a verbal duel between the defendant and Crown lawyers who
held all the advantages before a jury that was expected to deliver but one
verdict. Separated by a high barrier from the main part of Westminster Hall,

the spectacle – or what one contemporary, William Rastell termed 'this woeful tragedy' – would be played out in the court known as King's Bench.

In the meantime, Fisher had been brought from the Tower, it seems, 'part by horseback, part by water, because he was yet so little recovered of his feebleness and infirmity that he was not able to walk or go anything'. But Rastell's account adds, too, how he travelled 'with a great number of bills, and glaives and halberts and the axe of the Tower borne before him'. Wearing 'a black cloth gown', he had known his fate, of course, long before the king's 'secret messenger' had finally elicited the necessary evidence from him, though he delivered, nevertheless, a plea of not guilty, on the grounds, Rastell tells us, that his final denial of the royal supremacy had been made upon the specific request of the king and under guarantee 'that I should never be impeached nor hurt by mine answer … which I would never have spoken had it not been in trust of my prince's promise and of my true and loving heart towards him'. Whereupon, Rastell continues:

> This shameless beast, this mischievous messenger [i.e. Richard Rich], said that true it was that he declared unto him that message from the king and by the king's commandment made him that assured and faithful promise from the king, and sware also to him as he said. 'But all this,' quoth this wicked witness, 'do not discharge you any wit.'

Even by the flimsy standards of the day, the evidence was not only tainted, but undisguisedly so. Yet on Richard Rich's testimony alone, Fisher's judges remained wholly entitled to conclude that 'he by the statute committed treason' and that 'nothing might discharge him now of the cruel penalty of death appointed by the statute for speaking against the king's supremacy, howsoever the words were spoken'.

Beyond the fact that the whole process was concluded within a day, little else is known of the trial. In 1836, the legal records of the Court of King's Bench were transferred to the custody of the Master of the Rolls, and among these was what had become known as the *Baga de Secretis*, comprising ninety-one pouches, the seventh of which contained the records of the trials of Fisher, More and the three Carthusian monks. But there was no record of evidence tendered or speeches made, and we are left primarily with the description left by Rastell, which also formed the basis of the account produced by the anonymous early biographer. Whether, therefore, the Crown had indeed done more to prove its case remains unknown, though Rich, as one more member of that merry band of ambitious *politici* who abounded in sixteenth-century affairs of state, would certainly play an identical role at Sir Thomas More's trial a fortnight later, while Rastell himself was certainly present at Fisher's execution and may well have been an eyewitness to the trial itself. Certainly, as a judge of the same court during the reign of Queen Mary, he was well placed to glean the evidence and gather the recollections of those who really were present. But now, in any event, John Fisher was at last a dead man, returning under sentence to the Tower, and followed – as the Imperial ambassador, Chapuys, told his counterpart Dr Ortiz in Rome – 'by a crowd of men and women in great grief who demanded his blessing when he crossed the water'.

EPILOGUE

We glide away as doth a shadow and wither as hay; thy time, Good Lord, is everlasting and thy memorial time without end.

Psalm 101:10. From The Penitential Psalms in the
English Version, John Fisher.

The former Bishop of Rochester had been sentenced to be hanged, drawn and quartered, but on the morning of his execution on 22 June this decision was altered, apparently for fear that if dragged on a hurdle for 4 miles to Tyburn there was every likelihood of his death along the way. Instead, the executioner's axe alone was to suffice at nearby Tower Hill, and at 5 a.m. on the day, shortly after dawn, he was informed that 'he should suffer that forenoon', after which the following exchange is said to have occurred with the Tower's lieutenant:

'Well,' quoth the bishop,' if this be your errand hither, it is no news unto me; I have looked daily for it. I pray you, what is it a'clock?'

'It is,' quoth the Lieutenant, 'about five.'

'What time,' quoth the bishop, 'must be mine hour to go out hence?'

'About ten of the clock,' said the Lieutenant.

'Well, then,' quoth the bishop, 'I pray you, let me sleep an hour or twain. For I may say to you, I slept not much this night, not for fear of death, I tell you, but by reason of my great sickness and weakness.'

With which answer the Lieutenant departed from him till about nine o'clock. At which time he came again to the bishop's chamber, and found him upward, putting on his clothes, and showed him that he was come for him.

There followed a request from Fisher that he be allowed to wear his fur shoulder cape 'to keep me warm for the while until the very time of execution', and when the lieutenant responded by asking why he was so careful of his health with 'little more than half an hour to live', the bishop confessed that:

> Though I have, I thank our Lord, a very good stomach and willing mind to die at this present ... yet I will not hinder my health in the mean time not a minute of an hour, but will preserve it in the mean season with all such discreet ways and means as Almighty God of his gracious goodness hath provided for me.

Racked by the gruelling chill of the Tower for months past, and unable, it seems, to take anything more than milk for his last breakfast, even John Fisher would not be denied one last fleeting comfort before he finally left his cell at the ordained hour, 'taking a little book in his hand, which was a New Testament lying by him' and making a cross on his forehead as he passed through the prison door, 'being so weak that he was scant able to go down the stairs'. Indeed, according to William Rastell's account, which differs slightly from that of Fisher's anonymous early biographer, the condemned man was actually 'carried down out of his chamber between twain in a chair' and thereafter conveyed to the Tower gate:

> Where, being delivered to the sheriffs of London, he was with great company of halberds, bills and glaives, carried in a chair by four of the sheriffs' officers, the sheriffs riding next after him, from thence not far off to a plain besides the Tower of London commonly called Tower Hill, otherwise called East Smithfield, where he was brought near to the scaffold on which he should be beheaded.

Yet the scaffold itself was still being completed, we are told, when Fisher arrived before it, resulting in a delay of at least an hour, since (according to Rastell, who was actually present) the bishop did not mount the steps to the waiting executioner until 'eleven of the clock'. In the meantime, the early biographer tells us, he had risen out of his chair, 'leaned his shoulder to the wall', and 'opened his little book in his hand' in search of an appropriate passage to glorify his Maker 'in this my last hour'. He had awaited the day of his ordeal in no little dread after Cromwell had first informed him of it – at the very same time that the pope had made him a cardinal – and now, though finally at peace, he had still longer to wait as he read in heavy silence amid the unfinished preparations. But when the arena for his suffering was finally ready, he nevertheless managed to make his ascent unaided – 'to no little marvel,' as Rastell noted, 'of them that knew his weakness and debility' – and was able to address the axeman 'with a bold courage and a loving cheer', forgiving him 'heartily' and telling him how he 'trusted on our Lord' that 'thou shalt see me die even lustily'. Nor, when he delivered his final words to 'the wondrous number of people gathered to see this horrible execution', did his strength falter either. On the contrary, Rastell tells us, he 'spake with a cheerful countenance and with such a stout and constant courage as one no wit afraid but glad to suffer death'.

By then he had removed his gown and cape, revealing 'a long, lean, slender body nothing in manner but skin and bare bones, so that the most part that there saw him marvelled to see any man bearing life, to be so far consumed'. But, notwithstanding his abject physical condition, he was still able, in the view of the Bishop of Faenza, 'to speak to the people boldly', telling them how he how had 'come hither to die for the faith of Christ's Catholic Church', while urging them at the same time to be loving and obedient to the king, who, though deceived in this matter, was good by nature. As for himself, he confessed that since he was only flesh, he feared death as any man would. Yet in doing so, he continued to speak, wrote Rastell, 'with such a strong and very loud voice that it made all the people astonished' – so much so, in fact, that many 'noted it in a manner as a miracle to hear so plain, strong and loud a voice come out of so old, weak and sickly a carcass'. After which, the executioner went quickly about his work, though leaving the 'headless body lying there naked upon the scaffold almost all day after' until about 'eight a'clock in the evening' when 'the dead body's privities' were finally conveyed to the parish church of All Hallows, Barking, and 'vilely' thrown – 'without any winding sheet or any other accustomed ceremonies' – into a grave hastily dug by guards with their halberds.

The final insult had been carried out, it seems, at the express 'commandment of the king', who had insisted that the body be buried 'very contemptuously'. Nor was there any visible hint of remorse on the king's part thereafter. On the contrary, Henry was soon remarking upon the lenity of Fisher's treatment, since he had been spared more agonising cruelty and

merely 'sworded'. And in the meantime, the bishop's few remaining personal possessions were duly taken to the king's use – among them a small
book with a gilt cover and the French king's arms on the inside, a mitre set
with a worthless stone and pearl, a pair of knitted gloves embossed with
gold, and some plate of silver gilt. But it was not merely Fisher's possessions
that preoccupied his former royal master in the wake of the execution.
For his head, which was subsequently placed on a pike on London Bridge,
remained 'fresher', according to a Spanish report, than the others perching
there in putrefaction, necessitating an order, a fortnight or so later, that it be
knocked into the Thames to quell suspicion among the credulous of divine
approval for the victim. In just over another fortnight, moreover, the head
of Thomas More would take its place on the self-same pike.

Yet while More's death would redound to his glory across the centuries,
John Fisher's sacrifice would never be burnished by posterity to anything
like the same degree. And though the names of both men are celebrated
with a joint feast in the calendar of the Roman Catholic Church, the equality of honour they enjoy in their sainthood by no means reflects an equality
they have received at the hands of historians, or, for that matter, their relative
historical importance within the English Reformation. Indeed, the massive scholarly attention lavished on More continues to dwarf the efforts of
the few who have chosen to study the career of his fellow martyr – even
in the realm of ideas where Fisher's work as a professional theologian was
undoubtedly more solid, enduring, original and influential. Nor is this discrepancy new. For even in 1535, when they were executed, the romantic
figure of the wary and witty lawyer, sharing *bon mots* on his way to the
scaffold, attracted wider popular attention and sympathy than that of his
altogether graver and more outspoken clerical counterpart. The first biography of More, the memoir by his son-in-law William Roper, was in print by
the end of Mary Tudor's reign. The first biography of Fisher, by contrast, was
completed only under Elizabeth, and was circulated solely in manuscript
form until the middle of the next century. Compiled by a few members
of St John's College, and written most probably, as we have seen, by John
Young, former Vice-Chancellor of Cambridge and Master of Pembroke
Hall, it was based on critical research into original documents and evidence
from Young's time of service within Fisher's own household. But its anonymous authorship and first appearance in print under the tainted editorship

of Thomas Bailey did nothing to enhance either its own reputation or that of its subject.

Nor were these the only – or for that matter the most important – reasons why John Fisher failed to achieve the recognition that his role undoubtedly merited. For Henry VIII's vengeance pursued him beyond the grave and involved nothing less than a systematic campaign not only to eradicate his memory at home but to blacken it abroad. Even before Fisher and More were brought to trial they were both the target of malicious sermons in London, and between the death of the former and the trial of his fellow martyr, the king ordered, too, that the 'treasons' of the two men should be publicly declared at the assizes throughout the country. Within a year, moreover, one of Fisher's sermons had been specifically banned by proclamation, while before long his treatises against the divorce were passed to a committee headed by Cranmer with a view to discrediting them once and for all, though the archbishop, no doubt wisely, stopped short of any attempt at refutation. And in the meantime, Thomas Cromwell made every effort on the international level to portray Fisher's execution as the result of political treason involving hostile foreign powers, while encouraging the propaganda slurs of, first, Stephen Gardiner and, later, Richard Sampson, Bishop of Chichester. Even at St John's, for that matter, Fisher's memory underwent steady onslaught. For although the college had protected itself by seeking generous patronage from Cranmer and Cromwell, it was soon obliged not only to abandon plans for the tomb that had been prepared for Fisher in its chapel – limestone slabs for which were discovered in 1773 amid rubbish being cleared from a disused chapel – but to efface the heraldic emblems relating to him that had been placed on much of the chapel furniture, and to eliminate all mention of his name within the college's statutes. Except, indeed, for a brief revival of Fisher's statutes during the reign of Mary Tudor, he was all but forgotten at St John's until the time of Thomas Baker, a fellow of the late Stuart period, whose political and religious principles caused him to be ejected from his fellowship.

The relegation of Fisher to the status of a non-person was effected with all the systematic thoroughness that one might expect for a perceived enemy of the Tudor state. But neither, of course, would the London Charterhouse escape suppression in the wake of the execution of its martyred members, notwithstanding the fact that the process would be conducted over all of two years,

since Cromwell, unlike his royal master, was unwilling to outrage public senti-
ment with too sudden a destruction of a community so generally esteemed.
Instead, after all further attempts at persuasion had finally failed, the tactic of
division was once again attempted, and on 4 May 1536, four of those considered most recalcitrant were sent to other houses: Maurice Chauncy and one
named Fox to Beauvale; John Rochester and James Walworth to Hull. A little
later, too, eight more were sent to the Bridgettines at Syon, in what proved to
be the largely vain hope that they might be won over by learned and obedient example to acceptance of the royal supremacy. Yet in May 1537, after a
threat from the council to suppress the Charterhouse out of hand, the Crown
did at last achieve some progress when a number of the monks, exhausted
by the persecution and anxious to save their monastery from dissolution,
finally agreed to renounce the authority of the pope. For without the solidar-
ity resulting from everyday contact with their peers, some, as Cromwell had
anticipated with characteristic shrewdness, were simply unable to sustain their
resistance. And among them was Maurice Chauncy, who would be loaded
with guilt for the rest of his life, while still maintaining to the very end that the
hearts and consciences of all concerned had always given lie to their lips.

Even so, however, it was not this way with all, since ten remained
'unmoved, unshaken, unseduced, unterrified'. Three were priests, one a
deacon and six were converses [i.e. not in preparation for ordination], all of
whom eventually found themselves lodged in a filthy Newgate cell. Unlike
their martyred predecessors, moreover, these Carthusians – the most numerous band of all – were to be denied even the dignity of a formal trial and
execution. Indeed, having sought to live as hidden servants of Christ within
the Charterhouse, they would now die hidden from the eyes of all, chained,
like Sebastian Newdigate before them, without possibility of movement in
a foul atmosphere, and systematically starved until, as Thomas Bedyll put it,
'dispeched by thand of God'. Abandoned by all, and dying slowly of hunger
and fever, they received, it is true, a solitary instance of love and a precious measure of succour from Margaret Gigs, the adopted daughter of Sir
Thomas More, who knew well of her father's admiration for their Order,
and who now bribed her way into Newgate, acting the part of a milkmaid,
to carry sustenance and clean linen in a bucket on her head. When discovered and barred from further entrance, she subsequently obtained access
to the roof and endeavoured, by removing some tiles, to let food down in

a basket. But her efforts were to little avail, since the monks continued to expire, one by one, throughout the summer months, the last being Thomas Johnson on 20 September, though a converse, William Horne, was for some reason removed beforehand and lived on in prison elsewhere until drawn to Tyburn on 4 August 1540, to suffer the same fate as his prior before him.

'And so this child', we are told, who had been 'tried longer and more severely than any other, followed his father, and died for the love of Jesus, and for the faith of His bride the Catholic Church', thus completing the tale of eighteen Carthusian martyrs in all, since two others of those exiled from London had been hanged at York in 1537. And nor, of course, would their spiritual home remain unspoiled. For the London Charterhouse was formally suppressed on 15 November 1538, to be used as a store for the king's pavilions, hunting nets and arms, after workmen, we are told, had seen fit to use its altars as gaming tables. By this time, many of the kingdom's other monasteries had suffered a similar fate. The bells of Jesus Tower, the *Chronicle of the Grey Friars of London* tells us, no longer rang, since they had been won at dice by Sir Miles Partridge, while, according to John Bale, precious books of all kinds, once belonging to monastic libraries, were now mainly in the hands of grocers and soap-sellers, 'some to serve their jakes, some to scour their candlesticks, and some to rub their boots'. At the same time, convent buildings erected for pious contemplation were soon housing factories, while friary churches had found a new role as government storehouses. In one case, the church of the Crutched Friars was serving as a stone quarry for the repair of the Tower, and, in another, St Mary Grace's was bursting with ship's biscuits baked in the huge ovens that had been installed there. The church of the Austin Friars had been bought by an enterprising nobleman to store his corn and coal supplies in the steeple.

And where, of course, valiant resistance had been offered by others than the Carthusians, this also proved largely futile in forestalling the full bureaucratic momentum of the State. Most notably of all, the Abbots of Glastonbury, Reading and Colchester refused to give up their abbeys voluntarily. But it was decided, nevertheless, that these should 'otherwise to come into the King's hands', and in the process Thomas Cromwell exhibited no hesitation in penning an infamous memorandum, which continues to darken his reputation down the years. 'The Abbot of Reading to be sent down to be tried *and executed* at Reading with his complices, similarly the Abbot of Glaston at

Glaston,' Cromwell recorded in advance of the trial, clearly confirming the limitations of due process as he conceived it, and which resulted in another ghastly spectacle as Richard Whiting, the elderly Abbot of Glastonbury, was subsequently dragged through the streets of his little abbey town and hanged, drawn and quartered on the Tor overlooking it. When the venerable cleric had first ridden up to London to face his inquisitors, the orchards of his monastery were red with fruit, but now the trees were bare and the majestic pile of his abbey already desolate. And as he surveyed from the gallows the slopes of the clouded hills to Brent Knoll and Steep Holm, over to the outline of the Quantocks and the darker Poldens, he did so in full knowledge of the similar fate awaiting his counterparts. For Hugh Cook, Abbot of Reading, was hanged on the same day, and thereafter Thomas Beche, Abbot of Colchester, was convicted on the slender evidence of John Scrope, a priest in the town, to be executed on 1 December 1539, a fortnight after Cook and Whiting.

Yet even before the following summer was out, the king had not hesitated to be swung by vengeful counsel against the very man responsible for all three abbots' deaths. For, having succumbed to a stillborn marriage to Anne of Cleves and facing a Protestant religious tide that he found as repugnant as his most recent bride, Henry VIII was fully prepared to sanction his chief minister's violent removal when on 10 June, wholly without warning, the captain of the guard entered the room at Westminster where the council was assembled and arrested Thomas Cromwell on a charge of high treason. In response, the wretched victim is said to have leapt to his feet and dashed his bonnet to the ground, calling on his colleagues to confirm his loyalty. But the minister's despairing outburst was to no avail as the Duke of Norfolk snatched the medal of St George from his neck and the Earl of Southampton stripped the Garter from his knee. After this their broken victim was taken by river to the Tower to suffer the justice of the bloody laws that he himself had fashioned. Later that evening when the king's archers were seen outside Cromwell's house, Londoners finally learned the news of his downfall, while men within, packing plate and money for the king's use, were soon discovering that the accused had salted away Church jewels to the value of £7,000.

Needless to say, Cromwell's subsequent frantic appeals to the king went unheeded, for on 3 July he wrote to Henry as his 'poor slave'. 'Most gracious Prince,' he implored, 'I cry for mercy, mercy, mercy', but no succour was forthcoming. Instead, Sir Richard Rich, whose testimony had already undone both John Fisher and Sir Thomas More, was now equally eager to report the treasonable sayings of the patron who had made his fortune. In the meantime, Cromwell was not allowed to be heard in his own defence, and in the trial that followed he was condemned to die by Act of Attainder – not for the numerous crimes of which he had been genuinely guilty, since the king himself had been party to them, but on the false accusation that he had opposed the master whom he himself had helped to make a tyrant. 'Full of pride', Cromwell had, it was declared, dealt in 'weighty causes' and, though of 'very base and low degree', he had boasted too freely of his power and influence. Early in 1540, for example, when taunted about his origins, he was alleged to have responded with a threat to the effect that 'if the Lords would handle him so, he would give them such a breakfast as never was made in England and that the proudest should know'. Predictably, he was accused also of heretical leanings, demonstrated by his encouragement of 'combinations' and 'conventicles'. But most damagingly of all, perhaps, he was said to have revealed intimate secrets about Henry's relationship with Anne Boleyn to an unspecified third party. In his desperation to make a success of the king's latest marriage Cromwell had, it seems, made a clumsy attempt to tutor Anne of Cleves in the arts of seduction by confiding to her certain sexual preferences of her husband. And more than any other single factor it was quite possibly this last revelation that rendered the king's fury uncontrollable.

In all, six weeks would eventually elapse between Cromwell's condemnation and his execution, since the king was determined to be rid of Anne of Cleves and, in this regard, there was still some further service to be had from the fallen minister, as Henry sent him fourteen questions concerning his marriage, which would confirm, among other things, that he had entered the match unwillingly and that the marriage had never been consummated. But in spite of final services rendered and further appeals for clemency, arguably the most curious of all Henry VIII's 'martyrs' was nevertheless gruesomely hacked on 28 July 1540 by a bungling headsman who required two blows to complete the task. In John Foxe's opinion, 'he patiently suffered the stroke of the axe, by a ragged, butcherly miser, which very ungodly performed the office'. And nor was it long, of course, before Henry's tortuous judgement was bemoaning the victim's fate, and convincing him that 'the best servant he ever had' had been condemned 'on light pretexts'.

But even this is not the most striking paradox surrounding Thomas Cromwell. For in spite of his clinical ruthlessness when occasion dictated, there had been little, if any, personal animus involved in any of his persecutions. Indeed, few revolutions of the kind he undoubtedly orchestrated have been ultimately accomplished with such limited bloodshed or judicial barbarity. Certainly, if obstacles to 'progress' like the Maid of Kent and her key adherents remained defiant, they could be hideously swept aside without the palest flicker of sympathy or remorse. But others of the Maid's same circle – and indeed those like them – were sometimes treated not only to mercy but to rehabilitation on what might well be considered remarkably generous terms. Both Richard Master and Edward Thwaites received not only absolute pardons in June 1534 at the intercession of Sir Christopher Hales, but full restoration in due course to their former status. During five years of amiable compliance and more than a little self-interested service, indeed, Thwaites gradually recovered his possessions in Calais and his position as a magnate in Kent, largely by acting as Cromwell's adviser on real-property investments, so that by 1539, he was back on the Bench of Magistrates, as well as the Commission for Sewage (inland waterways and drainage), and the Commission for Gaol Delivery with reference to Canterbury Castle, where the Maid and her companions, and possibly even he, too, had once been briefly incarcerated. Richard Master, likewise, was reinstalled in his Aldington rectory with full parochial responsibilities of the kind he had exercised when Elizabeth Barton's original confessor.

And this, too, was not the limit of the broader irony involved. For in accepting the oath of supremacy, neither Thwaites nor Master repudiated in practice either the old religion or, indeed, the memory of the Holy Maid who had, at one point, been arguably its most influential defender. Not only obstinately refusing to preach against her fame, Master would also persistently defy Thomas Cranmer's subsequent policy of protestantising the diocese of Canterbury, continuing to observe the Catholic calendar, to venerate the Blessed Virgin and the saints, to administer the sacrament of penance, and to preach the benefits of good works and of pilgrimage to Court-at-Street in particular. In 1550, moreover, at the age of 66, he would refuse to comply with the ordinance of Edward VI's reign, which required him to desecrate and break down the altars of his church, keeping faith with both the Maid and all the traditions she herself held dear, until his death not earlier than 1553 and perhaps as late as 1557 – by which time all links with Rome had been firmly re-established under Mary Tudor.

At the same time, notwithstanding Edward Thwaites's steady reacquisition of influence in local government, he too would ultimately follow a parallel path. For, if a tradition originating with the account of Nicholas Harpsfield is to be trusted, he dared to jeopardise all once more during 1539–40, to rescue the bones of St Augustine from a devastated Canterbury, and to re-erect the saint's shrine, albeit only briefly, in his parish church at Chilham. Nor is there any doubt of his involvement in the so-called Prebandaries' Plot of 1543, which nearly succeeded in bringing Cranmer to the stake for heresy. Indeed, when this scheme finally foundered on the rock of the king's affection for his archbishop, Thwaites crowned all with the greatest irony of any: the purchase of the very manor and chapel of Our Lady at Court-at-Street that had lain at the epicentre of Elizabeth Barton's former fame and glory. Though too late to save the wonder-working image, which had already been shattered to fragments on Cranmer's orders, it was not too late to protect the holy ground on which she had built her reputation, and which remained in the possession of Thwaites's family for almost half a century after his death in 1551.

Plainly, if the flesh of martyrs was perishable, the ardour of those who revered them sometimes proved less so. And the same was no less true, finally, of the bravery and fixation that continued to enthuse the likes of John Forest – last Provincial of the Greenwich Observants – who followed in their wake. Slowly roasted to death on a bed of chains at Smithfield on 22 May 1538, his pyre comprised the remnants of the wonder-working image of the ancient Welsh saint Dderfel Gadern, which, it was said, could destroy a forest by fire. Having first submitted to government threats, Forest had nevertheless recovered himself to deliver upon the scaffold before Thomas Cromwell, Lords of the Council, the Lord Mayor and the host of other dignitaries present, what represented, from some perspectives, a classic manifesto for all others of his kind:

I will die. Do your worst upon me. Seven years ago you durst not for your life have preached such words as these; and now, if an angel from heaven should come down and teach me any other doctrine than that I learned as a child, I would not believe him. Take me; cut me in pieces, joint from joint. Burn, hang, do what you will, I will be true henceforth to my faith.

A NOTE ON SOURCES

Most of the source material for Elizabeth Barton's life was written after her condemnation, when to admire her was treason. So efficient was the censorship of her day that if the Elizabethan antiquary William Lambarde had not salvaged one old pamphlet and substantially preserved it in his own *Perambulation of Kent*, written in 1570, we should have only government-inspired documents as our sources for her early life. The pamphlet concerned, printed in 1527, was Edward Thwaites's *A Marvellous Work of late done at Court-of Street in Kent and published to the devout People of this time for their spiritual consolation*, which consisted of twenty-four pages and set out to popularise the findings of Archbishop Warham's Episcopal Commission of 1526. Beyond this, aside from passing references to Elizabeth Barton in printed collections of contemporary sources, such as *Letters and Papers, Foreign and Domestic, of the Reign of Henry VIII*, we are largely dependent on only three other sources: *The Sermon against the Holy Maid*, composed by Nicholas Heath, amended by Archbishop Thomas Cranmer, and first delivered at Paul's Cross on 23 November 1533; Cranmer's letter to Archdeacon Hawkins, dated from Lambeth on 20 December 1533; and *An Act concerning the Attainder of Elizabeth Barton and others*, drafted under the supervision of Thomas Cromwell between January and February 1534. The first, which lacked its original introduction, was originally identified by Rev. L.E. Whatmore, who edited and printed it in *The English Historical Review* in 1943. The second was printed by H. Jenkyns in *The Remains of Thomas Cranmer* in 1833. The third was printed as C.12 of the *Statutes of the Realm* for the twenty-fifth year of King Henry VIII.

All later accounts of Elizabeth Barton's life prior to her opposition to the king's divorce are based on one or more of these four sources, and little other direct evidence relating to her activities is available beyond the following: a letter of Archbishop Warham dating to 1528; a brief and inaccurate memoir by Dom Edward Bocking written in 1533; the nominations to the Canonical Commission proposed by Prior Thomas Goldwell in 1533; references to Barton's fame and miracles made by William Tyndale between 1527 and 1530; and traditions of her oracles of 1526 recorded by Richard Morison in 1537. With regard to modern authorities, we are still comparatively reliant upon Alan Neame, whose book *The Holy Maid of Kent: The Life of Elizabeth Barton, 1506–1534* (London, 1971), remains the only specialised study of its kind.

Rather more extensive, though by no means exhaustive, are the resources available to researchers of John Fisher's life. Fr Thomas E. Bridgett's *Blessed John Fisher* (1888) was the first full-scale biography to be based upon a careful study of state papers, and the publication five years later in *Analecta Bollandiana* of Fernand van Ortroy's edition of the manuscript of the earliest life of John Fisher, written anonymously, was an event of the first importance. In all, there are eleven manuscript copies of the earliest biography, and also five copies of a Latin translation. The most important of the English manuscripts is Arundel 152, while another, Harleian 6382, was used for the Early English Text Society version of 1921. But the identity of the author remains unknown. Bridgett ascribed the original version to Dr Richard Hall (d. 1604), who for many years was a professor at Douai, while Van Ortroy tentatively proposed Dr John Young, fellow of St John's College and, under Queen Mary, vice-chancellor of Cambridge. Certainly, the author had contact with many who had known John Fisher personally, including the most informative source of all – who 'was but a young scholar of St John's College' – and a string of others including Robert Truslove, a chaplain in the bishop's last years; Thomas Watson, Fellow and Master of St John's, Bishop of Lincoln under Queen Mary, and for twenty years under restraint during the reign of Elizabeth I; Walter Phillips, the last prior of Rochester; a priest named Buddell of Cuxton, who was scribe to Fisher; as well as servants and others of the Rochester household. In addition, the earliest biographer employed extracts from a life of Sir Thomas More, written by his nephew William Rastell, who had witnessed Fisher's execution, and, as a lawyer, was in a good position to collect evidence about the bishop's trial even if he himself was not present, as he may have been.

The Registers for the years during which John Fisher was Bishop of Rochester have been preserved, as has the Act Book of his Consistory Court. But the information in the first, particularly, is largely routine, while the visitation records have not been preserved at all, and the Vatican archives remain particularly disappointing, consisting of commonplace references to the payment of first fruits, *ad limina* visits *per procuratorem*, and so on. Nor has Fisher received the attention that is his due from more recent authorities, though three specialist works remain of outstanding value: E. Surtz, S.J., *The Works and Days of John Fisher* (Harvard, 1967); R. Rex, *The Theology of John Fisher* (Cambridge, 1991); B. Bradshaw and E. Duffy (eds.), *Humanism, Reform and the Reformation: The Career of Bishop John Fisher* (Cambridge, 1989).

For Sebastian Newdigate and his fellow Carthusians, the most important source remains Dom Maurice Chauncy who, notwithstanding his tendency to embellish his accounts with supernatural detail, wrote a number of eyewitness works telling the story of his brethren, after he himself had taken the oath of supremacy. These works include: *Historia aliquot nostri saeculi Martyrum in Anglia*, etc. (Mainz, 1550, and Bruges, 1583); *Vitae Martyrum Cartusianorum aliquot, qui Londini pro Unitate Ecclesiae adversus haereticos* (Milan, 1606); *Commentariolus de vitae ratione et martyrio octodecim Cartusianorum qui in Anglia sub rege trucidati sunt* (Ghent, 1608), a portion of which was reprinted; and *Vitae Martyrum Cartusianorum aliquot, qui Londini pro Unitate Ecclesiae adversus haereticos* (Milan, 1606). There is also further relevant material in *Historia aliquot martyrum Anglorum maxime octodecim Cartusianorum: sub Rege Henrico Octavo ob fidei confessionem et summi pontificis jura vindicanda interemptorum a V. Patre Domno Mauritio Chauncy conscripta* (London, 1888). For details relating to Sebastian Newdigate's background, Henry Clifford, *The Life of Jane Dormer, Duchess of Feria* (London, 1887) provides additional information.

INDEX

IF YOU ENJOYED THIS TITLE FROM
THE HISTORY PRESS ...

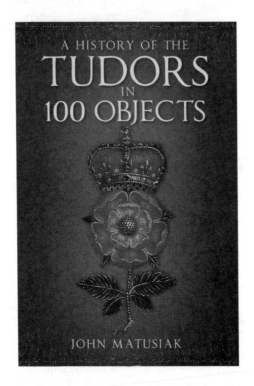

978 0 7509 9125 4